Instructor's Manual/Test Bank

to accompany

Interplay

The Process of Interpersonal Communication

NINTH EDITION

D1737322

Instructor's Manual/Test Bank

to accompany

Interplay

The Process of Interpersonal Communication

NINTH EDITION

Ronald B. Adler Santa Barbara City College

Lawrence B. Rosenfeld University of North Carolina at Chapel Hill

Russell F. Proctor II Northern Kentucky University

Original Contributions by Neil Towne

Prepared by

Ann Mitchell

Cami Bergquist

New York   Oxford

OXFORD UNIVERSITY PRESS

2004

Oxford University Press

Oxford   New York
Auckland   Bangkok   Buenos Aires   Cape Town   Chennai
Dar es Salaam   Delhi   Hong Kong   Istanbul   Karachi   Kolkata
Kuala Lumpur   Madrid   Melbourne   Mexico City   Mumbai
Nairobi   São Paulo   Shanghai   Taipei   Tokyo   Toronto

Published by Oxford University Press, Inc.
198 Madison Avenue, New York, New York, 10016
http://www.oup-usa.org

Oxford is a registered trademark of Oxford University Press

ISBN: 0-19-517192-6

Printing number: 9 8 7 6 5 4 3 2 1

Printed in the United States of America
on acid-free paper

CONTENTS

PREFACE

The hope of every instructor is that students will carry the knowledge bestowed upon them in class, beyond the classroom walls, into the real world. Showing students the relevance of *theory* to their *personal lives* is the best way to achieve that goal. This revised Instructor's Manual/Test Bank accompanying *Interplay*, Ninth Edition, provides novice and experienced instructors alike with strategies for presenting material in ways to keep the students thinking about the concepts after formal discussion is over.

Teaching, like any art form, is best regarded as a work in progress. Changes and enhancements can always be made to improve classroom effectiveness. This manual builds on earlier editions by Mary Bozik, Russ Proctor, Carol Dolphin and Derek Lane. To keep the focus on building analytical skills, the Portfolio Assignments (Part III) and Unit Wind-Ups (Part IV) originally presented in the seventh edition by Carol Dolphin have been retained, although the wind-ups have been updated to reflect changes in the ninth edition. In addition, Derek Lane's Team Learning instructional strategy presented in the eighth edition is included in Part I.

Newly developed chapter study guides are included as a tool to increase student responsibility for course material, and one new activity is presented for each chapter. Short Discussion Question & Activity assignments designed to aid classroom discussion have also been added for each chapter (Part III), as well as an in depth analysis of the film, "The Story of Us" as an option for semester review (Part III). Test bank questions have once again been modified to match *Interplay* ninth edition (Part V).

.   We would like to express our gratitude to the authors and publishers of *Interplay* for allowing us to share our perspectives on teaching Interpersonal Communication in this manual. We would also like to thank our families for supporting us in this endeavor, especially our children, for accommodating us with long naps so we could get some work done. Above all, we would like to wish good luck to all the instructors who will be using *Interplay* and this manual to teach students one of life's most fundamental skills: communication.

Cami Bergquist and Ann Mitchell

Instructor's Manual/Test Bank

to accompany

Interplay

The Process of Interpersonal Communication

NINTH EDITION

Part I: General Teaching Strategies

THE INSTRUCTOR IS THE MAIN INGREDIENT

The introductory course in interpersonal communication is unique in the college curriculum. When it is taught with the dual approach of theory and application as advocated by the authors of *Interplay*, it will lead students to an understanding of their own communication styles and those of others. Awareness and understanding are the first steps in empowering us to improve. As our students practice and acquire new expertise in daily "taken-for-granted" communication skills, they can actually *improve the quality of their lives*. This is a weighty claim for a single course!

Instructors of interpersonal communication, then, have a particularly challenging job. In addition to dealing with the various problems faced by all instructors in the classroom, the interpersonal communication teacher faces the challenge of connecting theory and daily reality as well as being a model interpersonal communicator for the class. To this end, it becomes important that interpersonal instructors are able not only to explain concepts and enhance the understanding of course materials, but to actually relate interpersonally to their students.

The single most effective way to do this is to participate actively in class exercises. While there will be many times in which the instructor must play a specialized role to facilitate an exercise, taking part on the same level as the student whenever possible pays dividends in two major ways:

1. It encourages participation from students. Sharing something of ourselves seems to increase interaction with the group. When students see that we are willing to share our experiences, they seem to be encouraged to do the same. (Remember the reciprocity factor in self-disclosure.) True to interpersonal studies that show that we are attracted to individuals who are competent but "human," it seems that we are most successful when we risk participating and making mistakes. Students seem to relate to and learning more easily from coping than from total mastery models.
2. Our participation gives us a good perspective on the students' experience in the class. Sometimes what appears to be a simple exercise is actually quite challenging; on the other hand, activities that appear valuable in theory may prove to be dismal failures in practice.

It is also essential that we relate comfortably with our students outside of the classroom, making ourselves available during office hours and dealing with students as individuals. The first step in this process is learning students' names as early as possible in the semester. Many instructors choose to increase their rapport with students by being on a first name basis with them.

FIRST DAY OF CLASS

The first day of class sets a tone for the remainder of the term, and, as such, it is a day on which instructors need to be most careful to create the impression of themselves and of the course that they want to remain in the students' minds. As research in impression formation indicates, the initial impression that students have of a class and of an instructor may give them an overall view of the course that endures throughout of the term. For the first class session, it is important to appear before students looking prepared, organized, and knowledgeable. Many of the people using this instructor's manual will be first-year instructors or graduate students who do not learn their teaching assignments until a day or two prior to the beginning of class. Complete preparation and organization of course lectures, exercises, and materials would be impossible only 24 hours before class starts, but strategies can be employed to make that first impression a positive one.

The first class session should include the following:

1. Introduce yourself and tell the students how you want to be addressed.

2. Distribute a course syllabus which includes the following:
   1. Course Name, Number, Meeting Times, Location, Teacher Name,
   2. Office Location, Phone Numbers, Office Hours, E-mail Address,
   3. Course Description
      - Catalogue description including prerequisites, additional description as needed
   4. Course Objectives
   5. Course Policies:
      - Attendance
      - Assignment Format Information
      - Make-up Policy
      - Class Participation
      - Plagiarism (reference to university policy)
   6. Grading Policy
      - Statement of how final grade will be determined, to include:
      - Grading Scale
      - Weight/Values for Various Assignments, Papers, Exams
      - Absenteeism, Extra Work, Late Work, In-class Participation
   7. Topics and Order of Coverage
   8. Key Dates:
      - Exams
      - Assignment Due Dates
      - Planned Absences
   9. Assignments:
      - Descriptions
      - Relative Weights
   10. Course Materials:
       - Texts
       - Supplies
       - Supplemental Readings
       - Fees
   11. Lab Policy (if applicable)

In addition, you may want to include the following paragraph, which is required by the North Central Accrediting Agency for Teacher Education. "(Name of your school) is an Affirmative Action Equal Opportunity Institution. Students with disabilities and other special needs should feel free to contact the professor privately if there are services or adaptations which can be made to accommodate specific needs."

3. Indicate what is expected of students before the next class meeting.
4. Introduction exercises (see activities in this manual at the end of Chapter 1 exercise section) can be used to "break the ice" and help create a supportive communication climate. (No student should leave the first class without having met at least a few new people.)

CLASSROOM ENVIRONMENT

If we expect students to interact comfortably with one another, it is important to create a conducive environment. The following suggestions have proven useful:

1. Chose a classroom with moveable chairs or desks that can be rearranged easily.
2. Arrange the classroom seating so that members of the group can see each other. If room and class size allow, a circle works best. This allows maximum face-to-face interaction and easy movement

into smaller circles for group exercises and discussion. Students become more willing to discuss with one another (rather than interacting with only the instructor) when they can see each other's nonverbal reactions. The circle formation also seems to keep students generally more involved and alert. (After all, it's more embarrassing to "drift off" if everyone can see you!)

3. Sit behind different members of the class and at different spots in the circle whenever possible to enhance the perception of dealing with students at the same level and to increase the chances of active interaction.

4. Encourage class participation by asking questions and enduring the silence until you get answers. Ask questions that may have a number of possible answers, and keep soliciting answers. Call on students by name.

5. If you're fortunate enough to have a classroom specifically designed for interpersonal communication classes, personalizing the environment creates a comfortable climate in which to interact. Carpeting the floor of the classroom provides students the option of sitting there in small group activities. This seems to increase informality and the amount of interaction that takes place. Other artifacts such as posters, plants, and bookshelves increase the "personalness" of a classroom environment and promote effective interpersonal communication.

THE IMPORTANCE OF EXERCISES

The unshakable belief on which this textbook and instructor's manual is based is that complete learning takes place only when the students understand a concept on an affective as well as a cognitive level. The authors would consider themselves to have failed if, by the end of a term, students could list the necessary elements of effective interpersonal communication but no longer cared about using this knowledge to improve their relationships.

This commitment to encourage readers to examine their everyday behavior explains the abundance of exercises in the textbook and instructor's manual. Participating in them should make a personal application of the subject almost inevitable. Every activity leads the reader to go beyond talking about how "people" communicate and ask "How do I communicate?" and, "How can I make my communication more appropriate and satisfying for myself and others?"

This emphasis on self-examination necessarily involves asking students to investigate (individually and as a group) feelings and behaviors that aren't often shared in academic settings. While very little growth comes without this kind of examination, it is absolutely essential not to push too hard, not to demand more self-disclosure than the group is ready to volunteer.

USE OF SMALL GROUPS

Many of the exercise in this manual depend on the use of small groups. Instructors may choose to place students in the variety of different groups throughout the semester (chosen by proximity, "counting off," drawing names, instructor assignment, etc.) or students may remain in the same group for longer blocks of time - throughout a unit, for example, or even for the entire semester. There are benefits to each of these formats. In the first case, students will have the opportunity to work with most or all of the individuals in the class. they will experience a larger number of personality styles and will be exposed to wider variety of ideas and examples. They will leave the class feeling that they "know" everyone to a limited degree. Also, if the class is "blessed" with an individual who clearly has problems relating to others and who tends to be a negative influence, everyone will have an equal opportunity to deal with this "challenge."

On the other hand, remaining in the same group for a longer period of times fosters a sense of dedication and devotion. Students may sometimes make a special effort to attend class because they know that their group is depending on them. Group members frequently develop a real sense of group identity and attain a high degree of comfort with one another. Most importantly, members of groups that are stable are more likely to achieve the trust level necessary for self-disclosure, and the group members often maintain their relationship after the semester ends.

Interpersonal communication instructors who prefer permanent teams and are interesting in a unique cooperative learning instructional strategy which can be effectively implemented in interpersonal communication classes will find the next section on **Team Learning** especially useful.

TEAM LEARNING[*]

Derek R. Lane, Ph.D.
Assistant Professor of Communication
University of Kentucky

Practical Aspects of Teaching and Learning

In his overview of research on teaching at the college and university level, McKeachie (1963) argues that the ultimate criteria of effective college teaching are changes in students toward the goals of higher education. These changes can be attitudinal and emotional as well as cognitive. He proposes that research evaluating the effectiveness of college instruction must consider "not only the accumulation of knowledge but the development of problem-solving skills and desirable attitudes" (p.1118). The development of instructional strategies that contribute to learning as an outcome is key to improving the educational process. While the general principles of learning (e.g., motivation, organization, feedback) are relevant to the choice of instructional strategies, McKeachie (1994) believes,

> Much of the progress made in understanding the practical aspects of teaching and learning has come from individual faculty members who have carried out studies in their own and colleagues' classes to get empirical evidence with respect to some issue, such as the effectiveness of some teaching innovation or the student characteristics affecting response to some aspect of teaching or testing (p.339).

Cooperative Learning

Johnson, Johnson and Smith (1991a) discuss two paradigms of college teaching and the change that is occurring within these paradigms. First, the old paradigm involves: (a) the transferring of knowledge from faculty to students, (b) the classifying of students by grade and category, © conducting education within a context of impersonal relationships among students and between faculty and students, (d) maintaining a competitive organizational structure, and (e) assuming that anyone with expertise in their field can tech without training to do so. This old paradigm uses a traditional, linear model where faculty knowledge is transferred to a passive student learner.

The second, new paradigm of teaching and learning involves collaborative methodology and assumes: (a) knowledge is constructed, discovered, transformed and extended by students; (b) students actively construct their knowledge; (c) faculty efforts are aimed at developing student's competencies and talents; (d) education is a personal transaction among students and between faculty and students as they work together; (e) the more pressure placed on students to achieve and the more difficult the material to be learned, the more important it is to provide social support within the learning situation; and (f) authentic learning takes place within a cooperative context.[†]

Cooperative learning is not a new idea. As early as the first century Quintilian (1875) suggested that students could benefit from teaching each other. The Roman philosopher Seneca advocated cooperative learning through such statements as "Qui Docet Discet" (when you teach, you learn twice). Johnson, Johnson, and Smith (1991a) state "in the late 1700's, Joseph Lancaster and Andrew Bell made extensive use of cooperative learning groups in England and the idea was brought to American when a Lancastrian school was opened in New York City in 1806" (p.16).

This paper is based on ideas from an article that was originally presented at the 1997 Southern States Communication Association entitled "The Use of Permanent Learning Teams In Teaching Introductory Communication Courses: A Theoretical Framework and Rationale for Assessing the Impact of Communication on Learning."

In the early 1960's, as a result of their work on cooperative learning, Johnson and Johnson (1991) developed the Cooperative Learning Center and the University of Minnesota. Since then, they have conducted over 85 research studies on cooperative learning and a series of meta-analyses of the last 90 years of instructional research containing a list of over 575 experimental studies and 100 correlational studies (Johnson & Johnson, 1989). The authors found that "cooperative learning promotes higher achievement that does competitive or individualistic learning" (p. 12). Other benefits of cooperative learning include: positive interpersonal relationships, higher levels of self-esteem, and the maximizing of social competencies (Johnson & Johnson, 1989). In addition, research has been compiled regarding knowledge attained through cooperative, competitive, and individualistic efforts (e.g., Johnson & Johnson, 1994; Johnson, Johnson & Holubec, 1990).

Johnson and his colleagues (1991a) suggest that "putting students into groups to learn is not the same thing as structuring cooperation among students" (p. 18). They discern five basic elements of a cooperative learning situation: (a) positive interdependence, (b) face-to-face promotive interaction, (c) individual accountability, (d) social skills (interpersonal and small group skills), and (e) group processing and evaluation (Johnson et al., 1990). One procedure for structuring cooperative learning groups is Aronson's "jigsaw" procedure, which involves a five-step sequence for structuring cooperative learning (Aronson, Blaney, Stephan, Sikes & Snapp, 1978).

Perhaps the most comprehensive group-based approach for harnessing the power of cooperative learning in higher education is that of Michaelsen and his colleagues (e.g., Michaelsen, 1994; Michaelsen & Black, 1994; Michaelsen, Fink, & Watson, 1994; Michaelsen, Jones, & Watson, 1993). Michaelsen, Jones, & Watson (1993) provide a distinction between Team Learning and Cooperative Learning. Both approaches make use of class time for group work and "build positive and supportive relationships between instructor and students while ensuring that students have immediate access to the instructor's task related expertise," but differences result from the "unique characteristics of the settings for which the two approaches were developed" (p. 140). Cooperative learning was developed for elementary students with a limited degree of self-control, while Team Learning was designed for professional business students capable of exhibiting a relatively high degree of self-control.

Cooperative Learning instructors define and structure individual member roles and train students to manage group processes. On the other hand, Team Learning emphasizes the application of concepts as opposed to merely learning about them. Team Learning provides the incentives and opportunities to students because: (a) a substantial part of the course grade is based on group performance and (b) groups receive regular and immediate feedback on their performance relative to other groups. As an instructional strategy, Team Learning provides the context and method for operationalizing an experimental instructional strategy.

Team Learning Methodology as a Theoretical Framework

Team Learning has the potential to better achieve the goals and objectives of the introductory, hybrid communication course because it offers students more opportunities to develop intellectual and professional skills through course content application. Team Learning helps students enhance their ability to establish positive interpersonal relationships, while increasing their self-esteem and maximizing their social competencies.

To understand how Team Learning strategies can enhance the achievement of classroom communication goals, one need only ponder the simple proverb: "I hear and I forget, I see and I remember, I DO and I understand." Instructional strategies incorporating Team Learning allow students to "do" and "understand."

The next section provides information regarding the use and utility of learning teams in instructional settings in three parts: (a) it provides a brief discussion of the nature of group dynamics and team learning and examines the benefits of team learning in the classroom; (b) it illustrates the necessary components of effective learning teams; and (c) it identifies procedures necessary for successful integration of learning teams into the instructional environment (i.e., course design, classroom management, student group composition, and performance evaluation).

Group Dynamics and Team Learning

A group is defined as "two or more persons who are interacting with one another in such a manner that each person influences and is influence by each other...Typically a group is composed of five or fewer members" (Shaw, 1991, p.8). Although the essential feature that distinguishes a group from an aggregate is interaction, there are three important aspects of a group: a group must (a) endure for a reasonable period (longer than a few minutes, at least), (b) have a common goal or goals, and (c) have developed at least a rudimentary group structure (Shaw, 1981, p. 8).

Team learning was originally designed to cope with the problems of large classes, over 120 students in an academic setting (Michaelsen, Watson, Cragin, & Fink, 1982). Team Learning primarily emphasizes learning to use concepts rather than merely learning about them. Michaelsen (1994) states: "Becoming a team is a process, not an event. Unless instructors facilitate the transformation of groups into teams, their success in using small groups is likely to be limited at best" (p. 2). The two distinctive features of instructional strategies incorporating learning teams are: (a) a redefinition of the primary roles and responsibilities in the learning process and (b) the formation of an operational learning environment which incorporates use of four new and essential operational tools (course design, classroom management, student group compositions, and performance evaluation).

Michaelsen and Black (1994) argue that instructional strategies that incorporate team learning require a learning model paradigm shift where the traditional model (which includes the roles (a) teacher as dispenser of knowledge and (b) students as passive receivers of information; subject mastery is determined by testing individual students) is replaced by a team learning model (which includes the roles of (a) instructor as course designer and manager of overall instructional process and (b) students as active participants who are accountable and responsible for their learning). Michaelsen, Watson, Cragin & Fink (1982) identify four primary features of team learning: (a) permanent and purposefully heterogeneous work groups; (b) grading based on a combination of individual performance, group performance, and peer evaluation; (c) the majority of the class time devoted to small group activities; and (d) a repetitive six-step instructional activity sequence (IAS) which assists students in developing higher level cognitive skills.

Necessary Components of Effective Learning Teams

There are five necessary and sufficient components which much be integrated into team learning instructional strategies. Omission of any of the components limits the ability of teams to be successful.

1. Heterogeneous composition of diverse interdependent work teams (comprising between 5-8 individuals) which minimize potential threats from cohesive subgroups.
2. Clear, specific, and widely shared group goals which encourage group cohesion.
3. Sufficiently difficult and meaningful group activities which do now allow one member of the group to accomplish the task alone.
4. Regular, descriptive, specific, relevant, timely and usable internal peer feedback.
5. External comparisons which are emphasized through immediate and ongoing feedback about organizational performance relative to other teams.

The next four sections describe the four essential operational tools that provide the foundation for the formation of an operational learning environment: course design, classroom management, student group composition, and performance evaluation.

Course Design

Michaelsen and Black (1994) argue that successful instruction using the Team Learning Model is dependent on course design in which "instructors must focus on creating two very different types of instructional activities. One type must focus on building a sound student understanding of basic concepts. The other is to design activities that focus on building students' higher level thinking and problem solving skills" (p. 3). Designing activities for the classroom is perhaps the most difficult obstacle to the successful use of learning teams. Michaelsen and Black (1994) developed four questions that assist instructors when making key strategic decisions:

1. What do I want the students to be able to <u>do</u> when they have completed this unit of instruction (desired educational outcomes)?
2. What will the students have to <u>know</u> to be able to do it (course content)?
3. How can I tell what students have <u>already learned</u> on their own or from each other so I could build from there (readiness assurance/assessment/feedback)?
4. How can I tell whether or not students can effectively <u>use</u> their knowledge (application of course concepts)?

Classroom Management

When using the team learning model, the majority of instructor effort occurs before the course begins. Preparation and organization are key to successful incorporation of the team learning model. While the primary classroom management tool in the traditional learning model is lecture, classroom management in the team learning model is accomplished through a six-step Instructional Activity Sequence (IAS) (Michaelsen, Fink, & Watson, 1994). The IAS is repeated for each major unit of instruction (typically five to seven times).

Michaelsen and Black (1994) believe "the most unique feature of the IAS is that there are no formal presentations by the instructor until the students have studied the material and completed the individual and group readiness assessment tests" (p. 5). The Instructional Activity Sequence includes working through the following six steps:

1. Individual Study
2. Individual Testing (Readiness Assurance Test—RAT)
3. Group Testing (Readiness Assurance Test—RAT)
4. Written Group Appeals
5. Instructor Feedback
6. Application-Oriented Activities

Step one (individual study) ensures that students prepare for class by studying assigned instructional materials. Steps two through five constitute the Readiness Assurance Process (RAP) (Michaelsen et al., 1985, Michaelsen, Fink & Watson, 1994). Step two (individual testing) provides a diagnostic tool for determining student readiness and promotes individual accountability. The individual test consists of 15-20 multiple choice and short answer questions taken from assigned readings and/or homework type problems. To provide immediate feedback to both instructor and students for a unit of instruction, both team and individual tests are scored in class. Step three (group testing) ensures group accountability and peer teaching. The group test is identical to the individual test and is taken after the completion of the individual exams. Immediate scoring provides instructor and students with feedback.

Step four (written group appeals) increases learning and enhances group cohesiveness. Michaelsen and Black (1994) believe that written group appeals "galvanize a group's negative energy from having missed questions into a focused review of potentially troublesome concepts" (p. 6). Written appeals may come from groups—no individual written appeals are accepted. If the team appeal is granted, however, individuals in the team writing the appeal should also be given credit. Step five includes providing feedback to students with additional explanation prior to the application of course concepts. Instructor skills such as processing, debriefing, and facilitating discussion, greatly affect the impact on student learning. These skills are similar to those required to lead discussions in a traditional instructional environment, but require more knowledge. Since the Team Learning Model encourages negotiation of the learning environment, it is likely that students will challenge an instructor's knowledge more than in traditional learning situations. Therefore, an instructor must be prepared, knowledgeable, and competent. This needs to be done without damaging the positive instructional environment (graduate teaching assistants must be cautious of power plays ["I'm right, You're wrong"] with students; or behaving in a condescending manner).

Step six requires the use of application-oriented activities to help students grow in self-confidence while developing a thorough understanding of the class concepts. This step can be problematic and even detrimental with ineffective group assignments. Michaelsen and Black (1994) believe that group assignments simultaneously accomplish four major objectives: promote learning of essential concepts or skills, build group cohesiveness, ensure individual accountability, and teach students the positive value of groups. Six characteristics of effective group assignments include:

1. Production of a tangible output.
2. Impossible to complete without comprehension of course concepts.
3. Sufficiently difficult to eliminate completion by an individual member.
4. Majority of time should be spent engaged in activities.
5. Applicable to real world issues or problems (pragmatic/applied).
6. Interesting and/or fun.

Michaelsen, Black, and Fink (in press) have recently compiled a manuscript which outlines detailed procedures for preventing group problems and developing effective assignments to be used in designing application-oriented activities. Michaelsen and Black (1994) suggest "the application activities, group projects, and exams employed should look and feel like that kinds of things you hope students would be able to do individually once they have completed the unit of instruction" (p. 6). The application of course concepts (step six) should constitute approximately 75% of total class time, whereas the readiness assurance process (first five steps) should constitute no more than 25% of class time.

Student Group Composition

The formation and development of learning teams enable students to move from a passive role in the traditional learning model to a more active role where they are accountable and responsible for their learning. Michaelson, Jones and Watson (1993) report that "the development of properly managed, permanent, and purposefully heterogeneous learning teams is key to successfully increasing students' willingness to accept responsibility to ensure that learning occurs" (p. 132).

Team Formation

Three key principles have been discussed (Michaelsen & Black, 1994) for the process of forming learning teams: (a) evenly distribute student assets among groups; (b) avoid unnecessary barriers to group cohesiveness by having teacher form the groups to eliminate students in groups with previously established relationships; and (c) make the group formation process as visible as possible.

Developing Performance-Oriented Group Norms

In order for performance-oriented group norms to be developed, students should: (a) see a clear relationship between individual member behavior and the success or failure of their team, (b) be able to monitor the extent to which members are complying with group norms, and (c) have feedback mechanisms available when individuals fail to comply with group norms. Michaelsen and Black (1994) suggest that the instructors can empower teams by: (a) providing comparisons to other teams, (b) requiring a peer evaluation, and (c) having students keep a record of attendance and performance.

Team learning can only be successful with a substantial part of the course grade is based on group performance and the groups receive regular and immediate feedback on how they are doing in relation to other groups (which causes students to take pride in their groups' success). Performance evaluation, therefore, is an important component in the team learning model.

Performance Evaluation

The final key procedure for the implementation of learning teams in the classroom involves three essential components related to performance evaluation: individual performance, group performance, and peer evaluation. Michaelsen, Cragin, & Watson (1981) encourage the involvement of students and teams in the development of fair and equitable grade weights. Their philosophy is that students will support a policy which they helped to create.

Essentially, the "learning teams" pedagogy includes a variety of student-centered activities both in and out of the classroom, including:

- Reading and lectures makes up 25% of the coursework; application of the material (various forms of experiential learning) is 75%.
- Teams of 4-5 students each are formed early in the course and maintained throughout.
- A substantial portion of the course deliverables (35-45%) is based on team performance.
- The class takes periodic "readiness assessment tests" covering the readings and class. material (first individually then immediately as a team) to ensure that they are prepared for the application portions of the course.
- The methodology ensures that students are exposed to the material at least four times before moving on to the application phase.
- The reward structure and class atmosphere is designed to facilitate cooperation *within* teams but competition *between* teams.

The learning teams approach to teaching requires substantial work—for the professor as well as the students—but it provides substantial rewards in terms of student learning in the interpersonal communication classroom.

References

Aronson, E., Blaney, N., Stephan, C., Sikes, J., & Snapp, M. (1978). *The jigsaw classroom.* Beverly Hills, CA: Sage.

Johnson, D. W., & Johnson, F. (1991). *Joining together: Group theory and group skills.* 4th ed. Englewood Cliffs, NJ: Prentice-Hall.

Johnson, D. W., & Johnson, R. (1978). Cooperative, competitive, and individualistic learning. *Journal of Research and Development in Education, 12,* 3-15.

Johnson, D. W., & Johnson, R. (1981). Effects of cooperative and individualistic learning experiences on interethnic interaction. *Journal of Educational Psychology, 73,* 454-459.

Johnson, D. W., & Johnson, R. (1985). Classroom conflict: Controversy vs. Debate in learning groups. *American Educational Research Journal, 22,* 237-256.

Johnson, D. W., & Johnson, R. (1989). *Cooperation and competition: Theory and research.* Edina, MN: Interaction Book Company.

Johnson, D. W., & Johnson, R. (1994). *Learning together and alone: Cooperative, competitive, and individualistic learning.* 4th ed. Boston, MA: Allyn and Bacon.

Johnson, D. W., Johnson, R., & Holubec, E. (1990). *Circles of learning: Cooperation in the classroom.* Edina, MN: Interaction Book Company.

Johnson, D. W., Johnson, R., Stanne, M., & Garibaldi, A. (1990). The impact of leader and member group processing on achievement in cooperative groups. *The Journal of Social Psychology, 130,* 507-516.

Johnson, D. W., Johnson, R. T., & Smith, K. A. (1991a). *Active learning: Cooperation in the college classroom.* Edina, MA: Interaction Books.

Johnson, D. W., Johnson, R. T., & Smith, K. A. (1991b). *Cooperative learning: Increasing college faculty instructional productivity.* Washington, D.C.: The George Washington University, School of Education and Human Development.

Lane, D. R. (1995). *Theoretical and methodological assumptions about learning: An overview of learning theory and its implications for instructional communication research.* Unpublished Manuscript, University of Oklahoma, Norman, OK.

Lane, D. R. (1996). *The use of permanent learning groups in teaching introductory communication courses: Assessing the impact of communication on human learning.* Unpublished Doctoral Dissertation, The University of Oklahoma, Norman, OK.

McKeachie, W. J. (1963). Research on teaching at the college and university level. In N.L. Gage (Ed.), *Handbook of Research on Teaching* (pp. 1118-1172) Chicago, IL: Rand McNally.

McKeachie, W. J. (Ed.). (1994). *Teaching tips: Strategies, research, and theory for college and university teachers.* 8th ed. Lexington, MA: D.C. Health and Company.

Michaelsen, L. K. (1992). Team learning: A comprehensive approach to harnessing the power of small groups in higher education. *To Improve the Academy, 11,* 107-122

Michaelsen, L. K. (1994). Classroom organization and management: Making a case for the small-group option. In K. W. Pritchard & R. M. Sawyer (Eds.), *Handbook of college teaching: Theory and applications.* Westport, CT: Greenwood Publishing Group, Inc.

Michaelsen, L. K., Black, R. H., & Fink, L. D. (1995). *Problems with learning groups: An ounce of prevention.* Unpublished manuscript. University of Oklahoma.

Michaelsen, L. K., & Black, R. H. (1994) Building learning teams: The key to harnessing the power of small groups in higher education, *Collaborative Learning: A Sourcebook for Higher Education* (Vol. 2,). State College, PA: National Center for Teaching, Learning & Assessment.

Michaelsen, L. K., Cragin, J. P., & Watson, W. E. (1981). Grading and anxiety: A strategy for coping. *The Organizational Behavior Teaching Journal, 6,* 8-14.

Michaelsen, L. K., Fink, L.D., & Watson, W. E. (1994). Pre-instructional minitests: An efficient solution to covering content. *Journal of Management Education, 18,* 32-44.

Michaelsen, L. K., Jones, C. F., & Watson, W. E. (1993). Beyond groups and cooperation: Building high performance learning teams. In D. L. Wright & J. P. Lunde (Eds.), *To improve the academy: Resources for faculty, instructional and organizational development* (pp. 127-145). Stillwater, OK: New Forums Press.

Michaelsen, L. K., Watson, W. E., & Black, R. H. (1989). A realistic test of individual versus group consensus decision-making. *Journal of Applied Psychology, 74,* 834-839.

Michaelsen, L. K., Watson, W. E., Cragin, J. P., & Fink, L. D. (1982). Team learning: A potential solution to the problem of large classes. *Exchange: The Organizational Behavior Teaching Journal, 7,* 13-22.

Michaelsen, L. K., Watson, W. E., & Schraeder, C. B. (1985). Informative testing: A practical approach for tutoring with groups. *The Organizational Behavior Teaching Review, 9,* 18-33.

Quintilian (Ed.). (1875). *Institutio oratio.* London: William Heinemann.

Shaw, M. E. (1981). *Group dynamics: The psychology of small group behavior.* 3rd ed. New York: McGraw-Hill.

Slavin, R. E., & Karweit, N. L. (1984). Mastery learning and student teams: A factorial experiment in urban general mathematics classes. *American Educational Research Journal, 21,* 725-736.

Watson, W. E., Michaelsen, L. K., & Sharp, W. (1991). Member competence, group interaction, and group decision-making: A longitudinal study. *Journal of Applied Psychology, 76,* 803-809.

GRADING SYSTEMS

A good evaluation system should achieve three goals:

1. It should give students feedback on their mastery of the skills under study, to answer the question, "How well do I understand the subject?"
2. It should give instructors feedback on how successful they have been in communicating the subject matter to students, to answer the question: "Which areas were taught successfully and which do I need to cover more or differently?"
3. It should avoid slipping into the trap of inviting and rewarding unproductive behaviors: busywork, plagiarism, or excessive verbosity.

Several alternatives for accomplishing these goals are available and can be used singly or in combination. The systems below are examined for both advantages and disadvantages.

Traditional Examinations

The biggest advantage of traditional examinations is the likelihood that students will read and study the text with care and reflect upon the objectives of each chapter. In addition to midterm or final exams, testing prior to discussion of each chapter works well to illuminate trouble sports and clear up any misunderstandings.

The principle disadvantage is that tests may not actually measure the most important goals of the class, namely, improving the student's everyday communication behavior. For example, it is entirely possible that a student could describe in writing a number of effective behaviors for coping with criticism and never practice any of them. Thus, tests may measure skill in taking tests about communication and little else.

Open Note Quizzes/Study Guides

In an effort to encourage reading before class discussion, an instructor may choose to incorporate open note quizzes into the curriculum. Chapter Study Guides are included for each chapter in the Part III Chapter Exercises Section. Instruct the students to read and take notes on each chapter using the study guides. At the beginning of the class allow students to ask clarification questions related to material they did not understand. Students may then use any notes they took off the study guide to complete a short (15 – 20 question) quiz on the chapter. It is then possible to discuss the concepts using the quiz as a guide.

There are 13 chapters, so an instructor may choose to drop 2-3 of the lowest quiz grades. The biggest advantage is decreased lecture time. Since the students have already read the material, an instructor can spend more class time exploring how students utilize course concepts in their everyday interactions.

The Study Guides were developed by Neil Gregersen, University of Wisconsin – Waukesha.

Group Study Exercises

For each chapter in the textbook, this manual provides a Matching Quiz entitled "Group Study Exercise." These questions generally require students to match particular examples with the theories that the situations illustrate. Because these exercises are completed in small groups, there is usually excellent discussion about the theory, and the students are able to see more clearly how it relates to "real life." Although an answer key is provided, instructors should exercise their own judgment as to whether or not a group can offer a reasonable explanation for other responses. (The real point is that the students *think*, not that they simply identify the correct letter.) The grades on these exercises may be recorded and used as a component of the Final Grade. Since all members of the group receive the same grade, the students' personal investment in the group is also increased.

Unit Wind-Ups

The concept of the Unit Wind-Up is tired closely to the link between theory and application. As instructors in interpersonal communication, one of our principal goals is that our students not only know/understand theory but also begin to apply the principles of communication to their daily transactions; it does not seem adequate that we test solely on content recall. The Wind-Up presents students with a scenario of interpersonal transaction. (Ideally, they will be able to both listen to the scenario on audiotape as well as reading it in hard copy. In this case, audiotape is superior to video since video introduces too many variables into the analysis.) After they have heard the conversation, students work in small groups to answer specific questions that analyze the interaction in terms of the theory of the particular unit. All members of a group receive the same grade on this in-class project.

Part IV in this manual offers a more complete explanation of the concept, development, and use of the Unit Wind-Up, as well as three Wind-Ups, one to follow each of the three units in the text. A scenario that can be used as a Final Exam—to be analyzed by each student individually—is also included. (The use of Unit Wind-Ups is built into the semester course plan, which follows in Part II.)

Student-Planned Examinations

In this variation of traditional examinations, students split into small groups that submit several possible examination questions. All questions then are given to the entire class, with the understanding that the instructor will select several of them for the actual test.

While this method carries the same disadvantage as the traditional method described above, students study the material more intensively as they select and draw up questions; personal involvement takes on even broader dimensions.

Student-Instructor Contracts

In this system, student and instructor develop a specific program of study that the student agrees to undertake in order to return for which he or she receives a predetermined grade. Contracts can cover work corresponding to units of study, or they can be written for term projects that may take the place of a final examination. Projects can take many forms: research papers, interviews, dramatic productions, surveys, journals.

There are two advantages to such a plan. First, it demands student initiative in proposing a course of study—a pleasant contrast to more passive types of assignments in which students play less creative roles. Second, such a format often allows students some latitude in choosing how to channel their energies. Research and experience show that the quality of work and motivation are higher when students work on subjects of personal interest.

Two disadvantaged often occur in the contract method. First, some tasks that students choose may not focus on concepts that the instructor deems most important. This difficulty can be remedied by defining acceptable areas of study. Second, some students lack the ability to be self-motivated scholars.

Journal Assignments & Portfolio Entries

In place of or in addition to examinations, instructors may use assignments in which students reflect on how topics under study apply to their personal lives. The advantage of such an approach lies in extending concepts discussed beyond the classroom and into the student's everyday relationships. The value of such applications is obvious in a course designed to improve communication skills, especially since students are forced to articulate their ideas in writing, rather than just "thinking about" their behaviors.

The Journal typically asks the student to write in response to something which (s)he has read or which (s)he has experienced in class. Students may, for example, be required to write one or two pages for each class session, of for two out of three session. Journal writing is usually fairly casual and may or may not be well focused; one potential disadvantage lies in the failure of journals to center clearly on key concepts discussed in class.

This can be remedied by using the more focused Portfolio Entries which are included for each chapter in Section III of the manual. These assignments are slightly more formal in their format and more clearly defined. These entries may ask students to examine their current behaviors, to try to solve a problem, or simply to use personal examples to illustrate the theory being studied. It is not likely that an instructor will have the time or inclination to use all of these assignments during a single semester; however, some of these assignments have had dramatic effects in improving students' interpersonal relationships.

Journal Assignments and/ore Portfolio Entries should be collected periodically (perhaps at the completion of each unit) throughout the semester. It should be noted that reading these assignments takes a good deal of time since each one is unique and needs to be responded to in a unique manner. Comments are critical—in addition to the grade. Instructors also need to assure students that anything that they write will be held in total confidentiality and that the grade will be a reflection of the quality of their work, not the quality of themselves as individuals.

Discussion Questions & Activities (D&A)

These short assignments can be given to students to encourage class discussion. Many students express frustration at coming up with real-life examples "on the spot" and these assignments help them think of personal examples ahead of time that can then be shared with the class. Assignments can be adapted from longer portfolio assignments and class activities outlined in Part III, selected from the activities list at the end of each chapter in the Interplay textbook, or developed based on essay questions at the end of each chapter in Part V. Sample D&A assignments are provided for each chapter in Part III Activities.

Assignments should be short, generally one page in length, and students should be given credit for completion rather than graded for content. The purpose in grading is to ensure the student thought about the concept, not necessarily whether they correctly applied it, although the instructor will have the opportunity to correct misunderstandings through discussion and written comments.

The advantage of such assignments is that students will have an example ready when asked to participate in discussion. An instructor will also be able to identify any troublesome concepts that need more class time based on responses.

There is a sample syllabus outlined in Part II showing how the above-mentioned open note quizzes and the D&A assignments can be integrated into the curriculum.

Book Reports/Exercises

Book reports may be assigned to students to encourage more in-depth study of a particular subject area.

The greatest disadvantage of book reports as a method of evaluation is that often students prepare book reports that merely repeat what was said in the book. To overcome this disadvantage, a requirement of the assignment can be that the student develop an activity that will illustrate the book's information. The activity should be designed to teach others in the class one important thing (cognitive or affective) that the student gleaned from the book and can take the form or a role-play, a questionnaire, or an exercise modeled on those in the text. Class sessions are periodically set aside for students to work out their activities with their classmates. Class members are asked to give feedback evaluating each student's exercise. The book report/exercise method seems to reinforce learning of the basic tenets of each book, and most students seem to enjoy sharing "discoveries" with their classmates.

Movie Analysis

The great thing about communication is that it permeates are lives, and popular culture often holds many examples for students to evaluate and learn from. Movies about relationships are great vehicles to use for course concept discussion. "The Story of Us," starring Bruce Willis and Michelle Pfeiffer, chronicles the 15-year relationship of a couple on the verge of divorce.

It is an excellent movie to generate discussion on relational development, intimacy and distance, climate and conflict – chapters 8-11. The movie can also be shown as a semester review for all 13 chapters. Discussion questions are included at the end of Part III for all 13 chapters.

The movie can either be shown during class, or assigned as an outside exercise. Discussion questions can be reviewed during class, or the questions can be assigned as an outside analysis paper.

Communication Skills Projects

This system allows students to focus on a process for altering their communication behavior by targeting a specific aspect of their behavior that they would like to improve, and then working through it in a series of steps from self-monitoring current behaviors to specifying desired changes, to practicing the skill in real-life situations. This procedure may involve:

1. keeping a journal of the problem behavior as it occurs verbally and nonverbally in terms of (a) the situation, (b) the actual behavior, (c) the preferred behavior for a specified time.
2. assessing the patterns that emerged in the journal entries.
3. observation and recording of people whose communication in the problem area is effective.
4. creating a specific behavioral goal including verbal and nonverbal choices.
5. covert rehearsal, or the imaginary practice of skills.
6. behavior rehearsal within the classroom among peers who provide feedback on what worked and what could be improved.
7. implementation in the actual situation followed by self-evaluation.

The Portfolio Entries for Chapters 7 and 8 are in format of Communication Skills Projects. The advantage of this method is that students learn at a process for gradually and systematically altering the behaviors they self-select, and can be repeated throughout their lives. Chapter objectives can be used to prime students' thinking about such behaviors.

The disadvantage is that students may not commit themselves to this process and turn in a fabricated project "completed" in a marathon session. Ongoing, in-class discussion of the stages of the project or draft versions will keep most students involved throughout the process.

Self-Assessment

Whether or not you choose to use it as a part of a student's grade, self-assessment is a critical element in the interpersonal communication course, as well as in our daily communication interactions. It is important for students to assess their skills and weaknesses at the outset of the course and to set semester goals (See Portfolio Entry for Chapter One). These goals should again be re-visited at the end of the semester when students assess their personal successes (and failures).

Some instructors may choose to use self-assessment as a factor in the final grade. This method operates on the assumption that in many respects students are in the best position to judge their own progress throughout the course. The self-assessment system asks each student to select a grade that reflects his/her effort and growth in understanding key concepts and/or progress toward meeting semester goals. This is followed by an explanation for the chosen grade based on specific criteria.

The advantage of this approach is its emphasis on self-judgment. It demonstrates that the student is responsible for his/her own growth and that whatever grade appears on his or her transcript is merely a symbol of that growth. Moreover, asking a student the question, "What do you deserve?" often generates much more self-reflection about effort expended than any other system of evaluation. It also encourages the student to pay careful attention to the achievement of his/her personal goals throughout the semester.

The most obvious disadvantage is the potential for abuse. There is no guarantee that a lazy student will not give herself or himself a high grade.

No matter which grading system you choose, it is very important to delineate clearly the assignments, the due dates, and the method of grading at the outset of class. It is also important to collect work on the assigned date. These practices reinforce the seriousness of the work involved, increasing respect for the instructor and the course.

INSTRUCTOR EVALUATION

Formal evaluations are an important tool in discovering how students perceive the course. They may be used periodically during the term to allow for ongoing adjustments or at the end of the term to obtain an overall evaluation and information for developing future courses. (For a succinct and readable summary of research on student evaluation of instructors, see William E. Cahin, "Student Ratings of Teaching: A Summary of the Research," IDEA Paper No. 20, Center for Faculty Evaluation and Development, Kansas State University, September, 1988.)

Forms can be designed to fit particular classroom situations but generally fall into two types: (1) open-ended specific response, and (2) objective/numerical rating. An example of each is provided below.

Open-Ended Specific

1. What expectations did you have for this course (units)? Has this course (unites) met you expectations? If not, why not?
2. Do you feel the workload was too light, too heavy, or just right? Were there any specific assignments on which you would like to comment?
3. Do you think that the grading has been done fairly? If not, why not?
4. What do you think of the classroom atmosphere? How would you like to see it changed?
5. Have the readings (text and outside) been satisfactory? Please make your comments specific.
6. Is the teaching style satisfactory? What do you like about your instructor's style? What do you dislike?
7. Please make any other comments you feel might be helpful. Do you have any suggestions for improvements? Is there anything you think particularly important that we should continue doing?

Objective/Numerical Rating

Please respond by giving each item a number.
5 = excellent, 4 = good, 3 = average, 2 = fair, 1 = poor
Instructor
_____ 1. The instructor defined the course goals well.
_____ 2. The instructor met the goals.
_____ 3. The instructor was well prepared for class meetings.
_____ 4. The instructor was knowledgeable in the subject matter of the course.
_____ 5. The instructor was effective in leading and administering the class.
_____ 6. The instructor was available to meet outside of class time to assist students.
_____ 7. The instructor was enthusiastic.

Assignments

  ____ 8. The effort required for the course was reasonable.

  ____ 9. The amount of time given for the completion of assignments was appropriate.

  ____ 10. The readings for the course were relevant to the subject matter.

  ____ 11. The amount of reading expected for the course was reasonable.

  ____ 12. The major text for the course was useful.

Grading and Evaluation

  ____ 13. The criteria used in assigning grades were clearly defined.

  ____ 14. The feedback provided by the instructor for class assignments was useful.

  ____ 15. The feedback provided by the instructor for class assignments was reasonably prompt.

  ____ 16. The class assignments and/or exams were appropriately difficult to challenge the student.

  ____ 17. The examinations and/or assignments were fair in their scope and expectations.

Overall

  ____ 18. Overall, I would rate this COURSE as (excellent, good, fair, poor).

  ____ 19. Overall, I would rate this INSTRUCTOR as (excellent, good, fair, poor).

GENERAL TEACHING STRATEGIES

You may want to consider using some of the following general teaching strategies from the *Communication Teacher* (previously published as *Speech Communication Teacher*), a quarterly publication available from the Speech Communication Association, 5105 Backlick Rd., Annandale, VA 22003. Specific strategies for teaching chapter content are listed in each chapter section of this manual. **A complete index to the *Communication Teacher* is available online at** www.natcom.org.

Alexander, B. K. (1998, Spring). Generating feedback in the classroom: Three teacher and student based tools of assessment, 12(3), 4-5.

Boileau, D. M. (1987, Summer). A summer quiz, 1(4), 5.

Brenner, D. (1990, Winter). Scholastic bowl exercise in the classroom, 4(4), 6.

Burke, J. (1987, Summer). Using numbers for greater participation, 1(4), 7.

Corey, J. (1989, Summer). Motivating students with service points, 3(4). 1-2.

Feezel, J.D. (1992, Spring). Applications to teaching, 6(3), 8-9.

Garrett, R. L. (1998, Fall). The interpersonal communication survey, 13(1), 9-11.

Gozzi, R. (1989, Spring). The ten-minute study method, 3(2), 11-12.

Gschwend, L. (2000, Spring). Every student deserves an assessment tool that teaches, 14(3), 1-5.

Haehl, A. (1988, Winter). Adapting to non-traditional students, 2(2), 12-13.

Hahn. D.F. (1992, Fall). To speak of many things, 7(1), 8.

Hall, D. (1991, Spring). Join the breakfast club, 5(3), 3.

Hauck, B. (1987, Fall). The 'people pyramid': A justification for communication studies, 2(1), 4-5.

Julian, F.D. (1991, Winter). Journal writing for the speech communication classroom, 5(2), 3.

Kuseski, B. K. (1999, Summer). Student-led exam review, 13(4), 5.

Langley, C. Darrell. (1989, Spring). The 'thought sheet': An interpersonal communication stratagem, 3(3), 13-14.

Lapakko, D. (1988, Fall). Sanctioned 'cheating' on exams, 3(1), 6.

Lesser, R. (1989, Fall). Lottery: Students teach the class, 4(1), 5-6.

Macky, N. (1990, Fall). Essential pursuit: A classroom review technique, 5(1), 8.

MacLenna, J. M. (1998, Summer). Teaching interpersonal communication: The personal icon assignment, 12(4), 13.

McSwain, J.E. (1986, Fall). A one-minute manager of instruction, 1(1), 13-14.

Mester, C. (1987, Fall). Peer support groups, 2(1), 2.

Miles, P. (1988, Summer). Teacher continuous feedback technique, 2(4), 4-6.

Noll, B. (1991, Fall). Learning through experimental research projects, 6(1), 4-5.

Pawlowski, D. (1999, Winter). Dialoguing the gender movements, 13(2), 4-6.

Presnell, S. (2000, Spring). BINGO: An interactive exam review exercise, 14(3), 11-12.

Ross, C. (1989, Winter). Suggestions for teaching international students, 3(2), 10-11.

Rumbough, T. B. (2000, Spring). 52 ways to break the ice, 14(3), 6-8.

Schnell, J. (1999, Fall). Ideas for including African-American perspectives in selected communication courses, 14(1), 12-13.

Schumer, Allison. (1988, Spring). Here now the news…,2(3), 6-7.

Smith, R. E., Jr. (2000, Spring). Communication images from art, 14(3), 10-11.

Smithson, S. (1990, Fall). Utilizing a teaching journal to increase teaching effectiveness, 5(1), 1.

Soller, R. and Benson, J. (1987, Summer). Using attendance sheets as feedback vehicles, 1(4), 1.

Stevens, S. R. (2000, Winter). How to go into the lion's den and bring out a kitty cat: First day strategies for graduate teaching assistants, 14(2), 10-12.

Tripp, E. (1987, Fall). The oral quiz, or letting students talk more while you talk less, 2(1), 1.

Zalewski, J. (1988, Fall). Using cartoons in test situations, 3(1), 1.

PART II: COURSE ARRANGEMENT

Text selection, difficult task that it is, may be one of the easier steps in the development of a course. Fitting the new book into your particular program really takes some thought and time, and it is difficult to know at the onset of a term just what emphasis and assignments will be most valuable by the end. Part II includes a semester course plan for using *Interplay* and the accompanying Instructor's Manual as the central resources for teaching the interpersonal communication course. This course outline is intended as a model which the instructor can use whole, in part, or simply as a guide to organizing a particular course. The manual contains numerous teaching exercises and a bibliography for reading assignments. The textbook contains discussion questions and activities in every chapter. The course outline below is a *starting point* for constructing a syllabus for a semester course in interpersonal communication. You will need to adapt it to your own specifications and interests. For those of you who are interested in Team Learning, there is a complete syllabus, course outline, necessary forms, and sample readiness assessment test provided following the generic outline below.

In addition to tailoring the schedule to the days/lengths of your course, here are some questions you'll want to consider when planning your own course:

1. This outline assumes three Unit Wind-Ups and a final. Do you want more or fewer exams? Do you plan to give quizzes? Will you use the Group Study Exercises? Do you plan to give assignments that will need to be explained in class?
2. This outline assumes you will cover all of the text's chapters and give them relatively equal attention. Do you want to cover every chapter? Do you want to address them in sequence? Do you want to devote more or less time to particular chapters and topics?
3. This outline assigns activity days for certain chapters. Do you want those activity days for those chapters? Do you want more or fewer activities? Which activities of the many in the manual will you choose to use? How long will they take?
4. An alternative ending to the semester might include the viewing/discussion of a feature film or student/guest presentations. Do you want to include these activities? Would you rather use speakers/films outside of class time? Would you rather use them throughout the course rather than at the end? How can you adjust the schedule to make room for these activities?

INTERPERSONAL COMMUNICATION: COURSE OUTLINE

When just the chapter and title are listed, the instructor needs to choose how the chapter materials (and other supporting materials) will be covered. How much will you lecture (as little as possible, it's hoped)? Will you use large or small group discussion? How will you involve students? What kinds of questions will you ask? What types of examples will you call for?

STANDARD INTERPERSONAL COURSE OUTLINE

Week One
Day One: Introduction to the course and each other
                 Reading Assignment: Chapter 1-Interpersonal Process
Day Two: Interpersonal Process
Day Three: Interpersonal Process

Week Two
Day One: Interpersonal Process Activities
                 Reading Assignment: Chapter 2-Culture and Communication

Day Two:	Intercultural Communication
Day Three:	Intercultural Communication

Week Three
Day One:	Intercultural Communication Activities
	Reading Assignment: Chapter 3-Communication and the Self
Day Two:	Self-Concept
Day Three:	Self-Concept

Week Four
Day One:	Self-Concept Activities
	Reading Assignment: Chapter 4-Perceiving Others
Day Two:	Perception
Day Three:	Perception

Week Five
Day One:	Perception
Day Two:	Perception Activities
Day Three:	UNIT WIND-UP #1
	Reading Assignment: Chapter 5-Language

Week Six
Day One:	Post Wind-Up Review
	Begin Language
Day Two:	Language
Day Three:	Language

Week Seven
Day One:	Language Activities
	Reading Assignment: Chapter 6-Nonverbal Communication
Day Two:	Nonverbal Communication
Day Three:	Nonverbal Communication

Week Eight
Day One:	Nonverbal Communication
Day Two:	Nonverbal Activities
	Reading Assignment: Chapter 7-Listening
Day Three:	Listening

Week Nine
Day One:	Listening
Day Two:	Listening Activities
	Reading Assignment: Chapter 8-Emotions
Day Three:	Emotions

Week Ten

Day One:	Emotions
Day Two:	Emotions Activities
Day Three:	UNIT WIND-UP #2
	Reading Assignment: Chapter 9-Dynamics of Interpersonal

Relationships

Week Eleven

Day One:	Relationships: Attraction Variables
Day Two:	Relationships: Models
Day Three:	Dynamics Activities
	Reading Assignment: Chapter 10-Intimacy and Distance in

Relationships

Week Twelve

Day One:	Relationships: Intimacy & Disclosure
Day Two:	Relationships: Self-Disclosure
Day Three:	Self-Disclosure Activities
	Reading Assignment: Chapter 11-Communication Climate

Week Thirteen

Day One:	Communication Climate
Day Two:	Communication Climate
Day Three:	Climate Activities
	Reading Assignment: Chapter 12-Managing Conflict

Week Fourteen

Day One:	Managing Conflict
Day Two:	Managing Conflict
Day Three:	Conflict Activities
	Reading Assignment: Chapter 13-Communicating with

Family/Work

Week Fifteen

Day One:	Communicating With Family and Work
Day Two:	Communicating With Family and Work Activities
Day Three:	UNIT WIND UP #3

"TEAM LEARNING" INTERPERSONAL COURSE OUTLINE

COM 252
Interpersonal Communication
General Course Outline
Fall 2003
http://www.uky.edu/~drlane/interpersonal

COM 252-000 Class Meets: 8:00 a.m. - 9:15 p.m. Tuesday and Thursday EGJ 225

Instructor Dr. Derek R. Lane drlane@pop.uky.edu Office: 238 Grehan Building 257-4651

Office Hours Wednesday 9:00 a.m. - 1:00 p.m. (and by Appointment)

Required Course Materials

Adler, R., Rosenfeld, L., & Proctor, R. (2004). *Interplay: The process of interpersonal communication*, Ninth Edition, New York: Oxford University Press.

Other supplemental readings will be provided throughout the course. Required reading material will be available in the Reading Room on the first flood of EGJ and/or in the W. T. Young Library of the reserve shelves.

Students will also be expected to purchase three packages of Scantron Forms #882-ES from the UK Bookstore.

Note: The benefits you receive in this class are directly proportional to your efforts in keeping up with the assigned reading and actively participating in class to build trust, cooperation, support and mutual respect.

Course Description

Interpersonal Communication (COM 252) is designed to increase your understanding and implementation of effective interpersonal communication behaviors and skills. Throughout the semester we will examine basic verbal and nonverbal elements effecting communication between individuals in family, peer groups, and work contexts. This course requires you to participate in activities designed to develop interpersonal communication skills and will actually improve the quality of your life if you keep an open mind and actively participate! Topics include: an introduction to interpersonal communication theory, strategy development, relationship and conversation management, effective listening, conflict management, defensive communication, communication anxiety, cultural/gender differences in communication style, ethics in communicating, relationship development communication climate, and intercultural communication.

Interpersonal communication introduces students to the complex interaction of social and psychological forces operating in human communication. The course is designed with a dual approach consisting of both theory and application that allows students opportunities to critically evaluate the intricacies of interpersonal relationships and the communication issues surrounding human interaction in various contexts. Theories will be considered based on relevance to empirical research, and various applied communication contexts (e.g., industry, education, medical and legal practice, etc.). There is an important distinction between social skills/manners and the interpersonal communication skills you are expected to develop in this course.

Course Purposes

1. The course seeks to increase student "relational sensitivity." Only as students become more socially sensitive can they recognize the various conditions that help and/or hinder the process of interpersonal communication.
2. The course seeks to increase student "behavioral flexibility." Only as students become more flexible in their behaviors can they select the appropriate behavioral responses to specific communication situations.
3. The course seeks to <u>motivate students</u> to demonstrate behaviors that facilitate competent communication and improve overall student and community life. *Enhanced communication skills create better citizens of the world.*

Competencies and Objectives[‡]

Students in this course will examine the dynamics of face-to-face encounters. A number of theories of communication will be examined that describe various aspects of the communication process. Many individuals believe that "communication" is so basic that it is taken for granted and not thought about seriously. Unfortunately, this attitude tends to result in such difficulties as misunderstandings, conflict, avoidance, and stereotyping. We will examine basic concepts, theories, and research findings relevant to initiating, developing, modifying, maintaining, and terminating relationships with an eye to the role of communication in the process. Lecture, discussion, response papers, in-and-out-of-class observations, and occasional "applied" assignments will be used to increase student knowledge and behavioral competence in interpersonal communication.

At the conclusion of the course it is expected that students will demonstrate knowledge and skills in several core areas. Specifically, students should demonstrate an increased understanding of:

1. The options and alternatives for action in a wide variety or interpersonal situations.
2. Individual preferences and an increased appreciation for the differences of others.
3. The dialectical tensions that can arise as students use communication to satisfy personal conflicting needs.
4. How the process of perception affects communication behavior.
5. The ethical dimensions of interpersonal communication.
6. The importance of nonverbal communication in developing successful interpersonal interactions.
7. Defensive and supportive communication climates.
8. Competence and an ability to assess the appropriateness and effectiveness of interpersonal strategies used in various interpersonal situations.
9. Why and how relationships develop and the role communication plays in determining the nature and quality of interpersonal relationships.
10. Interpersonal communication conflict and the application of conflict management principles.
11. The competencies related to communicating with individuals from other cultures and co-cultures.

In addition, COM 252 addresses the following University Studies Competencies:

Writing: To communicate effectively using standard written English (Students complete assigned written exercises designed for improved self-awareness of communication strengths and weaknesses.)
Reading: To understand, analyze, summarize, and interpret a variety of reading materials.

[‡] A special thanks to Russell F. Proctor, Ph.D., Northern Kentucky University, for permission to reprint instructions.

(Class discussions and examinations cover assigned required reading.)
Integrated Learning: To think critically and make connections in learning across the disciplines. (Students research, evaluate and organize information in order to complete written assignments and to develop an effective oral presentation in the form of a Group Workshop.)
Creative and Critical Thinking: To elaborate upon knowledge to create thoughts, processes, and/or products that are new to the students. (Students are challenged to incorporate strategies in their written assignments and oral presentations.)
Ethics/Values: To demonstrate awareness of ethical considerations in making value choices. (Students discuss value choices, personal and social ethics as related to interpersonal communication.)

Instructional Modes: Class Organization

This class will be organized into small learning teams. The majority of class time and several of the graded assignments will involve work in these teams. Class activities will include team exams, structured exercises, and workshops designed and managed by the teams. All team members will receive the same score on team exams and projects. The course combines lectures by the instructor, class discussion of assigned textbook readings, *group/team work*, audio/visual presentations emphasizing certain communication concepts and skills, oral presentations by the students, quizzes, exams, and classroom activities which will all contribute to your overall understanding of interpersonal communication. Out-of-class work may include written exercises (journals and communication improvement plans) and library research of communication concepts that are presented in a group workshop. Assigned chapters should be read *before* class so that you will be able to make a contribution to class discussions and activities and perform well on the quizzes and exams.

General Class Requirements

You are expected to:
- Be on time for all class meetings.
- Interact productively in class discussions and small group activities.
- Be prepared daily for discussions and quizzes by reading all assigned material BEFORE the day it is listed on the course schedule.
- Successfully deliver an instructional group presentation (workshop). FAILURE TO DO THIS ASSIGNMENT WILL RESULY IN AN 'E' FOR THE COURSE.
- Submit all written assignments TYPED at the BEGINNING of the class period on the designated date.

Classroom Civility

There are certain basic standards of classroom civility that should be adhered to, particularly in a communication course. Civility does not eliminate appropriate humor, enjoyment, or other features of a comfortable and pleasant classroom community. Classroom civility does, however, include the following:

1. Displaying respect for all members of the classroom community, both your instructor and fellow students.
2. Attentiveness to and participation in lectures, group activities, workshops, and other exercises.
3. Avoidance of unnecessary disruptions during class such as private conversations, reading campus newspapers, and doing work for other classes.
4. Avoidance of racist, sexist, homophobic, or other negative language that may unnecessarily exclude members of our campus and classroom community.

These features of classroom civility do not comprise an exhaustive list. Rather, they represent the minimal sort of behaviors that help to make the classroom a pleasant place for all concerned.

Reasonable Accommodation

The University of Kentucky is an Affirmative Action Equal Opportunity Institution. Students with disabilities and other special needs should feel free to contact the professor privately if there are services or adaptations which can be made to accommodate specific needs. If you have a special need that may require an accommodation or assistance, please inform the instructor of the fact as soon as possible and no later than the end of the second class meeting.

Criteria for Course Completion

This course consists of several assignments, each of which must be completed. **There are no optional assignments.** Course completion is accomplished when all necessary assignments (Quizzes, Workshops, Application Journals, Communication Improvement Plans, Interpersonal Assessments, Papers, Participation, and Exams, etc.) have been completed. Failure to submit ALL assignments will result in an E for the course—regardless.

Attendance Policy

ATTENDANCE IS REQUIRED. Readings, class discussions, group workshops, and in-class activities increase both your understanding of interpersonal communication theory and the development of your interpersonal communication skills. Class attendance and participation are important in accomplishing the goals of this course. If you are going to miss a class it is your responsibility to speak with the course instructor PRIOR to the class session you will be missing. In order to receive credit for attendance you must attend the ENTIRE class period. Failure to do so will result in an absence for the given class session.

If your class meets three times a week, you will be allowed three absences. If your class meets twice per week, you will be allowed two absences. If you class meets once a week, you will be allowed one absence (this is a total combination of excused and unexcused during the semester). However, you cannot make up work missed for unexcused absences—you simply receive a zero. **For each subsequent absence, 5% will be deducted from your final grade (students not attending class will not be given credit for any participation grade).**

For example, if your class meets twice a week and you finish the semester with a 91% average but have three absences (one more than is allowed) you will receive an 86%, which is a B. If you are late for your class, it is YOUR responsibility to make sure the instructor has not marked you absent for the day. This must be done on the day that you are late. Notice that you are given free absences for situations in which you are really sick or have to miss class. Do not use these "freebies" for blowing off the class and then come to the instructor later (after you have gone over the limit) when you are really sick or have an emergency and expect an excuse. The freebies *allow* for emergencies; please don't take advantage.

For any officially excused absence you are responsible for presenting official written documentation for the absence. For university-sponsored absences this notification is to be given to the instructor prior to the absence; for other excused absences, this documentation must be presented within two weeks of the absence. Students are responsible for arranging to make-up missed individual work. Missed group work cannot be made up. In other words: "To have an absence excused, you will need to give your instructor legitimate written proof from a recognized source explaining the absence…AND IT BETTER BE GOOD."

Please arrive to class on time. Tardiness is unprofessional and is not fair to me or to your classmates. Consequently, if you are consistently late, you can expect to have 1% deducted from your final grade for EACH tardy. Moreover, do not expect your instructor to cover any missed material.

Classroom Participation Policy

The quantity and quality of your contributions to class discussion and activities will be evaluated according to the following criteria:

1. Are you prepared for class discussions (e.g., completed reading, prepared for discussion questions)?
2. Are you able to relate your own experiences and observations to class concepts?
3. Do you respond to statements by others in an appropriate manner?
4. Do you move the discussion along, not derail it?
5. Do you ask questions and/or paraphrase when needed and appropriate?

If you do miss class, please see a classmate regarding class discussions and assignments. NO MAKE-UP WORK IS AVAILABLE for oral presentations, in-class exercises, quizzes, or exams.

Course Requirements

Oral Communication Skill Work

Since this is an oral communication skills course, we want to provide you with many opportunities to develop these skills. Aside from general class participation such opportunities may include the preparation for and performance and evaluation of role-playing activities, in-class presentations, and briefing sessions and discussion, analysis and critique of dyadic communication case studies, etc.

Written Work

You will be expected to use correct spelling in all written work. Use of appropriate grammatical skills in oral and written communication is also very important. Throughout the course you will expand your personal vocabulary through the study of terms related to the course. Your written work will be evaluated on both content and mechanics. Good writing should be reasonably free of mistakes and without composition errors which are called gross errors (sentence fragments, run-on sentences, subject-verb disagreement, misspelled words, and typographical errors which result in such errors). All of your work **MUST BE TYPED** (using no more that 12 point type with margins not exceeding 1 inch on the top, right, and bottom, nor 1.5 inches on the left) and double-spaced—unless otherwise indicated by the instructor. **You must also submit all written assignments using APA 4th Edition style guidelines.**

Reading

Your reading assignments are included in the course calendar. In addition to the textbook, you may, from time to time, be required to read other material that will be put on reserve in the Communication Reading Room in Grehan Bldg. If you do not do the reading, do not expect to benefit substantially from the course. **Class sessions are used to supplement rather that to review the reading material assigned.**

Exams and Projects

There will be twelve, short, true-false, multiple choice Readiness Assurance Tests (RATs) given during the course (approximately one at the beginning of each week). The same RATs will be given to individuals and teams. In addition, students will be expected to take a midterm exam (Chapters 1-8) and a comprehensive final, design a team workshop, participate in several interpersonal simulations, write a 2-4 page "I Am" reaction paper and write a 8-10 page Interpersonal Communication Analysis Paper which applies interpersonal communication theory and concepts to a student-selected interpersonal communication context.

Readiness Assessment Tests

You will be given twelve RATs. Each RAT will consist of multiple choice questions addressing the reading for that day.

"I Am" Paper

We will complete a class exercise called "I Am." Following this exercise you are to try it out on friends, family, etc. and write a two- to four-page typed paper. This paper will give students the opportunity to experience the editing/grading style of the professor before completing the major interpersonal communication analysis paper.

Interpersonal Communication Analysis Paper

You will select a context from which to analyze interpersonal communication, which is to be approved by the professor. You will apply what you have learned about interpersonal communication theory to the context you have chosen. The major content and ideas of the paper will be shared in an oral presentation to your peers.

Doing Your Own Work

We expect that all of the individual assignments you complete for COM 252 (and in all your other courses) are always your own work. We find, however, that many students are not exactly sure what the "your own work" means. So, please read again the information on plagiarism and cheating from your UK Student Rights and Responsibilities Handbook.

The sanction or punishment for a student who has either plagiarized or cheated is a minimum of an "E" grade for the entire course, but may involve suspension, dismissal, or expulsion from the University. As you can see, these are extreme measures for academic offenses which we believe are serious. If you have any questions about whether you may be plagiarizing in your work for COM 252, please be sure to contact me well in advance of the due date for your assignment.

Grading Criteria

The grades will be determined by scores in three major performance areas: *Individual Performance, Team Performance,* and *"Helping Behavior."* This course consists of several assignments, each of which must be completed. *There are no optional assignments.* Course completion is accomplished when all necessary assignments have been finished.

Grade Calculation

Individual Performance

Individual Readiness Assurance Tests	120 pts.
"I Am" Analysis Paper	50 pts.
Interpersonal Communication Analysis Paper	100 pts.
Midterm Exam (Chapters 1-8)	80 pts.
Oral Presentation of Interpersonal Analysis	50 pts.
Comprehensive Final Exam (Chapters 1-12)	120 pts.

Team Performance
Team Readiness Assessment Tests   _____ 120 pts.
Team   _____ 30 pts.
Peer Evaluation Procedures and Criteria   _____ 30 pts.
Team Workshop   _____ 200 pts.

Helping Behavior (Evaluated by Instructor and Peers)   _____ 100 pts.

TOTAL 1000pts _____ / 100

Helping Behavior

Each individual will rate the helpfulness of all the other members of their teams prior to the final exam. Individual helping behavior scores will be calculated using the mean of two score: (a) the average of the points they receive from the members of their group; and (b) the participation score they receive from the instructor. Assuming arbitrarily that (1) helping behavior is worth 10 points, and (2) that there are five members in a team, an example of this procedure would be as follows: Each individual must assign a total of 40 points to the other four members in their team. Not al group members contribute equally. Some members are more motivated or more communicative that others. For this reason raters must differentiate some in their ratings (This means that each rater would have to give at least one score of 11 or higher—with a maximum of 15—and at least one score of 9 or lower). The instructor will assign a participation grade for each of the members and this score will be averaged with the mean score from the group members to arrive at a comprehensive helping behavior score. The helping behavior scores will produce differences in grade only **within** teams. As a result, group members can't help everyone in their group get an A by giving them a high peer evaluation score. The only way for everyone in a group to earn an A is by doing an outstanding job on the individual and team exams and projects.

Determination of Final Grades

The final grades will be determined by adding the total points in each of the three performance areas: individual performance, team performance, and maintenance (helping behavior).
Grading Scale:
> *The plus/minus grading system is effective for this course.*

A+=100.00 - 96.45	A = 96.44 - 92.45	A- = 92.44 - 89.45	Students who attain points
B+ = 89.44 - 86.45	B = 86.44 - 82.45	B- = 82.44 - 79.45	that give them 59.44%
C+ = 79.44 - 76.45	C = 76.44 - 72.45	C- = 72.44 - 69.45	or less will receive a
D+ = 69.44 – 66.45	D = 66.44 – 62.45	D- = 62.44 – 59.45	FAILING GRADE of E.

Graded Individual Assignments

1. Individual Readiness Assurance Tests
2. "I Am" Reaction Paper
3. Interpersonal Communication Analysis Paper
   Students will be presented with specific information regarding this assignment during the first two weeks of the course. The length of the paper must be between 8 and 10 pages excluding the title page. Do not use a font size larger than 12 point nor margins larger than 1.5 inches on the left of 1.0 inches on the top, bottom or right.
4. Midterm Exam (Chapters 1-8)

5. Oral Presentation of Interpersonal Analysis
6. Comprehensive Final Exam

Graded Team Assignments

1. Team Readiness Assurance Tests
2. Design a Team Resume
3. Develop instruments and procedures for providing performance feedback to team members that will: 1) facilitate individual growth and learning and, 2) enhance the team's overall effectiveness.
4. Each team will design and manage a team workshop on specific concepts related to one of the following five major topics.

Workshop #1 Perceiving Others	Chapter 4	Thursday, September xx
Workshop #2 Language	Chapter 5	Thursday, October xx
Workshop #3 Nonverbal Communication	Chapter 6	Thursday, October xx
Workshop #4 Listening	Chapter 7	Thursday, October xx
Workshop #5 Emotions	Chapter 8	Thursday, October xx

These workshops will include: 1) a one page synopsis of the major conceptual issues; 2) a demonstration of key concepts; 3) a brief annotated bibliography of at least ten resources not included in the textbook, which much be integrated into the workshop; and 4) the opportunity for question from the class and instructor. The grade for these presentations will be determined by an evaluation by the members of the other teams and the instructor's evaluation. Grading criteria include research component, presentation style, distribution of effort, quality of handouts, quality of activity, video usage, wrap-up/debriefing linking activities to concepts.

More on Learning Team Assignments

The importance of your membership and participation in your learning teams cannot be overstated, since this is how the majority of your efforts in class will be evaluated. The learning team in which you are a participant will function in the following ways:

1. Each of you will be responsible for supporting, encouraging, and assisting other members of your group to read the assigned material, to participate actively in class and the interpersonal exercises and meetings, and to think about the issues raised in class sessions and readings.
2. Each of you will be responsible for evaluating other members of your team in a fair, mature, and well-substantiated manner. While it is up to the individuals within the team to determine evaluation criteria, the team is ultimately responsible for explaining and defending the criteria to the instructor based on the goals which the team wishes to achieve at the completion of the course. The team grading criteria will be evaluated based on comprehensiveness, rationale, and detailed substantiation.
3. Each team member will participate in four major assignments:
   a. The first major assignment is the active participation of all team members in the team readiness assessment tests.
   b. The second major assignment is to design a **team resume** which will assist team members in identifying strengths of individual members, develop mutuality of concern, and build cohesion. Strengths of all individual members of the team will be integrated in order to familiarize other teams with the "competition."
   c. The third major assignment will be to develop **instruments and procedures for providing performance feedback** to team members that will: 1) facilitate individual growth and learning and, 2) enhance the team's overall effectiveness. These criteria must be specific.

d. The fourth major assignment will be a **team workshop**. Each team will present a workshop which will include the selection of a specific movie clip which will be analyzed based on all information discussed in class and covered in the textbook. Each team will present their analyses to the class.

"I AM" PAPER GUIDELINES

The "I Am" exercise we did in class was an attempt to get you in touch with how you perceive yourself. The purpose of this assignment is to find out how *others* perceive you and to compare and contrast their perceptions with your own.

Give the slips of paper to a *minimum* of two other people who know you (the more people you ask, the more you'll learn). I recommend that you choose people who may have differing vantage points on your life (i.e., mother/boyfriend; close friend/casual friend; co-worker/family member). Ask them to construct a configuration (using the format from class) that typifies *you as they see you.* Request that they be as honest as possible, then leave the room while they work on it. Upon returning, discuss with them their rationale for the rankings they made (please do so in a supportive tone; your goal is to learn, not defend!).

The goal of your paper is to present what you learned, *applying concepts from lecture and text where appropriate.* Issues you may want to address include:

1. What were the major differences and similarities between the various configurations? How do you account for them?
2. You probably handed the slips to the respondents with some expectations of how they would rank you. Did their rankings match your expectations? (You may want to actually construct your expected rankings in advance, then compare and contrast).
3. What part did *meaning* and *perception* play in this assignment?

Feel free to run additional variations of this exercise. Some variations include:

"Turnabout is Fair Play"
Construct a configuration of the people who ranked you (and see if their evaluations of you have an impact on the way you assess them!

"Two Heads Are Better (or Worse) Than One"
Ask two or more people to work together on a configuration of you (and get ready for the sparks to fly!)

"Twice Removed"
Construct a configuration of how you think another person perceives a third person (the permutations on this are mind-boggling!)

This assignment is not so much a report or a research paper as it is a personal inventory, analysis, and reaction paper. As a result, it is appropriate (and recommended) to use first-person singular pronouns (I, me, my, mine) in describing what you experienced and learned. Avoid impersonal or collective pronouns (you, it, we)—speak for and about yourself. Please be sure to provide examples and specifics from this exercise, as well as from your interactions with the people who help you to complete this assignment. Your paper will be kept confidential; feel free to be as candid as is comfortable for you.

I am expecting a 2-4 page paper (excluding title/cover page), TYPED and STAPLED. Please use double-spacing, 1-inch margins, 10 or 12-point font, and do not right-justify your margins. I expect college-level writing and presentation: in other words, I want proper punctuation, spelling, and syntax;

complete sentences and paragraphs; no white-out, handwritten corrections, or typos. Failure to attend to these matters will result in a lowered grade. The assignment is due at the beginning of class on Thursday, September xx, 2003 (Late papers will not be accepted).

Tentative Schedule of Topics, Readings, and Labs

Thursday, August xx	Orientation to the course, expectations explored, Student Expectations/Team Formation Interpersonal Communication Defined
Tuesday, September x Thursday, September x	Overview of Interpersonal Communication—RAT #1, Chapter 1 Interpersonal Processes, Principles, and Preconditions *Peer Evaluation Procedures and Criteria Due*
Tuesday, September x Thursday, September x	Culture and Communication—RAT#2, Chapter 2 "I Am" Experiential Activity *Team Resume Due*
Tuesday, September xx Thursday, September xx	Communication and the Self—RAT #3, Chapter 3 Application Workshop *"I Am" Reaction Paper Due (2-4 pages)*
Tuesday, September xx Thursday, September xx	Perceiving Others—RAT #4, Chapter 4 *Team Workshop #1 w/film clip*
Tuesday, September xx Thursday, October x	Language—RAT #5, Chapter 5 *Team Workshop #2 w/film clip*
Tuesday, October x Thursday, October x	Nonverbal Communication—RAT #6, Chapter 6 *Team Workshop #3 w/film clip*
Tuesday, October xx Thursday, October xx	Listening—RAT #7, Chapter 7 *Team Workshop #4 w/film clip*
Tuesday, October xx Thursday, October xx	Emotion—RAT #8, Chapter 8 *Team Workshop #5 w/film clip*
Tuesday, October xx Thursday, October xx	*MIDTERM EXAMINATION*, (Chapters 1-8) *Interpersonal Communication Competence*
Tuesday, November x Thursday, November x	Dynamics of Interpersonal Relationships—RAT #9, Chapter 9 CMC Application Workshop
Tuesday, November xx Thursday, November xx	Intimacy and Distance in Relationships—RAT #10, Chapter 10 Application
Tuesday, November xx Thursday, November xx	Communication Climate—RAT #11, Chapter 11 Application *Interpersonal Communication Analysis Paper Due*

Tuesday, November xx	Managing Conflict—RAT #12, Chapter 12
Thursday, November xx	*Academic Holiday - Thanksgiving*
Tuesday, December x	*Oral Presentation of Interpersonal Communication Analysis*
Thursday, December x	*Oral Presentation of Interpersonal Communication Analysis*
Tuesday, December x	*Watch Video for Final Exam* - Evaluate Helping Behavior
Thursday, December xx	*Watch Video for Final Exam* - Course and Teacher Evaluation

Comprehensive Final Examination (covering all readings, lectures, and discussion)
COM 252-000   Wednesday, December xx, 2003, 8:00 a.m.   EGJ 225

TEAM LEARNING FORMS

Teacher Expectations—"Score Points With the Professor" (to be used first day)
Guidelines for Writing Appeals
Readiness Assessment Test Team Appeal Forms
Peer Evaluation Procedures and Criteria
End of Semester Helping Behavior Form
Sample Readiness Assessment Test—Chapter 1

How To Score Points With Your Professor!
Some Tongue-in-Cheek Tips for Impressing the Professor[§]

1. Try to arrive in class a few minutes late each day—that way, the class (and Dr. Lane) will be sure to notice you.

2. Be sporadic in your attendance. It's not a good idea to "wear out your welcome," and Dr. Lane won't mind.

3. Class time is a good opportunity for catching up on your work in other courses. It can also be well-spent reading the newspaper, talking with a friend, or taking a nap. Dr. Lane loves to see his students using their time efficiently.

4. Avoid coming to class prepared. Reading the text in advance, for instance, means you'll lose a sense of spontaneity. You wouldn't want to "spoil" Dr. Lanes lecture, would you?

5. Dr. Lane is really flexible about his assignment due dates. If you turn in something late, don't worry—it actually helps him spread out his workload. Penalties? NEVER!!

6. Only the things Dr. Lane puts on the board or the overhead are important. Keep this in mind and you'll take fewer notes.

7. Don't participate in class unless Dr. Lane calls on you. It's rude to ask questions and inappropriate to express opinions. Remember—this is education, not a talk show.

8. When someone else asks a question in class, pay no attention. Dr. Lane will be happy to answer the exact same question when you ask it a minute later.

9. Inasmuch as this is only an interpersonal communication course, don't worry about spelling, grammar or punctuation in your written assignments—that stuff is for English classes.

10. When you make spelling errors, inform Dr. Lane it's because you don't have a computer with a spell-checker. He certainly won't expect you to use a dictionary, for heavens' sake.

11. Remember, personality is more important than performance. If Dr. Lane likes you, you're guaranteed a good grade.

12. Nobody, especially Dr. Lane, still believes "C" means "average." Simply come to class and you're guaranteed _at least_ a "B."

13. If you're going to be absent, don't notify Dr. Lane in advance. Just show up several days later and ask, "Did I miss anything important?" (one of his favorite questions). Being the nice person he is, he won't hold you responsible for anything you missed while you were absent.

14. Here are some other of Dr. Lane's favorite comments:
    If you miss a question on an exam: "That's a trick question."
    If you do poorly on an assignment: "My mom (husband, dog, roommate) thought it was   great."
    If you won't be in class: "I need to study for another course."

15. Don't bother Dr. Lane with questions during his office hours; he has work to do. Instead, approach him one minute before class and ask him to look over the assignment you've just written.

16. Dr. Lane needs help remembering what time it is, so begin packing your books five minutes before class is over. He will appreciate the reminder and be impressed with your concern.

17. Wait until you are at the crisis point before asking for help; otherwise, he won't consider your problem important.

18. If you have a complaint or concern, don't discuss it with Dr. Lane—he won't listen or try to understand (after all, he doesn't really _believe_ in this communication stuff). Instead, talk about it with as many classmates as possible. Better yet, give Dr. Lane no clue that you are upset, then unload on him in your course evaluation. Now _that's_ effective communication!

[§]This exercise is based on ideas from a paper written by Russell Proctor entitlcd "Communicating Rules With a Grin" which was originally presented at the Central States Communication Association Annual Meeting in April, 1994.

19. Don't drop by Dr. Lane's office to chat—he's far too busy to be concerned about you. Remember, he's not in this profession because he loves working with students; he's in it for the money.

20. Don't keep this handout or a copy of the syllabus; Dr. Lane didn't mean for you to take them seriously. He just made them to have something to talk about on the first day of class. deposit them in the trash on the way out today.

Purposes of the Appeals Process

1. Clarify uncertainty about your understanding of the concepts.
2. Give additional recognition and credit when "missing" a question was caused by:
   - ambiguity in the reading material.
   - disagreement between the reading material and our choice of the "correct" answer.
   - ambiguity in the wording of the question.

Guidelines for Preparing Successful Appeals

Appeals are granted when they demonstrate that you understood the concept(s) when you answered the questions of that your lack of understanding was due to ambiguity in the reading material. As a result:

If the appeal is based on either inadequacies in the reading material or disagreement with our answer, you should:

1. state your reason(s) for disagreeing with our answer and,
2. provide specific references from the reading material to support your point of view.

If the appeal is based on ambiguity in the question, you should:

1. spell out why you thought the question was ambiguous and,
2. offer an alternative wording that would have helped you avoid the problem.

Readiness Assessment Test Appeal Forms

Readiness Assessment Test Appeal (Groups only)

Team Name _____ Test # _____ Question # _____

Proposed correct answer _____

Rationale for your appeal:

Supporting evidence:

Readiness Assessment Test Appeal (Groups only)

Team Name _____ Test # _____ Question #_____

Proposed correct answer _____

Rationale for your appeal:

Supporting evidence:

Peer Evaluation Helping Behavior

Many college students experience "group hate" because of past negative experiences working in groups. Most negative experiences, however, can be overcome by generating peer evaluation performance criteria and implementing simple evaluation procedures.

The creation of a peer evaluation process involves **two separate phases**:

Phase one is an *individual process* which requires each individual to generate two separate lists.

- List one contains individual goals and objectives which are to be accomplished during the semester.
- List two consists of *specific performance criteria* that is expected of all group members.

Phase two is a *group process* which requires the group to generate four specific products. The group must:

- Develop a list of group goals and objectives which subsumes ALL of the individual goals and objectives generated during phase one.
- Generate a list of group performance criteria which includes ALL of the individual expectations generated during phase one.

Produce a **well-organized document** that ***best communicates*** the group goals and objectives as well as group performance criteria to your instructor. *This document should be written in narrative form (using complete sentences) and be prepared using the procedure on the next page. It should be presented to the instructor in a **professional format.***

Create a **peer-grading form** which lists the specific criteria that your team will use to evaluate the participation of all team members (this includes a self-evaluation) throughout the course of the semester. Your peer grading form should be created on the computer so that revisions can be easily made. *This form should also be presented to your instructor in a professional manner.*

Peer Evaluation Procedures and Criteria

Instructions:

You are to develop a system for providing performance feedback to the members of your group in this class. Your group will use this procedure to provide performance feedback within the group at regular intervals during the semester.

In order to accomplish the task, each individual member will:

1. First, think about group experiences you have had in the past. If your experiences were negative, what made them negative? What did other group members do (or not do) that created problems? Now think about your positive experiences. What made those experiences positive?
2. Next, generate two lists. The first list should include specific INDIVIDUAL GOALS and OBJECTIVES you wish to accomplish during the course of this semester. The second list should provide specific PERFORMANCE CRITERIA that you expect from every group member (e.g., attendance, preparation, motivation, positive attitude, etc.).
3. Finally, share your list with your group. Pay close attention to details and similarities between individual goals, objectives, and performance criteria.

AS A GROUP you will then:

4. Develop two separate lists:
   List one should contain GROUP GOALS and GROUP OBJECTIVES;
   List two should contain PERFORMANCE CRITERIA.
   Both lists should be generated by combining all individual lists (both group lists should reflect an integration of individual goals and individual performance criteria).

5. Create a **document** that best communicates those team goals to your instructor. This document should be created in a professional format and include the following:

   a. A statement of specific team goals and objectives. Remember, these goals should reflect an integration of individual team members' goals. List them. Each goal should be a separate statement, usually in one sentence. Be specific.
   b. A description of how you intend to collect the data on which the feedback will be based. Please include copies of specific peer grading forms as examples of data collection instrument(s) and refer to these peer grading forms in your description.
   c. A description of the feedback process you intend to use. Please specify:
   When feedback will be give—provide specific dates and times.
   Who will give it to and to whom.
   d. An assessment of the difficulties that you are likely to encounter in implementing your performance feedback system and how these difficulties will be overcome using your procedures and criteria.
   e. A statement of how the system provides input into the grading process for the class.

6. Your team will create **a peer grading form** which lists the specific criteria that your team will use to evaluate the participation of all team members (this will include a self-evaluation) at least twice during the semester. The purpose of this evaluation is to allow team members to make *course* corrections in their helping behaviors before the end of the semester. This *form should be presented to your instructor in a professional manner.* Your document and grading form should be created on the computer so that revisions can be made easily.

The assignment will be evaluated using the following <u>criteria:</u>

1. Is the group collecting data that they will need to support the achievement of their individual and team objective(s)? Are the objectives clearly listed?
2. Will the procedures they intend to use support the achievement of their objective(s)? Do the procedures support objectives?
3. Are the procedures they intend to use practical (i.e., do they meet the guidelines set forth and can they be implemented effectively in the specific situation in which they will be used)? Is the assessment form consistent with guidelines and objectives?
4. Have they accurately anticipated the problems that they are likely to encounter in implementing the procedures? Are anticipated problems clearly stated? Are detailed strategies included for how the problems will be overcome?

End of Semester Helping Behavior Peer Evaluation

Please assign scores that reflect how you really feel about the extent to which the other members of your group contributed to your learning and/or your group's performance this semester. This will be your only opportunity to reward the members of your group who actually worked hard for your group. **If you give everyone pretty much the same score, you will be hurting those who did the most and helping those who did the least.**

Instructions: In the space below rate each of the **other** members of your group. Each member's peer evaluation score will be the average of the points they receive from the other members of the group. To complete the evaluation, you should:

a. List the *name of each of your group members in alphabetical order* by their last names. Include your name in the list but do not assign points to yourself.
b. Assign a total of 50 points.
c. Differentiate ratings among the group members so that at least one person scores 11 or higher (15 max.) and one score is 9 or lower.

Group Members	Scores
1) _____	_____
2) _____	_____
3) _____	_____
4) _____	_____
5) _____	_____
6) _____	_____

Additional feedback. In the space below, briefly describe your reasons for your *highest* and *lowest ratings.* These comments—but not information about who provided them—will be used to provide feedback to students who wish to receive it.

Highest ratings(s). Why did you assign this rating? (Use back side of paper. if necessary.)
Lowest rating(s). Why did you assign this rating? (Use back side of paper if necessary.)

Sample Readiness Assessment Test (RAT)

COM 252 Interpersonal Communication   **Readiness Assessment Test #1**
The University of Kentucky   Department of Communication

Multiple Choice Select the *best* answer. Record your answer three (3) times on the answer sheet. If you are not sure about the answer, you may "split" answers (e.g., a a c).

1-3. All of the following are valid reasons for studying communication *except*
    a. to learn new ways of viewing something already familiar.
    b. to discover weakness in others.
    c. it takes approximately 60% of our waking time.
    d. to be more successful in relationships.
    e. knowledge tends to increase effectiveness.

4-6.   Which of the following is a limitation of the interactive view of communication?
  a.   the implication that the roles of speaking and listening are done alternately
  b.   the portrayal of communication as a two-way activity
  c.   the emphasis on both verbal and nonverbal feedback
  d.   the portrayal of misunderstandings in terms of the participants' different environments
  e.   all of the above

7-9.   Your first encounter at a job interview is affected by the interviewer's scowling facial expression. Which characteristic of communication best describes the situation?
  a.   communication is irreversible.
  b.   communication is a transactional process.
  c.   communication is static.
  d.   communication is dependent on personalized rules.
  e.   none of the above describes it.

10-12.   In a survey of personnel managers, the ability to speak and listen effectively was rated as more important than
  a.   technical competence.
  b.   work experience.
  c.   academic background.
  d.   two of the above.
  e.   all of the above.

13-15.   The text suggests a "qualitative" definition of an interpersonal relationships. Which of the following is NOT one of the criteria for that definition?
  a.   context
  b.   irreplaceability
  c.   disclosure
  d.   interdependence
  e.   all are criteria

16-18.   Two friends, Jennifer and Kristi, have developed a way of dealing with each other when they are angry. The angry person puts a note on the refrigerator indicating the problem, and the other person writes on it a time when they can talk it over. This is an example of
  a.   truncated communication.
  b.   uniqueness.
  c.   impersonal communication.
  d.   face maintenance.
  e.   unintentional communication.

19-21.   Which of the following means the same thing as the statement in your text, "Communication is irreversible?"
  a.   Erasing or replacing spoken words or acts is not possible.
  b.   No amount of explanation can erase the impression you have created.
  c.   It's impossible to "unreceive" as message.
  d.   Words said are irretrievable.
  e.   All mean the same as the statement.

22-24. When a religious person listens to a speaker who uses profanity, he or she would experience
    a.   external noise.
    b.   cognitive complexity.
    c.   relational noise.
    d.   physiological noise.
    e.   psychological noise.

PART III CHAPTER EXERCISES
Chapter One Interpersonal Process

Introductions

Approximate Time: 30 minutes

Purpose: To enable the class members and instructor to learn the name of the members of the class: to establish early in the class a climate of trust and active interaction

Procedures:
1. Divide the class randomly into pairs (including the instructor if you wish). Be sure that the members of each dyad do not know each other.
2. Tell the class that they are going to spend ten minutes getting to know as much as they can about each other.
3. At the end of the ten minutes, bring the class together in a circle and announce that each person will now introduce her/his partner and will share with the class the single most distinguishing thing learned about her/his partner.

Alternate Procedures:
1. Arrange the class (including the instructor) in a large circle.
2. Beginning with the student to the instructor's left, ask each person to give his/her name, followed by answers to the same 2-3 "fun" questions, such as:
    a. If you could have anything to eat for lunch (dinner) today, what would you have?
    b. What song or artist would you like to hear on the stereo after class?
    c. What's the best birthday/holiday gift you've ever received?
    d. If you won the lottery, what's the first thing you'd buy?
3. After students offer their name and answer the question, ask them to recall the names of all the people who preceded them. Some tips:
    a. Don't allow students to write down name; the idea is to put names to memory.
    b. Offer hints/help to students having trouble remembering names. The game should be (and usually is) fun, not embarrassing.
    c. The instructor should be the last person the complete the task, naming all the students in the circle.

Another Alternative: The Name Game
1. Arrange the class (including the instructor) in a large circle.
2. Begin with the instructor stating his/her name and an animal that in reminiscent of him/her self or an animal which (s)he would like to be and why.
3. The student to the instructor's left continues by adding his/her name, animal and rationale for the choice and then repeating the name of the instructor and the animal (without the rationale).
4. The game continues with each student adding his/her name and reviewing all of the previous names and animals. The instructor concludes the game by repeating all of the names and animals.

Another Alternative: The Toilet Paper Exercise or The Candy Exercise
1. Arrange the class (including the instructor) in a large circle.
2. Begin with the instructor tearing off 5-6 sheets of toilet paper or taking 5-6 pieces of candy.

3. Hand the roll of toilet paper or candy to every student with the instructions "Take as much as you think you'll need for the class."
4. Once the entire class has taken the paper or candy, tell them you are going to go around the room (starting with the instructor) and have everyone take turns introducing themselves to the class. Everyone must include their name, what year they are, their major if declared, and then one piece of personal information for every piece of paper or candy they have. Some examples are favorite food, movie, how many siblings, etc.

The Team Resume

Approximate Time: 50 minutes

Purpose: To enable the class members and the instructor to learn each other's names; to establish a climate if trust and active interaction in the class; and to introduce students

A team resume is a fun way to help students become acquainted and identify strengths of all individual members of the team. The resume should include information that communicated the uniqueness of students and their respective teams.

Procedures:
1. Divide the class randomly into teams of no more than six students per teams. Be certain that each group has approximately equal resources in terms of diversity (age, gender, culture, academic major, distance to travel to attend class, etc.) and that the members of each team do not know each other.
2. Explain to the groups that they are going to spend twenty minutes getting to know as much as they can about each other and develop a team resume using the following format:
   a. Interview individual team members to obtain information that presents a team 'image" and sells the group as a whole.
   b. Develop a format for the team resume. Realizing that it can be presented on the chalkboard, an overhead transparency, or as a role-play or skit, it should be creative, introduce all members to the class, and incorporate most of the following data:
      Educational background; schools attended
      Knowledge about interpersonal communication
      Individual goals
      Team goals
      Job Experience
      Positions held
      Skills
      Interests
      Hobbies, talents, travel, family
      Accomplishments
   c. Determine Team Name, Team Logo (symbol) and Team Motto
   d. Prepare a 5-minute presentation to be delivered to the class.
3. At the end of the twenty minutes, each team will be given five minutes to introduce their team members and present their resume to the rest of the class.

First Impressions

Approximate Time: 50 minutes

Purpose: To enable the class members and the instructor to learn each other's name; to establish a climate of trust and active interaction in the class; and to introduce students to some of the concepts they will deal with in the course

Procedures:
1. Follow instructions in items 1 and 2 in Introductions.
2. After ten minutes, bring the class back together and announce that each person will give her/his first name. Have each class member quickly (in 5-10 seconds) write the first name, last initial, and a word or short phrase that is her/his "gut-level" first impression of the person who gave her/his name.
3. After first impressions have been made on each class member, have each person introduce the person she/he interviewed.
4. After the introductions, lead a discussion of how first impressions are formed, and how they may change or not change.

Principles Illustrated:
1. Many concepts covered in the course are related to first impressions—personal environments, stereotyping, sharing personal information, the role of nonverbal communication, feedback, self-fulfilling prophecies, qualitative communication, etc.
2. Unexamined first impressions may be problematic in communicating with others.

Extension of First Impressions

Approximate Time: 40 minutes (in addition to above time)

Purpose: To encourage more sharing of personal information; to examine the bases of first impressions; to explore differences in how we perceive ourselves, idealize about ourselves, and how others perceive us

Procedures:
1. Follow instructions in items 1 through 3 in First impressions.
2. Ask students to cut first impressions into strips for each person, and bring them to the following class. Tell them the first person into the room should begin laying them on the instructor's desk. Each person should follow suit, so there will be a stack of first impressions made on each class member by each of her/his classmates. (Note: Encourage students to keep strips in the order that they were written to expedite placing them in piles for each person.)
3. Give class members the stack of first impressions made about them by their classmates. Tell them to pick the first impression mad by others that is most like the way they see themselves and pick the first impression that is most different from the way they see themselves and to share these with the class.
4. After everyone has had a chance to share first impressions and get reactions from the class, the instructor should lead a discussion of how first impressions are formed, the impact of additional personal information upon first impressions, the usefulness of sharing others' perceptions in personal decision making, and the degree to which group members moved toward more qualitative interpersonal communication.

Principles Illustrated:
1. There are differences among self-perceptions based on our experiences, and those based upon what we might like to be, or think we are like.
2. You cannot not communicate. If someone sees you in a certain way, you are that way to that person.

What Is Interpersonal Communication?

Approximate Time: 30 minutes

Purpose: To familiarize students with the definition of interpersonal communication around which Interplay is structured

Procedures:
1. After students have a chance to read Chapter One, divide the class into group of 4-5.
2. Assign each group one of the following situation. Each group should decide if interpersonal communication has occurred in their assigned situation. (Where would they place it on a scale of one [interpersonal] to seven [impersonal]?) If the group decides that the situation is impersonal how might it be made interpersonal? The group should be able to justify its decision. Encourage the group to attempt to reach a consensus, rather that merely vote. Allow about ten minutes.

   Situation #1:
   While she is waiting in line at the supermarket check-out counter, a woman who is in line behind Maria comments, "Your coat look really warm. It must be nice and cozy on these cold winter days." Maria says, "Yes, it is, thank you." Before she moves up to the clerk, Maria chats with the woman about where she got the coat and how much she has used it.

   Situation #2:
   Ellen and Kendrick have known each other on a surface level for a couple of years. At a party they meet and strike up a conversation about a mutual friend Kendrick would like to date. During the course of the conversation, Ellen comments, "I know your type. You think you can use my personal credibility with Sharon."

   Situation #3:
   "Chandra, you know we promised each other on the night that we met that we'd always be honest no matter what. Now you can tell me what has happened."

   Situation #4:
   A student visits a professor to discuss an exam grad and before long they discover that they both grew up in northern Minnesota. For several minutes they recollect about the cold winters there.

   Situation #5:
   Jim is functioning as host for his organizations' funding-raising campaign dinner. He greets each member as they arrive and offers to take their coat and hat and directs them to the bar and hors d'oeuvres trays.
3. Meet again in the large class group. Have each group present its decision and rationale on whether their situation fulfilled the conditions of a definition of interpersonal communication. Have members of other groups raise issues and indicate the extent that they agree or disagree with the presenting group's decision and rationale.
4. Review the essential components of a developmental view of interpersonal communication.

Principles Illustrated:
1. Interpersonal interaction is characterized by individual regard.
2. Interpersonal relationships are characterized by the development of individualized rules.
3. Interpersonal relationships are characterized by the amount of personal information the partners share.

THE COMMUNICATION BLITZ

An Introductory Exercise About the Phenomenon of Communication
(An Exercise developed by Carol Z. Dolphin, University of Wisconsin–Waukesha)

Approximate Time: 30 minutes

Purpose: To emphasize various channels and modes of communication, as well as its pervasive nature in our society today

Procedures:
1. When students enter the classroom for their class meeting, they find the desks arranged in a circle. They are placed fairly close together with enough seats for each registered student, the instructor. (A few extras may be warranted if it is the first day of class.) Prior to the students entering, place the following on each desk: a sheet of typing paper to use as a name card, a brightly colored index card, a copy of a brief "Interpersonal Communication Quiz" (this could be the Communication Principles Survey at the end of this section or it could be based on the Communication Misconceptions which appear in Chapter One), and a piece wrapped candy. There are also magic markers placed on a few of the desks.
2. When the session begins and before taking roll, tell the students to be sure to pay close attentions to what is going on around them, to what they are doing, to what is being said, and to their affective responses.
3. Before beginning roll, tell students that while you are taking roll they should share the magic markers and place their first names of the typing paper—which they will then hang over the fronts of their desks and use as name placards for the first few weeks.

    Also, ask them to place the following information on the index card: name, address, phone number. Previous communication courses, and major. (You might want to write this list on a transparency and place it on the overhead projector as well.) Finally, they should complete the quiz. The candy may be opened and eaten at any time. Begin playing a background of classical music.

4. After each few names have been called, add cumulative communication stimuli:
    a. First, begin to pass around a number of objects which have varying textures (a plush stuffed toy, a piece of sandpaper or emery board, a brass weight, a piece of silk, perhaps a hot or cold pack, etc.). Students are told to touch each objet long enough to feel the texture/temperature and to notice a distinguishing feature about each object.
    b. After a few more names, turn off the lights in the room and do something to add the element of smell. Such as a lightly scented room spray. You could also pass around hand lotion, which the students may choose to use.
    c. Next, turn on a radio or tape with popular music with a good beat. This should be music that is readily familiar to the majority of the students. Turn on the lights again.
    d. Next, add the element if a video tape. The tape might vary according to the nature of the class. A Chaplin silent movie (one that they will recognize somewhat but without the distraction of additional sound) is a good choice. In a unit on intercultural communication, a foreign language film—using the most common second language of the class members (i.e., those with facility in that language would pay more attention than those not familiar with it)—is a good choice.
5. When this has gone on 'long enough" (you'll be able to tell by the nonverbals of the students), give them at least five minutes to write about the following:
    a. Describe what just happen. Use only sense data (facts). List all of the things you were aware of. Star the ones you heard and circle the ones you listened to. Again, limiting your observations to

sense data, what did you notice about the behavior of others?
    b.   Describe you own behavior and your feelings.
6.   Divide the students into small groups of about five members each. In the small groups, they are told to share their written reactions and discuss the exercise:
    a.   Did you recall different parts of the exercise than other members of the group? Why do you think this happened?
    b.   What made some factors which influenced what you remembered and what you neglected to remember?
    c.   What made this a difficult situation?
    d.   Based upon your discussion and other lifetime experiences, determine five barriers to effective listening.
    e.   Based upon your discussion, determine three general statements (principles) about listening (or communication).

Principles Illustrated:
1.   Communication takes many forms.
2.   Communication is always taking place; we can't not communicate.
3.   All communication comes to us via the channels of our senses.
4.   We cannot attend to all of the communication which takes place around us.
5.   Different people attend to different stimuli for a variety of reasons.
6.   We can identify a number of common barriers to effective listening.
7.   Our ability to attend effectively may be influenced by our affective responses.
8.   Although we may all receive the same sensory stimuli, it possible to interpret the stimuli in a variety of ways.

Communication Misconceptions

Approximate Time: 30 minutes

Purpose: To familiarize student with communication principles and misconceptions; to provide a simple non-threatening task for group early in the semester. (Note: This exercise world as early as the first day of the semester.)

Procedures:
1.   Type the following misconceptions about communication on an index card—one misconception per card.
    a.   Communication will solve all our problems.
    b.   We need more communication.
    c.   Communication can break down.
    d.   The more we communicate, the better.
    e.   Words have meaning.
    f.   Communication is a verbal process.
    g.   All communication is intentional.
    h.   Telling is communicating
    i.   Communication is natural human ability.
    j.   Feeling should be communicated spontaneously, not bottled up.
2.   Divide the class into groups of 4-5, and give each group two index cards with a misconception printed on them. (This is assuming a class of 20-25. A good way to get interaction later is to make sure that at least one of every group's misconceptions is duplicated in another group.)

3. Do not tell the class that the statements are misconceptions. Tell them that these are statements frequently made about communication, and that they have about 10 minutes to agree on a position relative to the statement. They should attempt to reach a consensus, rather that use majority vote. Of course, those who have read Chapter 1 may recognize the statements, but, interestingly, some waving usually occurs as a result of a conflict between the textbook and students' "common sense" view of communication as impacted by peer pressure.
4. After 10 minutes bring the groups back together. Let each group present its "consensus." Ask questions and try to get each member to speak. Encourage members of other groups to refute the conclusions of the group reporting. (Discussions can become rather lively, if a group which had the same statement disagrees with the conclusions of the first group called upon.) Write each statement and the group's consensus on the board, but do not comment on the validity of its conclusions until all groups have reported.
5. After all group have reported, point out that those who study communication say that all the statements are false, and lead the class in a discussion of why this might be said. Provide an alternative to each statement similar to these:
    a. Communication may create or help solve problems.
    b. Quality of communication is more important than quantity.
    c. One cannot no communicate.
    d. Communication is a tool. It has no moral quality.
    e. Meanings are in people.
    f. Communication is both verbal and nonverbal.
    g. Communication is both intentional and unintentional.
    h. Saying something is not the same as communicating it.
    i. Communication is learned.
    j. Feeling need to be shared appropriately.

Communication Myth Survey

Approximate Time; 35-40 minutes

Purpose: To introduce students to a number of concepts to be covered in the course; to establish a climate conducive to interaction and discussion

Procedures:
1. Without prior discussion distribute the Communication Principles Survey on the next page and allow students 5-7 minutes to fill it out.
2. Without collecting the surveys go through the items and solicit answers from the class. Ask students to discuss the reasons why they responded the way they did.
3. Make the point that there are no right or wrong answers. Many who study communication do not agree on all these points, but certain perspectives will be supported in this course.

Principles Illustrated:
1. Review of Chapter One and overview of several concepts which will be developed in this course.
2. There are no absolute truths in communication studies.

COMMUNICATION PRINCIPLES SURVEY

Circle the numbers on the following scales which most closely represents your belief.

1. People are _____ aware of their own communication patterns.

    100%   75%   50%   25%   0%

2. Male and female communication patterns are

    extremely   the

    different   same

    10   9   8   7   6   5   4   3   2   1

3. All communication behaviors are

    learned/   innate/

    changeable   fixed

    10   9   8   7   6   5   4   3   2   1

4. The language that we use is _____ factor in shaping self-concept.

    a primary   a secondary   not a

    10   9   8   7   6   5   4   3   2   1

5. Everyday language use _____ be altered.

    should   should sometimes   should not

    10   9   8   7   6   5   4   3   2   1

6. Everyday language usage can be altered.

    totally   somewhat   not at all

    10   9   8   7   6   5   4   3   2   1

7. The ultimate meaning of words is determined by

    people alone   people/words   words alone

    10   9   8   7   6   5   4   3   2   1

8. Nonverbal messages make up _____ of our communication behavior.

    100%   75%   50%   25%   0%

9. Most people are _____ as listeners.

    highly skilled   competent   unskilled

    10   9   8   7   6   5   4   3   2   1

10. Communication patterns and skills _____ the way our relationships turn out.

    completely   have   have

    determine   some effect on   no effect on

    10   9   8   7   6   5   4   3   2   1

PORTFOLIO ENTRY

Interpersonal Communication: A Personal Assessment

(Note: Students should be asked to reassess their skills and progress toward goals at the end of the semester.)

Think about your current communication skills. You might consider your general communication skills (such as expressing yourself clearly, think before you speak, making up your mind firmly, saying "no" without feeling guilty), your self-awareness skills (such as understanding your won strengths and weaknesses, being able to identify your values, recognizing the impact of your behavior on others, setting realistic goals), and your interpersonal skills (such as listening with an open mind, being a good "people reader," expressing feeling appropriately), etc.

In narrative (essay) form, respond to the following questions: What do you identify as your two or three most significant strengths in the area of communication? Illustrate each of these strengths by a specific personal example. What do you identify as your one or two most significant weaknesses? Illustrate (specifically) why you fell these are problem areas. Now determine three to five goals (in the area of interpersonal communication) which you would like to set for yourself this semester. What is one specific thing that you could do now in order to reach toward one of those goals?

D & A

(another version of the portfolio above)

1. What do you identify as your one single major strength in the area of interpersonal communication? Illustrate your response by giving two specific personal examples of times when you displayed this strength.
2. What do you identify as your one significant weakness? Give one example (specifically) to illustrate why you feel this is a problem area for you.
3. How do your strength and weakness relate to the communication competence section in chapter 1? Make sure to use course terminology in your discussion.

GROUP STUDY

The following matching exercise could be used as either a group study too or as a "group quiz" exercise. (See the Introductory Essay for further information.) The following directions should be included for each Group Study Exercise given through the manual:

All members of the group must decide upon a single answer. When you have finished the exercise, ALL members of the group should sign off on a single copy; however, all copies must be handed in. (Groups have the right to exclude the name of any member who is unprepared and/or does not contribute to the discussion.)

Answer directly on this sheet. Begin by clarifying the terms as they have been defined in your test. When doing the exercise, pay particular attention to underlined words and phrases

CHAPTER ONE

Match the letter of the communication process element with its description found below.

a. encode
b. decode
c. channel
d. message/feedback
e. noise
f. environment

_____ 1. The children make a <u>videotape</u> of themselves to send to their grandparents instead of <u>writing a letter</u>.
_____ 2. Majorie tries to <u>decide the best way</u> to tell Martin that she can't go to Hawaii with him.
_____ 3. Martin <u>decides Majorie means</u> she doesn't love him when she says she can't go to Hawaii.
_____ 4. It's <u>so hot and smoky</u> in the room that Brad has a hard time concentrating on what his partner is telling him.
_____ 5. Linda <u>smiles</u> while Larry is talking to her.
_____ 6. Brooke is <u>daydreaming</u> about her date while Allison is talking to her.
_____ 7. Since Jacob <u>has never been married</u>, it's difficult for him to understand why his <u>married</u> friend Brent wants to spend less time with him.
_____ 8. Whitney says, <u>"I'm positive about my vote."</u>
_____ 9. Richard <u>thinks Jon wants to leave</u> when he (Jon) waves to him (Richard).
_____ 10. Laura <u>winks</u> when she <u>says</u> she's serious and <u>gestures</u> with her arms.
_____ 11. Erin is from a <u>wealthy family</u> and Kate from a <u>poor one</u>. They have a serious conflict about how to budget their money.
_____ 12. Jack has been <u>feeling a cold coming on</u> all day while he has sat through the meeting.
_____ 13. Levi <u>constructs the best arguments</u> to convince his parents to buy him a new car.
_____ 14. Jessica <u>decided to lie</u> to her group members about the reason she missed the meeting last night.
_____ 15. <u>"I refuse to go,"</u> said Jeremy.

ANSWER KEY:

1. c	6. e	11. f
2. a	7. f	12. e
3. b	8. d	13. a
4. e	9. b	14. a
5. d	10. c	15. d

TEACHING ACTIVITIES FROM THE *COMMUNICATION TEACHER*

Berko, R. (1993, Winter). *Getting to know you and talking about it, 7(2)*, 5-6.

Bozil, M. (1988, Summer). *Who said that? 2(4)*, 6.

Bozik, M and Beall, M. (1994, Winter). *Modeling metaphorical thinking, 8(3)*, 1-3.

Garrett R.L. (1998, Fall). *The interpersonal communication survey, 13(1)*, 9-11.

Gill, B. (1998, Fall). *Understanding communication through popular music, 13(1)*, 11-12.

Myers, S. A. (1998, Summer). *Developing student awareness of interpersonal communications competence, 12(4)*, 6.

Oetzel, J. G. (1994, Fall). *The skills project, 9(1)*, 1-2.

Phillips, T. G. (1996, Winter). *Name that analogy: The communication game, 10(2)*, 10-11.

Ringer, R. J. (1989, Summer). *Pre-post test for interpersonal communication classes, 3(4)*, 4-5.

Rumbough, T. B. (2000, Spring). *52ways to break the ice, 14(3)*, 6-8.

Wilson, W. (1989, Winter). *Sex role stereotypes: What do we see in them? 3(2)*, 15.

Chapter Two: Communication and the Self

Accentuate the Positive

(Adapted from Games Trainers Play by Edward E. Scannell)

Approximate time: 10 minutes

Purpose: To break down self-imposed barriers that don't allow people to "like themselves"; to enhance one's self-image by sharing comments and personal qualities.

Procedures:

Most of us have been brought up to believe that it is not "right" to say nice things about one's self or, for that matter, about others. This exercise attempts to change that attitude by having teams of two persons each share some personal qualities with one another. In this exercise, each person provides his or her partner with the response to one, two, or all three of the following suggested dimensions.

1.   Two physical attributes I like in myself.
2.   Two personality qualities I like in myself.
3.   One talent or skill I like in myself.

Explain that each comment must be a positive one. No negative comments are allowed. (Since most people will not have experienced such a positive encounter, it may take some gentle nudging on your part to get them started.)

Discussion Points:
1.   How many of you, on hearing the assignment, smiled slightly, looked at your partner, and said, "You go first?"
2.   Did you find this to be a difficult assignment to start on?
3.   How do you feel about now?

Four facts

Approximate Time: 45 minutes

Purpose: To encourage more sharing of personal information; to examine the bases of first impressions; to explore differences in how we perceive ourselves, idealize about ourselves, and how others perceive us

Procedures:
1.   Divide the class into teams of no more than six students per team. Be certain that each group has approximately equal resources in terms of diversity (age, gender, culture, academic major, distance to travel to attend class, etc.) and that the members of each team do not know each other.
2.   Distribute the "Four Facts Exercise" form to every student.
3.   Instruct students in each team to take 3-5 minutes and independently list four " facts" not themselves. Three of them should be true (but not obvious). One of them should be false.
4.   As a group every individual should complete the following steps:
     a.   List below the name of each person in your group on the form.
     b.   Each person reads the four statements aloud.
     c.   As each person reads the four statements, list next to his/her name the number of statement you

think is false about them and <u>why</u>.

    d. Once each person has completed sharing the statements, take one person at a time and have each of the remaining people tell which statements is false and why. Then the person who shared the four statements originally can reveal which one was really false.

    e. Repeat the procedure for each of the people in your group.

5. ***Designated team leader*** should ***process*** and ***debrief*** the following four questions with all the other members of the team (make certain <u>everyone</u> participates):

    a. Were you surprised at some of the "fact" that people shared? Which? Why?

    b. How good were you as a group, and individually, at picking the false statement? What does this tell you about making assumptions and judgments about people?

    c. Were some of the statements made by different people similar? What reasons could you give for this?

    d. Were some of the "facts" quite different? What reasons could you give for this?

"THE FOUR FACTS EXERCISES" FORM*

Simulation adapted from Resources for Organizations, Inc. 1992

Part I ***Independently***, list four "facts: about yourself. Three of them should be true (but not obvious). One of them should be false.

    1.

    2.

    3.

    4.

Part II ***As a group***, do the following steps, in order:

1. <u>List</u> below the name of each person in your group.

2. Each person <u>reads</u> their four statements aloud.

3. As each person reads the four statements, list next to his/her name the <u>number</u> of statement you think is false about them and <u>why</u>.

4. Once each person has completed sharing the statements, take one person at a time and have each of the remaining people tell which statements is false and why. Then the person who shared the four statements originally can reveal which one was really false.

5. Repeat the procedure for each of the people in your group.

Name _____ Statement # _____ is false
because _____.
Name _____ Statement # _____ is false
because _____.
Name _____ Statement # _____ is false
because _____.
Name _____ Statement # _____ is false
because _____.
Name _____ Statement # _____ is false
because _____.
Name _____ Statement # _____ is false
because _____.
Name _____ Statement # _____ is false
because _____.

Part III ***Designated team leader*** should ***process*** and ***debrief*** the following four questions with all the other members of the team (make certain <u>everyone</u> participates):

1. Were you surprised at some of the "fact" that people shared? Which? Why?
2. How good were you as a group, and individually, at picking the false statement? What does this tell you about making assumptions and judgments about people?
3. Were some of the statements made by different people similar? What reasons could you give for this?
4. Were some of the "facts" quite different? What reasons could you give for this?

Self-Concept Object

Approximate Time: 50 minutes

Purpose: To help students become aware of how they view themselves and to illustrate differences among the perceived, ideal, and presenting selves

Procedures:
1. Have each student bring to class a small object which she/he thinks is somewhat symbolic of the way that she/he views her/himself (e.g., a watch, a colorful bottle with a cork, a book, a teddy bear, etc.).
2. At the next class period, ask students to form a large circle and show their self-concept objects. As each object is shown, have the class speculate as how the presenter views her/himself. Then, have each presenter tell why she/he chose that object.
3. Lead discussions relating the presentations to the content of Chapter 4.

Principles Illustrated:
1. Differences in perceived, ideal, and presenting selves.
2. How labels are a part of reflected appraisals.
3. Aspects of self-concept that develop by social comparison.
4. How feedback from others influences the development of self-concept.
5. How self-fulfilling prophecies are formed.
6. How self-concept can change in positive ways.

The Self-Concept Bag

Approximate Time: 50 minutes

Purpose: To help students become aware of their own self-concept and to illustrate differences among the perceived, ideal, and presenting selves

Procedures:
1. Tell students to bring to the next class period a "bag" of their self-concept. They should get a large paper bag and on the outside of the bag they should construct a collage that symbolizes what they know of themselves that is also know by others. Some students will cut pictures from magazines and advertisements, while other will want to exercise their own creativity and artistic talents.
2. Instruct students to place inside the bag pictures, labels, or objects which symbolized what they know of themselves that it not known by others.
3. Inform students that at the next class period they will have the opportunity to talk about their bag. They must bring the bag to class, but will be allowed to talk about as much or as little of it as they like. Let students know in advance that they will not be forced to talk about themselves.
4. At the next class period, have students form a circle. They should discuss the outside of the bag and then share one or more picture from the inside.

Principles Illustrated:
1. Differences in perceived, ideal, and presenting selves.
2. How labels are a part of reflected appraisals.
3. Aspects of self-concept which develop by social comparison.
4. How feedback from others influences the development of self-concept.
5. How relationship stages alter self-perceptions.
6. The role of self-disclosure in the creation of self-perceptions.
7. How self-fulfilling prophecies are formed.
8. How self-concept can change in positive ways.

Addressing One's self and Values

Approximate Time: 20 minutes

Purpose: To increase students' awareness of self

Procedures:
1. Have each students answer each question below spontaneously and quickly.
2. Have each student go back and reflect upon and answer each question again, coming up with personal examples of what they did and how they communicated in the past under these circumstances.
3. Ask students to share answers they are comfortable sharing.
   a. I am happiest when…
   b. I am most secure when…
   c. When I am home alone I…
   d. If I could change two things about myself, I would …
   e. I believe in…
   f. I trust those who…
   g. When I chose I…
   h. My advice to someone who wants to let her/his true self emerge or actualized would be…

Principles Illustrated:
1. Some aspects of our self-concept are revealed by analyzing our responses to questions.
2. Some aspects of our self-concept are revealed by comparing our responses to those of others.

"I Am"

Approximate Time: 30-60 minutes, depending on time allotted to discussion

Purpose: To help students become aware of their self-concepts and how they were formed

Procedures:
1. Type (or photocopy) the following phrases on a sheet of paper. Substitute different adjectives if you'd like, but keep the total at 16.
   I AM ATTRACTIVE
   I AM LONELY
   I AM INTELLIGENT
   I AM MERCIFUL
   I AM PERFECTIONISTIC
   I AM SERIOUS

I AM HUMOROUS
I AM ENTHUSIASTIC
I AM GENEROUS
I AM POPULAR
I AM SHY
I AM CONFIDENT
I AM FEARFUL
I AM EMOTIONAL
I AM COURAGEOUS
I AM OPINIONATED

2. Cut the phrases into slips of paper, then put a paper clip around them. Make one of these 16-slip packets for each student.
3. Instruct the students to arrange themselves in the classroom in such a way that they can conduct an exercise on their desks in privacy. They may necessitate moving desks and chairs.
4. Give each student a packet. Tell them to arrange the 16 slips to represent "the way you see yourself." They should use the following configuration: (Note—this portion of the exercise could be done out of class.)

C1	C2	C3	C4	C5	C6	C7
		SLIP				
	SLIP		SLIP			
	SLIP		SLIP	SLIP		
SLIP		SLIP		SLIP	SLIP	
SLIP		SLIP		SLIP		
	SLIP		SLIP			
		SLIP				

The slip in column 7 (C7) should be the phrase that MOST describes the way they see themselves. The slip in column 1 (C1) should be the phrase that LEAST describes the way they see themselves. The other columns are then a continuum between LEAST and MOST. For columns with multiple slips (i.e., C4), there is no rank difference between slips within in the column.

Discussion Questions:
1. What part did "reflected appraisal" play in building your configuration? Did you hear voices of significant others in your mind as you were arrange the slips? What about "social comparison?"
2. What is the relevance of "meaning is in people' to this exercise?
3. Might your configuration have looked different last week? Last year? Yesterday?
4. Were there any "strange bedfellows"—that is, slips in the same column that would seem to be contradictory?

Variations:
There are variations and extensions for this exercise. Variations include asking students to arrange the slips into a configuration of the person they would *like* to be. Extensions include having each student ask two significant others to offer their perceived configuration of the student, then analyzing the similarities and differences in a paper.

Principles Illustrated:
1. There are differences between perceived, desired, and presenting selves.
2. Self-concept us shaped by reflected appraisal and social comparison.
3. Self-concept is relatively stable but flexible.

PORTFOLIO ENTRY

Understanding Myself

(Note: This can be a very powerful exercise. When students "lose" some of their essential characteristics, they frequently increase their owe appreciation for who they are.)

Referring to the exercise in the beginning of Chapter 3, make a list of ten words or phrases that describe the most important features of who you are. Now arrange then ten characteristics in order of their importance to your own self image. Continue the exercise, following the directions carefully and writing your responses. Your written report should include your list of the ten fundamental items and the answer to the following questions; How do you change after each step? How do you feel about the "new you" which is created? (Make your descriptions specific. It is not enough, for example, to say, "Without my friendliness, I wouldn't have any friends, and I'd be lonely," or "Without this quality, I'd feel empty." Truly try to imagine the change which losing this characteristic would make in your basic perceived self.) What does this exercise tell your about yourself? Are these perceptions about yourself you would like to change?

D & A

Who Do You Think You Are?
1. Fill out the "Who Do You Think You Are" Survey. For the purposes of this exercise, you should include both positive and negative descriptors.
2. From each of the eight groups of terms, choose and circle one word or phrase that you think describes you best.
3. For each of the eight words or phrases, discuss how you came to believe you have that trait. Identify a specific person or event that helped develop each of the eight parts of your self-concept.
4. Be sure to include terms from the chapter to help explain your self-concept development.

WHO DO YOU THINK YOU ARE?
1. What moods or feelings best characterize you? (cheerful, considerate, optimistic, crabby, etc)
        a._____   b_____   c_____
2. How would you describe your physical condition and/or appearance? (tall, attractive, weak, muscular, etc)
        a._____   b_____   c_____
3. How would you describe your social traits? (friendly, shy, aloof, talkative, etc)
        a._____   b_____   c_____
4. What talents do you possess or lack? (good artist, bad writer, great carpenter, competent swimmer, etc)
        a._____   b_____   c_____
5. How would you describe your intellectual capacity? (curious, poor reader, good mathematician, etc)
        a._____   b_____   c_____
6. What beliefs do you hold strongly? (vegetarian, Christian, pacifist, etc)
        a._____   b_____   c_____
7. What social rules are the most important in your life? (brother, student, friend, bank teller, club president, etc)
        a._____   b_____   c_____
8. What other terms haven't you listed thus far that describe other important things about you?
        a._____   b_____   c_____

*NOTE: If using the Two-Views Portfolio, an option is to ask students to refer back to this exercise when analyzing why they and their partner may have different perceptions.

GROUP STUDY

(See the Introductory Essay for further information. Consult the Group Study Section in Chapter One for additional direction to students.)

CHAPTER TWO

Match the letter of the term which best identifies each of the situations below. Be sure that you clarify the terms before you begin, and pay particular attention to underlined words, and phrases. Identify which principle influences the self-concept in each example.

a. cognitive conservatism
b. reflected appraisal
c. distorted feedback
d. significant other

e. social comparison
f. "facework"
g. self-fulfilling prophecy

_____ 1. Your father has always told you that you have mechanical abilities. He first time you try to fix your bike, your fail miserably.

_____ 2. Your always scored more points than anyone else on your team, in high school. You still think you're the best even though your college teammates out-score you in every game.

_____ 3. Even though Jim is six feet tall, he describes himself as "a shrimp" when he is with his friends who are members of The Milwaukee Bucks.

_____ 4. Kerby knows that his usual use of grammar is often incorrect and sloppy. At his boss's party, he carefully monitors himself so that he appears educated and intelligent.

_____ 5. Because Peggy's parents and teachers have always encouraged her in her undertakings, Peggy sees herself as a worthwhile human being.

_____ 6. Sheila is doing average work in college, but she likes to hang around with her friends who are working in a factory because it makes her feel smart.

_____ 7. Your parents tell you, their friends, and all your relatives about all your wonderful accomplishments, even though you have only average achievements.

_____ 8. You anticipate that the party on Saturday night will be boring; when you go, you have a terrible time.

_____ 9. Although Jerry is late for his job interview because he took a wrong turn in the way, he tries to preserve his image by commenting on the long train which he also encountered.

_____ 10. High school senior Kim really admires her English teacher, Ms Rudolph. When Ms. Rudolph suggests that Kim consider a career in education, Kim pays special attention to her.

_____ 11. Even though he doesn't know his fiancée Amy's parents well, jasper listens carefully to their advice.

_____ 12. Your father has always told you that you have above average mechanical abilities. The first time you try to fix your bike, you succeed easily.

_____ 13. Ever since the third grade when Erin's teacher told her that she war poor at art. Erin believes that she is non-artistic.

_____ 14. Because of your preparation and positive attitude, you feel assured of success at your job interview; you get the job.

_____ 15. You still think of yourself as a shy fifth grader despite being at the hub of social activity in at least three clubs on your college campus.

ANSWER KEY:

1.	c	6.	e	11.	d
2.	a	7.	c	12.	g
3.	e	8.	g	13.	b
4.	f	9.	f	14.	g
5.	b	10.	d	15.	a

TEACHING ACTIVITIES FROM THE *COMMUNICATION TEACHER*

Adams, J. (1991, Summer). *The mask, 5(4)*, 11.

Bashore, D. 91991, Fall). *The resume as a tool for self concept confirmation, 6(1)*, 10.

Berko, R. (1985, Fall). *Intra-interpersonal goal* setting, 8.

Berko, R. (1996, Fall). *The public 'I' and the private 'I', 1(1)*, 6.

Crawford, L. (1993, Winter). *Silence and intrapersonal observation as an initial experience, 392)*, 11-12.

DeWitt, J., & Bozik, M. 91997, Spring). *Interpersonal relationship building along the information superhighway: E-mail business across two states, 11(3)*, 1-2.

Eisenberg, R. (1987, Summer). *Talking to a machine, 1(4)*, 12-13.

Garrett. R. L. 91992, Summer). *The onion concept of self, 6(4)*, 6-7.

Johnson, C. (1987, Summer). *A day in the life..., 1(4)*, 11.

Overton, J. (1995, Spring). *On the line: A self-concept discovery activity, 9(3),* 8.

Nagel, G. (1989, Fall). *'Peculiarity': An exercise in sharing, caring, and belonging, 4(1)*, 3-4.

Rumbough, T. B. (2000, Spring). *52 ways to break the ice, 14(3)*, 6-8.

Shumer, A. (1991, Summer). *Speech communication via critical thinking—it's in the bag, 5(4)*, 4.

Smith, K. A. (1997, Spring). *Negotiation of self in nickelodeon's 'Rugrats,' 11(3)*, 9-10.

Chapter Three: Perceiving Others

The Lemon Exchange

(Adapted from "Games Trainers Play" by Edward E. Scannell)

Approximate Time: 20-30 minutes

Purpose: To vividly illustrate the importance of individual differences, the need for astute observational skills, and sensitivity to personal characteristics.

Procedures: Bring an adequate supply of lemons (or almost any fruit)
1. Distribute one lemon to each member of the class. Direct each person to examine their lemon carefully by rolling it, squeezing it, fondling it, inspecting it, etc. Ask them to get to know their lemon (always good for a few laughs). Tell them to pick a name for it. Encourage them to identify in their minds the strengths and weaknesses of their lemon.
2. Collect all the lemons and visibly mix them up in front of the class.
3. Spread out all of the lemons on a table, and ask all persons to come forward and select their original lemon. If conflicts develop over their choices, assist the parties in reconciling their differences, or simply note the failure to agree and use that as a basis for later discussion. (Note: The vast majority usually successfully identifies their own lemon.)

Discussion Questions:
1. How many are very sure they reclaimed their original lemon? How do you know?
2. What parallels are there between differentiating many lemons and differentiating many people? What differences are there?
3. Why can't we get to know people just as rapidly as we did our lemons? What role does the skin play (for lemons and for people)?
4. What action principles of human behavior does this bring to light?

"Computer-Mediated Perceptions"

Approximate Time: 50 minutes

Purpose: To introduce students to the factors that may influence our perceptions when interpersonal communication is mediated across time and space by technology

Procedures:
1. Divide the class into groups.
2. Tell the students that they will be "meeting" another group (from a distant university) in cyberspace. Provide each group with a list of email address from a randomly chosen group from the distant university and distribute the assignment sheet below.
3. Allow student groups one week to "meet" in cyberspace. This should provide sufficient time for groups to complete the assignment.
4. Student groups will present their "findings" to the class and discuss reasons for their perceptions.
5. Hold a large group discussion on the many factors which might influence our perceptions.

NOTE: the teacher will need to collaborate with a colleague from another university and prepare several lists of email addresses (one for each university).

CMC ASSIGNMENT SHEET

OVERVIEW

In 1961 Marshall McLuhan, wrote the medium is the message. By this McLuhan meant that the mediums by which communication occurs, such as the telephone, the television, or through handwriting, is more influential shaping one's understanding of a message than the content of the message itself McLuhan concluded that the same message content communicated over different mediums, such as television, radio, or printed material would be interpreted differently by message receivers.

Remember that during the early 1960s when McLuhan explained the relationship between mediums and their effects on understanding, television, itself, was a new medium whose effects were not fully understood. McLuhan believed that understanding the effects of a medium and the public's ability to adopt to a new medium or technology, took 20 years.

We are now facing a new communication technology whose effects we do not yet know: the World Wide Web [WWW or the Web]. Research suggests that we will witness increases in the number of people working at home and using the Web in the future, and you will need to know how to best communication using this medium.

To help you prepare for the future of the Web, you will explore the effects of communication that is mediated through technology by solving a problem with another learning team using the Web to communication (called Computer-Mediated Communication).

ASSIGNMENT

A learning team from your class will work with a learning team from another university to solve a problem. Once the problem is solved each team will present the results to their respective classes.

THE PROBLEM:

What is the best way to communicate with people or groups on the Web to ensure that the receiver accurately understands your message?

In solving this problem consider the following:

- How do relationship develop differently using the Web than from using other technologies, such as the telephone, or letter writing? What are the benefits and shortcomings of relationship development via the Web? How can deficiencies be overcome?
- What effect does the Web have on productivity? What effect does it have on the quality of work, and the rate at which it is completed?
- What makes the Web essentially different from any medium we have encountered thus far? What ONE thing makes it different from ANY other medium, and not the same as television, radio, letter writing, face-to-face communication, telephone, etc.?
- How are your perceptions influenced by Computer-Mediated Communication?

WHAT YOUR PRESENTATION SHOULD INCLUDE:

Your team will present your findings to your class. Your presentation should address the above questions while leading to a set of "rules" for ensuring our message is accurately interpreted on the Web. You will explain to your class the problems of communicating on the Web and how we can overcome them (via your rules), so that we can be better users of this new technology.

Additionally, promptly after your class presentation, your team will submit a one-page synopsis of your findings and your rules for better communicating on the Web.

Shopping List

(Developed by Kathleen Valde, University of Iowa, adapted from John R. Johnson (1989). "The nature of inner speech-instructional exercise." University of Wisconsin-Milwaukee)

Approximate Time: 15 minutes

Purpose: To introduce students to the myriad of factors which may influence our perceptions
(Note: This is a good, quick exercise to introduce the unit on perception.)

Procedures:
1. Divide the class into dyads.
2. Place the following list on the board or on a transparency:
   >milk
   >toothpaste
   >veggies
   >bread
   >detergent
   >cereal
   >pop
   >cookies
3. Tell students to assume that this list has been given to them by their partner as items to be purchased at the store. Based on their own habits and what they may know about their partners, students are to jot down exactly which items they would buy. (i.e., a quart of whole or a gallon of skim milk, etc.)
4. Students compare lists with partners and discuss reasons for their perceptions and misperceptions.
5. A large group discussion is held on the many factors which might influence our perceptions.

Perceptual Differences

Approximate Time: 20 minutes

Purpose: To demonstrate how physiological factors can lead to perceptual differences

Procedures:
1. From the biology department or chemical supply house, obtain strips of litmus paper treated with PTC (phenyl-thio-caramide).
2. Distribute the strips of paper to all members of the class. Have them tastes the strips at the same time.
3. How many found the paper to be salty? sweet? bitter? tasteless?
4. Discuss the differences. Then ask students to think of other situations which people perceive differently because of physical influences. Relate these to the textbook discussion of physical influences on perception.

Principles Illustrated:
1. People perceptive identical stimuli in vastly different ways.
2. Physical differences in people can lead to perceptual differences.
3. People need to be aware that not everyone perceives food, temperature, and interpersonal events in the identical way.

The Overhead Projector

Approximate Time: 20-30 minutes

Purpose: To heighten student awareness of perceptual differences and stereotyping tendencies when viewing an inanimate object. (It is sometimes less threatening to initiate discussions about stereotyping with exercises involving objects rather than people.)

Procedures:
1. Have students take out a sheet of paper.
2. Direct their attention to an object at the front of the room. An overhead projector is ideal and will be used in this exercise description.
3. Without calling it by name or turning it on, point to the overhead projector and tell the students they have five minutes to "write a description of this."
4. After five minutes, have students read their descriptions aloud (you can have every student read or select certain students). After each reading, discuss the unique features of the description, such as:
   a. What was emphasized and what was ignored?
   b. What words were used for colors, measurements, materials, etc. did those words differ from other students' descriptions of the same items?
   c. How did point of view affect perception?
   d. What other perceptual filters/influences affected perception?
5. Inevitably, some students will describe assumptions rather than facts. For instance, if the overhead projector is not on, then those who write about light bulbs they cannot see, cooling fans that aren't running, or enlargements that aren't on the screen are assuming that the projector is operational and functions like others they have seen before. (And as we instructors know, believing that an overhead is operational can be faulty assumption!) Using the exercise as an example, discuss the following stereotypical statements:
   a. If you've seen one projector, you've seen 'em all.
   b. I've worked with a lot of projectors, and they're all alike.
   c. A projector is a projector; don't expect anything different from this one.
6. Discuss the pros and cons of assigning characteristics of one projector to another projector. Discuss how this becomes even complex and hazardous when dealing with human beings.

Principles Illustrated:
1. People perceive identical stimuli in vastly different ways.
2. Physical and social perspectives influence one's organization and interpretation of an object.
3. Stereotyping is both natural and potentially hazardous.

Role Reversal in Perceptual Differences

Approximate Time: 45 minutes

Purpose: To illustrate how different persons' perceptions of events may be and to identify reasons for the differences

Procedures:
1. Divide the class into groups of five. If the class works better as a large unit, this exercise can be adapted to one done by the large group.
2. Select one issue that affects everyone in the group, such as class assignments, testing, grading policy, room location, or scheduling. Note both the group's perception of the situation and the perception of

another party who might see it quite differently, e.g., the professor, or administrative person who schedules class times.

3. Answer the following questions, keeping in mind the group perceptions and the perspective of the other person. Give the groups 20-25 minutes to do this.
    a. What is the problem area?
    b. How is information about the "problem" selected and organized by the other party?
    c. What is the other party's interpretation of the situation?
    d. How is information about the "problem" selected and organized by you?
    e. What is your interpretation of the situation?
    f. What physical filters affect the other party's perception? What social filters affect the other party's perception?
    g. What physical filters affect your perception of the event? What social filters affect your perception of the situation?
    h. What conclusions can you draw about different perceptions in this example?
    i. What different approaches might be taken to address the problem?
4. If you have divided into smaller groups, report to the class the basic problem on which you worked, the reasons for perceptual differences, and suggestions for action.

Principles Illustrated:
1. The same event can be perceived in different ways by different people involved in the event.
2. Physical and social perspectives influence one's selection and organization of an event.
3. Some misunderstandings are the result of differing perceptions more than differences in opinion.
4. Clear communication, "perception checking" and extensive feedback can help clarify misunderstandings.

Inkblot Test

Approximate Time: 35 minutes

Purpose: To demonstrate to students that people have different perceptions of the same object due to background differences

Procedures:
1. Make a series of inkblots. You will need 10 to 15 sheets of paper. Artist's sketch paper works well. You will need tempera or watercolors in black. Draw a design on one side of the middle of the piece of paper and then press the other side against it so you have the same thing on both sides.
2. Bring the inkblots to class and tell the students that you are going to conduct a communication experiment and that your are interested in their individual responses to a series of inkblots.
3. Have students take a sheet of paper and number one line for every inkblot, then write down their majors and interests at the bottom of the sheet.
4. Have students sit in a semicircle, and request that they do not talk while this exercise is going on.
5. Pick up the first inkblot and, starting at one end of the semicircle, walk in front of the students, standing in front of each one for a few seconds—just long enough for them to get a good look at the inkblot. Ask them to write on their papers what the inkblot reminds them of. Continue with this procedure until you have shown the students all the inkblots.
6. Once you have finished showing the students the inkblots, ask them to share their responses to the various shapes and designs. Hold up each inkblot as you do this so students may see why the others responded as they did.

Discussion Points:
1. How does perception differ from person to person?
2. Discuss the reasons why some of the responses were similar and different.
3. Discuss past results of responses to the inkblots if you have done them previously.
4. Determine if there is a correlation between similar majors and interests and responses to the inkblots.

Principle Illustrated: The same event can be perceived in vastly different ways by different people.

Stereotyping

Approximate Time: 30 minutes

Purpose: To heighten student awareness of the effects of stereotyping on thought and communication

Procedures:
1. On the basis of past experiences and attitudes, have each student describe to the group his or her perceptions of a "type" of person (e.g., a teacher, a police officer, a politician, etc.).
2. Through small group interactions, have the members of each group pool their ideas until they can agree on one "type."
3. In each small group have one group member write a list of the "attitudes" of the selected stereotype until a basic description of the "type" evolves.
4. After 5 minutes, stop the discussion and have each group present its "stereotype" to the rest of the class. Let other groups guess the type of person being described.

Discussion Points:
1. Do we oversimplify or distort reality? Why does this happen?
2. How can stereotyping hamper productive communication?

Principles Illustrated:
1. We select, organize, and interpret stimuli in ways important to us, given our background and past experiences.
2. Our attitudes toward others may be influences by a number of influences, such as culture, social, and role expectations. Often resulting conclusions are unquestioned and rigid.
3. We often make decisions about others based upon information which is unrelated to present "reality."
4. Communication may be difficult if parties are unable or unwilling to examine their differing stereotypes of objects or people.

Variation: Sexual Stereotyping

Approximate Time: 50 minutes

Purpose: To heighten student awareness of the effects of sexual stereotyping on though and communication

Procedures:
1. Follow steps 1 through 4 previous "Stereotyping" activity.
2. After the class has completed Step 4, ask them t go back to their group, and decide if their descriptions were gender-related. If their description was of masculine characteristics, ask them to list the attitudes of their selected type if he/she were of the opposite sex.

66

3. Have each group present these characteristics to the class. Ask the class to examine the positive and negative attributes assigned upon the basis of gender.

Principles Illustrated:
1. We perceive information differently based upon whether the actor is male or female.
2. We tend to be negative in the attributes assigned to those who are not in expected gender roles, and we are more negative when men are in traditional female roles.
3. Expectations based upon sex roles influence interpersonal communication.

PORTFOLIO ENTRY

(Based on an assignment in Ron Adler & Neil Towne's *Looking Out/Looking In*, 5th edition)

Two Views
1. Choose a disagreement you presently have with another person or group. The disagreement might be a personal one—such as an argument about how to settle a financial problem or why you should not have a curfew—or it might be a dispute over a contemporary public issue such as the right of women to obtain abortions on demand or the treatment of AIDS patients.
2. Describe the background of the situation sufficiently so the instructor will be able to understand the remainder of the exercise. (This section will vary in length according to the complexity of the problem.)
3. Write a personal letter to your "opponent" stating your arguments and why you take the position you take. Your letter should be long enough to develop your ides—approximately 300-350 words.
4. Now put yourself in the other person's position. Write a letter to you, as if written by your "opponent" in which you present his/her side of the issue. This letter should also be 300-350 words in length.
5. Now show the description you wrote in Step 4 to your "partner," the person whose beliefs are different from yours. Have that person read your account and correct any statements that don'ts reflect his/her position accurately. Remember, you're doing this so that you can more clearly understand how the issue looks to the other person. (Of course, you may also share your view with him/her.)
6. Make any necessary corrections in the account you wrote in Step 4, an again show it to your partner. Unless there are major problems, it is not necessary to rewrite the entire letter. If you do choose to write a new letter, please include your first attempt with the assignment. When (s)he agrees that you understand his/her position, have her/him sign your paper to indicate this.
7. *Now record your conclusion to this experiment. Has this perceptual shift made any difference in how you view the issue or how your feel about your partner?
   * This is the single most important assignment in the first Journal. BE SURE TO COMPLETE ALL PHASES OF THE ASSIGNMENT!

D & A

Review the Common Tendencies in Perception section in the chapter and choose three to discuss. Think of a time when you have experienced each one. What were the outcomes? Would they have been different if the common tendency hadn't played a part in your perception?

GROUP STUDY

(See the Introductory Essay for further information. Consult the Group study Section for Chapter One for additional directions for students.)

CHAPTER THREE

Mark the letter of the term which best identifies each of the situations below. Be sure that you clarify the terms before you begin, and pay particular attention to underlined words, and phrases.

a. punctuation
b. interpretation
c. empathy
d. closure
e. generalizing
f. androgynous behavior
g. sympathy
h. selection

_____ 1. Holly communicated her understanding of her friend's housing problem to that friend.
_____ 2. Susan assumes that her friend's silence in class mean that she has nothing to say; Ye Sun believes that this same silence indicated respect for authority.
_____ 3. Now that he is shopping for a car, Ken seems to notice more car advertisements.
_____ 4. You figure your friend's smile means she's happy.
_____ 5. You show you're sorry that your friend was robbed.
_____ 6. Tracy exhibits both sensitivity and strength when faced with a difficult decision.
_____ 7. You say you're late because your partner's never ready on time; your partner says she takes her time getting ready because you're always late.
_____ 8. Although she has never met Sam before, Shannon assumes that he is a Clinton supporter because they are both attending a Young Democrats Meeting.
_____ 9. Even though Peter isn't especially interested in the life cycle of a worm, he listens carefully in class because he knows the material will be on the test.
_____ 10. Your best friend Betsy doesn't even have to complete her sentences in order for you to predict how they will end.

For each of the following, identify which element of the perception-checking statement is missing.

a. This statement doesn't describe behavior.
b. This statement doesn't give two distinctly different interpretations.
c. This statement neglects to request clarification of the perception.
d. There is nothing missing from this perception-checking statement.

_____ 11. "When you told everyone my parents own the company, you must have been indicating I was hired here only because of them. Is that what you think?"
_____ 12. "Dad, when you told my friend Art what a great athlete you think I am, I though you were either really proud of me and wanted to brag a little, or maybe your wanted to see what Art and I had in common by the way he responded. What were you up to?"
_____ 13. "I'm really wondering—are you angry with me or just sulking?"
_____ 14. "When your told me you expected to get an outline with my report, I though you were trying to trick me into doing more work, or maybe you didn't realize that wasn't part of my job."
_____ 15. "Why is it you're smiling all the time today? Did you win the lottery or get a new job? What's up?"

ANSWER KEY:

1. c	6. f	11. b
2. b	7. a	12. d
3. h	8. e	13. a
4. b	9. h	14. c
5. g	10. d	15. d

TEACHING ACTIVITIES FROM THE *COMMUNICATION TEACHER*

Anderson, J. (1986, Fall). *Communication crossword puzzle, 1(1)*, 4.

Blythin, E. (1988, Winter). *Communication crosswords, 2(2)*, 15-16.

Bozik, M. (1988, Summer). *Who said that?, 1(1)*, 6.

Cohen, M. 91986, Fall). *A grin-and-bear-it quiz*, 5.

Hall, D. (1987, Fall). *Interpersonal messages in music, 2(1)*, 7.

Hankins, G. (1991, Summer). *Don't judge a book by its cover, 5(4)*, 8.

Hochel, S. (1999, Fall). *Analyzing how others see the dominant U. S. culture, 14(1)*, 4-5.

Jensen, M. (1989, Summer). *Listening with the third ear: An experience in empathy, 3(4)*, 10-11.

Johnson, C. (1989, Summer). *Empathy interview, 3(4)*, 4.

Kassing, J. W. (1994, Summer). *The color of perception, 8(4)*, 4-5.

Lau, J. (1988, Winter). *Women and men, men and women, 5(2)*, 9.

Litterst, J. (1988, Winter). *Observation project, 2(2)*, 10-11.

Patterson, B. R. (1994, Fall). *An experiential vehicle for instructor on human perception, 9(1)*, 7-8.

Ross, R. (1991, Spring). *What is in the shoe box/, 593)*, 12.

Schnell, J. (1992, Winter). *The china protests as a perception case study, 6(2)*, 13.

Schrader, D. (1992, Winter). *A demonstration of the impression formation process, 6(2)*, 6-7.

Wakefield, B. (1990, Fall). *Are we aware?, 5(1)*, 5.

Walters, K. (1987, Spring). *Perception assignment: Moving beyond biases, 1(3)*, 4-5.

Zalewski, I. and Waters, L. (1989, Spring). *Using popular games to teach communication, 3(3)*, 13.

Chapter Four: Language

"Unraveling Periphrastics"

Approximate Time: 10-15 minutes

Purpose: To demonstrate how language can impact the process of communication

Procedures:
1. Distribute a handout similar to the one on the next page.
2. Allow students 10 minutes to identify the meaning of each of the seven common phrases below.
3. Debrief with students by discussing, as a class, the answer to each of the seven phrases.

Answers:
1. A rolling stone gathering no moss.
2. Don't count your chickens before they hatch.
3. All that glitters is not gold.
4. Too many cooks spoil the broth.
5. Curiosity killed the cat.
6. You can lead a horse to water but you can't make her drink.
7. All work and no play make John a dull boy.

Unraveling Periphrastics

Circumlocution is a verbal vice opposed to the virtue of brevity. It consists of making the simple complex, the obvious obscure, and at times the familiar enjoyably strange. Here are a number of circumlocutions, known as PERIPHRASTICS. Unravel them.

1. A mobile section of petrified matter agglomerates no bryophytes.

_____

2. Desist from enumerating your fowl prior to their emergence from the shell.

_____

3. Scintillation is not always identification for an auric substance.

_____

4. A plethora of culinary specialists has a deleterious effect upon the quality purees, consommé, and other soluble pabula.

_____

5. A chronic disposition to inquiry deprived the domestic feline carnivorous quadruped of its vital quality.

_____

6. It is in the realm of possibility to entice an equine member of the animal kingdom to source of oxidized hydrogen; however, it is not possible to force him to imbibe.

_____

7. If John persists without respite in a constant prolonged exertion of physical or intellectual effort, he will develop into a youth slow and bunted in perception and sensibility.

_____

How Often Is Often?

Approximate Time: 20-30 minutes

Purpose: To demonstrate that words can mean different things to different people

Procedures:
1. Distribute a handout similar to the one below.
2. Discuss differences in responses. Even on words that sound fairly precise, people have diverse interpretations. Encourage students to give reasons for their choices.

HOW OFTEN IS OFTEN?

Below is a group of words often used to indicate degrees of frequency with which events tend to happen. The words mean different things to different people.

Beside each word indicate how many times out of 100 you think the word indicates an act is likely to happen. For example, if "seldom" indicates to you that a thing should happen about 10 times out of 100, you should mark a 10 in the space before the expression. If it means about 2 times in 100, then mark 2.

_____ 1.	almost never	_____ 11.	hardly ever
_____ 2.	very often	_____ 12.	seldom
_____ 3.	always	_____ 13.	never
_____ 4.	very seldom	_____ 14.	rather often
_____ 5.	about as often as not	_____ 15.	not often
_____ 6.	usually not	_____ 16.	rarely
_____ 7.	frequently	_____ 17.	now and then
_____ 8.	usually	_____ 18.	once in a while
_____ 9.	generally	_____ 19.	occasionally
_____ 10.	sometimes	_____ 20.	often

How many are:
A. _____ a few?
B. _____ several?
C. _____ many?
D. _____ not many?
E. _____ a lot?

Principles Illustrated:
1. Meaning is in people, not in words.
2. Even words that sound precise may different interpretations for different people.
3. Use words as precisely as possible when clarity is your goal.

What I Really Mean Is...

Approximate Time: 30 minutes

Purpose: To discuss the nature of language and its role in human communication

Procedures:
1. Divide the class into groups of 4-5. This exercise may be done in the large class unit if desired.
2. Assign each group one of the following quotations:

a. "I know you believe you understand what you think I said, but I'm not sure you realize that what you heard is not what I meant."
b. "When I use a word," Humpty Dumpty said, in a rather scornful tone, "it means just what I choose it to mean—neither more nor less."
c. "Learn a new language and get a new soul." (Czech proverb)
d. "A rose by any other name would smell as sweet."

3. Each group should spend 15 minutes discussing the meaning of the quotation and come up with a concrete example of the point that is made in the quotation.
4. Return the larger group and report findings.

Principles Illustrated:
1. Meanings are in people, not in words
2. Language is arbitrary.
3. Language that is used habitually shapes perception.
4. Meanings change.

Abstract Language

Approximate Time: 20-25 minutes

Purpose: To demonstrate that seemingly concrete words can have different meanings for different people

Procedures:
1. With no previous discussion, write the following words on the board and ask students to jot down the first word or phrase that comes to mind when reading each word.

preacher	farmer
artist	football captain
teenager	librarian
soldier	atheist
prostitute	Miss America
construction	model
worker	Texan
feminist	Communist

Go around the room asking for responses. Lean a discussion on why there are different responses and at what point any given response may have originated in a student's past.

Principles Illustrated:
1. Meanings are in people, not in words.
2. Even words that sound precise may different interpretations for different people.

Cleaning up Your Act

Approximate Time: 15 minutes

Purpose: To demonstrate the power of language to affect emotions and to demonstrate the impact of perception upon language choice (Note: It is important that the instructor feel comfortable with the language used in this exercise.)

Procedures:
1. Ask students to take out a sheet of paper—which will not be handed in. tell them that you will give them a few simple directions which they are to follow without making any comments or asking any questions.
2. Give the students the following direction: "Write down all of the dirty words you can think of." Remind them again that they are to respond in whichever way they perceive the direction. Do not answer any questions or allow students to ask for clarification.
3. Have the students write down their won brief definitions to the word "clean" and "dirty."
4. Have students share their words and definitions. (Students tend to be more comfortable doing this in dyads or small groups.)
5. Conduct a discussion in the large group covering the following points:
   - How did you react when you received the initial direction? Why did this seem unusual to you?
   - What kinds of words did you think of? (Most students will respond with the typical four letter "cause words," but some will note words which refer to "real" dirt, such as mud, filth, grime, etc. the more creative my choose words such as war, hate, violence, AIDS, cancer, fear; or even calories, fat, or cholesterol.)
   - What do "clean" and "dirty" mean to you" who taught you the meanings of these words? Can you think of any specific incidents which had an impact on you? Times when language choice led to conflict?
   - How does language use affect your perception of others?

Principles Illustrated:
1. We adjust our language according to environment and situation.
2. Language can be a powerful affector of the emotions.
3. Meanings are in people, not in words.
4. Language choice has an impact on our perceptions of others.
5. Language choice is a learned behavior.

The Words We Buy

Approximate time: 20-30 minutes

Purpose: To demonstrate how dependent retailers are on the use of language to persuade consumers to purchase their products.

Procedure:
1. Ask students to bring in one example of an ad – it can be from a magazine, newspaper, or they can write down the words used in a radio or TV ad.
2. As a group discuss the language
   a. Key words, phrases – what message are we supposed to get? EX: "Just do it" "It's Miller Time" "$10 hotdog, $30 tickets, Spending time with your son, priceless"
   b. What values are being communicated?
   c. Who do you think the target audience is?
   d. Is the ad successful?
   e. Discuss ambiguous and abstract language EX: Natural flavors, made with real cheese flavor, new and improved

Principles Illustrated:
1. We are influenced by words
2. Words can illicit feelings towards objects

PORTFOLIO ENTRY

The Language Key

Identify three (3) specific personal examples of times when choice of language led to positive or negative results in your own interpersonal relationships. For each situation, cite the person(s) involved, the place of the occurrence, the situation, and the language used. Then identify the type of language problem (ambiguous language, relative words, euphemism, static evaluation, fact/inference problems, etc.) and note the results of each incident. How did language play a pivotal role in these experiences? (Each example should illustrate a different type of language problem.)

D & A

The Language Key outlined above

GROUP STUDY

(See the Introductory Essay for further information. Consult the Group study Section for Chapter One for additional directions for students.)

Label the examples of language given below by writing the letter of the language type illustrated on the line in front of the example. Be sure that you clarify the terms before you begin, and pay particular attention to underlined words and phrases.

a. inference
b. relative word
c. euphemism

d. emotive word(s)
e. equivocal language
f. static evaluation

_____ 1. John didn't call so he must be angry.
_____ 2. Look at this headline: "Massive organ draws crowds!"
_____ 3. That restaurant is too expensive.
_____ 4. My best friend is the friendliest and most helpful person in the world!
_____ 5. I'd like recognition for my work.
_____ 6. "Whew! This bathroom needs some air."
_____ 7. Sue is always on time. She's late today; she must have had an accident.
_____ 8. The funeral director pointed out the slumber room.
_____ 9. He showed up; so he must agree.
_____ 10. My daughter is so precocious when she interrupts my adult conversation.
_____ 11. My brother is a sanitation engineer.
_____ 12. Ian gave a long speech.
_____ 13. My grandfather is young.
_____ 14. My sister is a pill.
_____ 15. My sister is a little monster.

ANSWER KEY:

1. a	6. c	11. c
2. e	7. a	12. b
3. b	8. c	13. b
4. f	9. a	14. d
5. e	10. d	15. f

TEACHING ACTIVITIES FROM THE *COMMUNICATION TEACHER*

Bollinger, L., Sandarg, J. (1998, Winter). *Dare to go where others fear to tread, 12(2)*, 1-3.

Bozik, M. (1985, Fall). *Words and gender, 6.*

Hochel, S. (1990, Winter). *Language awareness and assessment, 4(2)*, 4-5.

Hopson, C. (1986, Fall). *What am I describing?, 1(1)*, 5.

Jensen, M. (1988, Summer). *Revising speech style, 2(4)*, 3-4.

McGrath, R. (1987, Fall). *The slang game, 291)*, 5.

Phillips, T. G. (1997, Summer). *Introducing gender-braised language: Much ado about something, 11(4)*, 3-4.

Rockwell, P. (1988, Winter). *Wheel of phonemes, 2(2)*, 5.

Rowley, E. N. (1992, Fall). *More than mere words, 7(1)*, 5.

Weaver, R. L. II. (1995, Winter) *Responsible communicators own their messages, 9(2)*, 8-9.

Young, K. S. (1999, Summer). *Proving the importance of inclusive language in the basic course*, 13(4), 7-8.

Zizik, C. H. (1995, Summer). *Powerspeak: Avoiding ambiguous language, 9(4)*, 8-9.

Chapter Five: Nonverbal Communication

"Let's Talk"

(Adapted from Games Trainers Play by Edward E. Scannell)

Approximate time: 10-15 minutes

Purpose: To illustrate one's use of gestures and how natural these gestures are to us in verbal communication. This exercise can also demonstrate that verbal communication may be awkward for us when nonverbal gestures or actions are prohibited.

Procedures:
1. 1. Tell the group that the next few minutes will be devoted to a simple activity wherein they will turn to a person seated nearby and just talk for 2-3 minutes. The subject matter is unimportant; you'd merely like them to converse with someone else (2 to a group) for a few minutes. (You may want to write some suggested topics in front of the room for encouragement)
2. After a 2-3 minute period, ask them to stop and tell their partners what they noticed about the other's nonverbal behavior; for example, the person kept fiddling with a pencil, or continually was tapping their fingers on the desk, etc. After these gestures have been identified, acknowledge that most of us do these movements almost unknowingly.
3. After each person has received a "critique" from their partner, tell the group to resume their conversations, but now they must make a conscious effort to use absolutely no nonverbal movements. Have them continue their conversations for 2-3 more minutes.

Discussion Questions:
1. Were most of us really aware or cognizant of our nonverbal movements in the first conversation?
2. Did you find any of your partner's gestures distracting or even annoying?
3. How did it "feel" when we were forced into a strictly verbal discussion? Was the communication as effective without our gestures?

Five Squares

Approximate Time: 30-40 minutes

Purpose: To increase awareness of the impact of nonverbal behavior on the process of communication

Procedures:
1. Before class, prepare a set of squares and an instruction sheet for each group.
2. A set consists of five envelopes containing pieces of stiff paper cut into patterns that will form five 6"x 6" squares, as shown in the diagram below. Several individual combinations will be possible but only total combination will form the five squares.
3. Cut each square into the pieces (a through j) and lightly pencil in the letters. Then mark the envelopes A through E and distribute the pieces thus:

Envelop A:	pieces i, h, e;
Envelop B:	pieces a, a, b, c;
Envelop C:	pieces a, j;
Envelop D:	pieces d, f;
Envelop E:	pieces g, g, b, f, c, h.

4. By using multiples of three inches, several combinations will form one or two squares. Only one combination will form 6"x 6" squares. Erase the small letters from the pieces and write instead the envelope letters A through E, so that the pieces can be easily returned for reuse.
5. Divide the class into groups of five and sea each group at a table equipped with a set of envelopes and an instruction sheet. Ask that the envelopes be opened only on signal.
6. Begin the exercise by asking about how nonverbal behavior impacts the process of communication.
7. Describe the exercise as a puzzle that requires cooperation. Everyone has to understand the problem. Everyone has to believe that s/he can help. Instructions have to be clear. Everyone needs to think of other person as well as himself.
8. Read the instructions aloud, point out that each table has a reference copy on them, then give the signal to open the envelopes.

The instructions are as follows:
1. Each group should have give envelopes, each containing pieces for forming squares. One individual from the group should take one of the envelopes. Not everyone in the group may have an envelope if the group has more than five members, At the signal, the task of the group is to form five squares of equal size. The task is not completed until everyone has before her/him a perfect square and all the squares are of exactly the same size.
2. There are three rules:
   a. No member may speak.
   b. No member may ask for a card or in any way signal that s/he wants one.
   c. Members may give card to others.

Discussion Points:
        When all or most of the groups have finished, call time and discuss the experience. Ask questions such as:
1. What were the nonverbal behavior that were most pervasive the simulation?
2. How did you "read" the nonverbal behavior? How accurate were you?
3. How did you feel when someone held a piece and did not see the solution?
4. What was your reaction when someone finished his/her square and then sat back without seeing whether her/his solution prevented others from solving the problem?
5. What were your feelings if you finished your square and then began to realize that you would have to break it up and give away a piece?
6. How did you feel about the person who was slow at seeing the solution?
7. If you were that person, how did you feel? Was there as climate that helped or hindered?

        If students help to monitor, they may have observations to share. Focus the discussion on nonverbal behaviors which demonstrate trust and cooperation—and the opposite.

Five Square Puzzle Exercise

DIRECTIONS
        Each group will be given give envelopes containing pieces of stiff paper cut into patterns that will form five squares of equal size.

DO NOT OPEN THE ENVELOPES UNTIL YOU ARE SIGNALED BY THE INSTRUCTOR.

        Each group should have five envelopes containing pieces for forming squares. At the signal, the task of the group is to **form five squares of equal size**.

The task is not completed until everyone has before him or her a perfect square and all of the squares are of the same size.

There are three rules:
1. No member may speak.
2. No member may ask for a card or in any way signal that s/he wants one.
3. Members may give card to others.

Nonverbal Environment

Approximate Time: 30 minutes

Purpose: To make students more aware of the impact of the environment on communication

Procedures:
1. After reading chapter Six, describe the nonverbal environment in which the class meets. Have students note space usage, color, furniture arrangement, lighting, distance, smell, temperature, etc.
2. Have students list the ways that this classroom affects the goal of the class.
3. Have each individual student make one recommendation for how the classroom environment could be changed to improve the class and give a reason for each recommendation.
4. Gather as a class and share the recommendations.

Variation:
Have students tour various areas of the campus and draw conclusions about the environments. Which are most welcoming? Most forbidding? Why?

Principles Illustrated:
1. Nonverbal communication is more than body language.
2. Environment can have a profound impact on communication patterns.
3. Many attainable changes can be made to improve an environment so that it facilitates the goals of the people meeting in it.

Analyzing Communication of Clothing

Approximate Time: 50 minutes

Purpose: To acquaint students with "object language": personal artifacts and clothing

Procedures:
1. Hold a general discussion of the communicative nature of clothing and artifacts (rings, etc.) then direct each student to categorize his or her own clothing as:
   a. formal wear
   b. informal
   c. intimate
   d. private
   e. functional
2. Have each student describe articles of clothing he or she would never wear to church, to work, in a locker room, in front of his or her parents.
3. Catalogue each item of clothing with regard to why it was purchased in terms of:

a. function
b. sexiness
c. daring
d. role-fulfillment
e. outrageousness
f. expense
g. fashionableness
h. funkiness

4. Finally, have students design a hypothetical wardrobe by having them name ten items they would love to own, regardless of price, and identify what is communicated by each item of clothing.

Principles Illustrated:
1. How we dress communicates.
2. There is a relationship between personality type and clothing choice.

Object Communication

Approximate Time: 35-40 minutes

Purpose: To illustrate that an object can reveal a person's values

Procedures:
1. Students bring to class an object special to them that reflects their personality. Make it clear that one else is to see what they bring.
2. Collect the objects of six persons (male and female) and place them in a large box. No one should see what goes into the box.
3. Those six students whose objects were collected sit in a row in front of the class.
4. Hold up an object, one by one, and have the remainder of the class guess to whom that object belongs on the basis of the following questions:
   a. What type of values do you believe the person has who owns the object? Why?
   b. What clues lead you to place the object with its supposed owner?
5. After attempting to match the items with their owners, have the six students identify their objects and explain how it reflects their personality.
6. Repeat with the rest of the students.

Discussion Points:
1. With what types of objects is it easiest to tell a person's values? Which types are more difficult?
2. Why is it dangerous to make inferences about a person's values from objects?
3. How much can objets tell you about a person's values/
4. How much can a person's car, hair clothes, club memberships, etc. tell you about the person?

Paralanguage: Learning From Vocal Cues

Approximate Time: 30 minutes

Purpose: To discover the kinds of information that can be obtained from vocal cues

Procedures:
1. Prior to class obtain a short taped message of any available speaker and a tape recorder to play it on. Make a copy of the *Paralanguage Quiz* for each student and devise one answer sheet to the quiz based on the speaker chosen.
2. Without previous discussion, announce that the class will hear a tape recording of a speaker, and that students are to listen carefully to the recording.
3. Play the tape recording.
4. After the tape is played, distribute a copy of the *Paralanguage Quiz* to students and instruct them to complete it.

PARALANGUAGE QUIZ

Complete each of the following questions according to the information you were able to obtain from the tape recording you have just heard.

1. What sex was the speaker? Male _____   Female _____
2. What was the approximate age of the speaker?
          under 10 years _____
          10-15 years _____
          16-20 years _____
          21-30 years _____
          31-40 years _____
          41-50 years _____
          51-60 years _____
          above 60 _____
3. From what part of the world does the speaker come? _____
4. What level of education has this person attained?
   Elementary (1-6) _____   Junior High (7-9) _____   High School (10-12) _____
   College (13-16) _____   Graduate (16 and up) _____
5. To what extend did this person seem to be introverted or extroverted (circle a umber)?
          introverted   1   2   3   4   5   6   7   extroverted
6. What were the speaker's political leanings?
          conservative   1   2   3   4   5   6   7   liberal
7. How would you rate the speaker's leadership ability?
          good   1   2   3   4   5   6   7   bad
8. How attractive is this speaker?
          attractive   1   2   3   4   5   6   7   ugly
9. Did the speaker seem too energetic?
          energetic   1   2   3   4   5   6   7   lazy
10. Was the speaker honest?
11. What was the speaker's body type?
          heavy   1   2   3   4   5   6   7   thin
12. What race is the speaker? _____

Discussion Points:
1. Why is it possible to answer questions correctly merely by hearing the speaker?
2. Which vocal cues provide information about each of the questions?
3. How effective are vocal cues in revealing information about a speaker?

Nonverbal Observation

Approximate Time: To make assignment: 15 minutes
Discuss in net period: 30 minutes

Purpose: To heighten student awareness of the differences in nonverbal communication between men and women

Procedures:
1. Divide the class into two groups: facial expression and movement. Tell them that they will be doing "field observation" of movement.
2. Instruct facial expression observers to: observe smiling and frowning facial expressions of a person interacting in 1) a classroom, 2) the checkout line of a grocery store, 3) a restaurant, 4) a bank, 5) a gas station, 6) a coffee break, and 7) a meeting of an organization.
3. Instruct facial expression observers to respond to the following questions:
   a. Who smiles most frequently? Least frequently?
   b. What purpose do smiles and frowns seem to serve?
   c. What relation do sex, status, and personality bear on smiling and nonsmiling behavior?
4. Instruct movement observers to observe pedestrian traffic 1) on the street, 2) in grocery stores, 3) in a shopping mall, 4) in the corridors of a building, 5) in line at a movie theater.
5. Instruct movement observers to respond to the following:
   a. Which person tends to give way or walk around the others
   b. Which tends to persist or continue on course, claiming the right of way?
   c. Formulate some hypothesis on the basis of your observations.
6. Discuss the following at the next class meeting.

Principles Illustrated:
1. Actual differences exist between the sexes in nonverbal communication.
2. Females tend t use less space, and males tend to use more space in movement.
3. Smiling behavior seems to be a more dominant characteristic of women than of men.

Body Language Quiz

Approximate Time: 10 minutes

Purpose: To illustrate the complexity of nonverbal communication (kinesics)

Procedures:
1. Distribute and have students complete the following matching quiz handout.
2. Share the answer, as determined by Julius Fast's research.
3. Compare Fast's responses with those of the students and discuss how easy it is to mis-read kinesics.

Principles Illustrated:
> It really isn't possible to "read a person like a book."

BODY LANGUAGE QUIZ

	BODY LANGUAGE SIGNALS		MESSAGE CONVEYED
1.	Stand rigidly	a.	stressfulness
2.	Raise one eye brow	b.	intimacy
3.	Rub you nose	c.	puzzlement
4.	Cross your arms	d.	hands off
5.	Shrug your shoulder	e.	forgetfulness
6.	Wink an eye	f.	disbelief—no trust
7.	Slap your forehead	g.	isolate/protect yourself
8.	Tap your fingers	h.	nervousness
9.	Play with hair or jewelry	i.	indifference
10.	Bite fingernails or crack knuckles	j.	impatience

ANSWER KEY:

1.	d	5.	i	9.	h
2.	f	6.	b	10.	a
3.	c	7.	e		
4.	g	8.	j		

Space Invasion

Approximate Time: 20 minutes

Purpose: To experience how the four proxemic distances identified by Hall affect communication

Procedures:
1. Have the students pair off into dyads. Be sure that there both mixed sex and same sex dyads.
2. Tell the students that they will be carrying on a conversation. They can talk about what they did last weekend or will do next weekend as a starting point or anything else they choose. (The topic is not important.)
3. Have one member of each dyad come to the center of the room and turn out to face his/her partner. The partner should place him/herself as far away from the partner as possible within the confines of the room. (Public Distance)
4. The conversation begins and continues for approximately two minutes.
5. Stop the conversation (a whistle is helpful) and have the partners move in toward one another until they are just touching finger tips. They drop their arms and continue the conversation at this distance. (Social Distance)
6. After a few minutes, again stop the conversation and have the students move in so that they can place a hand on their partner's shoulder. They drop their arms and continue the conversation at the distance. (Personal Distance)
7. Finally, have the students move toward one another until they the tips of their shoes are touching. The conversation continues. (Intimate Distance) BOTH feet should be touching; this needs to be monitored by the instructor.
8. After a maximum of two minutes at this close proximity, have students return to their seats and discuss the experience.
   a. What were your reactions to conversing at Public Distance? How did the distance make a difference in your conversation (degree of intimacy, vocal volume, number of exchanges)?
   b. How did this change when you moved in to the Social Distance? For how many of you was this the most comfortable distance?

c. What changes occurred as you moved in to the Personal Distance? For how many was this the most comfortable?

d. How did you respond to the Intimate Distance? How might you have reacted had this exercise been done on the first day of class? How did your posture change at this distance? Did you do anything to compensate for the closeness? (limited exe contact, change in posture, fold arms)

e. How well do you know your partner? To what extent did this make a difference in your level of comfort? (Male/female dyads, male/male dyads, female/female dyads will have varying responses.) how might culture make a difference?

Principles Illustrated:
1. The use of varying proxemic distances has an impact on the intimacy and comfort of conversation.
2. Different people will be most comfortable at different distances.
3. When individuals are forced into uncomfortably close proximity, they will do something to compensate for the lack of physical distance.

PORTFOLIO ENTRY

Nonverbals I Have Known

Give a personal example (a total of 10 examples) of how you have used each of the types of nonverbal communication discussed in Chapter Six: face and eyes, kinesics, touch, paralanguage, proxcmics (personal space), territory, chronemics, physical attractiveness, clothing, and environment. Note that these examples should reflect *specific incidents*, not just general tendencies. Based on these examples, personal reflection, and comments which have been made to you by others, how do you rate yourself as a nonverbal communicator in terms of frequency, awareness, and accuracy of decoding messages? Again, be specific.

D & A

Nonverbals I Have Known outlined above. An instructor may choose to shorten this to ask students to select five of the ten to discuss.

GROUP STUDY

(See the Introductory Essay for further information. Consult the Group study Section for Chapter One for additional directions for students.)

CHAPTER FIVE

Match the letter of the term which best identifies each of the examples given below. Begin by clarifying the terms as they have been in your text.

a. kinesics   d. territoriality
b. paralinguistics   e. environment
c. proxemics   f. chronemics

_____ 1. The executive folded her arms and stood ram-rod straight while she made her report to the Board.
_____ 2. Jeremy put a "NO ENTRANCE" sign on the door to his room.
_____ 3. The students placed the classroom chairs in a circle to facilitate interaction.
_____ 4. Anne stepped back three feet from her friend.
_____ 5. Martin turned his body away from his brother.
_____ 6. Rob's voice softened when he spoke to her.

_____ 7. Chrissie <u>waited three days</u> before answering Erin's e-mail message.

_____ 8. Even though she was really busy, Susan <u>found time</u> to spend with Todd.

_____ 9. Mitchell <u>sighed</u> audibly.

_____ 10. Kevin was annoyed that someone else was <u>sitting in "his seat"</u> in class.

_____ 11. Nick and Brad <u>decorated their dorm room</u> with posters and lights.

_____ 12. The officer <u>pointed</u> in the correct direction.

_____ 13. When Jennifer got into the elevator, she chose to <u>stand in the corner farthest away from the other passengers</u>.

_____ 14. The lovers were sitting <u>only inches</u> apart.

_____ 15. No one dared to sit in <u>Archie Bunker's chair</u>.

ANSWER KEY:

1.	a	6.	b	11.	e
2.	d	7.	f	12.	a
3.	e	8.	f	13.	c
4.	c	9.	b	14.	c
5.	a	10.	d	15.	d

TEACHING ACTIVITIES FROM THE *COMMUNICATION TEACHER*

Booth-Butterfield, m. (1992, Summer). *Analysis of an audiotaped conversation with a friend, 6(4)*, 14-15.

Bozik, M. (1984, Winter). *A picture's worth a thousand words, 1(2)*, 5.

Coakley, C. (1991, Spring). *Getting acquainted nonverbally, 5(2)*, 15.

Demo, N. (1991, Spring). *The game of twister—an exercise in proxemic interaction, 5(3)*, 2.

Johnson, C. (1987, Fall). *People's court comes to the classroom, 2(1)*, 10.

May, S. T. (2000, Winter). *Proxemics: The hula hoop and use of personal space, 14(2)*, 4-5.

Overton, J. (1993, Summer). *Look and learn: using field observation in the nonverbal course, 7(4)*, 4.

Parker, R. G., and Leathers, D. G. (1992, Fall). *You be the judge: Impression management in the courtroom, 7(1)*, 4.

Rollman, S. (1988, Spring). *Classroom exercises for teaching nonverbal communication, 2(3)*, 13.

Schnell, J. (1988, Summer). *Experimental learning of nonverbal communication in popular magazine advertising, 2(4)*, 1-2.

Schreier, H. N. (2000, Winter). *Experiencing persuasion and the persuader, 14(2)*, 7-9.

Siddens, P. J. III. (1996, Spring). *Touch, territoriality and nonverbal communication, 10(3)*, 2-4.

Sims, A. (1987, Winter). *Survey research on projected impressions, 1(2)*, 7.

Spicer, K. L. (1988, Summer). *Developing nonverbal skills through finger-plays, 2(4)*, 14.

Valentine, C. A., and Arnold, W. E. (1992, Summer). *Nonverbal scavenger hunt, 6(2)*, 14-15.

Chapter Six: Listening

Listening with Interest

(Adapted from "More Games Trainers Play" by John W. Newstrom)

Approximate time: 5-10 minutes

Purpose: To show that listening can be improved when one's interest is induced. To further illustrate that most of us listen at a relatively low level of efficiency on matters of little or not interest to us.

Procedures:
1. Take any article (two-three paragraphs) from a magazine or newspaper. The article should be of a non-business nature and preferably one in which most students would have little interest.
2. With little introduction, read the article to the group. Upon finishing, ask the group to write down three to four things they heard.
3. Then read an article (three-four paragraphs) from a trade journal or magazine in which most students can identify with, i.e., their school, city or other such areas of interest. After reading this to them, again ask them to write down as much as they can remember about the story. Compare the results.

Discussion Points:
1. Why did most of us "flunk" the first quiz? (no interest, "why bother," no purpose, etc.)
2. Research shows that immediately upon hearing something, most of us forget 50% just that fast. Why then, in the second example, did many of us score so well?)
3. What additional barriers to listening does this illustrate?

Most Effective Communicator

(An exercise developed by Laura A. Janusik, University of Maryland at College Park)

Approximate Time: 30 minutes

Purpose: To apply concepts from the listening chapter while interviewing a competent communicator

Procedures:
1. Distribute copies of the *Most Effective Communicator Interview Assignment sheet* and discuss the three major parts of the assignment: pre-conversation, conversation, and analysis. Be certain students are clear about the expectations of the assignment and how it related to the chapter.

MOST EFFECTIVE COMMUNICATOR INTERVIEW ASSIGNMENT

Purpose: through the course we've discussed a number of communication concepts, each of which can assist one in becoming a more effective or a less effective communicator. By this time, you have probably learned some concepts with which you fully agree, and other with which you disagree. This assignment will give you the opportunity to talk about a number of these concepts with an individual whom you respect in an effort to gain further insight into communication effectiveness. This assignment consists of a pre-conversation plan, an audiotaped conversation with your most effective communicator or someone whose communication skills you greatly respect, and a written analysis of the conversation.

Part 1: The Pre-Conversation Plan (Note: This part MUST be completed and approved before you go to Part 2.)

Develop at least ten (or more) questions that focus on problems, awareness, or interests in interpersonal effectiveness. The question should span at least three to four broad topic areas. Each question should be logically arranged under its appropriate topic, and each question should also have one to two additional probes. A probe is an additional question that refocuses the larger question into a more specific area. They are used in the event that you become "stuck," or they also assist in gaining additional information. Develop questions that are sophisticated enough for the savvy communicator with whom you'll be conversing. Note: the questions should be open-ended. In other words, they must allow for an explanation, not a clear-cut yes/no or good/bad or agree/disagree response. The questions should reflect areas of your personal interest in terms of communication.

For example, the start of one topic area may look like this:

Listening

We learned that to be an effective communicator, one must be effective listener, and that the listener is responsible for at least 51% of the conversation. Please explain why you would agree or disagree with this.

1. How does the ability to listen manifest itself at your workplace?
2. Recent studies suggest that listening is tied to leadership. What do you think about hose findings?
3. Do you think it's more important to listen better to friends or acquaintances? Why?
4. Do you think males and females listen differently? If so, how? Why do you suppose that is?
5. What listening tips would you recommend to help one become a more effective communicator?
6. According to the Sapir-Whorf hypothesis, people who have more words for something experience it differently. Do you agree or disagree, and why?

On a separate piece of paper, write YOUR responses to each question and probe.

Part 2: The Conversation

Schedule a time to meet with the other persons in a comfortable setting. Allot a minimum of one hour for your conversation. Explain that this is a class assignment and your will need to audiotape your conversation.

Meet with the individual and introduce the individual on tape to gain his/her consent for taping your conversation.

Next have a conversation with the person. Since this is a conversation, it should be a give and take interaction. You are in command of the direction of the conversation because you called the meeting and have the questions; however, using the norm or reciprocity, you should share your answers to the questions as well. Don't feel that you need to agree, but definitely discuss the underlying assumptions of your differences. DO NOT fire off your questions like an interrogation. Your goal is not to simply get the other person's response; it is to identify similarities and differences in the underlying assumptions of communication. It is quite likely that if you both really listen to each other's responses, your individual initial answers may shift.

Part: 3: Analysis

In a 3-6 page paper, analyze your efforts. Include your general reaction to the assignment, findings that were consistent or inconsistent with what you've learned, different perspectives you've never considered, and how you believe your perceptions toward interpersonal communication have either been changed or strengthened due to the interview. (Note: If they were not strengthened or changed, them you were not an effective interviewer.)

Your analysis should be written in APA style with a cover sheet and Reference page. Additionally, staple the approved questions and answers to the back.

Factual Listening

Approximate Time: 30 minutes

Purpose: To demonstrate to students how the tendency to selectively perceive information affects listening

Procedures:
1. Have students take out paper and pencil.
2. Instruct them that you are going to tread a series of statements and questions which will require a number, word, or phrase to be written in response.
3. Read the items which make up the "Factual Listening Exercise." Read each item only once, and read at a constant pace, allowing enough time for students to write an answer, but not enough time to reflect on the items.

FACTUAL LISTENING EXERCISE

1. How many members of each species did Moses take aboard the ark?
2. Can a man in South Carolina marry his widow's sister?
3. If a farmer lost all but nine of his 17 sheep, how many would he have?
4. Does England have a fourth of July?
5. How many months have 28 days?
6. How many two-cent stamps in a dozen?
7. What was the president's name in 1970?
8. You are a baby bull. You have been away from home for a long time and are in need of loving. To whom would you go, mama bull or papa bull?
9. You are pilot of an airliner flying between New York and Chicago. The copilot is five years younger than the pilot. The copilot's spouse is three years younger than the pilot's spouse. The interior of the plane is blue, and the seats are red. How old is the pilot?
10. A plane crashes on the border between the United Stated and Canada. In what country would you bury the survivors?

4. Share and discuss the answers.
Answers:
1. Moses took none; it was Noah.
2. No, he would be dead.
3. Nine.
4. Yes, it's just not a holiday.
5. All, some just have more.
6. Twelve.
7. Same as it is now.
8. Papa bull—there are no mama bulls.
9. Same age as you are, "You are…"
10. Survivors won't get buried.

Principles Illustrated:
1. We often judge prematurely when listening to familiar words or phrases.

2. Cultural background influences listening.
3. Poor listening habits may be problematic even in the simplest listening situation.

Noninteracting Dyad

Approximate Time: 5 minutes

Purpose: To reveal to students the role that nonverbal feedback plays in the listening process and the degree to which they give nonverbal feedback without being conscious of it.

Procedures:
1. Instruct each class member to turn and face the person beside him or her until each person in the class has a partner.
2. Tell each dyad to decide who will be in the listening role and who will be in the speaking role.
3. The speaker should take a moment to think of something she/he can easily talk about for one or two minutes.
4. The listener must give absolutely no verbal or nonverbal feedback while the speaker is talking—no facial expression, no nods, no leaning in, no nonverbal vocalizations. The listener is for all practical purposes a brick wall.
5. Instruct the dyads to begin and give them 1 to 2 minutes before stopping them and telling them to switch roles. Allow the second "conversation" to go on for 1 to 2 minutes.

Discussion Points:
1. Ask the speaker, how did you feel? Think you must be terribly boring? Feel dumb?
2. Ask the listener, how did you feel? Rude? Unnatural? Have to struggle to "control" yourself from responding nonverbally?

Principles Illustrated:
1. Nonverbal feedback is important in the listening process.
2. Feedback is an essential component of listening.

The Rumor Game—'The Amazing Squirrel Story"

(An exercise developed by Lisa, B. Callihan, Gadsden State Community College, Gadsden, Alabama)

Approximate Time: 45 minutes

Purpose: To experience and observe the process of information change and listening recall in the serial reproduction of information

Procedures:
1. Have four to seven members of the class leave the room and remain far enough away so that they cannot hear what is going on in the room.
2. Read "The Amazing Squirrel Story" to the remaining members of the class. Note taking is not allowed.
3. Call in the first subject and have a volunteer (or someone you or the subject designates) retell the story as accurately as possible. The subject should be told to listen very carefully because he or she will be asked to retell the message for the next person. Questions may be asked of the teller, but the audience should not participate in responding to questions.
4. Audience members are each given a response sheet for notations during each of the story retellings.

5. Call in the next person and have the first subject retell the story to subject two as the class listens. Repeat this process until all subjects have returned to the room and heard the story. The final subject should also retell the story to the entire group.

THE AMAZING SQUIRREL STORY

Once upon a time, there were three sorority sisters Bitsy, Bopsie & Boopsie. They had had a rough and exhausting day on the intramural sports field, and so they headed back to the sorority house for a refreshing shower. Bopsie talked about how she loved Harry Connick, Jr., and she began to sing her favorite tune, "Strangers in the night, exchanging glances…"

Boopsie was already showering in the end stall near an open window, when, much to her surprise she realized that she had no shampoo. Immediately after lathering up, Boopsie was attacked by a deranged squirrel who refused to release its vice-like grip from Boopsie's head.

Boopsie began to shriek like a fire engine and flail her hands madly about! She streaked from the shower stall nude, out into the corridor of her hall and down the stairs with her towel-clad friends, Bitsy and Bopsie, in hot pursuit. As she burst forth from the main entrance of her sorority house into the front yard, she could be heard screaming, "Monster! Monster! Help me! It's a demon!" She finally fell face first into the fountain at the center of the courtyard. At this time the squirrel scurried off and climbed an oak tree.

When Boopsie arrived at the police station, she was covered in nothing except for Office Black's jacked. Her parents were summoned by the captain. He stated, "Mr. and Mrs. Rosenstein, your daughter is being held with a bail of five thousand dollars, pending her psychological evaluation." When Boopsie's father asked the captain the charge, he was told, "The charges are indecent exposure, public nuisance, and apparent solicitation to commit prostitution.'

Boopsie's parents were returning her to school after posting bail when Boopsie spied the attacking squirrel. It was right beside an animal rights activist who was protesting in front of a restaurant called "Lambchop Heaven." In heavy traffic Boopsie leapt from the moving car, intent upon revenge against the squirrel. The squirrel ran between the legs of the activist and again escaped but no before Boopsie had unfortunately plowed the activist down accidentally. His sign, which read, "VEGETARIANISM, MAN!," flew into the gutter. His pamphlets, which outlined the dangers of red meat consumption, flew through the air.

"You know, " said Mrs. Rosenstein, "Maybe she should seek professional help. I don't know why she got so upset just because that man's a vegetarian! People should be allowed the right to free speech and to eat whatever they want!" Mr. Rosenstein replied, "I wonder what her bail will be for assaulting an old hippie?"

a newlywed couple saw the whole thing and correctly realized that the squirrel had actually been Boopsie's target. The lady opened her car door just in time for the squirrel to jump in. They sped off to their honeymoon feeling as if they had done the right thing in saving the animal.

THE AMAZING SQUIRREL STORY LISTENING EXERCISE

Please don't let this sheet intimidate you, as each person speaks, there will be fewer and fewer instances where you will circle a number. Did the third person remember a name? If so, circle the number 3, after the name which was remembered. At the bottom page you can add some of the things which were made up by the more dramatic speakers, and circle the number of that speaker. If you don't catch it all, don't worry.

SORORITY	1	2	3	4	5	6	7
BITSIE	1	2	3	4	5	6	7
BOPSIE	1	2	3	4	5	6	7
BOOPSIE	1	2	3	4	5	6	7
STRANGERS IN THE NIGHT	1	2	3	4	5	6	7
SHAMPOO	1	2	3	4	5	6	7
SQUIRREL	1	2	3	4	5	6	7
NUDE	1	2	3	4	5	6	7
TOWEL CLAD	1	2	3	4	5	6	7
MONSTER	1	2	3	4	5	6	7
FOUNTAIN	1	2	3	4	5	6	7
OAK TREE	1	2	3	4	5	6	7
POLICE STATION	1	2	3	4	5	6	7
MR. OR MRS. ROSENSTEIN	1	2	3	4	5	6	7
$5,000 BAIL	1	2	3	4	5	6	7
INDECENT EXPOSURE	1	2	3	4	5	6	7
APPT. SOLIC. PROSTIT.	1	2	3	4	5	6	7
ANIMAL RIGHTS ACTIVIST	1	2	3	4	5	6	7
LAMBCHOP HEAVEN	1	2	3	4	5	6	7
LEAPT FROM CAR	1	2	3	4	5	6	7
VEGETARIANISM MAN	1	2	3	4	5	6	7
FREE SPEECH	1	2	3	4	5	6	7
OLD HIPPIE	1	2	3	4	5	6	7
NEWLY WED COUPLE	1	2	3	4	5	6	7
HONEYMOON	1	2	3	4	5	6	7
SAVED THE ANIMAL	1	2	3	4	5	6	7

ITEMS DELETED FROM STORY (Note which teller)

ITEMS ADDED TO THE STORY (Note which teller)

Discussion Points: What Happened to the Message?
1. What kinds of information were reproduced accurately, omitted, added, and changed? Why were some of the details harder to recall than others?
2. How do the circumstances of this exercise differ from normal rumor transmission situations? Do these differences make the reproductions in the exercises more or less accurate than would occur in normal life?
3. How much should a person depend on the accuracy of information reproduced from memory through several individuals/
4. What methods can be used to improve the accuracy with which information is reproduced?
5. How is this exercise related to earlier communication concepts (perception, nonverbal communication apprehension, etc.)?

Principles Illustrated:
1. How well we listen is affected by a host of variables.
2. Feedback is important for accurate listening.

Becoming an Effective Listener

(Created by Gregory Lamp, University of Wisconsin Center—Rock County)

Approximate Time: 40-50 minutes or two 25 minutes segments

Purpose: To afford students the opportunity to practice the skills of listening for information and listening for feelings in a positive environment

Procedures:
1. Divide the class into groups of three. Designate the students as A, B, and C. the will rotate roles as the speaker, the listener, and the observer.
2. Have each student list the information which follows on Listening for Facts and Listening for Feelings, as well as the two check lists.
3. Begin by having student A serve s the speaker and B as the listener. A begin to speak, discussion one of his/her "beefs" about school, work, social life, or home (or any other topic of the students' or instructor's choice). Speakers converse for at least one minute without any substantive verbal feedback from the listener. Student C serves as the observer, using the "Observer's checklist" form.
4. When the speaker has finished, the listener provides feedback in the form of a paraphrase.
5. Observers offer their comments to the listener.
6. Students rotate positions so that each has an opportunity to be the speaker and the listener and the observer.
7. Large group discussion may follow at this point or the triads may be instructed to continue with the second part of the assignment, Listening for Feelings.
8. Follow a similar format for the second part of the exercise, Listening for Feelings, being sure to choose a topic that will arouse emotional reactions in the students. This time, the listeners and the observers will focus beyond what the speaker is saying to what (s)he is feeling. Some suggested topics are:
   > your most embarrassing moment
   > your most meaningful/significant relationship
   > the most exciting event in your life
   > the saddest event in your life
   > your feelings toward the opposite sex
9. Continue with steps 4, 5, and 6. Follow with a large group discussion.

Discussion Points:
1. How effectively did you find that people listened?
2. Did you find yourself listening differently in this situation that you ordinarily do?
3. Which role was the most difficult (speaker, listener/paraphraser, observer)? Why?
4. Did it make a difference to you as a speaker knowing that your words and behaviors were being carefully attended to?
5. What applications and ramifications does the exercise have for you as a "real life" listener?

Principles Illustrated:
1. We use different techniques for listening in different ways.
2. Listening is an active a process and takes effort an concentration.
3. Our listening abilities can be improved with practice.
4. Effective listening requires a commitment o understanding the other person.

PART I: PARAPHRASING—LISTENING FOR FACTS

Objectives: Restatements are used to:
1. Indicate your desire to understand the speaker's thoughts and to think with the speaker.
2. Check your listening accuracy and to encourage further discussion.
3. Let the speaker know you are committed to grasping the facts.

Method:

> Focus on the content of the speaker's message.
> Identify key ideas.
> Listen until you experience the speaker's point of view.
> Wait for a natural "break" in the conversation.
> Briefly restate the speaker's ideas, emphasizing the facts.
> State the essence of the speaker's content.
> Respond with your own words to what the speaker has said.
> Request feedback.

Listener Response Format:

> "As I understand it, you are saying that…Is that what you intended?"
> "What I think you said was…Is that right?"
> "Let me see if I have this right…Is that what you said?"

Message Communicated from the Listener to the Speaker:

> "I'm interested in you as a person, and I think that what you feel is important. I respect your thoughts, and ever if I don't agree with them, I know they are valid for you. I want to understand you. I think you're worth listening to, and I want you to know that I'm the kind of person you can talk to." (Carl R. Rogers)

Procedure for Paraphrasing:
- Make the decision to listen.
- Reduce any outside interference.
- Distance your emotions.
- Temporarily set aside your own opinion.
- Take a listening posture—
    - face the speaker
    - make eye to eye contact
    - lean forward
    - have an open, receptive posture
    - establish a close, but not uncomfortably close, interactional distance
    - maintain responsive facial expressions
- Listen for facts
- Verbalize brief and encouraging expressive (mm-hmmm; uh huh, I see, right).
- Without judgment. (Do NOT evaluate; do NOT agree or disagree.)
- If necessary, ask for clarification, examples, or more helpful detail.
- Speak in a warm and pleasant voice tone.
- Feed back the message as you understand it to see if that is what the speaker untended.
- Request feedback to check your perceptions.

OBSERVER'S CHECKLIST: LISTENING FOR FACTS
      In the spaces provided, place a "+" if the listener demonstrated the behavior and a "-"if the listener did not.

Did the listener…
_____ face the speaker?
_____ make eye to eye contact?
_____ lean forward?
_____ have an open, receptive posture?
_____ establish a close, but not uncomfortably close, interactional distance?
_____ maintain responsive facial expressions?
_____ listen for understanding first?
_____ verbalize brief and encouraging expressives?
_____ without judgment. (did not evaluate; did not agree or disagree?)?
_____ wait for a natural "break" in the conversation before asking questions or restating the speaker's idea?
_____ if necessary, ask for clarification, examples, or more helpful detail?
_____ briefly restate the speaker's ideas, emphasizing the facts to see if that was what the speaker intended?
_____ state the essence of the speaker's content.?
_____ respond in his/her own words to what the speaker has said?
_____ speak in a warm and pleasant voice tone?
_____ request feedback?

Additional Comments:

PART II: LISTENING FOR FEELINGS

Objective:
      Responding in a way to show that you have listened for feelings is used to…
      Show your desire to feel with the sender.
      Reduce anxiety, anger, or other negative feelings.
      Verify the listener's perception of the sender's feelings.
      Let the other person know you are working to understand how s/he feels.

Method:
      Reflect the other persons' feelings.
      Observer body language.
      Note the general content of the speaker's message.
      Focus on the feeling words and nonverbals.
      Match the speaker's depth of meaning, light or serious.
      Ensure accurate communication of feelings by matching the speaker's meaning.

Listener Response Format:
      "You feel that you didn't receive the proper treatment, is that right?"
      "It was unjust as you perceived it, is that it?"
      "I sense that you like doing the job but not sire how to go about is, right?"
      "It's frustrating to have this happen to you, right?"

Procedure for Listening for Feelings:

    Follow the pointers given above—plus—
- Focus on the feeling words.
- Reflect the speaker's feelings nonverbally.
- Feedback the feelings as you understand them to see if that is what the speaker intended.

OBSERVER'S CHECKLIST: LISTENING FOR FEELINGS

    In the spaces provided, place a "+" if the listener demonstrated the behavior and a "-"if the listener did not.

Did the listener…

_____ face the speaker?
_____ make eye to eye contact?
_____ lean forward?
_____ have an open, receptive posture?
_____ establish a close, but not uncomfortably close, interactional distance?
_____ maintain responsive facial expressions?
_____ observe the speaker's body language?
_____ reflect the speaker's feelings nonverbally?
_____ verbalize brief and encouraging expressives?
_____ without judgment. (did not evaluate; did not agree or disagree?)?
_____ wait for a natural "break" in the conversation before asking questions or reflecting the speaker's feelings?
_____ if necessary, ask for clarification, examples, or more helpful details?
_____ briefly restate/reflect the speaker's feelings?
_____ speak in a warm and pleasant voice tone?
_____ request feedback?

Additional Comments:

Listening Challenge

Approximate Time: 30 minutes

Purpose: To illustrate how people fail to listen to others because they often prepare their next statements while others are talking

Procedures:
1. Divide the class into dyads.
2. Write several controversial topics on the board, such as abortion, gun control, the president's budget. Ask the students to take opposite sides on the issue, even if they disagree with the position they will have to argue.
3. Direct the dyads to begin debating the issues. After 3-5 minutes of debate, tell them to switch sides. After a period of time, tell them to switch sides again.
4. Discuss what happened. What feelings were generated? Hostility? Frustration? Empathy?
5. Ask the same dyads to select a different topic. This time, each person has to restate the other's position before he or she can speak for his or her own position. Let this discussion proceed for 5-8 minutes.

6. Contrast the second situation with the first. Was it equally (or more) frustrating? What were the merits of each approach? Problems?

Principles Illustrated:
1. We often fail to listen effectively because we are preparing our statements in advance.
2. Effective listening is challenging; it is difficult and tiring.
3. Listening effectiveness can be improved with effort.

PORTFOLIO ENTRY

Listening Diary

(Based on an exercise in Mary O. Wiemann's Activities Manual for *Looking Out/looking in*, 8th edition)

Nobody's a perfect listener. Here's a chance for you to see how often you truly listen and how much of the time you just pretend.

Purpose:
1. To help you to identify the styles of listening/non-listening you use in your interpersonal relationships.
2. To help you to identify your response styles.
3. To help you to discover the consequences of the listening styles you use.

Background:
Your text discusses several types of listening/non-listening and styles of feedback:

Listening	Non-listening	Response Styles
To Understand & Retain Information	Pseudolistening	Passive
	Stage Hogging	Active-
To Build & Maintain Relationships	Selective Listening	Questioning
To Evaluate Messages	Filling in the Gaps	Paraphrasing
	Insulated Listening	Empathizing
(To Appreciate & Enjoy	Defensive Listening	Directive-
This is another reason less clearly	Ambushing	Supporting
related to interpersonal communication	Analyzing	
why we might listen.)	Advising	
	Evaluating	

Instructions:
1. Before beginning your Diary, circle the three listening/non-listening styles and three response style that you think use the most frequently.
2. For the next five days, pay attention to your listening behavior. Don't try to change the way you act; just observe the times when you're really trying to understand someone and the times you're behaving in one of the nonlistening ways listed above.
3. Using the entry sheets provided, note FIVE listening experiences for each of the five days (a total of 25 entries). Be sure to include a weekend in your survey. Each entry should include following information:
   a. Time and Place
   b. People involved

c. Situation
d. Emotions—mood/atmosphere (Yours? Your parent's? Expressed or not?)
e. Style of listening used (See above.)
f. Response Style (Yours and/or your partner's)
g. Outcome (Did your listening and responses bring the situation to a satisfactory conclusion?)

While your entry sheets will be handed in with your Portfolio, the notes are for your benefit, not the instructor's. Be sure you include enough information so that you will be able to draw conclusions and support your conclusions with specific examples.

4. Using the information your recorder over the five days, analyze your listening behavior. Create a cohesive essay in which you discuss the following points. (Be sure to use specific examples from your data sheets to support and illustrate your points. Your essay should be approximately three typed, double-spaces pages.
   a. Did you anticipate the results of the diary? Why or why not? Did you find that the styles you used most frequently were the ones you circled prior to collecting the data?
   b. Which listening/non-listening and response styles did you use most frequently? Do you see any patterns in your listening behaviors? (Do particular situations or people or times of day regularly correlate with certain listening/non-listening behaviors or response styles?)
   c. What conclusions can you draw about your listening behavior?
   d. How effective are your listening patterns? How satisfied are you with your listening behavior? *Explain why you are satisfied or dissatisfied.* How would you wish to change? How can you begin to change?

Date: _____

Results	Response Style	Listening/ Non-Listening	Situation	Emotion(s)	Time/Place/ People

D & A

Review the poor listening habits discussed in the chapter. Describe as experience where you have either used or been subjected to dour of the seven habits. What was the outcome of each?

GROUP STUDY

(See the Introductory Essay for further information. Consult the Group Study Section in Chapter One for additional directions to students.)

CHAPTER SIX

PART I: TYPES OF NONLISTENING

a. pseudolistening
b. stage hogging
c. selective listening

d. filling in the gaps
e. insulted listening

f. defensive listening
g. ambushing

_____ 1. John couldn't wait for Sue to make a mistake so that he could jump on her for it.
_____ 2. Andi often appears to be paying attention in class even though her mind is miles away.
_____ 3. Keith thinks he knows what Craig is going to say because they are such good friends.
_____ 4. Regina seems to take everything anyone says as an attack
_____ 5. Dale never gives anyone else a chance to speak.
_____ 6. When Georgina's grandfather talks, she doesn't need to listen because she's heard it all already twenty times (at least).
_____ 7. Although Cynthia has been told at least three times that her boyfriend is cheating on her, she never seems to register the message.
_____ 8. Winston was able to tune out the conversation in the other room while he was studying—until he suddenly heard his own name come up.

PART II: RESPONSE STYLES

a. passive	d. empathizing	f. advising
b. questioning	e. supporting	g. evaluating
c. paraphrasing	f. analyzing	

_____ 9. "You're really facing a tough decision. Just remember that I'm your friend, and I'm behind you 100% no matter what you decide."
_____ 10. "I think you're probably just jealous because your dad let your sister have the car."
_____ 11. "And then what happened? Did Jack have anything else to add? Why did Amy think you left the party?"
_____ 12. "Well, that sounds like a pretty dumb move. Apparently, you didn't think thing through very well before you made that decision."
_____ 13. "I can understand how you must feel. I remember that I felt really alone when my grandmother died."
_____ 14. "So what you're saying is that you don't know whether to report the theft to your boss or no and this is making you feel stressed out."
_____ 15. "If I were you, I'd try talking to her. Just find a good moment and lay out the entire situation."

ANSWER KEY:

1. g	6. a	11. b
2. a	7. e	12. h
3. d	8. c	13. d
4. f	9. e	14. c
5. b	10. f	15. g

TEACHING ACTIVITIES FROM THE *COMMUNICATION TEACHER*

Bohlken, B (1994, Winter). *Learning to listen as you listen to learn, 8(2)*, 8-9.
Bohlken, B (1996, Spring). *Think about* listening, *10(3)*, 5-6.
Forestieri, M. (1987, Spring). *Listening instruction, 1(3)*, 14-15.
Garvin, J. A. (1990, Spring). *Where is it and how do we get there?, 4(3)*, 15.
Hyde, R. B. (1993, Winter). *Council: Using a talking stick to teach listening, 7(2)*, 1-2.
Jensen, M. (1989, Summer). *Listening with the third ear: An experience in empathy, 3(4)*, 10-11.
Johnson, M. (1991, Winter). *Student listening tests, 5(2)*, 5.
Kaye, T. (1990, Spring). *Respecting others' point of view, 4(3)*, 12.
Lamoureux, E. L. (1990, Summer). *Practice creative word choice with dialogic listening, 4(4)*, 4-5.
Loesch, R. (1987, Summer). *Three nonverbal listening styles: A demonstration, 1(4)*, 4.

Mallard, K. S. (1998, Winter). *The listening box, 12(2)*, 9.

McPeak, J. (1994, Spring). *Listening activities, 8(3)*, 15-16.

Mino, M. (1997, Fall). *Creating listening rules, 12(1)*, 8.

Potnoy, E. (1989, Spring). *Activities to promote students' speaking and listening abilities, 3(3)*, 14-16.

Rausch, R. (1985, Fall). *On-the-job listening*, 6.

Schneider, V. (1987, Fall). *A three-step process for better speaking and listening, 2(1)*, 10-11.

Starnell, B. (1986, Fall). *Critic's corner, 1(1),* 1-2.

Wallace, J. D. (1996, Fall. *The rumor game revisited, 10(1)*, 6-7.

Wirkus, T. E. (1993, Winter). *Creating student-generated listening activities, 7(2)*, 3-4.

Chapter Seven: Emotions

Debilitative Emotions: Thinking Things Through

Approximate time: 45-50 minutes

Purpose: To focus group discussion on the ways in which assumptions affect our interpretations and how we feel.

Procedures:
1. In your small group, consider the ten episodes below and discuss the following questions:
    a.   What irrational assumptions is the person making? What fallacies are present?
    b.   How do these assumptions cause the person to feel the way she does?
    c.   What rational assumptions does the person need in order to change her feelings into more positive feelings?
2. In your group, discuss assumptions each of you have that influence your feelings of depression, anger, frustration, distress, and worry. When you are experiencing each of these feelings, what assumptions are causing you to feel that way? How can you change these assumptions to make your life happier?

Episodes

1. Sally likes to have here coworkers place their work neatly in a pile on her desk so that she can add her work to the pile, staple it all together, and give it to their supervisor. Her coworkers, however, throw their work into the supervisor's basket in a very disorderly and messy fashion. Sally then becomes very worried and upset. "I can't stand it," Sally says to herself, "It's terrible what they are doing. And it isn't fair to me or our supervisor!"
2. Jill has been given responsibility for planning next year's budget for her department. This amount of responsibility scares her. For several weeks she has done nothing on the budget. "I'll do it next week," she keeps thinking.
3. John went to the office one morning and passed a person he had never met in the hallway. He said, "Hello," and the person just looked at him and walked on without saying a word. John became depressed. "I'm really not a very attractive person," he thought to himself. "No one seems to like me."
4. Dan is an intensive-care paramedic technician and is constantly depressed and worried about whether he can do his job competently. For every decision that has to be made, he asks his supervisor what he should do. One day he came into work and found that his supervisor had quit. "What will I do now?" he thought. "I can't handle the job without her."
5. Jane went to her desk and found a note from her supervisor that she had made an error in the report she worked on the day before. The note told her to correct the error and continue working on the report. Jane became depressed. "Why am I so dumb and stupid?" she thought to herself. "I can't seem to do anything right. That supervisor must think I'm terrible at my job."
6. Heidi has a knack for insulting people. She insults her coworkers, her boss, customers, and passersby who ask for directions. Her boss has repeatedly told Heidi that if she doesn't change she will be fired. This depresses Heidi and makes her very angry with her boss. "How can I change?" Heidi says. "I've been this way ever since I could talk. It's too late for me to change now."
7. Tim was checking the repairs another technician had made on a television set. He found a mistake and became very angry. "I have to punish him," he thought. "He made a mistake and he has to suffer the consequences for it."

8. Bonnie doesn't like to fill out forms. She gets furious every day because her job as a legal secretary requires her to fill out form and form after form. "Every time I see a form my stomach ties itself into knots" she says. "I hate forms! I know they have to be done in order for the work to be filed with the courts, but I still hate them!"
9. Bob is very anxious about keeping his job. "What if the company goes out of business?" he thinks. "What if my boss gets angry with me?" "What if the secretary I yelled at is the boss's daughter?" All day he worries about whether he will have a job tomorrow.
10. Jack is a very friendly person who listens quite well. All his coworkers tell their problems to Jack. He listens sympathetically. Then he goes home deeply depressed. "Life is so terrible for the people I work with," he thinks. "They have such severe problems and such sad lives."

Principles Illustrated:

1. The assumptions we make greatly influence our interpretations of the meaning of events in our life. These interpretations determine our feelings.
2. The same even can be depressing or amusing, depending on the assumptions and interpretations we make.

Alligator River Story

Approximate Time: 40 minutes

Purpose: To introduce students to some of the basic concepts about emotions and their expression while participating in interactive scenario

Procedures:
1. Distribute the story to each student in class.
2. Give each student approximately five minutes to read the story and rank the characters.
3. After reading the story, the students will privately rank each of the five characters from most offensive to least objectionable.
4. Students will then assemble in their learning teams (or in groups of 5-6) to rank, as a group, the characters from most offensive to least objectionable. The students should attempt to come to a consensus as a group. THIS RARELY OCCURS.
5. After approximately 20 minutes, stop the discussion and debrief the simulation as a class.

Questions could include:
1. How comfortable do you feel expressing your emotions? Why/when do you NOT express your emotions?
2. What about the climate allowed you to express your emotions? Which emotions?

THE ALLIGATOR RIVER STORY*

*Adapted from: *Values clarification: A handbook of practical strategies for teachers and students.* 1972, Hart publishing Company, inc., New York.

After you read the story, rank privately the five characters from most offensive to the least objectionable.

Once upon a time, there was a woman named **Abigail** who was in love with a man named **Gregory**. Gregory lived on the shore of the river and Abigail lived on the opposite shore of the river. The river that separated the tow lovers was teeming with man-eating alligators. Abigail wanted to cross the river to be with Gregory. Unfortunately, the bridge had been washed out. She was wearing a tight skirt and a low-cut blouse because she wanted to look sexy for Gregory. **Sinbad**, the ferry caption, said that he would take her across; however, the look in his eyes frightened her. **Ivan**, a close friend of Abigail's, did not want to be involved at all in the situation. Abigail felt that her only alternative was to take the ferry, even though she did not trust Sinbad.

After leaving the river shore, Sinbad told Abigail that he couldn't control himself and had to go to bed with her. When Abigail refused, he threatened to throw her overboard. He also said that is she complied, he would deliver her safely to the other side. Abigail was afraid of being eaten alive by the alligators, and didn't see any other alternative for herself, so she did not resist Sinbad.

When Abigail told Gregory about what happened to her, he viewed her as asking for it because of the way she was dressed. He saw her as unclean and cast her aside with disdain. Heartsick and dejected, she turned to **Slug** who was a black belt in karate. Slug felt anger at Gregory and compassion for Abigail. He sought out Gregory and beat him brutally. Abigail was overjoyed at the sight of Gregory getting his just due. As the sun sets on the horizon, we hear Abigail laughing at Gregory.

1.
2.
3.
4.
5.

You and Your Feelings

Approximate Time: 40 minutes

Purpose: To introduce students to some of the basic concepts about emotions and their expression

Procedures:
1. Divide the students into groups of 5 to 7 each.
2. Give each group two large pieces of newsprint, magic markers, and copies of the discussion questions.
3. Allow about 25-25 minutes for discussion in small groups.
4. Groups each post their "finding" to share with the entire class.
5. The instructor leads a discussion on the questions and uses student responses as a stepping off point for introduction beginning theory.

Questions for Discussion:
1. Take two minutes to write down (individually) as many emotions as you can think of. Now, take about 5 minutes to brainstorm with other group members to list as many emotions as possible. (Can you identify 50? More?) Write these on he newsprint. (Remember to write large enough so that the list will be able to be seen by the rest of the class.)
2. Circle the tow emotions which <u>each</u> of you <u>feels</u> the most frequently.
3. Star (*) the two emotions which each of you <u>expresses</u> the <u>most</u> frequently.
4. Place an X next to the two emotions which each of you expresses <u>least</u> frequently. (Note that the same emotions may be both starred and "X'ed.")
5. Where (in your body) do you (individually) "feel" emotions? (List these on another sheet of newsprint.)
6. How comfortable do you feel expressing your emotions? Why/when do you NOT express your emotions?

7. With whom do you express emotions? Which emotions? (Note that you may express different emotions with different people.)
8. What conclusions/generalizations can you draw from your discussion of the above points? Determine at least two ideas which your groups will share with the entire class.

Principles Illustrated:
1. The repertoire of emotions which come to our minds for instant recall is limited. (Brainstorming with a group helps significantly.)
2. The emotions that we feel the most, how we experience them, and those emotions that we express the most and the least vary one person to another.
3. Most of us feel more comfortable expressing positive, rather than negative, emotions.
4. Society has played a powerful role in determining the freedom with that we express our emotions.
5. We feel comfortable expressing different emotions with those whom we know well than with those whom we do not know well.

Identifying Feelings

Approximate Time: 30 minutes

Purpose: To assist students in identifying the various feeling they experience and to widen the scope of their emotions vocabulary

Procedures:
1. Divide the class into triads.
2. Each person should share with the other two members of the triad a feeling (s)he has experienced in the past few days, sharing both the inner and outer physical signs that accompanied the feeling.
3. Each student also explains to the other two what (s)he did with the feeling. Was it ignored, denied, listened to, or dealt with? What happened? Were they satisfied with the outcome?
4. When the triads have finished sharing a minimum of three feelings each, move into the large class again and report the different feelings that were identified.
5. Have one person record all the different emotions on the blackboard.

Principles Illustrated:
1. Emotions are ever present and connected to every act and thought.
2. Our vocabulary for expressing emotions is limited and can be expanded to be able to better describe what we are feeling.

Rational Thinking

Approximate Time: 30 minutes

Purpose: To sharpen students' skills at thinking rationally on the spot

Procedures:
1. Before class, generate a list of four or five "scenes" that are interpersonal in nature and are likely to have anxiety connected to them for anyone experiencing a similar situation in real life.
   Potential scenes are:
   a. A potential employee just beginning a job interview.
   b. A couple just beginning their first date.
   c. A teacher or boss criticizing a student or employee for showing up late.

2. Ask for three volunteers from the class to act out each scene: a "subject," a second person, and the subject's "little voice"—his or her thoughts.
3. Have the students play out each scene by having the subject and the second party interact, while ht "little voice" stands just behind the subject and speaks the thoughts that the subject probably is having. For example, in a scene where the subject is asking an instructor to reconsider a low grade, the voice might say, "I hope I haven't mad things worse by bring this up. Maybe he'll lower the grade after rereading the test. Maybe he'll see something else wrong that he missed before. I'm such an idiot! Why didn't ii keep my mouth shut?"
4. Whenever the voice expresses an irrational though, the observers who are watching the skit should call out "foul." At this point the action is stopped while the group discusses the irrational thought and suggests a more rational line of self-talk. The players then replay the scene with the voice speaking in a more rational way.

Principles Illustrated:
1. Often what we think about an event causes us to have negative feeling about it.
2. Irrational self-talk can be overcome and replaced with rational internal monologues.

Find the Feeling

(Based on an exercise in Mary O. Wiemann's Activities Manual for *Looking Out/looking in*, 8th edition)

Approximate Time: 15-20 minutes

Purpose: To help students to distinguish between true and counterfeit expressions of emotions and to give students the opportunity to gain experience in expressing feelings accurately

Procedures:
1. Divide the class into small groups of 5 to 7 members.
2. Distribute the handout that follows and review the directions.
3. Review the correct responses—either with the individual groups or in the large group.

The exercise appears deceptively simple. Many students have a considerable amount of difficulty distinguishing between the "real" feelings statements and the counterfeits. In the statements below, only number 4 give an absolutely clear statement of the speaker's feeling. Number 8 is also acceptable as a metaphor; however, many students may find it too vague to be acceptable and may choose to to-write it as well.

FIND THE FEELINGS

Instructions:
1. Identify any true feeling statements below.
2. Analyze the other statements to determine WHY they are not true expressions of feelings.
3. Re-write the statements so that they accurately express the speaker's feeling.

HINT: Statements which could be prefaced with "I think" are not expressions of emotions. If the statements could be preceded by "I am," they are likely to express feelings.
Example: "That's the most disgusting thing I've ever heard."
Analysis: We know that the speaker thinks something is disgusting, but we do not know how (s)he is reacting to this assessment. Is (s)he truly disgusted? Amused? Offended?
Re-Write: "I really felt disgusted by the way that movie portrayed women."

1. "That was a great evening!"
        Analysis:

        Re-Write:

2. "You're being awfully sensitive about that."
        Analysis:

        Re-Write:

3. "I can't figure out how to approach him."
        Analysis:

        Re-Write:

4. "I'm confused about what you want from me."
        Analysis:

        Re-Write:

5. "I don't know how to tell you this…"
        Analysis:

        Re-Write:

6. "I feel as if you're trying to hurt me."
        Analysis:

        Re-Write:

7. "It's hopeless."
        Analysis:

        Re-Write:

8. "I feel like the rug has been pulled out from under me."
        Analysis:

        Re-Write:

Principles Illustrated:
1. Many of the statements which we make that wound like authentic expressions of feelings are really expressions of though or opinion.
2. Expressing feelings accurately improves communication.

PORTFOLIO ENTRY

Emotions: Thinking, Feeling, and Acting

We all experience emotions, but identify them and express them with varying degrees of expertise. The purpose of this exercise is to have you focus on the role which emotions play within your daily life.

1. Complete the three day survey by filling out the entry sheets. You should note **five** different experiences for each of the three days. (While you will be asked to hand in your entry sheets, the notes are for your benefits, not the instructor's. be sure to include enough information so that you will be able to draw conclusions and support your conclusions with specific examples. You may use any kind of personal shorthand that is meaningful for you.)
2. Using the data on your entry sheets, analyze the role of emotions in your life during this three day period and in general.
   a. How easy were the emotions for you to identify? Which methods did you use for the purpose of identification: proprioceptive stimuli (physical reactions)? nonverbal manifestations? cognitive interpretations? Illustrate your response with two *specific* examples.
   b. Analyze the types of emotions which you experiences. How wide a range of emotions? Re they mainly primary or mixed/ are most of them facilitative or debilitate? Illustrate by giving specific examples.
   c. Do you think that this three day period provides a "typical" sample of your emotions? If not, explain why not.
   d. Did you find evidence that you subscribe to any of the fallacies given in your text? Give two example of incidents when you did subscribe to a fallacy. (Your may go outside of the three day period if you wish.)
   e. How freely do you express your emotions? With whom do you express yourself most freely? Least freely? Why?
   f. How comfortable are you with your emotions? What is the impact of emotions in your daily interpersonal relationships?
   g. Make any other observations which you'd like based on your entry sheets or other thinking that you have done on this topic.

Date: _____

Results	How Expressed?	How Recognized?	Fac/Deb	Situation	Pri/Mix	Emotion(s)	Time/Place People

D & A

Complete Invitation to Insight #4, Fallacy of Helplessness at the end of Chapter 8.

GROUP STUDY

(See the Introductory Essay for further information. Consult the Group Study Section in Chapter One for additional directions to students.)

CHAPTER SEVEN

Match the letter of the irrational fallacy with its description of self-talk found below.

a. the fallacy of perfection	e. the fallacy of causation
b. the fallacy of approval	f. the fallacy of helplessness
c. the fallacy of shoulds	g. the fallacy of catastrophic expectations
d. the fallacy of overgeneralization	

_____ 1. "I really don't like rock concerts, but I go so that the others won't think I'm a loser."

_____ 2. "She'll really upset me if she comes late again."

_____ 3. "She's a totally cold fish; I'm lucky if I get a little kiss on the cheek!"

_____ 4. "You ought to drink less."

_____ 5. "What with the food, the water, and the transportation problems, you're going to die going to Mexico at spring break."

_____ 6. "I've had a class in interpersonal communication; I can't believe I used the wrong words and insults her just now."

_____ 7. "I know I'll make Shelly feel terrific if I come to her party."

_____ 8. "It's not even worth trying to reach him. I know I can't make him listen to me."

_____ 9. "There's no point in going to that job interview. I'll just turn twelve shades of red, say stupid things—if my voice even worked—and I won't get the job anyway."

_____ 10. "No matter what I do, I just can't seem to manage my time."

_____ 11. "You never tell me how you feel."

_____ 12. "You should really be more patient about learning how to play the piano."

_____ 13. "I can't afford it, but if I don't lend Rob $50, he probably won't like me anymore."

_____ 14. "Look at this rotten paper! I got an "A," but I missed these two dumb typos.'

_____ 15. "getting that "A" in math made me so happy!"

ANSWER KEY:

1. b	6. a	11. d
2. e	7. e	12. c
3. d	8. f	13. b
4. c	9. g	14. a
5. g	10. f	15. e

TEACHING ACTIVITIES FROM THE *COMMUNICATION TEACHER*

Coakley, C. (1986, Fall). *Feelings, 1(1)* 16.

Huntchinson, J. A. (1988, Winter). *The love debate, 2(2)*, 13-14.

Lane, S. D. (1997, Spring). *Communicating emotions, 11(3)*, 2-4.

Chapter Eight: Dynamics of Interpersonal Relationships

Mission Possible; Breaking Bread with Strangers

Approximate Time: one class period

Purpose: To simulate the development of a relationship between two strangers and reflect on the relationship using interpersonal communication theories and concepts

Procedures:
1. Ask students to bring something to eat and to drink that can (and will) be shared with another person for the next class period. Make sire that students also bring whatever utensils are needed to make sharing possible.
2. Ask students to pair off with a person in class that they do not know and share their food. Before they leave the classroom, provide each dyad with their "mission, " which is not to be read until after they finished eating.
3. After they have both finished eating they should be instructed to read their "mission." Everyone has the same statement.

You have just shared food with someone that you did not know. Reflect on what transpired over the last 3040 minutes. Explain your feelings and the events in terms of Knapp's Relationship Development Theory. You should also include in your discussion other theories and concepts from Chapter Nine. After your discussion, each of you (individually) should *type* a 2-3 page reaction paper that is both specific and descriptive.

New Relationships

Approximate Time: one class period

Purpose: To simulate the development of a relationship between two strangers

Procedures:
1. Ask students to pair off with a person in class that they do not know.
2. Ask them to write down in two to three words their feelings about pairing off with a stranger.
3. Instruct the dyads to get to know each other as well as possible in 20minutes. They may leave the classroom if they wish.
4. In 20 minutes, reconvene and ask them to write down their feelings at the beginning of the conversation. They should also write down what they think their partners were feeling.
5. Allow dyads to compare notes briefly.
6. Discuss the exercise, emphasizing the commonality of anxiety and uncertainty about a new relationship. Note changes in the feelings throughout the 20 minutes. Did the discussion topics change? Ask students to identify their feelings about their partners now that the exercise is over. Note how this exercise was different from and similar to real-life relationship formation.

Principles Illustrated:
1. Relationships develop I fairly typical patterns.
2. Most people feel anxiety at the onset of a relationship.
3. Feelings about a relationship change during the course of the relationship.

Wanted: Relationships

Approximate Time: 30 minutes

Purpose: To have each student assess the type of person he or she prefers in various situations; to demonstrate that relationship needs differ from situation to situation

Procedures:
1. Have each student write and bring into class three "want ads" (of the singles magazine variety) advertising for people to fill three different types of relationship "vacancies" in their lives. The student should also describe him/her in each of the ads.
   a. Advertise for a person with whom you wish to establish a working relationship.
   b. Advertise for a person with whom you wish to have a friendship.
   c. Advertise for a person with whom you would like to develop a long-term spousal relationship.
2. Divide the students into groups of about five members. Give them the following directions: in your small group, share the ads which have been written by each member. For each person, compile two lists, one which shows the characteristics which are uniform in all three ads and those which are distinct from one ad to another.
   - Are there strong similarities among the members of the group?
   - What might account for the differences between the members?
   - How do the ads reflect your goals for each of these relationships?
   - What role does impression management play in these ads? Do you present the same "self" for each of the ads?
   - What does the exercise tell you about yourself? About others in the group?
   Choose a number of ads and insights from your group to share.
3. Conduct a large group discussion based on the questions above.

Principles Illustrated:
1. There are situational elements in relationship needs.
2. People have an "implicit" personality theory that informs them of what type of person they need, or want, in a relationship.

Dyadic Interview

Approximate Time: one class period

Purpose: To provide students with an opportunity to practice and sharpen the basic skills of reception and transmission. It is also intended to represent, in capsulated form, the kind of talk people engage in at various levels of relationship, as they attempt to move from stranger to acquaintance to friend. The goal is not self-disclosure or friendship, but rather a clearer understanding of a process through which "close" relationships can occur.

Procedures:
1. Arrange to carry out the dyad interview in a quiet place, where other people, loud music, telephone calls, etc., will not intrude. Try to make this communication event as free from "noise" as possible.
2. Statements should be completed in the order in which they appear. (Each student should answer the question before going on to the next item. Individuals may wish to alternate which of them responds to each question first.)
3. Students may decline to answer any question.
4. All of the personal data discussed should, of course, be considered confidential.

5. Conduct the interview as a conversation, taking time with each question.
6. It is most helpful to students if the above purposes statement and procedures are printed on the handout used in the interview process.

DYADIC INTERVIEW

1. My name is...
2. My hometown is...
3. I come from a family of...
4. I am planning a career in...
5. One of the most important skills in getting to know another person is listening. In order to check on your ability to understand what your partner is communicating, the tow of you should go through the following steps *one at a time*.

   Decide which of you is to speak first. The first speaker is to complete the following item using two or three sentences:

   When I think about the future, I see myself living a life...

   The second person repeats in his or her own words what the first speaker has just said. The first speaker must be satisfied that he or she has been heard accurately. Then the second speaker completes the item, and the first speaker paraphrases what the second speaker just said, to the satisfaction of the second speaker.

   Share what you may have learned about yourself as a listener. The two of you may find yourselves later saying to each other, "What you seem to be saying is..." to keep a check on the accuracy of your listening and understanding.

1. When I am in a new group, I...
2. When I enter a room full of people, I usually feel...
3. When I am feeling anxious in a new situation, I usually...
4. I like to be quiet and let other people take charge when...
5. In a group, I usually get most involved when...
6. One thing that people who know me well probably would say about me is...
   (Conduct a Listening Check here.)
7. The thing that I am most concerned about when I am getting to know someone is...
8. The thing that interests me most is...
9. The thing that turn me off most is...
10. When I am alone I usually...
11. I am rebellious when...
    Checkup: Have a two- or three-minute discussion about this experience so far, and try to evaluate how well you are listening.
12. The emotion I have the most trouble expressing when I want to is...
13. I love...
14. What's really lovable about me is...
15. I tend to express anger...
16. Right now I'm feeling...
17. I am afraid of...
18. I believe in...
19. I was very pleased with myself...
20. I felt most comfortable during this exercise when you...
    Instructors (or students) can add other statements as they wish.

Principles Illustrated:
1. Active listening plays an invaluable role in understanding others and in and developing interpersonal relationships.
2. The developmental nature of interpersonal relationships as communication moves from impersonal to interpersonal to relatively intimate information.

Considering Friendship

Approximate Time: 30-40 minutes

Purpose: To allow students to discover and discuss the dimensions of friendship

Procedures:
1. Divide the students into groups of 5 to 7.
2. Distribute the following discussion sheet. Be sure that someone from each group from each group take notes to report back to the large group. (If time is short, different groups can be assigned to discuss different questions.)
3. After a prescribed amount to time, meet back in the large group to share responses.

CONSIDERING FRIENDSHIP

Some questions for discussion...
- How would you define the word "friends?"
- What are the most important characteristics of a friend? Brainstorm to come up with at least fifteen characteristics. Then try to come to consensus on rack-ordering the top five characteristics.
- What role does honesty play in your friendships? Is absolute honesty necessary? Possible? Desirable? What are the potential advantages and dangers of honesty in interpersonal situations? Is there a form of "pure" honesty which people can determine for themselves and always depend upon using or does what is "honest" sometimes vary with the situation or with how much information is available? Is there a difference between lying and not telling the whole truth? Discuss some situation is which "complete" honesty either strengthened or harmed an interpersonal relationship.
- What is necessary in order to foster a friendship? Do you spend time on your friends? How many is "enough" friends? How/when do friendships deteriorate? Have you ever had to "break off" a relationship? How did you do it? How did you feel about it?
- Do you see differences between male/male, female/female, and male/female relationships? Does it make a difference whether or not your are "attached (regularly dating, living with someone, married)?

PORTFOLIO ENTRY

Analyzing a Relationship

This entry covers the theory found in Chapter 9 and 10.

Using an essay format, analyze one of your most important relationships. Begin by identifying the individual and briefly describing the relationship. Then, use the principles in the chapters to analyze this relationship.

1. Consider the variables of why we form relationships (attraction, similarity, complementarity, proximity, etc.) How did these variables function in the beginning of your relationships/ how do the variables function now that your have a more established relationship?
2. Discuss your relationship in terms of Knapp's Stages of Coming Together/Apart. How did you move from one sage to another? Where are you now? What tells you this?
3. How do the dialectical tensions function in this relationship? Give at least two specific examples and describe how you managed the tension.
4. What types of compliance-gaining strategies do you use in this relationship? What kind does your friend use? Give at least two specific examples of the use of these strategies.
5. What role does self-disclosure play in this relationship? Why do you self-disclose (See Chapter 10). What benefits have you found in self-disclosure in this relationship? How important is honesty in this relationship? Do you ever use? Alternatives" to self-disclosure (lies, "white lies," equivocation, hinting)? What are the results of such behavior? Give a specific example.
6. What role does metacommunication play in this relationship?
7. Who would you describe the "social penetration" of this relationship?
8. What is your level of satisfaction in the relationship? What could/should be changed? What is your prediction for the future?

D & A

Consider the reasons we form relationships outlined in the chapter. Choose a relationship and discuss each variable and its role in your relational development. How do they affect your relationship differently now that it is established?

MOVIE ANALYSIS

See the movie analysis of "The Story of Us" at the end of this section.

GROUP STUDY

(See the Introductory Essay for further information. Consult the Group Study Section in Chapter One for additional directions to students.)

CHAPTER EIGHT

Match the description with the term below.

a. avoiding	f. experimenting	k. intensifying
b. bonding	g. expression/privacy dialectic	l. metacommunication
c. circumscribing	h. initiating	m. stability/change dialectic
d. differentiating	i. integrating	n. stagnating
e. exchange theory	j. integration/separation dialectic	o. terminating

_____ 1. Jason and Claire are in the process of a divorce. Instead of seeing one another or talking on the phone, they try to call on e another at times when they will be able to use voice mail instead.

_____ 2. Jason and Claire spend more and more time together; they admit to one another that they are "in love."

_____ 3. Jason and Claire discover that they both enjoy basketball, romantic movies, and Chinese food.

_____ 4. Jason and Claire have a wedding with over three hundred guests.

_____ 5. Jason and Claire continue their conversation to "safe" topics, like dinner and what's on the news.

_____ 6. Jason and Claire meet at a party. They are attracted to one another so they both try to present as positive an image of themselves as possible.

_____ 7. Jason enjoys being able to think he knows how Claire will respond, but he also enjoys a few surprises now and then.

_____ 8. Jason and Claire's divorce is final. They decide that they will move to different cities and begin life anew.

_____ 9. Claire likes the feeling that she get from sharing her private thoughts and feelings with Jason, but there are some things that she still prefers to keep to herself.

_____ 10. Jason and Claire frequently strengthen their relationship by discussing their strengths and weaknesses in the area of communication.

_____ 11. Jason and Claire talk as little as possible. He knows that if he talks about family, she will complain his mother. She knows that if she talks about going to see a movie, he will complain that they always have to see what she wants to see.

_____ 12. "You should really be more patient about learning how to play the piano."

_____ 13. Jason and Claire are seen as a couple. They receive joint invitations to parties and weddings.

_____ 14. Jason and Claire enjoy spending quality time with one another, but they each also value their own independence and sense of individual identity.

_____ 15. Jason and Claire begin to discover that they are not so alike at all. She loves to shop and go to the theatre, and he would rather stay home and read a book or watch a football game.

ANSWER KEY:

1.	a	6.	h	11.	n
2.	k	7.	m	12.	e
3.	f	8.	o	13.	i
4.	b	9.	g	14.	j
5.	c	10.	l	15.	d

TEACHING ACTIVITIES FROM THE *COMMUNICATION TEACHER*

Ayres, J. (1990, Spring). *How to use relationship to get more out of theory, 4(3),* 13-14.

DeVito, J. (1987, Winter). *Interpersonal relationships related in card and songs, 1(2),* 4.

DeWitt, J., & Bozik, M. (1997, Spring). *Interpersonal relationship building along the information superhighway: E-mail buddies across two states, 11(3),* 1-2.

Kassing, J. W. (1996, Winter). *Can you hear what else I'm saying?, 10(1),* 4-5.

Masten, R. (1989, Winter). *Conversation, 3(2),* 12-13.

Rivers, M. J. (1994, Fall). *Friendship network, 9(1),* 12-13.

Rozema, H. (1988, Summer). *Using literature to teach interpersonal communication concepts, 2(4),* 10-11.

Stahle, R. B. (1991, Spring). *What's the attraction?, 5(3),* 6.

Tolar, D. L. (1989, Fall). *Carl Rogers' three characteristics of a growth-promoting relationship, 4(1),* 4-5.

Chapter Nine: Intimacy and Distance in Relationships

Self-Disclosure Scenes

Approximate Time: 50 minutes

Purpose: To identify appropriate and inappropriate examples of self-disclosure.

Procedures:
1. Assign students a partner.
2. Give each pair 10 minutes to plan a role-play scene in which one person self-discloses to the other. Before each pair performs their scene they should describe the setting and the relationship depicted.
3. After each scene, discuss the self-disclosure in terms of risk, candor and equivocation, and the guidelines in Chapter 10.

Principles Illustrated
1. Self-disclosure has a variety of risks and benefits.
2. Many factors influence the appropriateness of self-disclosure.

Johari Window Survey

Approximate Time: one class period

Purpose: To identify elements of Johari Window as they relate to student self-disclosure patterns

Procedures:
1. Distribute a copy of the following form to each class member.
2. Discuss the results either in a small group or as an entire class.

JOHARI WINDOW QUESTIONNAIRE

Instructions:

Read each numbered item carefully. Read the statements marked "A" and "B." assign a point value to the A and B statements as follows: The total point value for A and B together is five (5). If statement A is most similar to what you would do, mark 5 for A and 0 for B. If A is not wholly is true. If B is best, mark 5 for B and 0 for A and so on.

1. If a friend of mine had a "personality conflict" with a mutual acquaintance of ours with whom it was important for him/her to get alone, I would:
   _____ A. Tell my friend that I felt s/he was partially responsible for any problems with this other person and try to let him/her know how the person was being affected by him/her.
   _____ B. Not get involved because I wouldn't be able to continue to get along with both of them once I had entered in any way.

2. If one of my friends and I had a heated argument in the past and I realized that s/he was ill at ease around me from that time on, I would:
   _____ A. Avoid making things worse by discussing his/her behavior and just let the whole thing go.
   _____ B. Bring up his/her behavior and ask him/her how s/he felt the argument had affected our relationship.

3. If a friend began to avoid me and act in an aloof and withdrawn manner, I would:
   _____ A. Tell him/her about his/her behavior and suggest that s/he tell me what was on his/her mind.
   _____ B. Follow his/her lead and keep our contact aloof since that seems to be what s/he wants.

4. If two of my friends and I were talking and one of my friends slipped and brought up a personal problem of mine that involved the other friend, of which s/he was not yet aware, I would:
   _____ A. Change the subject and signal my friend to do the same.
   _____ B. Fill my uniformed friend in on what the other friend was talking about and suggest that we go into it later.

5. If a friend of mine were to tell me that, in his/her opinion, I was doing things that made me less effective than I might be in social situations, I would:
   _____ A. Ask him/her to spell out or describe what s/he has observed and suggest changes I might
   _____ B. Resent his/her criticism and let him/her know why I behave the way I do.

6. If one of my friends aspired to an office in our organization for which I felt s/he was unqualified, and if s/he had been tentatively assigned to that position by the leader of our group, I would:
   _____ A. Not mentions my misgivings to either my friend or the leader of our group and let them handle it in their own way.
   _____ B. Tell my friend and the leader of our group of my misgivings and then leave the final decision up to them.

7. If felt that one of my friends was being unfair to me and his/her other friends, but none of them had mentioned anything about it, I would:
   _____ A. Ask several of these people how they perceived the situation to see if they felt s/he was being unfair.
   _____ B. Not ask the others how they perceived our friend, but wait for them to bring it up with me.

8. If I were preoccupied with some personal matters and a friend told me that I had become irritated with him/her and others and that I was jumping on him/her for unimportant things, I would:
   _____ A. Tell him/her I was preoccupied and would probably be on edge for a while and would prefer not to be bothered.
   _____ B. Listen to his/her complaints but not try to explain my actions to him/her.

9. If I had heard some friends discussing an ugly rumor about a friend of mine which I knew could hurt him/her and s/he asked me what I knew about it, if anything, I would:
   _____ A. Say I didn't know anything about it and tell him/her no one would believe a rumor like that

_____ B. Tell him/her exactly what I had heard, when I had heard it, and from whom I had heard it.

10. If a friend pointed out the fact that I had a personality conflict with another friend with whom it was important for me to get along, I would:

 _____ A. Consider his/her comments out of line and tell him/her I didn't want to discuss the matter any further.

 _____ B. Talk about it openly with him/her to find out how my behavior was being affected by this.

11. If my relationship with a friend has been damaged by repeat arguments on an issue of importance to us both, I would:

 _____ A. Be cautious in my conversations with him/her so the issue would not come up again to worsen our relationship.

 _____ B. Point to the problems the controversy was causing in our relationship and suggest that we discuss it until we get it resolved.

12. If in a personal discussion with a friend about hi/her problems and behavior s/he suddenly suggested we discuss my problems and behavior as well as his/her won, I would:

 _____ A. Try to keep the discussion away from me by suggesting that other, closer friends often talked to me about such matters.

 _____ B. Welcome the opportunity to hear what s/he felt about me and encourage his/her comments

13. If a friend of mine began to tell me about his/her hostile feelings about another friend whom s/he felt was being unkind to others (and I agreed wholeheartedly), I would:

 _____ A. Listen and also express my own feelings to him/her so s/he would know where I stood.

 _____ B. Listen, but not express my own negative views and opinion because s/he might repeat what I said to him/her in confidence.

14. If I thought an ugly rumor was being spread about me and suspected that one of my friends had quite likely heard it. I would:

 _____ A. Avoid mentioning the issue and leave it to him/her to tell me about it if s/he wanted to.

 _____ B. Risk putting him/her on the spot by asking him/her directly what s/he knew about the whole thing.

15. If I had observed a friend in social situations and thought that s/he was doing a number of things which hurt his/her relationships, I would:

 _____ A. Risk being seen as a busy body and tell him/her what I had observed and my reactions to it.

 _____ B. Keep my opinion t myself rather than be seen as interfering in things that are none of my business.

16. If two friends and I were talking and one of them inadvertently mentioned a personal problem which involved me, but of which I knew nothing, I would:

 _____ A. Press them for information about the problem and their opinions about it.

 _____ B. Leave it up to my friends to tell me or not tell me, letting them change the subject if they wished.

17. If a friend seemed to be preoccupied and began to jump on me for seemingly unimportant things and to come irritated with me and others without real cause. I would:

 _____ A. Treat him/her with kid gloves for awhile on the assumption that s/he was having some temporary personal problems which were non of my business.

 _____ B. Try to talk to him/her about it and point out to him/her how his/her behavior was affecting people.

18. If I had began to dislike certain habits of a friend to the point that it was interfering with my enjoying his/her company, I would:

 _____ A. Say nothing to him/her directly, but let him/her know my feelings by ignoring him/her whenever his/her annoying habits were obvious.

 _____ B. Get my feelings out in the open and clear the air so that we could continue our friendship comfortably and enjoyably.

19. In discussing social behavior with one of my more sensitive friends, I would:

_____ A. Avoid mentioning his/her flaws and weakness so as not to hurt his/her feelings.

_____ B. Focus on his/her flaws and weaknesses so s/he could improve his/her interpersonal skills.

20. If I knew I might be assigned to an important position in our group and my friends' attitudes toward me had become rather negative, I would:

_____ A. Discuss my shortcomings with my friends so I could see where to improve.

_____ B. Try to figure out my own shortcomings by myself so I could improve.

JOHARI WINDOW SELF-RATING SHEET

Solicits Feedback		Willingness to Self-Disclose/Gives Feedback	
2B	_____	1A	_____
3B	_____	4A	_____
5B	_____	6A	_____
7B	_____	9A	_____
8B	_____	11A	_____
10B	_____	13A	_____
12B	_____	15A	_____
14B	_____	17A	_____
16B	_____	18A	_____
20B	_____	19A	_____
Total	_____	Total	_____

```
---------------------------------------------SOLICITS FEEDBACK--------------------------------------------
0     5     10    15    20    25    30    35    40    45    50
5
10
15
20
25
30
35
40
45
50
                                              open           blind
                                              hidden         unknown
```

116

Self-Disclosure Survey

Approximate Time: one class period

Purpose: To identify topics and contexts that are appropriate for self-disclosure

Procedures:
1. Distribute a copy of the following forms to each class member.
2. Discuss the result either in a small group or as an entire class. Were most responses similar? Different? Why? Why is self-disclosure risky? When is it appropriate? What can be gain by appropriate self-disclosure?

SELF-DISCLOSURE SURVEY

Directions: Working alone, label each of the statements below:
L (low risk), meaning you believe it is appropriate to disclose this information to almost any person;

M (medium risk), meaning you believe it is appropriate to disclose this information to persons you know pretty well and have already established a friendship relationship with;

H (high risk), meaning you believe it is appropriate to disclose such information only to the few friends you have great trust in or to the persons you regard as your most intimate friends; or

X (extreme risk), meaning you would disclose it to no one.

_____ 1. Your hobbies, how you like best to spend your spare time.
_____ 2. Your preferences and dislikes in music.
_____ 3. Your educational background and record and your feelings about them.
_____ 4. Your personal views on politics.
_____ 5. Your religious views and your religious participation.
_____ 6. Your personal habits that bother you.
_____ 7. Your personal characteristics that make you proud.
_____ 8. The details on the unhappiest moments in your life.
_____ 9. The details of the happiest moments of your life.
_____ 10. The actions you have most regretted and why.
_____ 11. Your guiltiest secret.
_____ 12. Your views on the way a husband and wife should live in their marriage.
_____ 13. The main unfulfilled dreams in your life.
_____ 14. What you do, if anything, to stay physically fit.
_____ 15. The aspects of your body you are most pleased with.
_____ 16. The features of your appearance you are most displeased with.
_____ 17. The person in your life whom you most resent and the reason why.
_____ 18. The person in your life whom you most admire and the reason why.
_____ 19. Your most significant fears.
_____ 20. The people with whom you have been sexually intimate and the circumstances of your relationship with each.

When you have completed this list for yourself, go back through it and label the items again, responding to each item with the label (L, M, H, or X) that you think represents the way "most people" would respond to it.

Principles Illustrated:
1. Self-disclosure is risky.
2. Self-disclosure, when appropriate, can improve relationships.
3. Context, topic and participants determine appropriateness.

DYADIC INTERVIEW

The Dyadic Interview Exercise described in the exercise section of Chapter 9 might also be used to illustrate the role of self-disclosure in forming relationships.

PORTFOLIO ENTRY

See Chapter 9 section for a description of Portfolio Entry which includes the concepts covered in both Chapter 9 and 10.

D & A

Select four different types of relationships in your life: friend, dating partner, parent, sibling or other close family member. Identify the types of intimacy present in each relationship. What is similar, different? How have they changed over time? OR

Have the students complete the Johari Window Survey outside of class.

MOVIE ANALYSIS

See the movie analysis of "The Story of Us" at the end of this section.

GROUP STUDY

(See the Introductory Essay for further information. Consult the Group Study Section in Chapter One for additional directions to students.)

CHAPTER NINE

Match the example with the theory/term it most correctly describes.

a. blind	f. facts	k. open
b. catharsis	g. hidden	l. physical intimacy
c. clichés	h. intellectual intimacy	m. self-disclosure
d. emotional intimacy	i. intimacy/distance dialectic	n. social penetration
e. equivocation	j. lie	

____ 1. Kerby greets her new friend Kendra with a warm hug.
____ 2. Kerby decides to share her feelings about her parents' divorce, something
____ 3. She has shared with very few people, even with Kendra. (TWO responses)
____ 4. Kendra enjoys her time with Kerby but she also likes to spend time by herself.
____ 5. Kendra asks Kerby how she likes her new boots. Although Kerby thinks Kendra's boots are ugly, she replies, "I love them!"
____ 6. In the same situation, Kerby replies, "Wow! They're different from anything else I've ever seen you wear!"
____ 7. Brett points out to Vince that he is very good with children, a thing which Vince had never realized before. This information was in Vince's _____ Johari Window pane.
____ 8. Vince, a Catholic, and Brett, a Christian Scientist, discuss the main beliefs of their religions.

_____ 9. Vince doesn't share with others the fact that he is afraid of snakes and spiders. This information is in his _____ pane.
_____ 10. The information that Vince and Brett share about themselves has both depth and breadth.
_____ 11. Vince sees himself as outgoing and friendly, and he projects this image to others. This information is in his _____ pane.
_____ 12. Brett shares with Vince the information that he just heard on TV about the most recent standing in the NFL.
_____ 13. Neither Vince nor his friends realized that he has an aptitude for microbiology. This information is in his _____ pane.
_____ 14. When Brett first sees Vince, he greets him by saying, "Hi! How are you doing?" Vince responds with, "Great. How's it going?"
_____ 15. Brett shares with Vince that he knows that Vince's girlfriend has been cheating on him. Brett says that he just has to "get it off his chest."

ANSWER KEY:

1.	l	6.	e	11.	k
2.	d/m	7.	a	12.	f
3.	m/d	8.	h	13.	o
4.	i	9.	g	14.	c
5.	j	10.	n	15.	b

TEACHING ACTIVITIES FROM THE *COMMUNICATION TEACHER*

Gill, M.(1988, Spring). *Successful self-disclosure, 2(3)*, 7, 16.

Goldberg, J. (1985, Fall). *Secrets*, 4.

Johnson, C. (1986, Fall). *Opening lines, 1(1)*, 4.

Owen, W. (1988, Winter). *Identifying and disclosing intentions, 2(2)*, 2-3.

Schelle, E. B., and Koester, S. H. (1990, Spring). *The alter ego: Self-disclosure without anxiety, 4(3)*, 2-3.

West, R. (1987, Summer). *First impression exercise, 1(4)*, 13.

Chapter Ten: Communication Climate

Communication Climate Survey

Approximate Time: 30 minutes

Purpose: To identify behaviors which demonstrate components of defensive and supportive climates

Procedures:
1. Put the following statements on the board or on a handout without the accompanying directions. Ask class members to work on them individually or in small groups.
2. Discuss as a large group. Note throughout that a perceived threat can create defensiveness even if the speaker does not intend to threaten.

COMMUNICATION CLIMATE SURVEY

Directions:
1. Identify the defensive behavior from the Gibb categories which is illustrated by each of the disconfirming messages given below.
2. Then re-write the statement so that it becomes a confirming message, conducive to creating a supportive climate. (The first one is done for you.)

_____ 1.   Sue, turn that off! Nobody can study with all that noise!
           (Sue, I'm having a hard time studying with that radio on.)

_____ 2.   Did you ever hear such a tacky idea as a formal reception with cheap paper plates?

_____ 3.   That idea will never work.

_____ 4.   Oh Hank, you're so funny for wearing a printed shirt with those pants. Well I guess that's a man for you.

_____ 5.   Terry, you're acting like a child.

_____ 6.   CLASS! BE QUIET!

_____ 7.   You may think you know how to handle the situation, but you really don't have the experience. I know when something's over your head.

_____ 8.   You have five minutes and that's it. Now get to work!

_____ 9.   Whatever you decide will be okay with me.

_____ 10.   (Spoken to your roommate) Every time I turn around, you have some friend over here eating the food that I've purchased. You are such a mooch!!!

Principles Illustrated:
1. Certain behaviors create a defensive climate.
2. Certain behaviors create a more supportive climate.
3. Statements can be altered to lessen their defensiveness.

Sending Confirming, Disagreeing, & Disconfirming Messages

Approximate Time: 20 minutes

Purpose: To give students practice in using various types of responses

Procedures:
1. Divide the students into small groups of 5-7.
2. Distribute a worksheet with the following information. (Leave room for student responses.)
3. Call on various groups to share their responses. Clarify any confusion about the various types of responses.

SENDING CONFIRMING, DISAGREEING, AND DISCONFIRMING MESSAGES

You are speaking to someone in this class. (S)he says to you: "This has been some (sarcastic) semester! I thought this was going to be my blow-off class. Instead, here I am working 30 hours a week, carrying 15 credits, and trying to get caught up by the end of the semester. The work in here is unreal! Does (s)he think this is the only class I'm taking? How am I supposed to do all of this and still maintain any sanity? There's **another** Portfolio due and everything to learn form the Final Exam. Besides that, I have plans to go to some great parties the next two weekends—and I'm sure not going to give up my fun time. Good grief! I don't know if I can possibly pull this all off!"

In your group, formulate a number of responses to this student—as directed below:

Confirming Message   (Your position is that you agree 100% with him/her.)

Disagreeing Messages   (You think that (s)he has been wasting time all semester and would probably be failing if it weren't for your group's help.)

Assertive Disagreeing Response
Argumentative Disagreeing Response
Complaining Disagreeing Response
Aggressive Disagreeing Response

Disconfirming Responses   (Your position doesn't matter here.)

Impervious Response
Interrupting Response
Irrelevant Response
Tangential Response
Impersonal Response
Ambiguous Response
Incongruous Response

Principles Illustrated:
1. Different responses create different responses.
2. We can choose a number of different ways to respond to any message.

Red/Green Game

Approximate Time: 30 minutes

Purpose: reveal to students their own competitive or cooperative natures in a low-risk collaborative situation

Procedures:
1. Divide the class into pairs and then put four pair together in a two-by-two person, square seating pattern, eight in each cluster.
2. Distribute to each pair within each cluster a sheet of paper with a green square on one side and a red square on the other. This will be their voting ballot.
3. With no prior discussion distribute the Red/Green Score Sheet.
4. Do not give instructions except to say that students will play 10 rounds of a game designed to win them as much money as possible.
5. Tell students that in each round they and their partner will decide, based on the amount it is possible to win, (listed in the win/lose box on the score sheet) whether to vote red or green. The "pay-off" for each round is dependent upon the pattern of choice made in the overall cluster.
6. Note that in round 1, 2, 3, 4, 6, 7, and 9, only the pairs discuss what their votes will be. In rounds 5, 8, and 10, the entire will confer, before going back to make the final decision.
7. Students will be confused at first, but just play the game and they will soon see what is happening. It will become clear that they can choose to compete with the rest for the cluster and attempt to win the most money for their particular pair or they can attempt to help the overall cluster finish in the "black," in the balance column at the end of the game.
8. A distinct communication climate—one of mutual trust or one of suspicion and competition—will develop very quickly in this exercise. Students are often surprised at the competitive natures revealed in the game.

SIN AS MUCH AS YOU CAN

Red/Green Sheet:

Directions: For 10 successive rounds you and your partner will choose either a red square or a green square. The "pay-off" for each round is dependent upon the pattern of choices made in your cluster:

        4 Red: Lose $1.00 each

        3 Red: Win $1.00 each
        1 Green: Lose $1.00 each

        2 Red: Win $2.00 each
        2 Green: Lose $2.00 each

        1 Red: Win $3.00 each
        3 Green: Lose $1.00 each

        4 Green: Win $1.00 each

ROUND	TIME ALLOWED	CONFER WITH	$WON	$LOST	$BALANCE
1	2 minutes	partner			
2	1 minute	partner			
3	1 minute	partner			
4	1 minute	partner			
BONUS—pay x 5					
5	3 minutes	cluster			
	1 minute	partner			
6	1 minute	partner			
7	1 minute	partner			
BONUS—pay x 5					
8	3 minutes	cluster			
	1 minute	partner			
9	1 minute	partner			
BONUS—pay x 10					
10	3 minutes	cluster			
	1 minute	partner			

Discussion Points:
1. What was your initial decision to compete or cooperate before you started seeing the results of what the other pairs were choosing?
2. Prior to this exercise did you feel that you were generally a cooperative or a competitive person?
3. How did it feel the first time a pair did not vote as agreed upon in the cluster conference? How did it affect your communication? Your behavior?
4. What are the origins of competitive behavior? Or cooperative behavior?
5. Do you think this exercise is reflective of people's actual personality types and behavior patterns?
6. What are the effects on communication climate, and ultimately interpersonal relationship, on competition?
7. How does communication change (or does it?) depending on whether the climate is cooperative or competitive?

PORTFOLIO ENTRY

Analyzing Defensiveness

Defensiveness implies protecting ourselves from a perceived threat. The universal tendency is to try to "save face" by defending our presenting self when we perceive that it has been attacked by what social scientists call 'face-threatening acts." Frequently, this results in creating a climate which leads to a negative defensive spiral. For this assignment, you will do the following:
1. Identify three different times when you perceived that you were under attack and responded by using one of the Gibb Defensive categories. Briefly describe each situation and your response.
2. Identify the Gibb category which you used.
3. Describe how you might have otherwise responded in order to create a more positive and supportive climate.

4. Analyze your defensive behavior. In general, do you consider yourself a "defensive" person? Why or why not? Are there certain topics which tend to trigger your defensiveness? Are there certain people with whom you are more defensive than normal?

D & A

Analyzing Defensiveness outlined above. An instructor may choose to have students cite only two examples.

MOVIE ANALYSIS

See the move analysis of "The Story of Us" at the end of this section.

GROUP STUDY

(See the Introductory Essay for further information. Consult the Group Study Section in Chapter One for additional directions to students.)

CHAPTER TEN

Match the letter of the defensive or supportive Gibb category with its description of behaviors below. Pay particular attention to the words which have been underlined.

a.	evaluation	g.	description
b.	control	h.	problem orientation
c.	strategy	i.	spontaneity
d.	neutrality	j.	empathy
e.	superiority	k.	equality
f.	certainly	l.	provisionalism

_____ 1. Gerry insists he has all the facts and needs to hear no more information.

_____ 2. Richard has a strong opinion but will listen to another position.

_____ 3. Linda kept looking at the clock as she was listening to Nan, so Nan thought Linda didn't consider her comments as very important.

_____ 4. "I know Janice doesn't agree with me," Mary said, "but she knows how strongly I feel about this, and I think she can put herself in my position."

_____ 5. "Even though my professor has a Ph.D.," Rosa pointed out, "she doesn't act like she's the only one who knows something; she is really interested in me as a person."

_____ 6. "Bob tricked me into thinking his proposal was my idea so I'd support it."

_____ 7. "Even though we **all** wait tables here, Evanne thinks she's better than any of us—just look at the way she prances around!"

_____ 8. Clara sincerely and honesty told Georgia about her reservations concerning Georgia's party.

_____ 9. The co-workers attempted to find a solution to the scheduling issue that would satisfy both of their needs.

_____ 10. "Its seems my father's favorite phrase is 'I know what's best for you; just let me tell you what to do' and that really gripes me."

_____ 11. "You drink too much!"

_____ 12. "I was embarrassed when you slurred your speech in front of my boss."

_____ 13. "The flowers and presents are just an attempt to get me to go to bed with him."

_____ 14. She looked down her nose at me when I told her I didn't exercise regularly."

_____ 15. "Well, if you need more money and I need more help around here, what could we do to make us both happy?"

ANSWER KEY:

1.	f	6.	c	11.	a
2.	l	7.	e	12.	g
3.	d	8.	i	13.	c
4.	j	9.	h	14.	e
5.	k	10.	b	15.	h

TEACHING ACTIVITIES FROM THE *COMMUNICATION TEACHER*

Nagel, G. (1989, Fall). *'Peculiarity': An exercise in sharing, caring, and belonging, 4(1)*, 3-4.

Weaver II, R. L. and Cotrell, H. W. (1990, Winter). *Role playing assertiveness scenes, 4(2)*, 13-14.

Chapter Eleven: Managing Conflict

Mediation: An Alternative to Dispute Resolution

Approximate Time: two 50 minute class periods
First Session: Preparation
Second Session: Mediation Application

Purpose: To identify mediation as a process for conflict resolution and provide an interactive simulation for demonstration ADR

Procedures:
1. Assign the four mediation readings.
2. Explain the four phases of the mediation process: introduction, storytelling, problem-solving, and agreement.
3. Ask students to volunteer to be mediators. This simulation works best if the co-mediators are male and female. This allows for the disputants to be male-male, male-female, or female-female without bias. For five separate mediations you will need 10 mediators and 10 disputants.
4. Ask students to volunteer to be disputants. You will need two disputants for every mediation.
5. Disputants should then brainstorm possible conflicts (roommate conflicts work best) and prepare to experience the simulation the following class period.
6. On the next class day, arrange the room so that clusters of four desks (two for mediators and tow for disputants) are facing each other. REMIND all students of the ground rules of the mediation process.
7. Process should begin by having all concerned parties read and sign the confidentiality agreement form. Mediation is complete when all parties have signed the Agreement Form.
8. After all mediations are complete, distribute the reaction and analysis assignment—which is due the following class period.

MEDIATION WORKSHOP

Mediation Process
I. **Introduction Phase.** Ground rules and definitions.
   A. Ground rules for mediation are described
      1. no name calling
      2. no interruptions
   B. Mediator(s) role and process are described
      1. The role of the mediator is to facilitate understanding of problems and a mutually satisfying agreement.
      2. The mediator does not solve the problems for the involved parties. The mediator never becomes and arbitrator.
      3. The goal of mediation is a collaborative effort of the parties toward a win-win end. Compromising is not the ultimate goal for this; it suggests a lose-lose scenario.
      4. Four stages form mediation: introduction, storytelling, problem-solving, and agreement.
   C. Confidentiality and non-binding or binding agreement is signed by parties and causing is defined.
      1. Each party agrees to keep confidential all information revealed vis-a-vis the mediation.
      2. At the onset, the parties will sign an agreement to bind/not bind the resolution reached. This is similar to binding arbitration and provides a legal agreement.
      3. A cause may be called by the mediators at any time to help identify root issues. One party is asked to leave the room at this time. This allows for the mediators to elicit "private" information.

II. **Storytelling Phase.** Each party states his/her case.
   A. Dispute A states case.
      1. The mediators restate or reframe the problems and ask if this is accurate.
      2. The mediators can then probe to clarify points and issues.
   B. Dispute A states case.
      1. The mediators restate or reframe the problems and ask if this is accurate.
      2. The mediators can then probe to clarify points and issues.
   C. The primary issues are then stated back to the disputants.
   D. The disputants are asked to prioritize the importance of these issues, one at a time.
III. **Problem-solving Phase.**
   A. Prioritize problems/issues are now assessed.
      1. Example: Boyfriend/Girlfriend dispute
         a. stop beating me—physical issue
         b. stop lying—trust issue
         c. staying the relationship—goal issue
      2. Which issue was most important or discussed first by each party?
   B. Attempt to find an issue which is easily solved and obtain concrete solutions from each party.
      1. Example: Bobby, stop hanging out with the boys.
      2. Example: Karen, give me some time to be alone.
   C. At this point you may go back to Phase II and hear more storytelling.
IV. **Agreement Phase:** Not all mediation will reach this phase.
   A. Each party agrees to abide by the solutions.
   B. Each party signs the agreement.

Things to remember about mediation
1. A co-mediation model is suggested with one male and one female mediator.
   a. One mediator holds the other in check.
   b. Gender differences may aid in perception and problem-identification.
   c. Parties won't feel "ganged up on."
   d. Balance of "powers"
2. Define difference between dispute
   a. offers win-lose situation
   b. compromise offers lose-lose proposition
   c. mediation offers win-win solution
3. Mediators have different styles, but re-framing points is essential for successful mediation.
4. Mediators have different listening styles which may impact the process. Also, mediators use different strategies for identifying problems, etc…
5. Model of Mediation:

   Party A
   _____ Mediator
   _____ Mediator
   Party B
   *Parties A and B are on an equal (nonverbal) plane
   *Mediators sit across from disputants to show non-bias nature

Mediation Assigned Readings

Sillars, A. L. (1980). Attributions and communication in roommate conflicts. Communication Monographs, 47, 180-200.

   After reading this article, you should be able to identify the three related tasks of the naïve social observer, inference to social attributions, which are important to communicative decisions in conflict interactions. They are: causal judgments, social inference, and the prediction of outcomes and behaviors. Further, each reader should be able to distinguish between conflict resolution strategies: passive-indirect, distributive, and integrative. A successful mediation depends upon the identification of strategies suggested by the parties in the storytelling phase. Problem-solving techniques should hinge upon a win-win solution and should de-emphasize individual outcomes and maximize mutual outcomes.

From the three propositions proffered, five predictions are proposed. Based on the mediation exercise you participate in, examine why you agree or disagree with these predictions. Use specific examples from the mediation in your analysis paper while integrating the language used for conflict resolution.

Donohue, W. A., Allen, M. & Burrell, N. (1988). Mediator communicator competence. Communication Monographs, 55, 104-119.

After reading this article, an understanding of behavior associate with mediator competence should be realized. An earlier model proposed by Donohue, Diez, and Weider-Hatfield (1984) holds that mediator's successful in facilitating an agreement between disputants are more competent in knowing when to interrupt the interaction and selecting the appropriate intervention to improve disputants' information exchange and decision-making. This article should stimulate thoughtful questions pertaining to which mediator intervention strategies/behaviors, in response to specific disputant negotiation strategies, are associated with achieving a mediated agreement. Also, knowledge of mediator as an interventionist should highlight contexts whereby this adaptive model should/could be utilized for maximum benefit.

Burrell, N. A., Donohue, W. A., & Allen, M. (1990). The impact of disputants' expectations on mediation: Testing an interventionist model. Human Communication Research, 17, 104-139.

This article should further enlighten the reader as to the goals and processes involved in mediation. Research on disputant expectations suggests that this variable impacts the outcome of a mediation. The control-based model utilized for this analysis presumes that a critical function of a mediator is to orchestrate the interaction by developing and extending the information resources, enforcing rules for the session (such as no name calling and no interruptions), and encouraging disputants to make constructive proposals to reach an agreement collaboratively. This study examines both the mediators; and disputants' assessments of their sessions. A mediator should be concerned and try to bring out/identify disputants' expectations in order to use adaptive strategies which will increase the likelihood of agreement.

Sillars, A. (1980), The sequential and distributional structure of conflict interactions as a function of attributions concerning the locus of responsibility and stability of conflict. In D. Nimmo (Ed.) Communication Yearbook, 4, 217-235.

Attributions are assumed to affect interpersonal conflict resolution strategies for two reasons. First, attributions influence emotional (affective) and evaluative (cognitive) reactions to individuals. According to tension-reduction theories, you can probably understand the importance of these issues, this is a write of a study that is similar to the finished product that we will have as a result of our class mediation data.

MEDIATION CONFIDENTIALITY STATEMENT

The following signature signifies that I have carefully read and agree to all statements includes on this page. I agree that no information revealed in this mediation will be discussed or in any way used against any person involved in the mediation process. Further, I understand that there are two rules which govern a mediation session. These rules are that there will be no name-calling or use of abusive language and that interruptions of mediators or disputants is not tolerated. Also, I understand that a caucus may be called by the mediators at any time whereby one of the disputants will be asked to leave the room for a few minutes. Finally, I hereby agree to abide by any solution which has bee reached, if any, during the agreement phase of the mediation. This agreement will be binding.

_____   Disputant A

_____   Disputant B

_____   Mediator A

_____   Mediator B

This confidentiality and agreement to abide by the rules of mediation was conducted at _____ am/pm on _____, 200__.

MEDIATION AGREEMENT FORM

We the undersigned agree to implement the following resolutions to our conflict as mediated by _____ and _____.

The following solutions are set forth:

1.

2.

3.

4.

5.

_____   Disputant A

_____   Disputant B

_____   Witness/Mediator A

_____   Witness/Mediator B

OR

We, the undersigned, agree that no resolution of this conflict can be agreed to at this point in time.

_____   Disputant A

_____   Disputant B

_____   Witness/Mediator A

_____   Witness/Mediator B

MEDIATION REACTION AND ANALYSIS

Congratulations! You have each successfully participated in a mock mediation training session. The demands of this analysis are few.

Briefly, in three to four pages discuss your opinion of mediation as an alternative to dispute resolution such as arbitration and litigation. Discuss the process of mediation and your feelings regarding the four-step sequence toward a win-win solution. Do you believe that mediation works, or can work? What type of disputes do you believe are best settled vis-à-vis this method?

Next, discuss your mediation session, what issues did you find most salient to the disputants? Did you employ any strategies to elicit information (such as causing), or to further probe? How successful were your attempts to facilitate viable solutions to the major issue? Discuss the cultural premises of the individual disputants. Did same sex or opposite sex disputants impact the outcome or the process of mediation? Explain.

Finally, as an observer (if you observed), provide insight as to turning points in the mediation or points in the mediation where a caucus was needed or where definite strategies may have been better suited to bring about resolution.

Good luck.

Perception of Conflict

Approximate Time: 20 minutes

Purpose: To identify common perceptions of conflict

Procedures:
1. Write the word "CONFLICT" on the board.
2. Ask students to down the first word that comes into their minds when they see the word ""CONFLICT." Write their words on the board.
3. Ask students to write down three or four things which they believe it is worth having a conflict about, i.e., things worth fighting for.
4. Have them jot down one or two things which others seem to have conflicts over but which they believe are silly to "fight about."
5. Go around the class and write all the words (from #2) on the board.
6. Ask what the words (at least most of them) have in common. (Most are likely to be negative.) Discuss the implications of this perception for conflict and conflict management.
7. Ask for student responses to the other two questions. Note that some topics (typically money, curfew, siblings) appear on both lists. What are the implications of this conflict resolution?
8. Discuss how conflict can be a beneficial force. Relate this discussion to the textbook identification of types of conflict resolution.

Principles Illustrated:
1. Conflict has a negative connotation for many.
2. Negative perceptions of conflict make us reluctant to welcome it for its positive value.
3. Conflict is inevitable.
4. Conflict can be a helpful, dynamic force in communication.
5. Perceptions of what is "important enough" to warrant conflict can differ from one person to another.

Conflict Styles Survey

Approximate Time: 20 minutes

Purpose: To heighten students' awareness of their patterns of conflict style and to launch the discussion of the variety of styles that they and others employ

Procedures:
1. Without prior discussion, distribute the Conflict Style Survey to class members and tell them to respond to the items. There are no right or wrong answers.
2. When students are finished, tell them the categories for each column and briefly discuss their findings. Use this exercise to lead into a lecture on the various conflict styles.

CONFLICT STYLES SURVEY

Directions: Indicate your opinion of each of the following short proverbs as a conflict strategy. In each case, ask the question: How desirable is this strategy as a method for resolving conflict?

Using the key, write the appropriate number in the blank to the left of each proverb.

1 = completely undesirable   4 = desirable
2 = undesirable   5 = very desirable
3 = neither desirable nor undesirable

_____ 1. You scratch my back; I'll scratch yours.
_____ 2. When two quarrel, he who keeps silent first is the most praiseworthy.
_____ 3. Soft words win hard hearts.
_____ 4. A person who will no flee will make his foe flee.
_____ 5. Come and let us reason together.
_____ 6. It is easier to refrain than t retreat from a quarrel.
_____ 7. Half a load is better than non.
_____ 8. A question must be answered by knowledge, not by numbers, if it's to have a right decision.
_____ 9. When someone hits you with a stone, hit him with a piece of cotton.
_____ 10. The arguments of the strongest always have the weight.
_____ 11. By digging and digging, the truth is discovered.
_____ 12. Smooth words make smooth ways.
_____ 13. If you cannot make a man think as you do, make him do as you do.
_____ 14. He who fights and runs away lives to fight another day.
_____ 15. A fair exchange brings no quarrel.
_____ 16. Might overcomes right.
_____ 17. Tit for tat is fair play.
_____ 18. Kind words are worth much and cost little.
_____ 19. Seek 'til you find, and you'll not lose your labor.
_____ 20. Kill your enemies with kindness.
_____ 21. He loses least in a quarrel who keeps his tongue in cheek.
_____ 22. Try, and trust will move mountains.
_____ 23. Put your foot down where you mean to stand.
_____ 24. One gift for another makes good friends.
_____ 25. Don't stir up a hornet's nest.

Transfer your rating numbers to the blanks below. The numbers correspond to the proverb numbers. Total each column.

5 ___	4 ___	1 ___	2 ___	3 ___
8 ___	10 ___	7 ___	6 ___	12 ___
11 ___	13 ___	15 ___	9 ___	18 ___
19 ___	16 ___	17 ___	14 ___	20 ___
22 ___	23 ___	24 ___	21 ___	25 ___

Total   ___   ___   ___   ___   ___

Here are the interpretations for the various columns:

1 – Problem Solving; Assertive
2 – Forcing; Aggressive
3 – Compromising
4 – Withdrawing; Non-Assertive
5 – Smoothing; Accommodating

Principles Illustrated:
1. Different individuals have different perceptions about conflict.
2. Different individuals approach conflict in different ways.

Understanding Conflict Styles

(From Mary O. Wiemann's Activities Manual for *Looking Out/looking in*, 8th edition)
Approximate Time: 40 minutes

Purpose: To understand the styles with which conflict can be handle

Procedures:
1. Hand out the sheet at the class prior to the day the exercise is being done. Ask students to complete the first step prior to coming to class.
2. Divide students into groups of 5-7.
3. Have them follow the directions in discussing their own responses and supplying additional responses to the exercise. Each group should plan to hand in a single copy of their responses.

UNDERSTANDING CONFLICT STYLES

Instructions:
1. For each of the situations give below, describe how you would **really** respond. Classify your response as nonassertive, aggressive, passive aggressive, or assertive. Do this part of the exercise **prior** to coming to class.
2. In your small group, share your responses. Do group members agree that you assigned the correct classification?
3. For each of the conflicts described below, write four responses illustrating nonassertive, directly aggressive, indirectly aggressive and assertive communication styles. Use as many of your own group's actual responses as you can.
4. Describe the probable consequences of each style.

EXAMPLE: Three weeks ago your friend borrowed an article of clothing, promising to return it soon. You haven't seen it since, and the friend hasn't mentioned it.

Nonassertive response: *Say nothing to the friend, hoping she will remember and return the item.*

Probable consequences: *There's a good chance I'll never get the item back. I would probably resent the friend and avoid her in the future so I won't have to lend anything else.*

Directly aggressive responses: *Confront the friend and accuse her of being inconsiderate and irresponsible. Say that she probably ruined the items and is afraid to say so.*

Probable consequences: *My friend would get defensive and hurt. Even if she did intentionally keep the item, she'd never admit it when approached this way. We would probably avoid each other in the future.*

Indirectly aggressive response: *Drop hits about how I loved to wear the borrowed item. Casually mention how much I hate people who don't return things. Gossip about the incident to others.*

Probable consequences: *My friend would be embarrassed by gossip. She might ignore my hints. She'll most certainly resent my roundabout approach, even if she returns the article.*

Assertive response: *Confront the friend in a noncritical way and remind her that she still has the item. Ask when she'll return it, being sure to get a specific time.*

Probable consequences: *The friend might be embarrassed when I bring the subject up, but since there's no attack it'll probably be okay. Since we'll have cleared up the problem, the relationship can continue.*

SITUATIONS

1. Someone you've just met at a party criticizes a mutual friend in a way you think is unfair.
2. A fan behind you at a ballgame toots a loud air horn every time ht home team makes any progress. The noise is spoiling your enjoyment of the game.
3. Earlier in the day you asked the person with whom you live to pick up the house for a party which you are planning for this evening. You arrive home about thirty minutes before the guests are to arrive and the place is still a mess!
4. You are explaining your political views to a friend who has asked your opinion. Now the friend obviously isn't listening. You think to yourself that since the person asked for your ideas, the least he/she can do is pay attention.
5. Last weekend, you invited a good friend (A) t go out for dinner and a movie. Your friend replied (s)he was tired and was planning on "laying low" for the evening. The next day, you spoke to another mutual friend (B) who reported that the first friend (A) had spent the evening (of your invitation) at a party at his house.

Principles Illustrated:
1. Different people respond to the same situation in different ways.
2. Different conflict management styles are likely to lead to differing degrees of success.

PORTFOLIO ENTRY

In class, you were given a Conflict Styles Survey which allowed you to see how you might be inclined to manage conflict. For you Portfolio Entry:

- Report the scores which you determined in each of the five categories.
- In essay format (1-3 pages) analyze the results for the survey. Do you agree that the scores reflect your style(s) in managing conflict? Use **specific personal examples** to support your conclusions.

FINAL SELF-ASSESSMENT

Now that we are nearly at the end of the semester, re-analyze your own interpersonal communication skills. What are your strengths? Your weaknesses? How does this list compare with the one you made during the first weeks of the semester? How much progress have you mad toward your goals? (1-3 pages)

D & A

Complete Invitation to Insight #2 Functional and Dysfunctional Conflicts at the end of the chapter.

MOVIE ANALYSIS

See the movie analysis of "The Story of Us" at the end of this section.

GROUP STUDY

(See the Introductory Essay for further information. Consult the Group Study Section in Chapter One for additional directions to students.)

CHAPTER ELEVEN

Choose the letter of the personal conflict style that is best illustrated by the behavior found below.

    a. avoidance
    b. accommodation
    c. direct aggression
    d. assertion
    e. indirect communication
    f. passive aggression

_____ 1. Stan keeps joking around to keep us from talking about commitment.
_____ 2. "I can't believe you were so stupid as to have erase that disk!"
_____ 3. Even though the wanted to the party, Allen stayed home with Sara rather than hear complain.
_____ 4. By mentioning how allergic she was to smoke, Joan hoped that her guests would smoke outside.
_____ 5. "When you smoke inside, I start to cough and my eyes water; so please go out on the balcony when you want to smoke."
_____ 6. Rather than tell Nick about his frustration over Nick's not meeting the deadline, Howard complained to others about Nick's unreliability while maintaining a smiling front to Nick.
_____ 7. Carol wouldn't answer the phone after their disagreement because she was afraid it would be Nancy on the other end.

_____ 8. Faced with obvious distress, Nikki put her important work aside to listen to Alonzo.

_____ 9. Even though Nikki could see Alonzo's distress, she told him she had a deadline to meet in one hour and asked if they could talk then.

_____ 10. (Sarcastically) "Oh, sure I *loved* having dinner with your parents instead of going to the party on Saturday night."

_____ 11. Even though Suzie really wanted to go bowling on Friday night, she agreed t go to the movies with her fiancé Bernard because it didn't really matter that much to her.

_____ 12. Mitzi was upset when she only get a "C" for the semester. Rather than talking to the instructor, she told everyone to sign up for a different professor because this one was unfair.

_____ 13. When Mitzi got her "C" grade for the semester, she went to see the instructor to try to find out the reasons why.

_____ 14. Pete seemed illogical at the meeting when he opening attacked Saul's ideas and shouted at him.

_____ 15. When they walked past the jewelry store window on February 12th, Sasha commented to her boyfriend Jay how much she loves jewelry.

ANSWER KEY:

1.	a	6.	f	11.	b
2.	c	7.	a	12.	f
3.	b	8.	b	13.	d
4.	e	9.	d	14.	c
5.	d	10.	f	15.	e

TEACHING ACTIVITIES FROM THE *COMMUNICATION TEACHER*

Hanna, M. S. (2000, Spring). *Design a role-playing case for study and practice, 14(3)*, 12-14.

McGowan, L. (1992, Spring). *St. Elmo's Fire as a tool for discussing conflict management, 7(3)*, 12-13.

Rancer, A.S. (1994, Spring). *Teaching constructive means of handing conflict, 8(3)*, 1-2.

Williams, D. (1990, Summer). *Interpersonal communication feud, 4(4)*, 8-9.

Chapter Twelve: Culture and Communication

Lifestyles Exercise

Approximate Time: To make assignment: 15 minutes
Discuss in second class period: 50 minutes

Purpose: To evaluate the extent to which various cultural patterns and communications styles are reflected in the literature we read and music we listen to

Procedures:
1. Discuss the influence of various cultural factors on our ability to relate and communicate.
2. Select various "subcultures" present in our society.
3. Assign individuals to examine representative literature and music of each group. Have them determine the extent to which various "styles" of communication are revealed, examined, or advocated in the music and literature.
4. Have students identify code words, phrases, and expressions used by the subculture.
5. Have the students report their "findings" and interpretations to the class in the next class session.

Welcome to Your New Culture

(Developed by Carol Z. Dolphin, University of Wisconsin—Waukesha, based on an exercise by Scott Johnson, Ithaca College)

Approximate Time: To make assignment: 60-75 minutes

Purpose: To simulate for students the effect of being introduced to a culture different from ones own and to experience the effect of culture on spontaneous interaction and problem solving

NOTE: This exercise is especially effective in situation where a class—and even a campus community—is very homogenous and where students have had little experience in interacting with individuals from other cultures.

Procedures:
1. Divide the class into three groups with at least six members in each group.
2. Distribute a different "Culture Information Sheet" to each of the three groups. Remind them of the rule at the bottom of the sheet that they are not to share this data with members of other groups (cultures). *These sheets must be distributed at the session prior to the one in which the exercise will take place.*
3. When students enter for the following class, they should meet in their culture groups. Following the "rules" for their new culture, they should take about 15 minutes to discuss the following:
   * What is the unique manner which you will use when greeting others?
   * In your **mixed culture** groups, how will you choose a leader? According to your new culture, what will be your criteria? (You do not have to choose a leader from your same culture group.)
   * What will you group's position be on the problem given on the Culture Information Sheet?
4. Divide the students into new groups with at least two to three representatives from each culture.
5. Provide students with the following directions for their mixed culture groups:
   * Choose a leader for your multi-cultural group.
   * Work together to come up with ideas to solve this problem:

136

The three countries in which you live are on the verge of suffering an intercultural crisis due to problems with the environment. This is particularly critical in the area of food production where you face a potential famine. Culture A is in the wealthiest position with a good supply of wheat and grains—but little in the way of other crops. Culture B is production adequate vegetable crops but faces a grain shortage. Culture C is in the worst shape, producing barely enough crops to stay alive. They are the only culture, however, to have any dairy products—but do no have a surplus. Always keeping your culture in mind, determine the outline of a plan. (You must come to consensus—if this is possible.)

- Discuss ways in which you can work together to help to alleviate the problems.
- Be sure to remember the characteristics and behaviors of your own culture while working with this new group.

After the exercise has been completed:

- Take a few minutes to write down as many characteristics of the other two cultures which you have been able to identify.
- Make a note about your most frustrating during the process of the exercise.
- In the large group, discuss the following:
    a) Who did you choose as the leader of your group? Which culture was represented? On what basis was the leader chosen?
    b) What plan did you come up with? (Leader should report)
    c) What were the culture characteristics?
    d) How did cultural differences help/hinder communication and decision making?
    e) What was your most frustrating moment?
    f) What was the impact of the subcultures on the communication process?
    g) What techniques might assist communication in the new groups?
    h) What similarities do these groups have with the real world?
    i) Now—do you agree or disagree that cultural differences should be ignored?

WELCOME TO YOUR NEW CULTURE

Information Sheet for Culture A

It is difficult to simulate what it is like to interact in a different culture. This exercise will place you in a culture which is unlike our own and unlike most of the other members in your group.

As a part of your new culture…

You will always wear only one shoe. If you are a male, you will wear your right shoe; if you are a female, you will wear your left shoe. The fact that others in your culture wear only one shoe gives you a special bond. If you like someone who is not a member of your culture, you may try to get him/her to also remove the appropriate shoe. (To remove the incorrect shoe exposes one to ridicule.)

You believe that it is essential to be a good listener. When other are speaking to you (and when you are speaking to them), you maintain good eye contact and react with your voice and body.

When you speak, you try to include everyone; however, you do no answer questions directly— and only if they are preceded by "please." (It is perfectly acceptable to hint to the questioner that some indication of courtesy is needed before you will respond.)

In terms of power, you believe that men are superior. Any man in your group should automatically be the leader, no matter how young or incompetent.

You prefer to conduct your transactions while seated in chairs in a circle, with the leader of the group at the focal point. People only sit on the floor when they are feeling ill.

You believe that laughter is critical in dealing with others. When you agree with someone, you respond with laughter to show your support. You nearly always laugh when someone of your own culture speaks.

You consider children the most important thing in your society. All members should be willing to share in order to be sure that children are safe and properly cared for.

You are a member of a collectivist society. You believe that working together is essential. You succeed or fail a group—not individually.

DO NOT SHARE THE INFORMATION ON THIS SHEET!

WELCOME TO YOUR NEW CULTURE

Information Sheet for Culture B

It is difficult to simulate what it is like to interact in a different culture. This exercise will place you in a culture which is unlike our own and unlike most of the other members in your group.

As a part of your new culture…

You will always wear a paper clip on your right lapel/collar/or neckline. People who do not do so are viewed as rude and ignorant. If you decide that you like someone who is not wearing a paper clip, however, you may give him/her one and get the person to wear it on the left lapel/collar/neckline. (Bring along an additional paper clip to class so that you can show your appreciation of at least one person from another culture in your new multi-cultured group.)

You believe that it is the polite thing NOT to react nonverbally to anything that others say. You listen to others with as little reaction or expression as possible. You look directly at them; however, you do not respond with any facial expression.

When you speak, you maintain eye contact only with those who are of the same sex. With members of the opposite sex, you look at the floor. You also always look at the floor when addressing the leader (out of respect). Having people of the opposite sex look you directly in the eye makes you very uncomfortable.

You believe that age is very important. You see the oldest member of a group as the most powerful and the leader. Because it is not always possible to determine age at a glance, it is perfectly acceptable for you to ask their ages. Remember that the oldest person should always be in charge.

You prefer to conduct your transactions while seated on the floor and encourage others to do the same. If they will not sit, that is OK—but your remain on the floor.

You are basically quite introverted. You have trouble sharing your thoughts (especially to your elders), and you believe that people who ask question s are rude and ignorant.

To you, the most important quality in life is equality. You do not consider anyone above anyone else and feel very strongly that all people should share equally in the wealth of a society.

You are a member of a collectivist society. You believe that working together is essential. You succeed or fail a group—not individually.

DO NOT SHARE THE INFORMATION ON THIS SHEET!

WELCOME TO YOUR NEW CULTURE

Information Sheet for Culture C

It is difficult to simulate what it is like to interact in a different culture. This exercise will place you in a culture which is unlike our own and unlike most of the other members in your group.

As a part of your new culture…

You will always cover your head. You believe that people who expose their heads are rude and ignorant. You will encourage people of other cultures to comply with your cultural more.

You believe that it is the polite thing to never look people directly in the eye. When someone is speaking t you, you will always aver your eyes, looking either at the floor or at the wall. You may, however, react in other ways—such as nodding or shaking your head or saying "yes" or "no," etc.—to the person. You nay even begin to speak while the other person is speaking if you have something important to say.

When you speak, you talk loudly enough for everyone to hear but you address your comments and look directly only at a person next to you.

In leadership and power positions, you believe that sex is very important. Women are seen as more powerful than men and are given positions of authority. If there is a mother in you midst, she is especially revered and should be given the place of honor in the group.

Women in your culture always converse with others while seated on the floor. (They deserve the honored position which is close to the Earth.) Men are seated on chairs, never on the floor. You encourage other cultures to follow this cultural tradition and are skeptical of those who do no comply.

You ask questions of others freely (lots of them) and answer them freely as well (often at great length). You are eager to share information and ideas. You believe that people should **say** what they mean.

You believe that money is critical in life. Relationships are secondary.

You are a member of a collectivist society. What is important is that YOU get ahead and are seen as successful and bright.

DO NOT SHARE THE INFORMATION ON THIS SHEET!

Culture Groups

(Adapted from an exercise developed by Scott Johnson, Ithaca College)

Approximate Time: 45-60 minutes

Purpose: To demonstrate the impact of culture differences on interpersonal and group interaction.

Procedures:
1. Divide the class into groups—4-6 members per group.
2. Given the groups approximately 15 minutes to develop a unique "culture." At minimum, each culture should include:
   a. One unique way of dressing (that can be displayed now)
   b. One unique ethical stand related to (your topic)
   c. Two unique manners of speaking
   d. Three unique beliefs that will NEVER be compromised
   e. Four words that only the group members will understand
3. Once the groups are done creating their cultures, divide them into new groups. Each new group should be composed of 2-3 PAIRS from the first groups (so each member of the group has an associate from the first group). Individuals in the new groups must live by the cultural rules they created in their first groups. They also must not explain those rules to their new group; they simply must abide by them.
4. Assign the groups a decision-making task and have them work toward consensus. Examples of tasks include a campus-related concern or a local community issue with which everyone is familiar. Allow approximately 15 minutes for the new groups to arrive at a decision.

Discussion Points:
1. How did cultural differences help/hinder communication and decision-making?
2. What might the impact of subcultures on the communication process?
3. What might happen if the group continued for several weeks?
4. What techniques might assist communication in the new groups?
5. What similarities do these groups have with the real world?

Culture in Change

Approximate Time: 30-40 minutes

Purpose: To discover and discuss the impact of culture on our daily lives and to investigate how culture changes over time

Procedures:
1. Divide the students into groups of 4-5 members.
2. Distribute the directions given below. (students could also be given these in the class prior to the exercise and asked to complete a worksheet before coming to class.)
3. After the groups have discussed, gather for general discussion with the entire class.

Culture in change

What we believe and value, how we behave, and how we view ourselves and others are strongly influenced by the culture in which we live. For each of the categories, discuss the following: 1) What is your own attitude toward the concept? (Your values?); 2) Give a specific example of a time when this attitude influenced your behavior. 3) How does your attitude/behavior contrast with that of your parents' generation? Your grandparents' generation? 4) How might your reactions be different if your came from another culture?

> Categories:
> > Time
> > Religion/Worship
> > Family
> Competition
> Dating/Marriage
> Homosexuality

Discussion Points:
1. What are some of the differing attitudes toward the above concepts?
2. What kinds of information do you need in order to understand the attitude that are different from your own?
3. What are the implications for your own interpersonal communication transactions?
4. Share at least two of the particular examples that you discussed in your small group.

Culture Groups

(Created by Jennifer A. Lundberg Anders, University of Wisconsin Center-Waukesha County)

Approximate Time: 25-30 minutes

Purpose: To examine how culture influences the roles and communication styles we enact in interpersonal communication. This exercise challenges students to recognize and evaluate their culturally influenced perceptions and work through intercultural communication concepts.

Procedures:
1. Distribute a copy of the following situations to all the class members at the class period *before* you plan to do the group discussion part of the exercise. Have the members read the cultural situations and respond to one or both of the situations.
2. Divide the class into groups—4-6 members per group.
3. Have the students enact and then evaluate their responses—were the responses based on stereotypes, how accurate do they think their responses were?
4. Have the students examine how the cultural role enactments and response evaluations influences their understanding of interpersonal and intercultural communication competency.

CULTURAL SITUATIONS AND ROLES

Directions: Read the following cultural situations and respond according to the assigned cultural role. Take 5-10 minutes and respond (in written form) to the situation as a member of the assigned cultures. Bring your responses to our next class.

Situation #1
Recently you and your family have had an important discussion at the dinner table about your future. Your parents announce that they have found the "right/appropriate mate" for you to marry. While you are casual friends and have talked with this person on several occasions, you have never spent any time alone wit him/her. Additionally, you have a college education and the opportunity for a good job in

the business world. You feel your life is really just beginning as you are well-educated and have many opportunities.

The first cultural role you must enact is that of an American female/male (depending on your gender). How would you respond to your parents' suggestion and what are the influential factors (in terms of values, attitudes, and beliefs)?

The second cultural role you must enact is that of an East-Indian female/male (depending on your gender). How would you respond to your parents' suggestion and what are the influential factors (in terms of values, attitudes, and beliefs)?

Situation #2

You are the owner of a construction firm. You have just received notification that one of the nearby Native American reservations is looking for a new company to build their community center. When you call the contact person at the reservation, they tell you that you must set up an appointment for a meeting with the tribal elders. The contact person at the reservation also informs you that the tribal elders will make the hiring decision for the construction job. A week later you travel to the reservation to meet with the elders in an attempt to convince them to accept your company's bid. At the meeting, the elders ask you to tell them a little about yourself and your company. Then the elders ask you to discuss what you can offer the reservation and tribal community and your qualifications for the job. You want to make sure that you "win the bid and that you prove to the elders that you and your company are "right for the job."

The first culture role you must enact is that of a white business owner. What do you do and/or say to prove your worth? You responses should reflect those of the typical interview/bid situations.

The second culture role you mist enact is that of a Native American. What do you do and/or say to prove your worth to the elders? Your responses should reflect what your have learned and know of the Native American culture.

How do you think the elders respond to each person? What can make us more culturally competent in such situations?

**Side note to instructor:* the typical response of many Native American elders in such a situation would be to hire those that demonstrate collectivism and use collectivist language (i.e. talks in terms of we, team, group, and community). Typically, many native American elders would be hesitant to hire someone who demonstrated individualism and uses individualistic language (i.e. talks in terms of I, personal achievements, personal goals, individuality) as such a person would conflict with the collectivist Native American culture.

Discussion Points:
1. How did student perceptions of the situation change based on the cultural role they enacted?
2. What was the impact of each cultural role on the outcome of the situation?
3. Did some of your perceptions and/or assumptions of the other culture change based on your enactment of a different culture role?
4. How might the different culture roles affect interpersonal communication?
5. Does the enactment of a cultural role encourage intercultural competency? If so, how?
6. In the first situation how was each of the following intercultural communication concepts illustrated?
   hard culture vs. soft culture/achievement vs. nurturing
   gender as a co-culture
   collectivist vs. individualist
   communication competency

7. In the second situation how was each of the following intercultural communication concepts illustrated?

> language-collectivist vs. individualist
> hard culture vs. soft culture/achievement vs. nurturing
> idea of self ·
> nonverbal language—eye contact
> language and identity—how do you describe yourself?
> high context vs. low context

Principles Illustrated:
1. Cultural conditioning (collectivistic vs. individualistic cultures, high context vs. low context, attitudes about gender rules, etc.) affects our responses in interpersonal situations.
2. We have a tendency to respond to less familiar cultures by the use of stereotyping.

Alien Encounter

Approximate Time: 30 – 40 minutes

Purpose: To examine how "taken for granted" certain cultural aspects are to people "living it."

Procedures:
1. Divide the students into groups of 4 – 5.
2. Distribute the directions below.
3. After groups have created their lists, come together as a group to discuss differences and similarities.

Alien Encounter

Imagine your group is introduced to an alien from outer space sent here on a communication mission. The alien is fluent in the English language but unfamiliar with the concept of culture. Your job is to explain to him what you believe to be the most important cultural "rules" of the United States. For example, how should he act (nonverbally and verbally) when he meets people? What rituals or customs might he observe? What subgroups might he encounter?

Discussion Points:
1. How different/similar were each of the lists?
2. Possible ritual/custom discussion points: Holidays (Halloween, 4th of July, Santa, religious holidays) weddings, funerals, professional sports, family living arrangements, etc.
3. How do you think someone traveling from a different culture might view these behaviors?
4. Why is it challenging to stand outside and look at these rituals/customs from an objective perspective?

PORTFOLIO ENTRY

Assessing Interpersonal Communication Competence

Using the guidelines in Chapter Two, assess your own Intercultural Communication competence. Some considerations:
1. To which cultures do you belong? Which co-cultures?
2. How much experience do you have interacting with individuals from other cultures of co-cultures? (Remember that cultural differences are not limited to race or ethnicity.)

3. How would you describe your motivation and attitude toward meeting people different from yourself? Do you feel comfortable approaching strangers? Does their culture make a difference? Provide an example to illustrate your tolerance (or lack if tolerance) for ambiguity.
4. Do you consider yourself open-minded? Give an example of an instance in which you stereotyped. What were the results?
5. How do you respond when your find yourself in a culture (or co-culture) different from your own. Relate a specific example.

D & A

Assessing Your Intercultural Communication Competency

Think of a time when you have been in a situation or place where you had to interact with people you perceived as culturally different from you.

Define different – was it race, socio-economics, education, age, religion, etc.?

How did you feel?

How did your emotions, attitudes and/or lack of knowledge affect your communication?

What were the outcomes of the interaction?

Do you think the outcome(s) of the interaction would be different if you had the same experience now, after taking this class? How?

Keep your answers brief, but thorough enough to aid you in a class discussion on the topic.

GROUP STUDY

See the Introductory Essay for further information. Consult the Group Study section in Chapter One for additional directions to students.)

CHAPTER TWELVE

Match the letter of the term which best identifies each of the situations below. Begin by clarifying the terms as they have been defined in your text.

a. collectivism
b. co-culture
c. ethnocentrism
d. high context culture
e. high power structure tolerance

f. individualism
g. intercultural communication
h. international communication
i. linguistic relativism

j. low context culture
k. low power structure
l. stereotyping
m. uncertainty

_____ 1. James, a British citizen, believes it is important for him to achieve on his own—and to be recognized for his accomplishments.
_____ 2. As an Arab, Habib sometimes finds himself standing at a distance which is uncomfortably close for his German friend, Gottfried.
_____ 3. Leonard, a gay male, recognized that he and other gays have certain unique characteristics problems.

_____ 4. Jason is proud of being a U.S. citizen because he considers his own culture superior to others in the world.

_____ 5. When Young Sun, a Japanese executive, continually proposes to take care of an issue "later," his subordinates understand that he is really denying their request.

_____ 6. Young Sun is especially proud of an award that names his unit of the company "Outstanding Division of the Year."

_____ 7. In her board meetings, Pamela Sils, an African American, is careful to express herself precisely so that her subordinates clearly understand their responsibilities.

_____ 8. Pamela Sils is especially pound of an award that names her "Executive of the Year."

_____ 9. Father Brady and Rabbi Silbert enjoy their friendly discussions about their different religious perspectives.

_____ 10. Jennie, a twelfth grader, feels comfortable challenging her teachers in class.

_____ 11. Wally, who works as a rancher in Wyoming, knows at least ten nouns that refer to different types of hoses.

_____ 12. Lana chooses not to travel into foreign countries because she is wary of new environments and customs.

_____ 13. Kim is given special respect in his family because he is the oldest brother.

_____ 14. Max, Frances, Louie, Enid, and Muriel, all octogenarians, enjoy their weekly card sessions at the Senior Center.

_____ 15. Because Amy is Chinese, the music teacher expected her to choose to play the violin.

ANSWER KEY:

1. f	6. a	11. i
2. h (g)	7. j	12. m
3. b	8. f	13. e
4. c	9. g	14. b
5. d	10. k	15. l

TEACHING ACTIVITIES FROM THE *COMMUNICATION TEACHER*

Baldwin, J. R. (1999, Fall). *Intercultural pals: A focused journal, 14(1)*, 13-14.

Bollinger, L., & Sandarg, J. (1998, Winter). *Dare to go where others fear to tread, 12(2)*, 1-3.

Bradford, L., & Uecker, D. (1999, Spring). *Intercultural simulations: Enhancing their pedagogical value, 13(3)*, 1-7.

Brunson, D. A. (2000, Winter). *Talking about race by talking about whiteness, 14(2)*, 1-4.

Brunson, D. A. (1994, Fall). *A perceptual awareness exercise in international communication, 9(1)*, 2-4

Corey, J. (1990, Fall). *International bazaar, 5(1)*, 4.

Dillon, R. K. (1998, Spring).*The diversity board, 12(3)*, 7-9.

Ekachai, d. (1996, Spring). *Diversity icebreaker, 10(3)*, 14-15.

Geyerman, C. B. (1996, Spring). *Interpretation and the social construction of gender differences, 10(3)*, 7-8.

Hankins, G. A. (1991, Summer). *Don't judge a book by its cover, 5(4) 8.*

Hart, J. L. (1999, Fall). *On parachutes and knapsacks: exploring race and gender privilege, 1491)*, 16-17.

Harvey, V. L. (1999, Fall). *Cultural musical chairs, 14(1)*, 6-8.

Hastings, S. O. (1998, Spring). *Increasing intercultural empathy: From principle to practice, 12(3)*, 9-10.

Hawkinson, K. (1991, winter). *Through the eyes of Djeli Baba Sissoko: the Malian oral tradition, 5(2)*, 1-2.

Hawkinson, K. (1993, Fall). *Two exercises on diversity and gender, 8(1)*, 2-4.

Hochels, S. (1999, Fall). *Analyzing how others see the dominant U. S. culture, 14(1)*, 4-5.

Hochels, S. (1994, Summer). *An exercise in understanding ethnocentrism, 8(4)*, 10-11.

Jensen, M. D. (1993, Fall). *Developing ways to confront hateful speech, 8(1)*, 1-2.

Kinser, A. E. (1999, Fall). *Diversity scrapbook, 14(1)*, 1-3.

May, S. T. (2000, Winter). *Proxemics: The hula hoop and use of personal space, 14(2)*, 4-5.

Pawlowski, D. (1999, Winter). *Dialoguing the gender movements, 13(2)*, 4-6.

Robie, H. (1991, summer). *A Native American speech text for classroom use, 5(4)*, 12.

Schnell, J. (1999, Fall). *Ideas for including African-American perspectives in selected communication courses, 14(1)*, 12-13.

Simonds, C. J. (1999, Fall). *Pennies form heaven, 14(1)*, 19-20.

Souza, T. (1999, Fall). *Framing equity: Examining approaches to diversity, 14(1)*, 5-6.

Walter, s. (1995, Summer). *Experiences in intercultural communication, 9(4)*, 1-3.

Yook, E. L. (1996, Fall). An experiential approach to diversity, 11(1), 12-13.

Chapter Thirteen: Communicating with Family and at Work

Minefield Exercise

Approximate Time: 45-60 minutes

Purpose: To enhance the understanding of students with regard to the aspects of communication and culture within organizations.

Procedures:
1. Materials needed:
    a. Objects of various size such as toys, stuffed animals, books, paper plates, plastic forks, spoons, etc. for the minefield)
    b. Masking tape
    c. Blindfolds
    d. String or rope - (optional) for hanging objects from the ceiling.
2. Prepare a minefield by taping off a large section of the room into the shape of a rectangle with masking tape. Note: You can create a different design and included as many entrances as you like, just make sure to have at least two openings/entrances; one at each end of the rectangle. Place objects (mines) randomly throughout the rectangle. You can use any type of objects such as paper plates, books, stuffed animals, toys, etc)
3. After all students arrive to class, separate them into 5-6 groups with 3-4 members each. Assign each group an organizational department (Human Resources, Marketing, Sales, Customer Service, Engineering, etc)
4. Explain the following scenario to the entire class.
    > You are at your place of employment within a large office building. While you are working, the lights suddenly go out and you hear a loud explosion. The power to the building has been cut off and there are fallen electrical wires everywhere.

    > Tell the group that they will have 20 minutes to work together to get everyone out of the building. After 20 minutes is up, a chemical fire will occur. In this case, the building is the minefield that you have prepared with the masking tape
5. Explain the following rules/guidelines to the class right away
    *   The goal is get all members out of the building within the 20 minute timeframe with the least number of hazard touches. (Note to instructor: Be purposely vague about how to do this. It is completely up to the groups to figure it out. Groups may choose to work together or separately etc.)
    *   All members of the group will be blindfolded with the exception of a couple of designated leaders who will have "night vision goggles" (individuals without blindfolds)
    *   The members of the group must begin at one entrance of the maze and exit at the other opening to the maze. Within the maze will be obstacles/hazards that must not be touched. So….the final rule is that no part of anyone's body is allowed to touch the ground or another person. ALL TOUCHES ARE HAZARDS. Members must talk each other through the maze to avoid all hazards- not touch or lead each other by the hands.
    *   You may also want to set up various safety guidelines. E.g. An exception to the no touching other people rule is, it is ok to grab someone's arm if you feel a classmate is going to actually hurt or endanger themselves. (fall or bang into something)
6. Allow the groups to have a few minutes to plan and strategize.
7. Have group members put on blindfolds. (At this time designate three people in the room to be leaders/managers who will get to go blindfold-free)

8. After group member's blindfolds are on, throw the various objects listed above into the minefield and then instruct the groups to begin.
9. After 20 minutes of working together, stop exercise and debrief.

Discussion Questions:
1. What communication strategies and tactics were used in accomplishing the group objectives? How did these strategies vary between members? Between members and leaders? Discuss how this relates to upward, downward and horizontal communication
2. What role did the leaders play? Did any other types of leaders emerge during the scenario? Discuss how this relates to the various types of power within organizations. (Designated power, expert power, reward power, coercive power, referent power)
3. Did the groups see themselves moving through the stages of working together that the textbook outlined? (Orientation stage, conflict stage, emergence stage, reinforcement stage)
4. How would you describe the culture within your organization and departments? Relate this to the dimensions of communication culture: Sociability, distribution of power, tolerance of new ideas, ways of managing conflict, emotional support. Was this a competitive or collaborate environment?
5. How did it feel to be blindfolded? How is this similar to how a new employee feels when beginning employment with a new organization?

20 Questions

Purpose: To allow students an opportunity to practice preparation for an interview and encourage career exploration.

Procedures:
1. Ask students to brainstorm 5-10 careers they may be interested in pursuing. From that list, ask them to pick the career they would most like to learn about. Assign students an out of class activity-- conduct an interview with someone who currently has the job they are interested in.
2. Provide students with the following information on a hand out.

In addition to participating in employment interviews, it is a good idea to practice gathering information about what's happening in an occupation or an industry you might be interested in. The best way to do this is to talk with people working in the field. This process is called INFORMATIONAL or RESEARCH INTERVIEWING.

An informational interview is an interview that **you** initiate; you ask the questions. The purpose is to obtain information, not to get a job.

Following are some good **Reasons To Conduct Informational Interviews**:
- To explore careers and clarify your career goal.
- To discover employment opportunities that are not advertised.
- To expand your professional network.
- To build confidence for your job interviews.
- To access the most-up-to-date career information.
- To identify your professional strengths and weaknesses.

Listed below are **Steps To Follow To Conduct An Informational Interview**
Step 1 →**Identify the Occupation or Industry You Wish to Learn About**
> Assess your own interests, abilities, values and skills, and evaluate labor conditions and trends to identify the best fields to research.

Step 2 →**Prepare for the Interview**

Read all you can about the field prior to the interview. Decide what information you would like to obtain about the occupation/industry. Prepare a list of questions that you would like to have answered. (suggested questions listed below)

Step 3 →**Identify People to Interview**

Start with lists of people you already know- friends, parent's friends, relatives, fellow students, present or former co-workers, neighbors, etc. Professional organizations, the yellow pages, organizational directories, and public speakers are also good resources. You may also call an organization and ask for the name of the person by job title.

Step 4 →**Arrange the Interview**

Contact the person to set up an interview:

- By telephone
- By a letter followed by a telephone call, or
- By having someone who knows the person make the appointment for you.

Step 5 →**Conduct the Interview**

Dress appropriately, arrive on time, be polite and professional. Refer to your list of prepared questions, stay on track, but allow for spontaneous discussion. Before leaving, ask your contact to suggest names of others who might be helpful to you and ask permission to use your contact's name when contacting these new contacts.

Step 6 →**Follow up**

Immediately following the interview, record the information gathered. Be sure to send a thank-you note to your contact within one week of the interview.

20 Questions

Prepare a list of your own questions for your informational interview. Following are some sample questions:

1. On a typical day in this position, what do you do?
2. What training or education is required for this type of work?
3. What personal qualities or abilities are important to being successful in this job?
4. What part of this job do you find most satisfying? Most challenging?
5. How did you get your job?
6. What opportunities for advancement are there in this field?
7. What entry level jobs are best for learning as much as possible?
8. What are the salary ranges for various levels in this field?
9. How do you see jobs in this field changing in the future?
10. Is there a demand for people in this occupation?
11. What special advice would you give a person entering this field?
12. What types of training do companies offer persons entering this field?
13. What are the basic prerequisites for jobs in this field?
14. Which professional journals and organizations would help me learn more about this field?
15. What do you think of the experience I've had so far in terms of entering this field?
16. From your perspective, what are the problems you see working in this field?
17. If you could do things all over again, would you choose the same path for yourself? Why? What would you change?
18. With the information you have about my education, skills and experience, what other fields or jobs would you suggest I research further before I make a final decision?
19. What do you think of my resume? Any problem areas? How would you suggest I change it?
20. Who do you know that I should talk to next? When I call him/her, may I use your name?

The Boundaries We Build and Tear Down

Approximate Time: 20 – 30 minutes

Purpose: To identify how boundaries in families are constantly changing.

Procedure:
1. Divide students into groups of 4 –5 each.
2. Ask the students to come up with 5 – 6 boundaries they remember having growing up. They can by physical, conversational, or systems related (curfew, how many friends could sleep over at a time, etc).
3. Ask them to review the list and reflect how these rules changed from age 12, 15, 18 or older. What brought about the change?
4. Discuss as a class.

Discussion Points:
1. List the boundaries on the board, noting similarities and differences.
2. Discuss the age factor and whether these boundaries were openly negotiated at any time.
3. Discuss the impact of culture and gender.
4. Discuss how the students envision boundaries being handled in their future families?
5. How can different expectations of boundaries cause conflict in new family systems?

Principles Illustrated:
1. Boundaries can be very family specific.
2. Boundaries often cause tension within the family system.
3. Boundaries can be difficult to change.

Conflict Role Play

Approximate time 30 – 40 minutes

Purpose: To explore how different conflict roles affect communication

Procedure:
1. Divide the students into groups of 4 - 6.
2. Give each group the conflict scenario outlined below.
3. Assign each group a different configuration of conflict roles. EX: one group might have one of each, another might have two parent placaters, one sibling blamer, and one sibling computer; another might have one parent blamer, one parent placater, one sibling blamer and sibling distractor, etc.
4. Allow the students 15 minutes to review the conflict situation, assign roles to group members (NOTE: if using groups with more than 4, some group members will help with set-up but will not participate in the actual role play) and discuss possible argument strategies. (EX: What would a blamer say?)
5. Have the groups take turns role playing the situation in front of the class.

Conflict scenario:
  Two kids, a girl, Sara, age 17 and a boy, Craig, age 15 are having a disagreement about their respective curfews with their parents. Sara's current curfew is midnight on weekends and 10:00 on weeknights. Craig's current curfew is 11:30 on weekends and 10:00 on weeknights. They both are good students, however, Craig does better academically than Sara. Sara plays varsity volleyball and Craig

plays JV basketball. Sara has a driver's license and is sometimes expected to drive Craig to and from social gatherings.

Possible Discussion Points:
1. How did the different role configurations affect the conflict?
2. How might gender affect boundaries such as curfews?
3. How might conversation and conformity orientation affect the conflict?

Principles Illustrated:
1. How different family communication can be if you change just one variable (systems)
2. How different roles can affect positive and/or negative outcomes.

Portfolio Assignment

Using an essay format, analyze the communication patterns in your family of origin. Answer the following questions, making sure to include course concepts in your explanation.
1. What couple type do you think your parents are? Explain
2. If you have siblings, what roles do you and your siblings play in each other's life?
3. Give at least two examples of how your family has interacted as a system.
4. What conflict roles do you and other family members play? Use at least two examples.
5. Do you have any family narratives? How did they develop?
6. What communication rules about conversation and conformity orientation exist? What type of family would you label yours? Provide specific examples.
7. Give at least two examples of family boundaries.
8. Do your family conflicts revolve around any repeating issues?

D & A

From Table 13-2, prepare answers for four of the nine employment interview questions.

Chapter Thirteen

Match the example with the theory/term it most correctly describes.

a. Traditional couple type	i. Conformity orientation	p. Conflict stage
b. Independent couple type	j. Chaotic	q. Emergence stage
c. Separate couple type	k. Rigid	r. Reinforcement stage
d. Blamer	l. Downward communication	s. Expert power
e. Placater	m. Upward communication	t. Reward power
f. Computer	n. Horizontal communication	u. Coercive power
g. Distracter	o. Orientation stage	v. Referent power
h. Conversation orientation		

_____ 1. "No Sally, I don't think we should be using this print layout for this ad." Sally replies, "I can't believe you'd say that, you don't know anything about print layout."

_____ 2. "If you cared about this family, you would follow the rules that are there to make life better for all of us."

_____ 3. In the Jones household, Jane always mows the grass and John likes to cook.

_____ 4. "I need everybody's month end numbers turned in by Friday at noon."

_____ 5. "Thank you for covering for me in front of the boss. You were a real life saver."

_____ 6. Jayne sticks her head in Susan's office and says "Excellent work on that presentation this morning. Why don't you take the rest of the afternoon off?"

_____ 7. "Hey, Jack, I'm so glad to hear you'll be working with me on this new advertising project." Jack replies, "Yeah, I'm so happy to be able to work with somebody with so much experience."

_____ 8. "Alright everyone, I guess Sally was right. I was just thinking the client wouldn't like it."

_____ 9. "Good work everybody. That was a great decision. I think the client will love that print layout."

_____ 10. "I really think we should all calm down before we blow this way out of proportion and look at this logically."

_____ 11. Tim always goes hunting with his buddies during his vacation while Joan vacations on the beaches with her friends.

_____ 12. "You never do anything right."

_____ 13. "If everyone doesn't dress more appropriately on business casual days, we'll go back to a formal dress code."

_____ 14. "I'd like to take next Monday for a vacation day. Can you approve that?"

_____ 15. Everyone jumps to help Jim reach his project deadline since Jim is highly liked and respected by the entire team.

_____ 16. "Can't we just forget about it for tonight and go to a movie?"

_____ 17. John enjoys the fact that everyone has to come to him when they need a report generated because he's the only one familiar with the new software.

_____ 18. "I can talk to my mom about anything."

_____ 19. "Whatever you decide is OK with me

_____ 20. "As long as you live under my roof you will obey my rules."

_____ 21. In the Smith household, mark always takes care of the outside of the house and Marge always takes care of the inside."

_____ 22. "I can't get an answer from Dad on whether I can go to the party tonight, and I don't know where Mom is."

Answer Key:

1. p	7. o	13. u	18. h
2. i	8. q	14. m	19. e
3. b	9. r	15. v	20. k
4. l	10. f	16. g	21. a
5. n	11. c	17. s	22. j
6. t	12. d		

"The Story of Us"

Discussion Questions Related to Chapters 8, 9, 10, & 11

Approximate Time: Two 1-hour 15-minute class periods
First session: Watch movie
Second session: Watch movie and discuss

Purpose: To give students experience identifying, analyzing and evaluating course concepts in a "real-life" relationship

Procedures:
1. Distribute the discussion questions listed below.
2. Have students view "The Story of Us."
3. Divide the students into groups of 3-4 members.
4. After the groups have discussed, gather for general discussion with entire class.

"The Story of Us" Discussion Questions

Chapter 8: Dynamics of Interpersonal Relationships

- What factors caused Ben and Katie to form their relationship at the beginning? How did those factors change over time?
- Map how Ben and Katie's relationship moves through Knapp's stages.
- Which dialectics do you see in Ben and Katie's relationship?
- Explain, based on exchange theory, how the Kirby's helped jumpstart Ben and Katie's relationship.

Chapter 9: Intimacy and Distance in Relationships

- What dimensions of intimacy are apparent in Ben and Katie's relationship?
- How does the dialectic of intimacy and distance affect Ben and Katie's relationship?
- How is the game high/low related to intimacy and self-disclosure?
- How do Ben and Katie use equivocation and "benevolent lies" to protect their children from their marital problems?
- How do Ben and Katie's perception shift relate to Johari's window?

Chapter 10: Communication Climate

- What role do confirming and disconfirming messages play in Ben and Katie's conflict?
- How do Gibb's categories reflect Ben and Katie's communication?
- What will they have to do differently in the future?

Chapter 11: Managing Conflict

- What styles do Ben and Katie use most?
- Is their style of conflict complementary, symmetrical, or parallel?
- Which intimacy/aggression style characterizes their conflict?
- What do you think Ben and Katie will have to do in the future to ensure positive conflict resolution?

Possible Discussion Points

Chapter 8: Dynamics of Interpersonal Relationships

- What factors caused Ben and Katie to form their relationship at the beginning? How did those factors change over time?

    Complementarity - breath of fresh air at the beginning – becomes a source of conflict later in their relationship

    Proximity – met while working for the comedy show

    Rewards – nothing better in the world than "being gotten"

- Map how Ben and Katie's relationship moves through Knapp's stages.

    Initiating: Ben initiated with the paper clips

    Experimenting: Dinner where Katie talks about crosswords and Ben plays checkers with the silverware/utensils; re-experimenting: trying to find common ground and history together – calling about the tree surgeon and caulking in the bathroom, Ben admitting to trying one of her crossword puzzles during dinner after being apart

    Intensifying: spoon story, re-intensifying: talking about therapists at dinner after being apart, playing hang-man "I hate Kirby's" "I do too"

    Integrating: Ben's marry me sign; short romantic clips of Ben and Katie and the family; giving Ben the spoon from soup in the park, high-low points of the day, apartment – "this is where we became an us," feet finding each other under the covers, re-integrating: Katie saying Chow Fun's at the end because "We're an us."

    Bonding: getting married

    Differentiating: when they have kids, their differences in life philosophy surface even more, windshield wiper fluid low, Harold and the purple crayon – differences were attractive to each other at first, now driving them apart "Where is the girl with the pit helmet?" "I don't know – you beat her out of me"

    Circumscribing: argue about the same thing over and over. Katie "You're not listening" and Ben "Everything is always my fault." Katie saying, "Fighting becomes the condition, not the exception"

    Stagnating: Katie talking about how after a while when arguing becomes the condition and you retreat in silence to neutral corners (while they are out to eat for their anniversary), calling about the postcards from the kids, but nothing else to say

    Avoiding: Ben moving out, Katie not answering Ben when he asks her why they're doing this they get back from dropping kids off at bus

    Terminating: Katie saying, "it's over," discussing one or two lawyers;

- Which dialectics do you see in Ben and Katie's relationship?

    Stability/change

        Ben is too spontaneous and Katie is too rigid

        Katie wants to write letter to kids before sex - Ben wants to have sex first

        Katie remembers tooth fairy during sex - needs it taken care of right away

        Katie not being able to count on Ben to stop the papers for vacation

    Integration/Separation

        Ben expressing the desire to have one look during the course of the day that would tell him they had a connection, they were on the same page

        Katie talking about them having less and less eye contact over the years

    Expression/Privacy

        Katie is hurt over his disclosure to another woman

        Ben discloses how miserable he's been during dinner, Katie mocks him with kitchenware,

Katie not telling Rachel right away, Stan telling Rachel after telling Ben he wouldn't

- Explain, based on exchange theory, how the Kirby's helped jumpstart Ben and Katie's relationship – comparison level for alternatives

Chapter 9: Disclosure & Intimacy

- What dimensions of intimacy are apparent in Ben and Katie's relationship?
    - Physical - sex
    - Emotional – "Everything important in the world is in this bed right now."
    - Intellectual – talking about their different therapists
    - Shared activities: through kids – soccer, baseball
- How does the dialectic of intimacy and distance affect Ben and Katie's relationship?
    - They want to be together, they make up reasons to call each other when they're apart, but they argue when together for any length of time
- How is the game high/low related to intimacy and self-disclosure?
    - It's a ritual developed to facilitate self-disclosure
    - Katie breaks the norm of reciprocity when Ben admits missing her as his low and she comments on the garlic press
- How do Ben and Katie use equivocation and "benevolent lies" to protect their children from their marital problems?
    - Katie says their anniversary is their "high"
    - Ben and Katie go out to dinner so the kids see themselves leaving and coming home together
    - At parent's weekend Ben tells Erin he made up the couch to do some reading
    - How do Ben and Katie's perception shifts relate to Johari's window?
    - Their character flaws (Ben – irresponsible; Katie – rigid) moves from their blind to their open area
    - Gender differences: men and women's table conversations

Chapter 10: Communication Climate

- What role do confirming and disconfirming messages play in Ben and Katie's conflict?
    - Confirming – playing hang-man in Italy; Katie's monologue at the end
    - Disconfirming – Katie hanging up while Ben's talking about their old apartment (impervious); yelling and name-calling (aggressiveness); Ben ignoring Katie while following the moving truck (impervious, irrelevant); Ben saying "isn't this when one of us is supposed to say this is stupid, we love each other?" - and Katie getting out of the truck without answering (impervious); Ben forgetting to stop the papers like Katie asked him to (impervious); Katie mentioning that they made less and less eye contact over the years (lack of recognition)
- How do Gibb's categories reflect Ben and Katie's communication?
    - Evaluation: Katie saying, "You're not listening to me."
    - Control: Katie saying "All we've proven is if we're apart weeks at a time we can have a civil dinner for a couple of hours…Ben, it's over."
    - Strategy: Ben saying, "In Europe, you would have made love first."
    - Neutrality: Katie saying, "Why don't you ask your girlfriend, I'm sure she can help us get back on track."
    - Superiority: Ben saying, "It isn't my fault you turned into your goddamn mother."
    - Certainty: Ben saying, "The kids need some spontaneity in their life."
    - What will they have to do differently in the future?

Chapter 11: Managing Conflict

- What styles do Ben and Katie use?
  - Passive aggression: Katie sighing when she sees the papers piled up outside their home
  - Direct Aggression: Most of their arguments; Ben saying "… a fucking watermelon." As he pulls the covers off the bed; Katie saying, "Fuck you."
- Is their style of conflict complementary, symmetrical, or parallel?
  - Symmetrical
- Which intimacy/aggression style characterizes their conflict?
  - Intimate- aggressive
- What do you think Ben and Katie will have to do in the future to ensure positive conflict resolution?
  - Discuss assertion

Additional Discussion points if using as a semester review

Chapter 1: Communication Process

- How does Katie's monologue about their relationship at the end of the movie reflect the qualitative definition of interpersonal communication?
  - Uniqueness: "I know what mood you wake up in by which eyebrow is higher and you always know I'm a little quiet in the morning and compensate accordingly. That's a dance you perfect over time."
  - Irreplaceability: "Building cities on top of cities – I don't want to build another city. I won't be able to say to a stranger Josh has your hands."
  - Interdependence: "We made two great kids. There were no people there and now there's people there." "I didn't even know the girl in the pith helmet existed until you brought her out in me."
  - Disclosure: "I'm no day at the beach."
  - Intrinsic rewards: "You're a good friend, and good friends are hard to find."

Chapter 2: Communication and the Self

- What role does self-concept play in their relationship?
  - Katie's monologue about "Harold and the Purple Crayon" because he was everything she is not vs. "Harold's wife," and her belief that Ben gave her the role of designated driver of their marriage (reflected appraisal and self-fulfilling prophecy)
  - Katie's moving the dry cleaning and Ben getting a watch with hands (identity management)
  - Katie responding to Ben's hi/low at dinner with cookware "all the while making myself more attractive" (identity management)

Chapter 3: Perceiving Others

- What role does perception play in Katie and Ben's conflict?
  - Ben: "I saw myself through your eyes tonight." (Empathy)
  - Katie: "We were just talking…" (Common tendencies in perception - We judge ourselves more charitably & Empathy)
  - Ben and Katie each focuses on the other's character flaws that annoy them the most (Common tendencies in perception - We favor negative impressions)
  - Katie assuming Ben is having an affair because she walks in on him sharing personal information with another woman (Common tendencies in perception – We are influenced by the obvious)

Discuss the perceptual shift they both experience from blaming their problems on the character flaws of each other to realizing they both are responsible (Punctuation)

Chapter 4: Language

Static Evaluation: She sees Ben as a third child, he sees Katie as uptight
Emotive Language: designated driver (implies she's the only one responsible)
Euphemism: watermelon under the bed
Euphemism: Fred and Ethel Mertz
Emotive: Crossword 7 down: "needs" direct attack
They both use a lot of "You" language
Naming and Identity: Dot

Chapter 5: Nonverbal Communication

- How does their nonverbal communication reflect changes in their relationship?
    Paralanguage: Yelling during their arguments, not yelling during their conversation at Ben's apartment
    Proxemics/Intimate space: Their feet finding each other under the covers, her moving her foot away from his
    Proxemics/Territoriality: Ben moving out of the house
    Chronemics: Ben's watch with no hands, getting a watch with hands, Ben wondering where the furniture guys have been
    Environment: Ben's apartment being organized, having different drinks; Chow Fun's; Stan not replacing the toilet paper roll
    Face and eyes: Her rolling her eyes when he wakes up the baby; smiling when the kids are watching them row the boat; Katie saying over time there were less and less times during the day when they made real eye contact
    Touch: Ben's irritation with Katie's checklist before they can make love
    Kinesics/manipulators: Katie taking a towel to answer the door
    Clothing: Katie shutting the bathroom door at the cabin

Chapter 6: Listening

- What poor listening habits do Ben and Katie exhibit?
    Pseudolistening: Katie when Ben calls about their old apartment
    Stage hogging: Ben at dinner with Rachel and Stan
    Insulated listening: Ben not hearing Katie when she talks about not being able to meet everyone of Ben's needs because she's busy with 5,000 things all day
    Defensive listening: Ben responding, "I am not a third child" when Katie tries to get him to understand the pressures of raising children; Katie saying, "What does that supposed to mean?" when Ben says "In Europe you would have made love first"
    Ambushing: Katie when Ben was trying to explain why he was talking to another woman

Chapter 7: Emotions

Social Conventions: Josh embarrassed by Ben's hug and crying at parents' weekend
Fallacies:
    The fallacy of perfection: Katie
    The fallacy of should: Ben and Katie
    The fallacy of overgeneralization: Ben and Katie

Recognizing feelings:

> Ben and Katie both express anger freely. What other emotions do you think are under the surface? Frustration, loneliness, neglected, defensive, disappointed, resentful, tired, detached, empty

Chapter 12: Intercultural

- Do Ben and Katie live in a high or low context culture? How would their interaction be different if they lived in the opposite?
    - Low. If lived in high they would both rely on more on contextual cues to let them know the other is unhappy
- Do Ben and Katie live in a collective or individualistic culture? How would their interaction be different if they lived in the opposite?
    - Individualistic. If they lived in collective they would both work harder at maintaining social harmony, their expectations might be different as well.
- Does power distance affect their relationship?
    - Low power distance

Chapter 13: Family and Work

- Which couple type do you think would best describe Ben and Katie's relationship?
    - Independent
- How do Ben and Katie's families of origin affect their current view of relationships and their behavior within their relationship?
    - Ben – parents more laid back, more pleasure oriented (discuss make-up sex and sing Andrew sisters song in scene where they're all in bed)
    - Katie – Dot has need for perfection, games are "childlike"
- What general principles would Ben and Katie do well to follow?
    - Don't sweat the small stuff (Ben's washer fluid)
    - Focus on manageable issues (Katie not commenting on directions)
    - Share appreciations as well as gripes (Katie complementing Ben at the end)
    - Seek win-win solutions (that satisfy Katie's need for order and Ben's need for spontaneity)

PART IV UNIT WIND-UPS

INSTRUCTION

The following paper was presented at the Speech Communication Association Annual Meeting in November 1995. It explains the concept behind the techniques of group study and use of the Unit Wind-Up. The ideas of the assessment of basic cross-disciplinary proficiencies is also inherent in this approach.

Assessment of Critical Thinking Skills Through Collaborative Testing and Case Study Analysis in the Interpersonal Communication Course

Carol Zinner Dolphin
Associate Professor of Communication Arts
University of Wisconsin Center—Waukesha County

Abstract

The basic course in Interpersonal Communication presents a unique blend of communication theory and application of theory to practical experiences, frequently with the aim of improving daily communication skills. While traditional testing methods—the objective/short answer/essay test—may be adequate in order to judge student understanding of theoretical concepts, these measures fall short in determining the ability of the students to think critically in applying theory to practical situations.

This paper describes an experiment conducts over a period of six semesters in which members of beginning interpersonal communication classes used collaborative learning and group testing experiences in order to link theory and application. The collaborative work was done with the hope that students would be better prepared to demonstrate individually their ability to identify and apply theory on the final exam/case study.

Final results of student grades compare favorably with those in previous semesters where these methods were not used. Notably, however, student satisfaction with this method is very high; in addition, students express a stronger sense of self-confidence about having integrated the theory into their own daily communication behaviors at least to some extent.

Instruction

The introductory interpersonal communication course can be approached in at least three different ways. The instructor may design the course purely as one in beginning theory in which examples are used only as they might illustrate the theory; in this case, the student's grade depends upon him/her mastery of the cognitive elements of theory. On the opposite end of the spectrum, the course might focus predominantly on application and analysis of student expertise in actual and/or role-played interpersonal transactions; in such classes, the student is graded upon the demonstrated ability of skillful interpersonal communication traits. The third—and most common—approach blends the first two methods, presenting a solid body of theory that students must then apply to read and hypothetical situations; with this approach, the student's grade is based upon the ability to master both theory and understanding of application—possibly without regard t the student's actual expertise in interpersonal transactions.

In my own teaching, I have long embraced the third philosophy. It is explicitly stated in the objectives of the course appearing in the syllabus and is emphasized by a number of portfolio or journal assignments that force students to make connections. In all of my lectures, I use personal and hypothetical examples and encourage student additions. I even tell students that, if they understand the theories of the course an learn to *use* what they learn in their daily communication transactions, they can improve the quality of their lives.

160

Clearly, then, this approach permeates my philosophy teaching the introductory interpersonal communication course. Nevertheless, when I reviewed my teaching materials a few years ago, I noticed one deviance. For many years, I had tested students by using three to four major exams (three "unit" tests and a final cumulative) which assessed primarily the students' understanding of theory. Using traditional objective (true/false and multiple choice) and short response questions, students demonstrated whether or not they had assimilated the information gathered via the textbook and class lectures. I justified this approach by telling myself that the purpose of the tests was, indeed, to test "knowledge" and that I was already evaluating application via the written assignments.

I realized that I had produced for myself a philosophy dilemma. Was I not being untrue to my supposed philosophy by the type of exams that I was administering? Why could not an exam, as well as a written assignment, test for both theory and application?

I had also done a good deal of work in the past years on the use of collaborative learning. In the interpersonal class, I always used carefully focused small group work, usually with positive results in terns of both student learning and satisfaction. In a course that focused on small group interaction, I had even introduced the practice of "group testing." I had found it encouraging, during this experiment, to hear students discuss with their peers the theories that I had presented in class and think through the applications out loud. Having a grade attached to the outcome seemed to enhance the seriousness of the work, as well as group productivity. I wondered if this technique could not be transferred successfully to the interpersonal course, frequently taken by first semester freshmen on our campus.

In addition, I had spent a number of years in investigating the impact of assessment techniques on student learning. From this work, I knew that the best measurement of potential student success is observation of behavior. Study of assessment also increased my awareness of the importance of direct feedback to the student.

This analysis was the seed for the experiment that is described in the following pages. It should be noted that, since this paper began not as a scholarly investigation but as an experiment in a pedagogical approach, it is written in this more casual spirit.

The First Experiment

During the first semester of the experiment (Spring 1993), I worked with a campus colleague, Associate Professor Therese Rozga. Together, we developed chapter quizzes that could be taken by students either individually or in small groups. Usually, these exercises consisted of a number of very brief descriptions of behavior, which students needed to match to the correct communication vocabulary or theory. In addition, students were expected to complete a short objective quiz one the contents of the chapter. (We were both using Adler, Rosenfeld, and Proctor's *Interplay* at the time and relied heavily on suggestions from the instructor's manual.)

Each of us taught two sections of the course. In one of each of our sections, students completed both sections of the quiz individually and then worked together in a small group to come to group consensus on the matching section of the quiz. As each group completed the matching section of the quiz, members received immediate feedback and assessment from the instructor to clarify any errors in thinking. Although all group members participated in the consensus exercise, only those who achieved a certain level on the first quiz were able to earn the group points.

Both of the instructors—as well as the students—liked the second method. It took longer, but it seemed to be time well spent. It was gratifying to hear students discussing the vocabulary and trying to recall text and class examples, thinking aloud and working together to make connections. The scores clearly showed that the students were helping each other to succeed, and many of them expressed satisfaction in a higher level of understanding. Even the better students who tended to contribute the most valuable insights to the group discussions said that they were helped by the interaction to see concepts more clearly. Students also benefited from the "live" feedback and explanations from the instructor, rather than relying solely on a score or other written comments. (Traditional unit tests were also retained at this stage in the experiment.)

But the real test of the process came at the end of the semester. For the final exam, we presented the students with a brief case study (written as a dialogue), which they had to analyze (via directive questions) in the light of the semester's theory. While students who had experienced the collaborative testing throughout the semester performed slightly better on the exam, individuals in all four sections generally did poorly on the final. They appeared overwhelmed with the instrument, and many almost gave up before they completed the entire exam. Only the best students persevered, and, despite the overall quality of the students, there were very few "A's" and many "D's" and "F's." Those who did well expressed satisfaction with the challenge and felt that they had really accomplished something when they had finished. Even some of the "non-performers" noted that the scenario was probably a good idea but that they felt unprepared for the demands of the exam.

The outcome created a dilemma with, I though, three possible explanations. Number One: We were both very poor teachers who didn't know how to teach interpersonal communication. Many years of prior successes (happily) negated this possibility. Number Two: The experiment was a dismal failure. The ideas of collaborative learning, assessment, and an exam that required theory application were all flawed. This second conclusion flew in the face of a great deal of prior research; also, a few students did, indeed, perform well on the exam. Number Three: The method was flawed. Most students were frustrated by the introduction of a new type of instrument along with the stress of a cumulative exam. There must be a better method to prepare students for the final exam.

The Revises Experiment

Despite students' frustration with the final exam, I decided hat there was too much promise in this method to accept failure. The second semester, I revised my approach somewhat. Concluding that the problem was not with the instrument itself but with the preparation of the students, I moved forward, applying the revised experimental method to all of my sections of the course. I am still using the following approach at this time.

The collaborative work on individual chapters has been retained; however, it is no longer linked to the quiz grade. Instead, at the request of a number of students, the quiz session begins with the group work, giving the opportunity for further clarification of terms. On these exercises, students earn "group points," which ultimately figure into the final grade, but the quiz is a separate grade.

Next, I have elaborated on the collaborative learning and substituted scenarios for the traditional "unit texts." A series of case studies has been developed, one for each major unit of study (Introductory Theory, Self-Concept, Perception; Listening, Language, Nonverbals; and Relationships and Conflict). Students analyze the case studies, called "Unit Wind-ups," in their small groups. (The groups have sometimes remained the same throughout the semester and have sometimes changed from unit to unit or even from chapter to chapter. This depends upon the particular mix of students in the class, although I prefer to maintain as much group stability as possible.) Just recently, after completing a "Wind-Up" exercise, two students, one who struggles with the concepts and one who assimilates information with ease, were overheard discussing the experience. Both noted how helpful the exercise was to them individually, how it "really showed what we've been learning" and made them "more confident about understanding the material."

A second significant change is that I have also audiotaped the case studies (using on-campus talent). In addition to the written copy, then, students are able to hear the voices of the "participants" and make more accurate judgments about the climate of the transaction by listening to the vocal cues. The tape is an especially helpful modification. I have purposefully chosen audiotape because I believe that it is extremely difficult to produce a quality video, and it is possible that the extra visual stimuli might serve to muddy rather than clarify.

Since the responses are generated by a group, thereby reducing the number of papers that need to be assessed by the instructor, the questions for the "Wind-Ups" have been fairly open-ended and require some degree of explanation. The "Wind-Ups" result in a real grade, and all members receive the same grade for the exercise.

Each analysis takes a full seventy-five minute class session. The process might be modified for a shorter session either by reducing the number and types of questions and/or distributing the case study at the previous meeting so that students could begin to familiarize themselves with the copy. Each of these would speed up the consensus process.

At the final exam session, students receive a similar case study—along with hearing an aural tape—which they must analyze on their own. In consideration of the typical end-of-semester time crunch, the questions on this exam tend to be more directive. For example, on the "Wind-Up," I might ask for them to locate an example of the use of proxemics in the scenario. For the final exam, I'd ask which category of nonverbal communication is illustrated in Speech 17. A sample of the final exam scenario and questions are include with this paper.

The Model

The model in Figure 1 attempts to illustrate the entire learning/assimilation process and to emphasize the key role played by assessment through the process. Initially, theory from a single chapter/topic is presented to students via textbook (or other written) materials, lectures, and discussion. Students' initial individual understanding of the theory is tested by an objective quiz (student behavior); feedback takes the form of individual grade and general clarification on information which was commonly confused. With a foundation in theory understanding, students can begin to use and develop critical thinking skills in the application of theory to practical communication situations.

Concurrent with an following the initial assessment, collaborative work begins using group exercises and testing. Observable behavior may include small group reports to the general session, written reports to the instructor, and consensus reports on group tests. Instructor feedback, directed to the specific group, is primarily oral. While these activities are occurring in the classroom, students are also individually completing a series of Portfolio assignments that require them to identify, explain, and apply the chapter theory to their own personal experiences. Prior to handing in their Portfolios, students are required to use a checklist in order to self-assess their own work. Portfolios are collected and graded three times throughout the semester, and students receive relatively detailed feedback from the instructor on their Portfolio materials.

Following each unit, students are required to integrate the theories from that unit by analyzing a scenario. These "Unit Wind-Ups" are collaborative efforts that require a written consensus report from the group. Assessment feedback is also written. Finally, for the final exam, students must individually analyze a case study in terms of all of the communication theory studies throughout the semester. The final assessment feedback comes in the form of the semester grade.

Results

The modifications to the initial experiment resulted in a significant improvement on the final exam scores. Whereas during the first semester the scores clustered in the "D" and "F" range, grades now represent the full spectrum and also tend to correlate closely with the grades the students have been receiving throughout the semester. Student surveys confirm that they feel that the group "Win-Up: exercise have prepared them for the type of exam they can expect for the final.

Somewhat to my disappointment, students are not scoring higher on the case study exam than they did on the more traditional instrument; however, I believe this is offset by the fact that they are being asked to perform at a more sophisticated cognitive level when they need to use critical thinking skills to *apply* theory, rather than simply identify or describe it. The final range of semester grades, then, has remained relatively constant before and during the experiment.

There have been some interesting subordinate finding s generated by a questionnaire completed by 128 students immediately following the final exam. It comes a no surprise that students express a high degree of satisfaction with the work done in their small groups and that a full 99 percent either strongly agree (73 percent) or agree (26 percent) with the statement, "I enjoyed the group work in COM 101." Clearly, the satisfaction is widespread and is not linked to any particular level of achievement in the course. That is, the "A" students—who might initially express some reservations—find the group work just as positives as the "C" students. In addition, 95 percent agree (agree/strongly agree) that the group exercises and discussions helped them to understand the course concepts; 92 percent agree that the group quizzes were helpful in learning/clarifying course concepts; and 80 percent agree that the group "Wind-Up" exercises helped to prepare them for the final exam. Casual comments and nonverbal indicators also demonstrate that students feel a heightened self-confidence about knowing the material as they enter the final exam situation. Interestingly, 84 percent report that they believe they "probably learned more from the small group work than they would have from additional lectures," possibly because they are forced to listen, think, and contribute in the small group situation.

In conclusion, I believe that, although this experiment took a different route than initially expected, it has been largely successful. There is no question that the students are applying theory with greater accuracy and assurance and that they are using critical thinking skills rather than relying strongly on memorization. In addition to test scores, I would point to an increased level of sophistication in their portfolio assignments and more thoughtful questioning during classroom sessions.

As a postscript on the questionnaire, I asked students, "What is the thing that you will remember most about this class?" A sample of responses follow:

"I really enjoyed working in groups. They helped me to remember things that we talked about for tests and quizzes."

"… the group helped me a lot. There are many times when one person doesn't know the answer, but someone else in the group usually does. What is one person's weakness could be another person's strength."

"…the information and how it was *used* in the class. This will be extremely helpful for me in the future. The class was oriented to tech and help the students involved to get good grades."

"…how to look at a situation, evaluate it, and figure out how others feel about it."

"I liked the way the group exercises, quizzes, and wind-up exercises functioned as group study."

"The things that I will remember most are those that I had to write about an make applicable to my own life."

"It has been helpful in my daily life and has improved not only my communication skills but my perception of the world to include a more realistic picture…I learned more about myself too."

"I will remember to ask myself why I am behaving the way I am. I will remember (hopefully) most of what I've been taught so that I may communicate on a higher level. Finally, I will remember most of the class, but especially my group and the professor."

As educators, what more could we ask?

UNIT WIND-UP #1: "YOU JUST DON'T UNDERSTAND..."

Chapters 1-3: Interpersonal Process, Communication and the Self, Perceiving Others

Procedure:
- Read through the questions at the end of the scenario.
- Read and/or listen to the following scenario carefully. You may mark up this paper in any way you wish.
- Work *as a group* to respond to the questions that follow. Each group will hand in one copy of the responses. The entire group will receive the same letter grade for the exercise, any member who does not participate may, by agreement of the rest of the group, be excluded from signing the group product; however, it is also the joint responsibility of all members to try to involve everyone in the decision-making process. You must work as a group and may not create sub-groups to work on different questions simultaneously. You may not use your text or any notes.
- In answering the questions, always explain and illustrate your repose by referring to course definitions and the particular case study. When appropriate, you need to both identify the specific Speech Line *and* briefly describe the situation. Monitor your time so that you are able to complete the exercise the time limit.

Case Study Participants;
1. Richard Karr, Ph.D. -- middle-aged college professor in the field of communication; well-known and well-liked by students; has a reputation for being open and understanding with a no-nonsense attitude
2. Cyndi Chambers -- freshman in her second semester at he university; average students with about a "C" GPA; outgoing and popular among her peers; school is not necessarily her number one priority

Situation:
Despite her usual grades of "C" or "D" in the exams in his communication course, Cyndi earned a high "B" on the last exam, leading Professor Karr to look more carefully at her paper. To his dismay, he noticed a number of striking similarities between Cyndi's responses and those of Jayne, an excellent student who sat immediately in front of Cyndi during the exam. Dr. Karr placed the earned grade of "B+" on Cyndi's paper with a request to see him in his office after class. Because she knows that she has cheated, Cyndi approaches this meeting with a churning stomach and a good deal of trepidation. The following scene takes place in Karr's office.

Case Study:
1. C *(Cyndi knocks timidly at the open door.)* You wanted to see me, Professor Karr?
2. K Yes, Cyndi, come in. (He gestures for her to sit in the chair next to his desk, and she sits—with some hesitation.) I wanted to talked with you about your test paper on the last unit.
3. C What about it? I was rally happy—I got a "B+"; that's pretty good for me.
4. K You're right. And you know, initially I was really pleased for you because it seemed as if you had studied hard and were understanding the concepts more clearly.
5. C Right—what do you mean "initially?"
6. K Because shortly after reading your paper, I came to Jayne's—who I recall was sitting right in front of you for the exam. (Cyndi begins to look down and shift uncomfortably in her chair.) Do you think that your grade has anything to do with the fact that there was a striking similarity between your answers and those of Jayne?
7. C What are you talking about? What kinds of similarities?

8. K   There were a number of times when you listed the characteristics of a theory in exactly the same orders as Jayne and at least twice you gave the identical examples.

9. C   Are you saying that I cheated? (She notices Karr nodding gravely.)

10. K   That's exactly what I am saying. I'm afraid that there were just too many similarities in you two papers for it to be accidental.

11. C   Well, you know that Jayne and I are friends. Maybe we just studied together.

12. K   Perhaps you did, but I don't think that this would account for answers using exactly the same words—or the same examples.

13. C   How do you know that Jayne didn't do the cheating?

14. K   Let's be logical, Cyndi. You are the one who had the opportunity to cheat, and, as you yourself mentioned, the "B" grade was pretty good for you. Jayne is someone who has done consistently well this semester while you have squeaked by with "Cs."

15. C   (She has been thinking things through and has decided to admit her guilt.) OK—you caught me. I confess! But I don't understand why this is such a big deal. I mean, everyone does it. In my last sociology test, I know of at least six other people who are cheating.

16. K   Do you mean that you've also cheated in sociology? (Cyndi nervously curls her hair around her finger.)

17. C   Well…I'm telling you, those tests are impossible. I mean, she takes sentence from the book, and leaves out any old word, and you're supposed to fill it in. Who can study all of that? It's not reasonable—so everyone…takes in a few notes.

18. K   Everyone?

19. C   No—not everyone—but a lot of people do.

20. K   And this makes it all right.

21. C   Well, sure. It's only a silly test. It doesn't really mean anything.

22. K   Do you think the sociology professor feels that way too?

23. C   Of course not—but if she expects people to be able to pass the tests, she has to make them reasonable for us to pass.

24. K   (He leans in toward her slightly.) Cyndi, I really do understand the pressures that students are under. I can remember feeling pretty stressed out myself when I was in school, but we're getting off the topic. Are you telling me that others also cheated on the communication exam?

25. C   No—not that I know of.

26. K   Then let's talk about the penalty you'll have to incur for this action.

27. C   (disgruntled) I suppose I have to give up my "B+" and go back to getting a mediocre "C."

28. K   A "C"? You didn't do your own work on the exam.

29. C   But I didn't cheat for all the questions, only a few. It's not fair to penalize me for the questions I answered on my own.

30. K   Cyndi, I don't think that you understand the seriousness of this situation.

31. C   (Beginning to get worried) You mean that I could get an "F" for the exam? I can't afford that! My grade is bad enough already, and I need at least a "C" in order to stay in school.

32. K   Perhaps you should have thought of that before you decided to cheat. Do you remember the policy on plagiarism that's printed in the syllabus?

33. C   Wait a minute—I didn't plagiarize. It's not like I went to the library and copied some research out of a book and just handed that in for a paper.

34. K   What exactly is plagiarism?

35. C   It's using someone else's work without giving credit.

36. K   And didn't you do exactly that?

37. C   No—not exactly. I just looked at someone's paper and wrote that down.

38. K   Isn't that using someone else's ideas?

39. C   But…

40. K   You did use Jayne's ideas, didn't you?

41. C Yes, but…

42. K And I didn't notice that you gave her credit on your paper…

43. C But…

44. K Cyndi, you don't seem to realize that this is really a very serious offense. I have a copy of the syllabus right here. You'll notice that I quoted the policy which explains the severity of the offense.

45. C It says that I could fail the course!

46. K Yes—and it says that you could be expelled from the university with a permanent notation on your transcript.

47. C You wouldn't do that, would you?

48. K I'm not exactly sure what's going to happen. I'm especially disturbed that you've already admitted that this wasn't a one-time event.

49. C It's the only time I've cheated in this class…

50. K But you have admitted to cheating in sociology as well. Ethically, I simply can't hide this—from your professor or from the university. Quite frankly, it makes me wonder how many other times you've used someone else's work and gotten away with it.

51. C This sound like you might even fail me for the semester!

52. K First of all, you chose to fail yourself when you chose to cheat. And secondly, I don't think you are hearing me yet. Your action has ramifications beyond this course. I'm going to have to report your academic misconduct to the administration. I've made a copy of our university's policy on this for you; I suggest you contact your advisor immediately. (He hands her the policy and rises to gather his materials for class.)

53. C Wait a minute, Professor Karr. Can't we talk about this? I had no idea that this was so important to you.

54. K It really has nothing to do with me personally. We are talking about ethical responsibility. Right now, I need to get going to my next class. Please see your advisor as soon as possible. I'm sure we'll be talking again in the near future.

Suggested Questions:

1. Of the three chapters in this unit (Communication Process, Self-Concept, and Perception) which is most involved in the disagreement in this case study?

2. Using a quantitative definition, does this interaction constitute interpersonal communication? Using a qualitative definition? Explain your response.

3. Is this interaction an example of linear, interactive, or transactional communication? Why?

4. What kind(s) of noise are represented during the interaction? Explain.

5. What is punctuation? How might Professor Karr and Cyndi *each* puncture this situation differently?

6. Formulate a perception check, which Professor Karr might have used at the beginning of the conversation.

7. Both Professor Karr and Cyndi were influenced by common tendencies of perception. List and define four of the six tendencies and provide one example of a tendency from this scenario.

8. How does Cyndi use impression management in this transaction? How do you think that her presenting self contrasts with her perceived self?

9. Do you find examples of self-fulfilling prophecy, social comparison, and/or empathy in the case study? If so, indicate the lines of the speeches in which they occur.

Brief Sample Answers:

1. Perception—student and professor differ in their perceptions of the severity of cheating.

2. Quantitative—yes; there are two individuals involved.
   Qualitative—depends upon the students' explanation.

3. Transactional; adequate parenthetical comments indicate that both individuals are sending and receiving messages simultaneously.
4. Psychological Noise—Cyndi: unrest about knowing that she has cheated Karr: concern for how to approach the topic
   Physiological Noise—Cyndi's churning stomach and feelings of unrest (External Noise—This could be introduced on an audiotape.)
5. Professor Karr—This situation exists because of Cyndi's cheating conduct and her attitude toward it. Cyndi—This situation exists because Professor Karr is making such a big deal out of nothing. He doesn't understand that everyone does it.
6. Karr: Cyndi, I've been wondering about the reason for your higher grade on this test. (Description) Did you study harder? (Interpretation # 1) or is it possible that you copied from Jayne's paper? (Interpretation # 2) What is your explanation? (Request for clarification)
7. Common tendencies in scenario: Karr is influenced by expectations (Cyndi's past work) and the obvious (Jayne is the better student and Cyndi had the opportunity to cheat); Cyndi assumes others are like her (that everyone thinks cheating is not a big deal).
8. Although she realizes that she is guilty of cheating and that this is a punishable act (Perceived Self), Cyndi uses Impression Management to try to present herself as innocent and naïve (Presenting Self).
9. Self-Fulfilling Prophecy—no
   Social Comparison—Speech # 18
   Empathy—Speech # 27

UNIT WIND-UP #2: "I JUST NEED SOMEONE TO LISTEN"

Chapter 4-7: Language, Nonverbal Communication, Listening, Emotions

Procedure:
- Read through the questions at the end of the scenario.
- Read and/or listen to the following scenario carefully. Mark up this paper any way you wish.
- Work *as a group* to respond to the questions that follow. Each group will hand in one copy of the responses. The entire group will receive the same letter grade for the exercise. Any member who does not participate may, by agreement of the rest of the group, be excluded from signing the group product; however, it is also the joint responsibility of all members to try to involve everyone in the decision-making process. You must work as a group and may not create sub-group to work on different questions simultaneously. You may not use your text or any notes.
- In answering the questions, always explain and illustrate your response by referring to course definitions and the particular case study. When appropriate, you need to both identify the specific Speech Line <u>and</u> briefly describe the situation. Monitor your time so that you are able to complete the exercise within the time limit.

Case Study Participants:
- Sonja Markios   Age 20; bank teller; intelligent, personable, attractive, well groomed
- Mick Grady   Age 20; graduate from high school with Sonja; unshaved, small and wiry; dressed in jeans with holes and a soiled flannel shirt
- Andrew Garrett   Age 22; graduate student; long time friend of Sonja; clean-cut and good looking with a strong physique

- Louanne Briggs   Mid-50s; waitress; short and overweight
- Situation:

Sonja and Andy have been good friends for over ten years. They both really enjoy each other's company and have found that they are soul mates. They have never been attracted to one another romantically. Sonja has made a mid-morning coffee date with Andy at a casual restaurant (such as Denny's, Big Boys, Shoney's etc.) to discuss a personal problem she is having. Sonja arrives at the restaurant first and is seated in a corner booth. While she is waiting, she notices Mick, a high school classmate whom she has not seen since graduation, approaching. She tries to avoid his eyes, playing close attention to the coffee in her cup, but he moves toward her table.

Case Study:

1. M *(His voice is loud enough to make Sonja cringe.)* Hey, Sonja, sweetheart! Long time no see, What's happenin'?
2. S (She looks up reluctantly, responding unenthusiastically) Oh, hi, Mick.
3. M Looks as if you're alone. How about if I join you, and me and you can catch up on old times? *(He sits down without waiting for her response and begins to move in toward her.)*
4. S Well, actually…
5. M Great. Good to see you. Looks like you're doin' pretty good for yourself, Sonja. All dressed up in that snazzy uniform. You must have some fancy job. Let's see what that says on your nametag. *(He moves in close to her to read nametag.)* "First National Bank—Sonja—How may I help you?" Sounds like an invitation to me. Hey, that java smells good. I've gotta get me some before we talk any more. Which girl is our waitress? *(He spots Louanne looking toward the table and waves at her.)* Hey, honey, bring me a cup of this, would ya?
6. S *(She has been quiet during all of this, sometimes almost cringing in embarrassment.)* Mick, if you don't mind, I'd really rather be alone right now.
7. M *(looking at her with interest, but not moving.)* Yeah, sure.
8. S I'm waiting for someone and my mind is—well, it's just some place else.
9. M Right, *(He has been keeping his eye on Louanne who has picked up two plates and is delivering them to an adjacent table.)* Hey, baby, don't forget about that coffee. *(To Sonja)* Huh, what was that you were saying?
10. S Never mind.
11. M It sure is terrific seeing you again after all these years. Time really flies, huh? Seems like just yesterday we were in Krupke's biology class dissecting that old frog. Say—are you busy tomorrow night? How about if you and me hit a few bars together?
12. S Mick—no, really. That's not exactly my style. Now, if you could please leave me alone; I'm kind of engaged…
13. M Kind of engaged? How can anyone be kind of engaged? Either you are or you aren't. Sounds like you and your old man are in trouble. I don't see no ring on that finger neither. What you need is a change, and, baby, I'm here to give it to you.
14. *(Andy arrives—just in time. Sonja jumps up to give him a welcoming hug which Andy returns warmly, also kissing her on the cheek. He eyes Mick questioningly. Mick is impressed with Andy's physical size.)*
15. S Mick, now if you wouldn't mind…*(She gestures for him to leave.)* Oh, this is Andy Garrett, my…
16. M Hey, I get the picture. You could have just told me, you know. Thanks a lot for embarrassing me. *(Disgruntled, the leaves the restaurant, just as Louanne arrives with his coffee. She looks at all of them, confused.)*
17. S *(Sonja speaks to Louanne, smiling.)* He's decided to leave. But I bet Andy would be glad to have that coffee.

18. A   Sure, thanks.

19. *(Louanne leave the coffee. Sonja and Andy settle into the booth for their conversation.)*

20. A   **Who** was that jerk?

21. S   **That** was Mick Grady. *(She rolls her eyes.)* He was my lab partner in high school biology class, and, yes, he was a lose even then. Guess who had to dissect the whole frog? *(She begins to laugh quietly.)*

22. A   What are you alighting at? You sounded so serious over the phone.

23. S   I just realized…I was trying to get rid of him; so I told him I was kind of engaged—since you were coming. When you showed up…

24. A   …he thought I was your fiancé?

25. S   Well, he took one look at you and bolted. It was wonderful.

26. A   The look on his face was pretty funny. I wondered what was going on.

27. S   I needed that laugh today. And, yes, what I want to talk about to you *is* serious.

28. A   *(He moves in to her slightly. Both of their voices become quieter.)* Well…

29. S   *(Talking a deep breath)* Well…*(Tears begin to well up in her eyes, and she twists the ring on her right hand.)* This is harder to talk about than I thought it would be. Last week, my mom told me that she and dad are getting a divorce.

30. A   I'm sorry.

31. S   She asked me not to tell anyone; I just had to talk to someone. I know you went through this a few years ago; so I hoped you could help me to sort this all out. I just don't know what to do.

32. A   Did this all really come as a total surprise to you?

33. S   Well…more or less. I know that there have been some rough times. A few years ago, we all even went to family counseling and that seemed to help. But lately, dad seemed to be spending less and less time at home. And mom seemed to be trying to be gone when he was home. I supposed I should have guessed that something was up, but it was easier not to face the truth. When I think about it, it's been a long time since we've all done much of anything as a family, except for the big holidays.

34. A   So you thought that the counseling worked but now you realize that maybe things haven't been all that great lately after all, and you're feeling sort of isolated and confused.

35. S   Some…but I think that what I'm mostly feeling is anger. I mean, Andy, they've been married for nearly 25 years. They've gone through dad's business failure and mom's illness, and they've raised three pretty decent kids. And now they're going to throw it all away. It really makes me mad!

36. A   It's OK to be mad. I remember how I felt when I found out about my parents' divorce. I just wanted to punch somebody—mostly them—or myself.

37. S   Yes, that's another thing. I keep thinking how **I** should have done things differently. I should have talked to both of them more. Or maybe I should have been less of a problem to them when I was in high school. At the very least, I should have recognized that this was all happening—and tried to do something.

38. A   *(He touches her arm, and she stops talking.)*

39. S   What?

40. A   You can't blame yourself for what's happening to them. Maybe they've worked really hard to keep things from you. Maybe they also thought that if they ignored the problems they would go away.

41. S   I guess. But it's so hard to see your whole life kind of change before your own eyes. I wish I could figure out what happened—and whose fault this all is. You'd think that someone who's had as many communication courses as I have would be able to handle something this close to home. I just feel like an awful failure.

42. A   I don't think that placing blame is going to help anything or anyone. What you need to do now is to keep the channels of communication open—and try not to take sides.

43. S   That's easier said than done. I've always talked to mom more than dad. After all, she's the one who told me about this whole awful situation. When I see dad staying out later and later and never spending any time with us, it's hard not to take sides.

44. A   Maybe you need to talk to your dad about this—alone.

45. S   Maybe—but I just don't think he's going to have much to say. *(Using a deeper voice)* "This is all between your mother and me. You kids aren't involved." That's what he'll say. But we ARE involved! He's so insensitive!

46. A   Do your brother and sister know about this yet?

47. S   No—and that's pretty awful too. Mom said that she was telling me because I'm the oldest and I deserve to know what's happening. I think that **they** deserve to know too, but mom disagrees. Still, I hate to go behind her back and make her feel ever worse.

48. A   It does seem pretty unfair to leave you caught in the middle of things.

49. S   Right—I'm really sorry to dump all of this on you, but I needed to talk to someone.

50. A   That's OK. You know I always have time to listen to you. Of course, I'm no professional. Have you thought about seeing that counselor again?

51. S   You mean the whole family? I don't know.

52. A   No, not the whole family. I mean just you. It sounds as if you could use someone to talk to who can be objective about things.

53. S   You know—that's really a good idea. I hadn't thought of it. Talking to you always helps. Thanks for being such a great friend, Andy. *(She squeezes his hand.)*

54. A   Any time, Sonja. After all, you've listened to me plenty of times.

55. S   Speaking of that, do you have a little more time? How about another cup of coffee and we can catch up on your life for a while.

56. A   Sorry, Sonja. I really do have to run now. I have a class at noon. Let's get together again soon though.

57. S   Soon? *(gently)* The last time we said "soon," it took us six weeks. How about right here next week at the same time?

58. A   You're on—and maybe then you can tell me some more about Mick. What a character!

Suggested Questions:

1. Your text discusses the link between languages and credibility and attraction. Based upon his use of language, what kinds of judgments might you make about Mick? Why? Be specific.

2. Find an example of each of the following in the scenario:

    Ambiguous Language

    Emotional Language

    Relative Language

    Sexiest Language

    Static Language

    Powerless Language

    In each case, identify the type of language, the specific Speech Number, the example itself, and explain *why* your example fits the criteria for this type of language.

    (An alternative approach would be to give the speech number and ask students to identify the type of language which is illustrated by each example.)

3. Make at least two observations about how this interaction does or does not illustrate the typical differences between genders in the use of language in communication.

4. How do fact and inference operate in this scenario?

5. According to your text, nonverbals serve five functions: to repeat, to substitute, to contradict, to complement, and to regulate. Give examples from the scenario of the following:

to emphasize

to regulate

to substitute

6. Briefly define and give examples of the following types of nonverbal communication:

    kinesics

    proxemics

    paralanguage

    chronemics

    What does the choice of the environment for this scene communicate?

7. Give one example of a nonlistening behavior (poor listening habit) which appears it the case study.

8. Your text discusses a number of listening response style. Give an example of four of the following from the case study: Active Listening Response Styles: Questioning, Paraphrasing, Empathizing; Directive Listening Response Styles: Supporting, Analyzing, Advising, Evaluating.

9. Give an example or two of the emotional fallacies that are discussed in your text. (Fallacy of approval, causation, catastrophic expectations, helplessness, overgeneralization, perfection, should)

10. In Speech # 40, Sonja talks about her anger. In this situation, is her anger a facilitative or debilitative emotion? Why?

11. Are the emotions exhibited by Sonja first or second order emotions? Explain.

Brief Sample Answers:

1. Students should refer to Mick's use of slang, his poor grammar, and, especially, his use of sexiest language.

2.
Ambiguous Language:	Speech #17-18 "engaged"
Emotional Language	Speech #25 "jerk"
	Speech #26 "loser"
	Speech #63 "character"
Relative Language	Speech #61-62 "soon"
Sexiest Language	Speech #6 "sweetheart"
	Speech #10 "honey"
	Speech #18 "baby"
Static Language	Speech #50 "He's so insensitive."
Powerless Language	Speech #11 "if you don't mind"

3. Sonja and Mick's interaction supports generalizations about gender differences: He talks more; he interrupts; he is playing a game; he is using conversation to assert his dominance. Sonja and Andy's interaction is not typical: She speaks more than he does; communication is used as a relational tool even by Andy; he exposes his feelings at this parents' divorce.

4. Fact: Sonja states that she is engaged. Inference: Mick infers that Sonja is engaged to be married to Andy.

    Fact: Sonja's parents are getting a divorce.

    Inference: Sonja makes a number of inferences about the causes of the divorce.

5.
To Emphasize:	Speech #34 "taking a deep breath"
	Speech #26 "rolling her eyes"
To Regulate:	Speech #43 "He touches her hand and she stops talking."
To Substitute:	Speech #20 "She gestures for him to leave."

6.
Kinesics—use of body	Speech #11 "cringing with embarrassment"
	Speech #20 "gestures for him to leave"
Proxemics—use of space	Speech #10 "He moves in closer to read her name tag."
	Speech #33 "He moves in to her slightly."
Paralanguage—use of voice	Speech #11 "keeping quiet"
	Speech #33 "Both of their voices become quieter."

Chronemics—use of time   Speech #55 "You know I always have time to listen."
     The coffee shop atmosphere is both public and private. This is not an intimate meeting, but it is less casual than meeting in a fast food environment. Typically, diners are not rushed and are left alone by the wait staff. The midmorning time would also be less crowed with more opportunity for private conversation.

7. Mick's entire "monologue" is an example of stage hogging. He also pseudolistens in Speeches #11-14.

8. Questioning: Speech #37
   Paraphrasing: Speech #39
   Empathizing: Speech #41
   Supporting: Speech #35
   Analyzing   Speech #45
   Advising: Speech #49
   Evaluating: Speech #53

9. Fallacy of Should: Speech #42
   Fallacy of Perfection: Speech #45
   Fallacy of Overgeneralization: Speech #50
   Fallacy of Causation: Speech #52

10. It is facilitative because she is expressing it calmly and coherently. There is no evidence that the anger is leaving her out of control or that it is an unreasonable emotion under the circumstance.

11. Second order.

UNIT WIND-UP #3: "CAN'T I PLEASE ANYONE?"

Chapter 8-12: Dynamics of Interpersonal Relationships, Intimacy and Distance in Relationships, Communication Climate, Managing Conflict, Culture & Communication.

Procedure:
- Read through the questions at the end of the scenario.
- Read and/or listen to the following scenario carefully. You may mark up this paper in any way you wish.
- Work *as a group* to respond to the questions that follow. Each group will hand in one copy of the responses. The entire group will receive the same letter grade for the exercise. Any member who does not participate may, by agreement of the rest of the group, be excluded from signing the group product; however, it is also the joint responsibility of all members to try to involve everyone in the decision-making process. You must work as a group and may not create sub-group to work on different questions simultaneously. You may not use your text or any notes.
- In answering the questions, always explain and illustrate your response by referring to course definitions and the particular case study. When appropriate, you need to both identify the specific Speech Line <u>and</u> briefly describe the situation. Monitor your time so that you are able to complete the exercise within the time limit.

Case Study Participants:
- Jack Lyons   19 year-old-college student; home for the summer after giving been away for the past year; working full time at a local grocery as an assistant manager. Jack has been romantically involved with Rachel since they met at freshman orientation. Rachel lives in the same hometown and is also home for the summer.

- Marjorie Lyons   Jack's mother, age 45; attorney. She and Jack had always had a very warm and open relationship, sharing easily with one another.

Situation:

Jack and Marjorie have had a difficult time adjusting to Jack's living at home again after a year away at school. Although Jack has never given her reason to doubt him, Marjorie remains concerned about his welfare. In this light, a curfew has been set for Jack, something which he resents in view of his year of independence. The scene begins at the kitchen table on a Sunday morning. It is about 11:00 am; Jack has just gotten up and is eating breakfast. Marjorie enters. She is annoyed about Jack's late arrival homes but not overtly angry.

Case Study:

1. M   So—did you have a good time last night?
2. J   *(Distracted)* Oh, yeah. I guess it was fine.
3. M   What time did you get in? *(Calmly)*
4. J   I don't know. Sometime after midnight, I guess.
5. M   *(A little more agitated)* You don't need to lie to me, Jack. Just because I'm in bed doesn't mean that I'm asleep. I heard you come in. it was 2:47!
6. J   *(Wearily)* Mom, look, I know that my curfew is 1:30 on weekends. It seems as if I can't please anyone these days. No matter what I…
7. M   What I don't need to hear right now is excuses. Jack, I'm just tired of you ignoring the rules of this house. *(Frustrated)*
8. J   Mom, could we please not talk about this right now?
9. M   Why not? You know the rules. You just can't keep disregarding them time after time. Having you back home for the summer after your year of freedom is hard on both of us, but you need to give a little effort too.
10. J   Mom, please, not now, OK?
11. M   We can't just keep avoiding the issue, Jack. If you really considered how much I worry when you're out till all hours, doing who knows what, with who knows whom, you'd be considerate enough to come in on time.
12. J   *(Serious, almost pleading)* Mom, please, I've got other things on my mind.
13. M   *(Changing tones—finally realizing Jack's distraction)* Yes—it sounds as if you really do. *(pause)* Do you want to talk about it?
14. J   No—well, yes—I guess I could use a good listener.
15. M   So—what's the problem? Does this have anything to do with Rachel?
16. J   You've got that one right. She told me last night that she wants to break up. That's why I was so late. We started to talk, and the time just got away on me.
17. M   Have you been having any problems to this point?
18. J   Not that bad. You know, I'm crazy about Rachel. From the first time I saw her at freshman orientation, I thought she was special. And then the next day, she showed up in the same English class, so we got to see a lot of each other. And we started talking and found out that we had so much in common. And I found out that she's smart too—not brilliant but really smart, especially in things like math that I'm not so good at. We always had such a great time together, and I honestly thought that this was really it for both of us.
19. M   And…?
20. J   And everything was great until this summer. Now it seems that I just can't please her. She wants to be together all the time. I'm trying to tell her that I really need some breathing space, but she doesn't seem to understand that. She wants me around just about every minute that I'm not working. As a matter of fact, she even thinks I'm working too much.
21. M   What exactly does she expect?

22. J   That's another problem. She always said that she loved the way I'm so steady and reliable, that she nearly always know what I'm thinking and what I'll say next. Now she says that she's beginning to think that I'm boring.

23. M   Go on…

24. J   So last night, I asked her where we stood. I told her that I would do whatever she wants. If she wants me around, I'll be around. If she wants me to do unexpected things, I'll try to do that. If she wants me to listen, I'll listen. If she wants me to talk, I'll talk. And she said that's not the point.

25. M   What do you think *is* the point?

26. J   It beats me! The next thing I knew she was calling me a wimp—and I was screaming back at her. It was pretty awful.

27. M   I guess so. I can understand why you're so upset about all of this.

28. J   It just seems as if I don't know Rachel anymore—even in some little ways. Last night, I bought tickets for the baseball game, and she said that she hates baseball. When I brought her a red rose, she said that she likes yellow roses. She didn't even like the music I chose on the radio. I feel as if she's a different person.

29. M   Can you just try to talk to her about all of this?

30. J   That's another thing. It seems that she wants to know every little last detail about me—what happened in my past and how I'm feeling about everything and who I've dated and—well, you get the picture.

31. M   And you don't feel comfortable with this?

32. J   I just don't think I always have to share everything I'm feeling all the time. But she tells me everything—and then I feel guilty when I don't do the same.

33. M   Have you explained this to her?

34. J   I've tried. Believe me, I've tried. Last night she ended up by saying that she really didn't care what I did. I should just please myself and not worry about her. That really made me mad.

35. M   Why?

36. J   Probably because I know she does care—or at least I sure hope she does. I don't know; we just couldn't stay on the topic last night. I got to the point where I almost made up some stories—just to give her something to think about.

37. M   That doesn't sound like such a good idea.

38. J   I know…but I was getting desperate.

39. M   So—what now?

40. J   I thought I'd give her a call and try to see her again tonight—to try to work something out. Maybe we do need some breathing time away from one another.

41. M   That sounds like a good idea.

42. J   Thanks, Mom. It really did help to talk about this.

43. M   Good. Now—what about that curfew issue? *(lightly)* Or did you think I was going to forget all about that?

44. J   Mom, you know I hate the curfew. I've just had a whole year on my own. I know that you worry, but I feel as if I'm being treated like a little kid again. Couldn't we work together to find a better solution?

45. M   Maybe we can work out a better deal. Could you at least promise—and I really mean promise—that you'll call when you're going to be late?

46. J   You mean that you'd be willing to get rid of the time limit as long as I call? That's a deal. Maybe we can both be satisfied with that arrangement. You know I don't stay out all that late very often.

47. M   Good—that's at least one problem settled then.

48. J   Thanks, Mom. I've got to get going. My shift starts in an hour.

49. M   Jack—I really do hope that things work out for you and Rachel. By the way, since you're going to work, we're almost out of milk.

50. J   Sure, I'll bring some milk home from the store. I'll drop it off before I go over to talk to Rachel. And yes, I'll call if I'm going to be late.

Questions:

1. Identify the speech in which Jack discusses attraction variables (why we form relationships). Then explain the variables which he talks about.
2. Mark Knapp has described five Stages of Coming Together (initiating, experimenting, intensifying, integrating, and bonding). At which stage are Jack and Marjorie? At which stage are Jack and Rachel? Knapp also identifies five Stages of Coming Apart (differentiating, circumscribing, stagnating, avoiding, and terminating). What stage are Jack and Rachel in? Why?
3. How do the dialectical tensions of connection/autonomy, stability/change, and openness/closedness function in this scenario? Give at least two specific examples.
4. Your text discusses a number of compliance gaining strategies. Identify at least two different strategies in the scenario and cite the speeches in which they occur.
5. Cite an example of equivocation from the scenario.
6. Identify two concepts about self-disclosure that are illustrated by this scenario.
7. Identify at least one example of a disconfirming response.
8. Recall the categories that Jack Gibb identified as helping to create defensive and supportive communication climates. Note—by speech and by identifying the category name—one example of defensiveness-creating behavior and one example of a supportive-creating behavior.
9. According to the definition of conflict given in the text, are Marjorie and Jack involved in a conflict? Are Jack and Rachel? Why?
10. Your text describes five individual conflict styles: nonassertion, indirect communication, passive aggression, direct aggression, and assertion. In addition, four methods of conflict resolution are discussed: Win-Lose, Lose-Lose, Compromise, and Win–Win.
    a. Which individual conflict style is used by Marjorie until Speech #14?
    b. Which method of conflict resolution is she using? Which individual style does Jack attempt to use?
    c. Which individual style is illustrated by Jack's response to Rachel as reported in Speech #27?
    d. Which style is reported in Speech #29?
    e. Give an example of a way in which Jack might have responded to Rachel using passive aggressive behavior?
    f. In order to resolve their initial conflict about the curfew, which individual conflict style(s) do Marjorie and Jack use? Which type of conflict resolution method does this resolution illustrate?
11. Do Jack and Marjorie live in a collective culture or and individual culture? Give at least one reason for your response. Describe at least two ways in which the interaction might be different if they came from another culture.
12. Do they live in a high-context culture or a low-context culture? Explain
13. Do they live in a culture with low or high power distance? Explain.

Brief Sample Answers:

1. Speech #21. Jack mentions appearance, similarity, complementarity, proximity, and competency in this speech.
2. Jack and Marjorie are probably in the bonding stage since they are "legally" paired as son and mother and because they share a healthy degree of intellectual and emotional intimacy. Jack and Rachel have clearly passed the initiating and experimenting stages and have not yet reached bonding. Students might make a case for either the intensifying or integrating stage.
3. Integration/Separation
     Jack and Marjorie: Tensions involved in growing up and letting go.
     Jack and Rachel: Rachel wants Jack all the time; Jack needs some freedom.

Stability/Change:

    Jack and Rachel: Rachel used to like Jack's predictability; suddenly she is finding him boring.

Expression/Privacy:

    Jack and Rachel: Rachel demands more of Jack in the way of self-disclosure than he is comfortable sharing.

4.   Speech #11 contains a direct request.

    Speech #14 contains a relationship appeal.

    Speech #52 contains an indirect request.

5.   Speech #7 illustrated the use of an equivocal response.

6.   There are gender differences in self-disclosure.

    Self-disclosure enhances relationships.

    There are numerous reasons for self-disclosure: catharsis, self-clarification, and reciprocity are particularly illustrated in this scenario.

    Self-disclosure has both depth and breadth characteristics.

7.   Speech #10 illustrates an interrupting response.

    Speech #7 illustrates an ambiguous response.

8.   Evaluation, Superiority, Control—Marjorie in Speech #10, 12, 14

    Neutrality—Rachel (reported by Jack) in Speech #37

    Empathy—Marjorie in Speech #30

    Problem Orientation—Jack and Marjorie in Speech #47-50

9.   Yes to both situations. Both parties are aware of a conflict situation, both see themselves as somewhat interdependent with the other party, both see scarce rewards, and the interference of the other in achieving their goals.

10. Marjorie begins the scene by using Direct Aggression in a Win-Lose conflict resolution style. Jack tries to use Avoidance to postpone the potential conflict situation.

    Speech #47: Non-Assertive Style

    Speech #49: Direct Aggression

    Possible Passive Aggressive Actions: He might have actually made up the stories as he threatened in Speech #39. He might have brought Rachel another red rose. They use Assertive Behavior leading to a   Win-Win Resolution.

11. Individualistic Culture—more concern for personal needs, not social harmony

    Other Culture—Son wouldn't question his mother, or in other cultures based on gender differences, a mother wouldn't question her son; more respect for house rules,

12. Low Context—situation was laid out very clearly by the use of language; little was left unsaid

13. Low power distance – Jack felt comfortable confronting parental authority.

FINAL WIND-UP: "WHOSE LIFE IS THIS, ANYWAY?"

Cumulative Exam: Chapter 1-13

Note to Instructors:

    The case study/scenario which follows was developed for use at the University of Wisconsin Center-Waukesha County. Waukesha is a community located just west of the city of Milwaukee. Chicago's O'Hare Airport is approximately 90 miles south of Milwaukee. Kenosha is located midway between Milwaukee and Chicago, UW-M is the University of Wisconsin-Milwaukee. Instructors are encouraged to alter the locations in this scenario according to the location of the individual campus.

    The exam would ordinarily be printed in such a manner as to leave enough room for students to respond to the questions directly on the test form.

Procedure:
- Read through the questions at the end of the scenario.
- Read and/or listen to the following scenario carefully. You may mark up this paper in any way you wish.
- Work *independently* to respond to the questions that follow. You may not use your text or any notes.
- In answering the questions, always explain and illustrate your response by referring to course definitions and this particular case study. When appropriate, you need to both identify the specific Speech Line <u>and</u> briefly describe the situation. Monitor your time so that you are able to complete the exercise within the time limit.

Case Study Participants:
- Sarah Barkley   Age 28; B.A. in Communication; employed full-time at Mitchell Field in Milwaukee as a ticketing agent for a small airline company. She is the major source of income for the family while husband Brad completes his M.B.A.
- Brad Barkley   Age 31; B.A. in Business; employed part-time as a shoe salesman while working on his M.B.A. full time at US-M. He expects to finish his degree in a year.
- Tony Barkley   Brad & Sarah's 18 month old son

Situation:
     Sarah and Brad have been married for four and one-half years. Although the going was pretty tough at first, they are now quite well settled into their current lives. They have just purchased an older home on the east side of Milwaukee—convenient to UW-M and not too long a commute to the airport. Although they need to watch their spending, their current incomes are adequate to manage the house payment, Tony's day care three days a week when Brad is not home to watch him, and even an occasional evening out.

     At the scene begins, Brad is just setting the table for their evening meal, which he has prepared. Tony is playing quietly in his playpen in the living room. It is approximately 6:00 pm when Sarah enters, wearing her airline agent's uniform. She is obviously excited as she rushes into the house, sweeps up Tony from his playpen and moves into the kitchen to involve the three of them in a family hug. During all of this, she is exclaiming...

Case Study:
1. S   I did it! I can't believe it! I did it, I did it! I'm so excited I can hardly stand it. Brad—I actually did it!
2. B   That's terrific, honey. What did you do?
     (Immediately the atmosphere changes; he has forgotten.)
3. S   You mean you forget? One of the biggest chances in my life, and you forget?
4. B   Aw—geez—I'm sorry. Of course I didn't forget...the big promotion interview. So I guess this means you got the job. *(Suddenly it dawns on him)* You got the job!!!! *(another hug and more squeals)* I told you you could do it.
5. S   You told me, and I told me...and it worked. I got it! *(to Tony)* What do you think, kid; your mom's going to be a department manager!
6. B   So tell me more. How did it go? What did they ask? When do you start? What do you do?
7. S   Well...the interview was at 11:00 this morning...When I walked into the office, I almost died. Six of the company's top execs were there, all staring at me...
8. B   Hey—wait a minute! This calls for a toast.
     (He moves quickly to the cupboard and takes out two wine glasses, goes to the refrigerator and fills them from the large box of wine in the fridge.)
9. S   *(talks sotto voce to Tony)*...and so your mom had to talk to all of those bigwigs. Pretty tough stuff, huh?

10. B   O.K. *(He hands her a glass)* To my wife, the department manager.
   (They clink glasses and drink. There is a brief pause.) So...go on...

11. S   So...there were all these people...

12.   *(The sound fades out as Sarah continues her story about the interview. The scene picks up ate the end of the description. By this time, Sarah and Brad have moved to the living room couch. Tony has been returned to his playpen and is quietly eating a graham cracker.)*

13. S   Its looks as if I'll have charge of the entire local staff for domestic reservations. That's over 100 people! And, of course, there's a nice raise to go along with this. I accepted on the spot!

14. B   100 people? I though the Milwaukee staff only had about 25.

15. S   Oh, oh. I guess I forget a little detail. We have to move to Chicago. The new position is at O'Hare Airport.

16. B   That's some little detail.

17. S   But, honey, it's such a great opportunity. I couldn't pass it up!

18. B   *(He begins to speak more loudly.)* Opportunity or not, this is *our* life, not just yours. Don't you think you should have at least consulted me! I guess this shows what you really think about my going to school.

19. S   Brad, that's not fair!

20. B   Not fair? What is this? Some kind of game we're playing?

21. S   Well, maybe it is! The game of life!

22. B   You know, you're making me mad. How about your making a major life-changing decision without any input from me? I'm really getting fed up with the way you're always making *our* decisions for us without even talking to me.

23. S   Brad—I can't believe you're reacting like this. This is such a great opportunity. Talk about breaking somebody's bubble.

24. B   Sure it's great opportunity—for you. What about me? There's my job and my education to consider too you know.

25. S   Look, let's be realistic. We have a child to take care of. We sure can't do this on your flunky's salary as a part time shoe clerk! As for school—you can do that anywhere. Heaven knows there are plenty of shoe stores and colleges in Chicago! *(sarcastically)*

26. B   *(angry)* I don't want to talk about this any more. It's pretty clear how much *I* count in this relationship. I'm going to check on the dinner that *I* made for *all of us* while *you* were at your high-class job! *(He storms out of the room.)*

27. T   *(Begins to cry)*

28. S   Now look what you've done!

29.   *(Sarah and Brad eat a very silent dinner, broken only occasionally by Tony's babbles. After dinner, Sarah proceeds to clean up—according to their regular routine—while Brad gets Tony ready for bed. After he is tucked in Brad returns to the living to try to do some homework; Sarah goes to a small office area in their bedroom where she frequently works or reads. After a few minutes, Brad gets up and goes to Sarah in the bedroom. A radio is playing in the background.)*

30. B   Honey, I'm sorry. Can you talk about this now?

31. S   Is there anything to talk about?

32. B   Of course there is. It's just that you sprang this on me so fast that I didn't have time to think.

33. S   *(slightly defensive)* Oh—so it's my fault. Why can't anything be your fault?

34. B   *(calmly)* Nothing is anybody's fault. *(He turns off the radio.)* Your news really is terrific. I'm awful proud of you...really. *(He gives her a kiss.)*

35. S   *(She responds coolly, her body still tense.)*

36. B   Honey—are you listening? I mean it. *(He kisses her again.)*

37. S   *(She relaxes a little.)* Does that mean that you've though this through and you agree with me? That you'll move without kicking and screaming?

38. B   No…I didn't say that.

39. S   Then what's the point of all of this? *(Sarah throws up her hands, rises, and moves away from Brad.)*

40. B   Wait…wait…wait…Can't we talk about this like two adults?

41. S   So—talk.

42. B   I can understand how you were so excited that you just accepted the offer right away. But how about if we try to look at the situation objectively and weight the alternatives.

43. S   What alternatives? I have a promotion offer, which happens to be in Chicago. Either I take it or I'm stuck here—probably for the rest of my life!

44. B   Please, can't we just *try* this?

45. S   Well, O.K.

46. B   How about if we start by looking at the positives: I'll start. First of all, it's a great opportunity for you in a job and with a company that you like.

47. S   *(She likes his beginning.)* And there's a nice salary increase.

48. B   Chicago isn't too far away. We could still easily visit our parents and Tony could see his grandparents. And it *is* a pretty neat city.

49. S   *(tentatively)* And you *could* find a job at another shoe store, even with the same chain. I guess I have to admit that switching schools isn't such a great idea.

50. B   Now—what about he bad stuff? Want to start this round?

51. S   Well, we've just bought the house; we'd have to go through the hassle of selling and finding a new place…

52. B   One that we could afford—remember, Chicago is more expensive…

53. S   No fair—it's my turn. And even though you could ask for a transfer, you would have to find another job…and we'd have to find a day care place for Tony. And there is the issue of your degree. It doesn't really make much sense for you to change schools at this point. This isn't as much fun as listing the positives.

54. B   And there's one other thing I just though of. We'd be new residents of Illinois. We'd have to live there a year before I could get in-state tuition.

55. S   And if you commuted to Milwaukee to finish, you'd have to pay out of state tuition. Yikes! I never though of that.

56. B   And remember—Chicago is more expensive in general. We'd have to take a look at how far tat extra salary would really go.

57. S   O.K. You're right—anything else?

58. B   Not that I can think of right now. So—how about if we brainstorm for solution…

59. S   What do you mean? It seems to me that either I take the job and we move and have to put up with all of those hassles. Or I turn down the promotion and I'm just stuck here with the boredom. It's a no-win situation. One of us is going to be miserable.

60. B   You know, it was pretty quiet at dinner. I had a little time to give this some thought, and I think I might just have something that would work. It's not perfect, but…

61. S   Go ahead. I'm listening.

62. B   Well, how about if we move some place between here and Chicago?

63. S   What do you mean?

64. B   Well, we could move somewhere along I-94—like near Kenosha maybe.

65. S   Oh—I don't know about that. How does that solve anything? That way we could both have enormous commutes!

66. B   Listen—it could work. We'd have to sell the house, but we could rent somewhere until I'm finished with school next year. You could take the bus to work—it takes less than an hour and goes right to O'Hare—so we wouldn't need another car, and you could work or sleep on the way.

67. S   The rents would be a lot cheaper than Chicago…

68. B   I could probably transfer to a store in Kenosha for my job, but I could continue to commute to Milwaukee for school.
69. S   And you could also Tony to day care? That way we wouldn't have to change something we're really happy with.
70. B   Sounds good to me…
71. S   And by the time you're through with school, we'll have had time to decide if Chicago is the place to relocate.
72. B   And there's always the chance that I'll get a job offer somewhere else in the country…
73. S   …and I'll be the one who has to re-locate.
74. B   What do you think? It could work.
75. S   I say we give it a try.
76. B   Congratulations, Manager!
77.   *(They both laugh and embrace.)*

FINAL EXAM QUESTIONS
Respond to the following questions.
    IMPORTANT: When appropriate, you *must* provide BOTH the speck number and the example itself. Explain if you wish—of if indicated in the question. Note that the same speech if the scenario may be used to illustrate more than a single in interpersonal communication phenomenon. Please write or print legibly; answers that cannot be read easily will be counted as incorrect.

1.   The scenario illustrates an example of transactional communication. Explain why or how.
2.   Is there an example of self-fulfilling prophecy in this scenario? If so, give the speech where it appears.
3.   Illustrate the concept of interpersonal "punctuation" about the conflict in this situation. What might Sarah's interpretation be? What might Brad's view be?
4.   Note an example of facilitative emotions in the scenario. Why are they facilitative in this case? Note an example of debilitative emotions. Why are they debilitative?
5.   Your text discusses a number of fallacies of thinking: approval, catastrophic, expectations, causation, helpless, overgeneralization, perfection, shoulds, etc.
        Which fallacy is illustrated by Speech #26 in which Brad says, "You know you're really making me mad.?"
        Which fallacy do you see in Speech #63 in which Sarah says, "One of us is going to be miserable.?"
6.   Identify and give an example of one type of nonlistening which you find in the scenario.
7.   Which of the listening response styles is illustrated by the following speeches in the scenario? Why? (Explain the style[s] being used.)
        Speech #10:
        Speech #22:
        Speech #46 illustrates two response styles. They are:
8.   Design an empathic response that Sarah might have made following Speech #28.
9.   Brief define the following types of "troublesome language": emotive words, ambiguous words, static evaluation, euphemisms, relative words
        Speech #29: "your flunky's salary…"
        Speech #69: "enormous commutes…"
        Speech #23-25: "fair…game"
10. Brief define each of the following types of nonverbal communication and give an example of each from the case study: kinesics, proxemics, chronemics, paralanguage
11. What does it mean to say that nonverbals may be used to *regulate*? Give an example from the scenario.

12. Give one example of a dialectical tension that Brad and Sarah are experiencing in this scenario.
13. Mark Knapp discussed five "Stages of Coming Together" (initiating, experimenting, intensifying, integrating, bonding). And five "Stages of Coming Apart" (differentiating, circumscribing, stagnating, avoiding, terminating). Where would you place Sarah and Brad in this taxonomy? Why?
14. Jack Gibb identified six pairs of behaviors that are likely to create defensive or supportive climates (evaluation/description; strategy/spontaneity; control/problem orientation; neutrality/empathy; superiority/equality; certainty/provisionalism). Which one of these behaviors is illustrated by each of the following:

    Speech #46: "I can understand how you were so excited that you just accepted the offer right away."

    Speech #46: "But how about if we try to look at the situation objectively and weight the alternatives."

    Speech #27: "You sure can't do that on your flunky's salary...!"
15. Your text discusses a number of disconfirming responses. Identify one type of disconfirming response that appears in the scenario.
16. Does Sarah and Brad's situation fit the definition of conflict as given in your text? Why or why not? Is this a functional or dysfunctional conflict? Why?
17. Briefly explain each of these styles of managing conflict (avoiding, accommodating, compromising, competing, collaborating). Chart the use of conflict in this cast study.

    The conflict begins at Speech # _____.

    From this point until Speech #30, the main management style used is:

    Speech #30-33 illustrate this management style:

    The remainder of the case study primarily uses which management style? *Why*?
18. Culture affects our communication. Is the United States a collectivist or individualist society? How is this illustrated in the case study? How might the situation (and outcome) have been different if Brad and/or Sarah had come from a different culture or cultures? (Give at least two specific examples.)
19. What conflict roles do Brad and Sarah play?
20. Give an example of family systems present in this scenario.

Brief Sample Answers:
1. Sarah and Brad are sending and receiving messages simultaneously.
2. Yes—Speech #9
3. Sarah's View: This conflict started because Brad only thinks about himself—his job and his school. He doesn't care about my opportunity for advancement.

   Brad's View: This conflict started because Sarah went ahead and made a life-changing decision without consulting me.
4. Any number of speeches might be cited for this response.
5. Speech #26: fallacy of causation

   Speech #26: fallacy of overgeneralization

   Speech #26: fallacy of catastrophic expectations
6. Any number of speeches might be cited. Pseudolistening, defensive listening, ambushing, and stage hogging are all present at some point.
7. Speech #10: Questioning

   Speech #22: Evaluating

   Speech #46: Supporting (or Empathizing) & Advising
8. It sounds as if you are really feeling upset because I went ahead and jumped at this opportunity without consulting you—even though this decision really affects both of us.
9. Definitions are found in the text glossary.

   Speech #29: emotive words

   Speech #69: relative language

Speech #23-25: equivocal language
10. Definitions are found in the text glossary. Any number of examples might be cited.
11. There are a number of times when nonverbals are used to regulate in the scenario. Speech #22, 30, and 43 are all examples.
12. Support might be found for any of the dialectical tensions discussed in the text. The most obvious is that of stability/change.
13. According to Knapp, Sarah and Brad are in the bonding stage because they are married. The argument is also evidence of differentiating.
14. Speech #46: empathy
    Speech #46: problem orientation
    Speech #27: evaluation
15. There are a number of disconfirming responses through the scenario.
16. Yes, this does fit the definition. The conflict involves a disagreement that is recognized by both parties; they are clearly inter-dependent; and they believe (initially) that the solution is Win/Lose. Although the conflict might have escalated to be debilitative, it is solved in an equitable manner. It is a facilitative conflict, and their relationship is stronger as a result.
17. The conflict begins at Speech #19-22
    Competing—Aggression—Win-Lose
    Avoiding—Nonassertion—Win-Lose
    Collaborating—Assertion—Win-Win
18. The United States is an individualist culture, Sarah might not even be working outside of the home, much less consider making a life changing decision without her husband.
19. Sarah plays the blamer, and Brad plays the computer/placater.
20. Tony starts crying when Brad and Sarah are fighting (family members are interdependent); Sarah's need for career development is hindered by the size of local airport which affects their relationship (family systems are affected by their environment); They may need to move for Brad next (family members are interdependent)

PART V TEST QUESTIONS

Code for Test Items

QUESTION TYPES (TYPE):

T = True/False
M= Multiple Choice
K= Matching
E= Essay
Note that multiple choice directions should include the statement: "Select the *best* answer."

COGNITIVE TYPES (COG):

R= Recall
C= Conceptual
A= Application

CHAPTER ONE: INTERPERSONAL PROCESS

True/False

1. Effective communication can satisfy identity needs.
  ANSWER: T TYPE: T COG: R
2. We gain an idea of who we are from the way others define us.
  ANSWER: T TYPE: T COG: R
3. Recent studies confirm that people get just as much psychological relief from thinking privately about a negative experience as by talking about it.
  ANSWER: F TYPE: T COG: C
4. In scientific jargon, any interference with communication is termed "noise"
  ANSWER: T TYPE: T COG: R
5. Most people can learn to communicate more effectively.
  ANSWER: T TYPE: T COG: R
6. Recent studies have shown that interpersonal communication mediated by the computer can be just as deep and complex as personal contact.
  ANSWER: T TYPE: T COG: R
7. Communication is not something people do to one another, but a process in which they create a relationship by interacting with each other.
  ANSWER: T TYPE: T COG: R
8. According to the qualitative definition, all two-person interaction is interpersonal.
  ANSWER: F TYPE: T COG: R
9. In interpersonal contexts, the content dimension is more important that the relational dimension of a message.
  ANSWER: F TYPE: T COG: R
10. Most people operate at a level of communication effectiveness equal to their potential.
  ANSWER: F TYPE: T COG: R
11. Communication competence is defined as the ability to get what you are seeking from others in a manner that maintains the relationship on terms that are acceptable to both you and the other person.
  ANSWER: T TYPE: T COG: R

12. Communication competence is a trait that a person either possesses or lacks.

    ANSWER: F   TYPE: T   COG: R

13. Interpersonal/human relations skills have been identified as most important for career success.

    ANSWER: T   TYPE: T   COG: R

14. Cognitive complexity is the term describing the process of paying close attention to one's behavior.

    ANSWER: F   TYPE: T   COG: R

15. Self-monitoring is the ability to construct a variety of different frameworks for viewing an issue.

    ANSWER: F   TYPE: T   COG: R

16. Communication plays a role in satisfying the five human needs that Abraham Maslow calls basic to living a safe and fulfilled life.

    ANSWER: T   TYPE: T   COG: R

17. At the present time, there is no research to support the hypothesis that a connection exists between social interaction and physical health or longevity.

    ANSWER: F   TYPE: T   COG: R

18. According to the transactional model of communication, at any given point in time a person is sending a message *and* receiving a message.

    ANSWER: T   TYPE: T   COG: R

19. The qualitative view of communication is more *impersonal* than the quantitative view of communication.

    ANSWER: F   TYPE: T   COG: R

20. Communicators who adapt their talk to differing situations possess a characteristic of interpersonal effectiveness.

    ANSWER: T   TYPE: T   COG: R

21. From a qualitative perspective, a telephone operator and caller are probably not communicating interpersonally with each other.

    ANSWER: T   TYPE: T   COG: A

22. Feedback is the listener's verbal and/or nonverbal response to messages received from the speaker.

    ANSWER: T   TYPE: T   COG: R

23. The term "feedback" may be useful in everyday conversations, but it doesn't reflect the nature of communication as defined in your text.

    ANSWER: T   TYPE: T   COG: R

24. Communication as defined in the text is always intentional rather than unintentional.

    ANSWER: F   TYPE: T   COG: R

25. In some interpersonal contexts the relational dimension of the message may be more important than the content of the message.

    ANSWER: T   TYPE: T   COG: R

26. It is a misconception to assume that more communication will always make tense interpersonal situations better.

    ANSWER: T   TYPE: T   COG: R

27. Sometimes computer-mediated communication goes beyond normal patterns of interpersonal communication and becomes what researcher Joseph Walther calls "hyperpersonal."

    ANSWER: T   TYPE: T   COG: C

28. The effective communicator is going to both make a commitment to the other person and be concerned with profiting from the relationship.

    ANSWER: T   TYPE: T   COG: C

29. There is evidence that indicates communication is so important that it's necessary for physical health.

    ANSWER: T   TYPE: T   COG: R

30. The ability to ask yourself mentally how you're doing and to change your behavior if necessary is termed *self-monitoring*.

    ANSWER: T   TYPE: T   COG: R

31. Qualitatively, interpersonal communication is relatively infrequent, even in many close relationships.
    ANSWER: T   TYPE: T   COG: R
32. A chat conducted via e-mail or on the Internet is a good example of transactional communication.
    ANSWER: F   TYPE: T   COG: A
33. The concept of communication competence suggests there is no single "ideal" or "effective" way to communicate in every situation.
    ANSWER: T   TYPE: T   COG: R
34. Cognitive complexity and self-monitoring are both identified as factors that impede (reduce) communication competence.
    ANSWER: F   TYPE: T   COG: R
35. The transactional nature of communication suggests that communicators who are personally effective may not always be relationally successful.
    ANSWER: T   TYPE: T   COG: C
36. From a quantitative perspective, the terms "dyadic communication" and "interpersonal communication" are interchangeable.
    ANSWER: T   TYPE: T   COG: R
37. Personnel directors tend to recognize communication skills as more important than recommendations or grade point averages.
    ANSWER: T   TYPE: T   COG: R
38. Research suggests that communication competence is an inborn rather than a learned characteristic.
    ANSWER: F   TYPE: T   COG: R
39. Even positive qualities such as self-monitoring and cognitive complexity can be ineffective when carried to excess.
    ANSWER: T   TYPE: T   COG: C

Multiple Choice

40. Which of the following allows us to use the terms *dyadic communication* and *interpersonal communication* interchangeably?
    a. quantitative
    b. qualitative
    c. situational
    d. functional
    e. interactional
        ANSWER: a   TYPE: M   COG: R
41. Post WWII Americans attend _____ club meetings, family dinners and social gatherings with friends than pre WWII Americans.
    a. fewer
    b. more
    c. the same number of
    d. none of the above
        ANSWER: a   TYPE: M   COG: C
42. An example of psychological noise is
    a. cigarette smoke in a crowded room
    b. fatigue
    c. insecurity
    d. poor sound
    e. illness
        ANSWER: c   TYPE: M   COG: A

43. Which of the following is not a valid reason for studying communication?
    a. wanting to learn new ways of viewing something already familiar
    b. wanting to discover weakness in others
    c. understanding that it takes approximately 60 percent of our waking time
    d. desiring to be more successful in relationships
    e. increasing effectiveness through knowledge
        ANSWER: b   TYPE: M   COG: C

44. Abraham Maslow identified five basic types of human needs, which he termed "hierarchical," meaning
    a. the higher-level needs are always the most important
    b. the different needs hold differing degrees of importance
    c. lower-level needs must be largely satisfied before higher-level needs become important
    d. higher-level needs rely more on communication than lower-level needs
    e. none of the above applies
        ANSWER: c   TYPE: M   COG: R

45. A discernible response to a message is
    a. encoding
    b. channel
    c. feedback
    d. noise
    e. none of the above
        ANSWER: c   TYPE: M   COG: R

46. Your first encounter at a job interview is affected by the interviewer's scowling facial expression. Which characteristic of communication best describes the situation?
    a. Communication is dyadic
    b. Communication is a transactional process
    c. Communication is static
    d. Communication is dependent upon personalized rules
    e. None of the above describes it
        ANSWER: b   TYPE: M   COG: A

47. Because it's often impossible to distinguish sending and receiving, your text's communication model replaces these roles with the more accurate term:
    a. speaker
    b. listener
    c. communicator
    d. empathizer
    e. none of the above
        ANSWER: c   TYPE: M   COG: R

48. Which of the following characterizes transactional communication?
    a. Communication is continuous
    b. Communication involves communicators occupying different but overlapping environments
    c. We may be receiving and responding to messages from another person at the same time that she or he is receiving and responding to us
    d. Noise may be both physical and psychological
    e. All of the above characterize it
        ANSWER: e   TYPE: M   COG: R

49. The first communication models characterized communication as:
    a.   a ping-pong game
    b.   a one-way event
    c.   a transactional event
    d.   an ongoing process
    e.   none of the above
                ANSWER: b   TYPE: M   COG: R
50. The idea that it is often necessary to negotiate a shared meaning in order for satisfying
    communication to occur relates to which characteristic of the communication model?
    a.   sending and receiving are usually simultaneous
    b.   meanings exist in and among people
    c.   environment and noise affect communication
    d.   channels make a difference
    e.   none of the above
                ANSWER: b   TYPE: M   COG: R
51. That fact that college students who have been enrolled in debate classes tend to become more
    verbally aggressive than those who have not, is related to which communication concept?
    a.   external noise
    b.   channel
    c.   transactional
    d.   environment
    e.   none of the above
                ANSWER: d   TYPE: M   COG: C
52. Research conducted by Patrick O'Sullivan to learn about preferences for face-to-face versus
    mediated channels for sending messages concluded that
    a.   face-to-face is always better than mediated channels
    b.   negative messages should be sent face-to-face
    c.   positive messages should be sent using mediated channels
    d.   mediated channels are appealing for sending negative messages
    e.   channels people choose for sending messages don't contribute to communication competence
                ANSWER: d   TYPE: M   COG: R
53. Environments are also referred to as:
    a.   contexts
    b.   homes
    c.   relationships
    d.   cognitive complexity
    e.   self-monitoring
                ANSWER: a   TYPE: M   COG: R
54. Which of the following are outlined in your text as important characteristics of communication?
    a.   sending and receiving are usually simultaneous
    b.   meanings exist in and among people
    c.   environment and noise affect communication
    d.   channels make a difference
    e.   all of the above
                ANSWER: e   TYPE: M   COG: R

55. The text suggests a "qualitative" definition of an interpersonal relationship. Which of the following is *not* one of the criteria for that definition?
    a. context
    b. irreplaceability
    c. disclosure
    d. interdependence
    e. all are criteria
        ANSWER: a   TYPE: M   COG: R

56. Two friends, Terrell and Bart, have developed a way of dealing with each other when they are angry. The angry person puts a note on the refrigerator indicating the problem, and the other person writes on it a time when they can talk it over. This is an example of
    a. truncated communication
    b. uniqueness
    c. interpersonal communication
    d. face maintenance
    e. unintentional communication
        ANSWER: b   TYPE: M   COG: A

57. Which of the following is an accurate statement about communication?
    a. Much communication is unintentional
    b. With concentration we can control when and what we communicate
    c. Words have meanings independent of people's use of them
    d. More communication is always better
    e. Communication ability is natural
        ANSWER: a   TYPE: M   COG: R

58. The idea that "nothing" never happens refers to which communication principle?
    a. Communication is transactional
    b. Communication can be intentional or unintentional
    c. Communication has a content and relational dimension
    d. Communication is irreversible
    e. None of the above
        ANSWER: b   TYPE: M   COG: A

59. Sandra interprets her co-worker's comment "thanks a lot" as negative. This is an example of which communication principle?
    a. content dimension
    b. relational dimension
    c. noise
    d. communication is unintentional
    e. communication is irreversible
        ANSWER: b   TYPE: M   COG: A

60. The explicit, dictionary definition of a message is referred to as:
    a. content dimension
    b. relational dimension
    c. context dimension
    d. relative dimension
    e. none of the above
        ANSWER: a   TYPE: M   COG: R

61. Mike and Sue are happily married and always say, "I love you" before ending their telephone conversations. The fact that the words do not have the same emotional impact as the first time they were spoken is indicative of:
    a. communication is transactional
    b. communication is unrepeatable
    c. communication is unintentional
    d. communication is irreversible.
    e. none of the above
        ANSWER: b   TYPE: M   COG: A

62. Communication is more effective when the communicator
    a. is sending intentional messages only
    b. has little personal commitment in the message outcome
    c. takes responsibility for making the message clearly useful to the listener
    d. has less to gain, and, therefore, is willing to compromise
    e. concentrates more on the content than on the relational aspect of the message
        ANSWER: c   TYPE: M   COG: C

63. When a religious person listens to a speaker who uses profanity, he or she would probably experience
    a. external noise
    b. cognitive complexity
    c. relational noise
    d. physiological noise
    e. psychological noise
        ANSWER: e   TYPE: M   COG: A

64. Being unable to hear a speaker's remarks because you are sitting in the rear of an auditorium is an example of:
    a. external noise
    b. psychological noise
    c. physiological noise
    d. static
    e. none of the above
        ANSWER: a   TYPE: M   COG: A

65. An example of physiological noise is:
    a. anger
    b. poor sound
    c. insecurity
    d. fatigue
    e. none of the above
        ANSWER: d   TYPE: M   COG: R

66. A typewritten love letter not having the same impact as a handwritten one is related to the _____ of the message.
    a. channel
    b. context
    c. noise
    d. environment
    e. none of the above
        ANSWER: a   TYPE: M   COG: A

67. The dynamic process that participants create through their interaction with one another is termed:
    a. environment
    b. noise
    c. transactional
    d. context
    e. none of the above
    ANSWER: c   TYPE: M   COG: R

68. Which of the following is not true about communication competence?
    a. There is no single "ideal" or "effective" way to communicate
    b. Competence is situational
    c. Competence can be learned
    d. Competence involves a large repertoire of skills
    e. None of the above
    ANSWER: e   TYPE: M   COG: C

69. Which of the following means the same thing as, "Communication is irreversible?"
    a. Erasing or replacing spoken words or acts is not possible
    b. No amount of explanation can erase the impression you have created
    c. It's impossible to "unreceive" a message
    d. Words said are irretrievable
    e. All mean the same as the statement
    ANSWER: e   TYPE: M   COG: C

70. Effective communication includes the dimension(s) of
    a. commitment to the other person
    b. commitment to the relationship
    c. concern about the message being received
    d. a desire to make the relationship useful
    e. all of the above
    ANSWER: e   TYPE: M   COG: R

71. According to researcher Mark Redmond, which kind of message is communicatively competent by definition?
    a. an assertive message
    b. an empathic message
    c. a feedback message
    d. a linear message
    e. all of the above
    ANSWER: b   TYPE: M   COG: R

72. Which characteristic applies to interpersonal communication?
    a. intentional or unintentional
    b. impossible not to communicate
    c. irreversible
    d. unrepeatable
    e. all of the above
    ANSWER: e   TYPE: M   COG: R

73. Which is true of communication?
    a. Everyone does it
    b. More is always better
    c. It can solve all problems
    d. It is a natural ability
    e. All of the above are true
    ANSWER: a   TYPE: M   COG: R

74. Which of the following is a reason to study communication?
    a. It gives you a new look at a familiar topic
    b. We spend a staggering amount of time communicating
    c. None of us communicates as effectively as we could
    d. All of the above are reasons
    e. Only a and b are reasons
             ANSWER: d   TYPE: M   COG: R
75. We need to communicate because of which needs?
    a. physical
    b. ego
    c. social
    d. all of the above
    e. b and c only
             ANSWER: d   TYPE: M   COG: R
76. Which of the following are social needs met by communication?
    a. inclusion
    b. control
    c. affection
    d. all of the above
    e. a and c only
             ANSWER: d   TYPE: M   COG: R
77. Communication is defined as
    a. continuous and transactional
    b. having overlapped environments
    c. simultaneously sending and receiving messages
    d. distorted by physical and psychological noise
    e. all of the above
             ANSWER: e   TYPE: M   COG: R
78. Interpersonal relationships are distinguished from impersonal ones by
    a. a minimum of stereotyping
    b. development of unique rules
    c. increased self-confidence
    d. all of the above
    e. a and c only
             ANSWER: d   TYPE: M   COG: R
79. When compared to face-to-face interactions, communication via computer is
    a. less personal
    b. more personal
    c. either less or more personal depending on the individuals involved
    d. the medium has no bearing on how personal the interaction is
    e. none of the above
             ANSWER: c   TYPE: M   COG: R
80. A study conducted by Patrick O'Sullivan revealed that undergraduates would prefer to use e-mail to send which type of message?
    a. confess
    b. boast
    c. accuse
    d. praise
    e. none of the above
             ANSWER: a   TYPE: M   COG: R

81. Sarah and Kim are driving to a friend's house. She is about to suggest a different route when she stops herself because she knows Jim hates it when she "takes over" while he's driving. This is an example of which communication concept?
    a. self-monitoring
    b. cognitive complexity
    c. communication is unrepeatable
    d. content messages
    e. none of the above
        ANSWER: a   TYPE: M   COG: A

Essay

82. Has there ever been a time when a communication problem "made you (or someone you know) sick?" Why do you think this happened? What is the implication of this? If you have never experienced this, use an example form a TV show, movie, or book, or present a fictionalized account. In your response, briefly describe the situation and then explain it using the terms and theories presented in Chapter One.
        ANSWER: TYPE: E   COG: A

83. Virginia Satir uses the metaphor of an umbrella to explain communication. Select a different metaphor and describe how it can be used to explain the concept of communication.
        ANSWER: TYPE: E   .COG: C

84. List and give an example of the three types of noise that can disrupt communication.
        ANSWER: TYPE: E   COG: R, A

85. Your book claims that the transactional communication model is more like a motion picture than a book. Explain why this is true. Can you think of another pair of words to fit the sentence: "The transactional communication model is more like a _____ than a _____?"
        ANSWER: TYPE: E   COG: A

86. Discuss the content and relational dimensions of the statement, "I'm glad you're here." How might your interpretation differ if the two individuals were siblings? Lovers? Working partners? Enemies?
        ANSWER: TYPE: E   COG: A

87. The communication model depicted in the text suggests three reasons receivers may not hear a message as the speaker intended. They are: differing environments, psychological noise, and physical noise. Choose one of those terms, define it, and give a specific example of how it can inhibit effective communication.
        ANSWER: TYPE: E   COG: A

88. Discuss how the quality of parent-child interaction is a transactional process.
        ANSWER: TYPE: E   COG: A

89. Discuss the idea that communication can be intentional or unintentional.
        ANSWER: TYPE: E   COG: C

90. Explain how social rituals we engage in reflect the idea that not all communication seeks understanding.
        ANSWER: TYPE: E   COG: C

91. Below are three important characteristics of the definition of communication:
    a. Communication is a transactive process
    b. Communication is irreversible
    c. Communicators are simultaneously senders and receivers

Choose one of these characteristics, explain it, and then illustrate it with an example from your experience.
        ANSWER: TYPE: E   COG: A

92. Consider a recent student-teacher interaction that you experienced or observed, and provide examples for each of the following elements of a communication model:
    a. student's personal environment
    b. teacher's personal environment
    c. channels
    d. physical noise
    e. psychological noise
        ANSWER: TYPE: E   COG: A
93. When compared with face-to-face interaction, communication via computer is both less personal and more personal. Explain how this is possible.
        ANSWER: TYPE: E   COG: A
94. Discuss one of the reasons critics argue that CMC is inferior to face to face interaction?
        ANSWER: TYPE: E   COG: C
95. List and explain three of the seven characteristics of communication competence.
        ANSWER: TYPE: E   COG: R
96. According to the qualitative definition of communication, it is neither possible or desirable to communicate interpersonally all the time. Consider the following relationships:
    a. A newly married couple
    b. A couple celebrating 25 years of marriage
    c. Siblings
    d. Friends
    e. Student/teacher
How do you think their communication is reflected on the interpersonal/impersonal continuum?
        ANSWER: TYPE: E   COG: A
97. Discuss the difference between effective communication and appropriate communication as they relate to communication competence.
        ANSWER: TYPE: E   COG: A
98. Define the difference between cognitive complexity and self-monitoring.
        ANSWER: TYPE: E   COG: C
99. Discuss one of the reasons your text cites for why CMC can increase both the quantity and quality of interpersonal communication?
        ANSWER: TYPE: E   COG: C

Matching

100. Match the social needs on the right with the statements illustrating them on the left

        _____ 1. "to put off doing something I should be doing"   a. pleasure
        _____ 2. "because it allows me to unwind"   b. affection
        _____ 3. "because it makes me less lonely"   c. inclusion
        _____ 4. "because I want to do something for me"   d. escape
        _____ 5. "because it's fun"   e. relaxation
        _____ 6. "because it helps others"   f. control
        ANSWER: d,e,c,f,a,b   TYPE: K   COG: R

CHAPTER TWO: COMMUNICATION AND THE SELF

True/False

1. Research suggests that children tend to focus on classmates' traits and characteristics that differ from the norm.
   ANSWER: T   TYPE: T   COG: C

2. Self-concept is a relatively *stable* set of perceptions you hold of yourself.
   ANSWER: T   TYPE: T   COG: R

3. At about six or seven months of age, a child begins to recognize "self" as distinct from surroundings.
   ANSWER: T   TYPE: T   COG: C

4. At the stage of infancy, self-concept is almost exclusively physical.
   ANSWER: T   TYPE: T   COG: C

5. In reflected appraisal, messages received from significant others are particularly powerful.
   ANSWER: T   TYPE: T   COG: C

6. Nonverbal statements play a minor role in shaping children's feelings about being "OK" or "not OK"
   ANSWER: F   TYPE: T   COG: R

7. Self-esteem has a powerful effect on communication behavior.
   ANSWER: T   TYPE: T   COG: C

8. Late in life, the looking glass of the self-concept may become so distorted that it shapes the input of others to conform to our existing beliefs.
   ANSWER: T   TYPE: T   COG: C

9. The significance we attach to the features of the self is unrelated to the opinions of others.
   ANSWER: F   TYPE: T   COG: C

10. We create our environment as well as respond to it.
    ANSWER: T   TYPE: T   COG: C

11. People seldom look at others as a way of judging themselves.
    ANSWER: F   TYPE: T   COG: C

12. Social comparison offers a way of reshaping unsatisfying self-concepts in that we control who is available for comparison.
    ANSWER: T   TYPE: T   COG: R

13. The principle of distinctiveness illustrates the power of social comparison to shape identity.
    ANSWER: T   TYPE: T   COG: R

14. The way we view ourselves is usually identical with others' perception of us.
    ANSWER: F   TYPE: T   COG: C

15. The tendency to resist revision of our self-perception is strong.
    ANSWER: T   TYPE: T   COG: R

16. Research shows that people are more critical of themselves when they are in a positive mood than when they are in a negative mood.
    ANSWER: F   TYPE: T   COG: C

17. Our beliefs are so important to us that we will do anything to keep them intact.
    ANSWER: T   TYPE: T   COG: C

18. The tendency to seek information that conforms to an existing self-concept has been labeled cognitive conservatism.
    ANSWER: T   TYPE: T   COG: R

19. Unfortunately, self-concepts are fixed and not subject to change.
    ANSWER: F   TYPE: T   COG: C

20. The self-concept can actually affect the future behavior of others.
    ANSWER: T   TYPE: T   COG: C

21. The reference groups against which we compare ourselves play an important role in shaping our view of ourselves.
    ANSWER: T   TYPE: T   COG: R
22. Self-concept can be defined as the image you hold of yourself.
    ANSWER: T   TYPE: T   COG: R
23. Research shows that people with low self-esteem are inclined to seek out people who view them favorably.
    ANSWER: F   TYPE: T   COG: C
24. Communicators who believe they are incompetent are more likely than others to pursue rewarding relationships.
    ANSWER: F   TYPE: T   COG: C
25. Specific, influential individuals are the single source of self-concept information.
    ANSWER: F   TYPE: T   COG: C
26. While children may be born with some social characteristics, self-concept is almost totally determined by social interaction.
    ANSWER: T   TYPE: T   COG: R
27. Few "other people" have a greater influence on an adult's self-concept than romantic partners.
    ANSWER: T   TYPE: T   COG: C
28. One reason for negative evaluation of self is that our culture subscribes to the myth of perfection.
    ANSWER: T   TYPE: T   COG: C
29. People often cling to outmoded and unrealistic self-concepts even when the new image would be more favorable than the old one.
    ANSWER: T   TYPE: T   COG: C
30. Our society tends to see self put-downs as "modesty" and self-endorsements as "bragging."
    ANSWER: T   TYPE: T   COG: C
31. People with positive self-esteem are likely to think well of others, while those with negative self-esteem tend to think poorly of others.
    ANSWER: T   TYPE: T   COG: R
32. Self-fulfilling prophecies occur when strong expectations of an even make the expected outcome more likely than it otherwise would have been.
    ANSWER: T   TYPE: T   COG: R
33. Research has shown that communicators who consider themselves to be incompetent are less likely to have strong relationships and more likely to sabotage their own relationships than individuals who consider themselves competent communicators.
    ANSWER: T   TYPE: T   COG: R
34. Self-concept is almost totally a product of social interaction.
    ANSWER: T   TYPE: T   COG: R
35. To connect the concept of self-fulfilling prophecy with "the power of positive thinking" is an oversimplification.
    ANSWER: T   TYPE: T   COG: R
36. Once the self is firmly rooted, only a powerful force can change it.
    ANSWER: T   TYPE: T   COG: R
37. Self-concept must change in order to stay realistic.
    ANSWER: T   TYPE: T   COG: R
38. For most people, their physical appearance is the most important component of their self-concept.
    ANSWER: F   TYPE: T   COG: R
39. A significant other is someone who has given us primarily positive reinforcement.
    ANSWER: F   TYPE: T   COG: R
40. The term "face" is used by social scientists to describe the presenting self.
    ANSWER: T   TYPE: T   COG: R

41. Fluctuations in self-concept are especially possible during adolescence and young adulthood (the ages from 14 to 23).

        ANSWER: T   TYPE: T   COG: R

42. Each of us possesses several selves, not merely one self.

        ANSWER: T   TYPE: T   COG: R

43. Facework refers to the degree to which people act to maintain their own presenting image.

        ANSWER: T   TYPE: T   COG: R

44. Cognitive conservatism is the tendency to seek information that fits our self-concept.

        ANSWER: T   TYPE: T   COG: R

45. People are likely to reveal all of their perceived self to others.

        ANSWER: F   TYPE: T   COG: R

46. People rarely manage impressions to accomplish personal goals.

        ANSWER: F   TYPE: T   COG: C

47. The decision to be spontaneous can be a form of impression management.

        ANSWER: T   TYPE: T   COG: R

48. Low self-monitors express their thoughts and feelings without paying much attention to the impression they are creating.

        ANSWER: T   TYPE: T   COG: R

49. The text clearly indicates that high self-monitoring is better than low self-monitoring.

        ANSWER: F   TYPE: T   COG: C

50. "Face Management" is something that is only necessary in actual face-to-face encounters.

        ANSWER: F   TYPE: T   COG: R

51. Identity management is not as pervasive in computer-mediated communication as it is in face-to-face interaction.

        ANSWER: F   TYPE: T   COG: C

52. Daniel Brouwer's research indicates that people who are HIV positive advertise their health status through tattoos to present a negative self image.

        ANSWER: F   TYPE: T   COG: R

Multiple choice

53. The view that self-concept can be seen as a product of the messages you've received throughout your life is known as
   a.   reflected appraisal
   b.   social comparison
   c.   multidimensional self
   d.   subjective self-concept
   e.   self-fulfilling prophecy

        ANSWER: a   TYPE: M   COG: R

54. Which of the following is supported by research related to how the self-concept develops?
   a.   Self-concept does not exist at birth
   b.   Self-concept is almost totally a product of social interaction
   c.   Children recognize "self" as distinct from surroundings at about age six or seven months
   d.   All of the above are supported
   e.   None of the above are supported

        ANSWER: d   TYPE: M   COG: R

55. For a reflected appraisal to be regarded as important it must be
    a.   from a competent source
    b.   perceived as highly personal
    c.   reasonable in light of what we believe about ourselves
    d.   consistent and repeated
    e.   all of the above
         ANSWER: e   TYPE: M   COG: C

56. You can use a social comparison to fool yourself by
    a.   arguing that those who don't approve of you have worthless opinions
    b.   setting up standards that only you and a few others meet
    c.   offering a way of reshaping an unsatisfying self-concept
    d.   all of the above
    e.   a and b only
         ANSWER: e   TYPE: M   COG: C

57. Which of the following is *not* a characteristic of self-concept?
    a.   denotative
    b.   multidimensional
    c.   subjective
    d.   flexible
    e.   resists change
         ANSWER: a   TYPE: M   COG: R

58. The communication strategies people use to influence how others view them is called
    a.   cognitive conservatism
    b.   impression management
    c.   reflected appraisal
    d.   self-concept
    e.   social comparison
         ANSWER: b   TYPE: M   COG: R

59. Compared to low self-monitors, people who are high self-monitors
    a.   have a more simple, focused idea of who they are
    b.   can easily identify their true feelings
    c.   are typified by the phrase "What you see is what you get"
    d.   are good "people readers"
    e.   have a narrow repertoire of behaviors
         ANSWER: d   TYPE: M   COG: C

60. Which of the following is *not* true about persons with positive self esteem?
    a.   They work harder for undemanding, less critical people
    b.   They are inclined to feel comfortable with others they view as superior
    c.   They are able to defend themselves against negative comments of others
    d.   They expect to be accepted by others
    e.   They are likely to think well of others
         ANSWER: a   TYPE: M   COG: R

61. When some professional athletes doggedly insist they can be of value to the team when past their prime, they are displaying which characteristic of self-concept?
    a.   multidimensional
    b.   subjective
    c.   flexible
    d.   resists change
    e.   none of the above
         ANSWER: d   TYPE: M   COG: A

62. Rosenthal and Jacobson's report that a change in teachers' expectations of randomly selected "special" children led to an actual change in their intellectual performance most nearly illustrates
    a. changing self-concept
    b. characteristics of self-concept
    c. self-fulfilling prophecy
    d. social comparison
    e. psychological vultures
    ANSWER: c   TYPE: M   COG: A

63. If you ever gave a speech and forgot your remarks, not because you were unprepared by because you were afraid, saying "I know I'll blow it," you experienced
    a. changing self-concept
    b. characteristics of self-concept
    c. self-fulfilling prophecy
    d. social comparison
    e. feedback
    ANSWER: c   TYPE: M   COG: A

64. You can change your self-concept by having
    a. realistic expectations
    b. a realistic perception of yourself
    c. the will to change
    d. the skill to change
    e. all of the above
    ANSWER: e   TYPE: M   COG: R

65. The communication strategies people use to influence how others view them is called
    a. public self strategies
    b. social comparison strategies
    c. reflected appraisal strategies
    d. identity management strategies
    e. perceived self strategies
    ANSWER: d   TYPE: M   COG: R

66. Children with cruel "friends" suffer from
    a. bragging
    b. inaccurate feedback of others
    c. perfection
    d. multidimensional self-concept
    e. subjective self-concept
    ANSWER: b   TYPE: M   COG: C

67. Even though others disagree, Diandra thinks of herself as a tremendously effective communicator. She enforces this image by surrounding herself with people who are very shy and socially naïve. Diandra's unrealistic handling of this situation provides an example of
    a. the theory of significant others
    b. social comparison theory
    c. self-discipline theory
    d. similarity theory
    e. consistency appraisal theory
    ANSWER: b   TYPE: M   COG: A

68. Which of the following is (are) *not* characteristics of identity management?
    a.   We strive to construct multiple identities
    b.   Identity management is collaborative
    c.   Identity management can be unconscious
    d.   People are equally aware of their identity management behaviors
    e.   Both c and d
            ANSWER: d   TYPE: M   COG: A
69. People manage impressions to
    a.   follow social rules
    b.   make others feel comfortable
    c.   accomplish personal goals
    d.   All of the above are correct
    e.   Only a and c are correct
            ANSWER: d   TYPE: M   COG: C
70. Which of the following has the power to be a self-fulfilling prophecy?
    a.   astrological horoscopes
    b.   placebos
    c.   sex-linked stereotypes
    d.   labels of shyness
    e.   all of the above
            ANSWER: e   TYPE: M   COG: A
71. Which of the following is used in face-to-face interactions to manage impressions?
    a.   physical appearance
    b.   words and verbal action
    c.   personal items
    d.   physical setting
    e.   all of the above
            ANSWER: e   TYPE: M   COG: R
72. Two concepts that describe how interaction shapes the way individuals view themselves are
    a.   comparison appraisal and social reflection
    b.   reflected appraisal and social comparison
    c.   social reflection and intrapersonal comparison
    d.   self-esteem and self-concept
    e.   reflected comparison and social appraisal
            ANSWER: b   TYPE: M   COG: R
73. Significant others are those people
    a.   whose evaluations are especially influential to us
    b.   who were a negative force in our lives
    c.   whom we view as highly competent
    d.   with whom we spend a great deal of time
    e.   c and d
            ANSWER: a   TYPE: M   COG: R
74. Social comparison allows us to decide
    a.   if we are superior or inferior to others
    b.   if we are the same or different from others
    c.   if we like or dislike others
    d.   all of the above
    e.   a and b only
            ANSWER: e   TYPE: M   COG: R

75. Seeking information that conforms to an existing self-concept is called
    a.   presenting self
    b.   reflected appraisal
    c.   cognitive conservation
    d.   self-fulfilling prophecy
    e.   social comparison
          ANSWER: c   TYPE: M   COG: R

76. Which of the following is *not* true about identity management in computer-mediated communication (CMC)?
    a.   Identity management is just as pervasive in CMC interactions
    b.   CMC is preferred when self-preservation is threatened
    c.   CMC is not as effective for identity management as face-to-face communication
    d.   CMC can actually be an advantage for communicators who want to manage the impressions they make
    e.   CMC allows communicators to choose the desired level of clarity
          ANSWER: c   TYPE: M   COG: R

77. The "Michelangelo phenomenon" describes
    a.   How individuals resist negative feedback about themselves.
    b.   How we strive to construct multiple identities.
    c.   How we manage impressions.
    d.   How significant others sculpt one another's self-concept.
    e.   How the self concept fulfills its own prophecy.
          ANSWER: d   TYPE: M   COG: R

78. Even though he has a nice singing voice, Kevin still believes he is a terrible singer because his first grade teacher told him he couldn't sing well. This is an example of how _____ shapes our self concept.
    a.   Reference Groups
    b.   Reflected Appraisal
    c.   Self Esteem
    d.   Dyadic Communication
    e.   None of the above
          ANSWER: b   TYPE: M   COG: A

79. Joe thinks he is smart compared to everyone else in his algebra class. This is an example of how _____ define(s) our self concept.
    a.   Self Monitoring
    b.   Facework
    c.   Identity Management
    d.   Cognitive Conservatism
    e.   Reference Groups
          ANSWER: e   TYPE:M   COG: A

80. Still thinking you are a good student even after failing classes for two years is an example of which reason for having a self concept others would regard as unrealistically favorable?
    a.   Low self-esteem
    b.   Distorted feedback
    c.   Obsolete information
    d.   A and C
    e.   None of the above
          ANSWER: c   TYPE: M   COG: A

81. The fact that being ignored by an acquaintance hurts more than being ignored by someone familiar to us tells us that
    a.   People are poor judges of their own communication skills.
    b.   The self concept is objective.
    c.   Family plays a strong role in shaping our identity.
    d.   Who counts as a significant other isn't always obvious to us.
    e.   None of the above.
          ANSWER: d   TYPE: M   COG: C
82. When studying the relationship between individual's self evaluation as communicators and their ability to perform those communication skills, researchers found that
    a.   Subjects accurately evaluated their performance.
    b.   Subjects inaccurately judged their own abilities.
    c.   Subjects predictions were inaccurately negative when they were in a good mood.
    d.   Subjects succumbed to a self-fulfilling prophecy.
    e.   None of the above
          ANSWER: b   TYPE: M   COG: R
83. The Myth of Perfection describes
    a.   How self esteem is affected by societal models that are unrealistically perfect.
    b.   How our self concept is formed based on distorted feedback.
    c.   How social comparison theory isn't perfect in nature.
    d.   How we used identity management to appear more perfect than we are.
    e.   How no one comes from a perfect family.
          ANSWER: a   TYPE: M   COG: R
84. Seeing yourself as being "patient at work, but not patient at home" demonstrates how
    a.   Cognitive conservatism works.
    b.   The self concept does not resist change.
    c.   The self concept is flexible.
    d.   The self concept is objective.
    e.   All of the above.
          ANSWER: c   TYPE: M   COG: A
85. The person you believe yourself to be in moments of honest examination is your
    a.   intuitive self
    b.   perceived self
    c.   public self
    d.   presenting self
    e.   both c and d
          ANSWER: b   TYPE: M   COG: R
86. The term used to describe the verbal and nonverbal ways we act to maintain our own and others presenting images is called
    a.   facework
    b.   multiple identity construction.
    c.   self presentation.
    d.   identity performance.
    e.   self esteem maintenance
          ANSWER: a   TYPE: M   COG: R

87. When we used items such as cars to influence how others see us, we are managing impressions by using
   a. setting
   b. manner
   c. appearance
   d. attitude
   e. B & C
   ANSWER: a   TYPE:M   COG: C

88. Since studies show that Chinese, Germans, Japanese and Americans all manage identities differently in conflicts, we can deduce that facework is influenced by
   a. conflict
   b. self Esteem
   c. culture
   d. social comparison
   e. impression management
   ANSWER: c   TYPE: M   COG: C

Essay

89. Discuss the meaning and significance of the following line from Dorothy Nolte's *Children Learn What They Live:* "If a child lives with encouragement he learns confidence."
   ANSWER: TYPE: E   COG: C

90. Explain the subjective, resistant nature of the self-concept.
   ANSWER: TYPE: E   COG: C

91. List three aspects of your self-concept. Then list a reference group you would use for each of the three
   ANSWER: TYPE: E   COG: C

92. How is it possible to change one's self-concept?
   ANSWER: TYPE: E   COG: A

93. Discuss the relationship between these terms: perceived self, presenting self, impression management, honesty, and communication competence. Offer an example that illustrates the relationship in action.
   ANSWER: TYPE: E   COG: C

94. What is the nature and extent of identity management?
   ANSWER: TYPE: E   COG: A

95. Explain how messages shape the self-concept by comparing and contrasting reflected appraisal and social comparison.
   ANSWER: TYPE: E   COG: A

96. Describe two specific strategies that can be used to improve your self image.
   ANSWER: TYPE: E   COG: A

97. Discuss the three primary characteristics of the self-concept.
   ANSWER: TYPE: E   COG: R

98. What are the four requirements that must be met for an appraisal to be regarded as important?
   ANSWER: TYPE: E   COG: R

99. What are the primary influences that shape development of the self-concept?
   ANSWER: TYPE: E   COG: R

100. Compare and contrast identity management in face-to-face interaction with identity management in computer-mediated communication. Under which circumstances would you use one over the other?
   ANSWER: TYPE: E   COG: A

CHAPTER THREE PERCEIVING OTHERS

True/False

1. Research suggests that typical dyads can only interpret and explain 25 to 50 percent of each other's behavior accurately.
    ANSWER: T   TYPE: T   COG: R
2. Motives determine how we perceive people.
    ANSWER: T   TYPE: T   COG: R
3. Excessive stereotyping can be overcome by decategorizing others.
    ANSWER: T   TYPE: T   COG: R
4. *Interpretation* is a term used by communication theorists to describe the determination of causes and effects in a series of interactions.
    ANSWER: F   TYPE: T   COG: R
5. The way a communication sequence is punctuated affects its perceived meaning.
    ANSWER: T   TYPE: T   COG: R
6. Age, health, fatigue, and hunger are all psychological factors that influence perceptual judgments.
    ANSWER: F   TYPE: T   COG: R
7. Within a single, national culture, regional and ethnic differences can create very different realities.
    ANSWER: T   TYPE: T   COG: R
8. Sandra Bem's sex type research suggests that stereotypical masculine and feminine behaviors are opposite poles of a single continuum.
    ANSWER: F   TYPE: T   COG: C
9. There's nothing wrong with generalizations as long as they are accurate; in fact, it would be impossible to get through life without them.
    ANSWER: T   TYPE: T   COG: R
10. Narratives generally evolve with conscious strategies by the participants.
    ANSWER: F   TYPE: T   COG: R
11. People commonly imagine that others possess the same attitudes and motives that they do.
    ANSWER: T   TYPE: T   COG: C
12. Pearson's research on long-term happy marriages asserts that one key to a happy marriage is to tell yourself and others that you have one and then to behave as though you do.
    ANSWER: T   TYPE: T   COG: C
13. *Attribution* is the term social scientists use to describe the process of attaching meaning to behavior.
    ANSWER: T   TYPE: T   COG: R
14. When others suffer, we often blame the problem on their personal qualities; when we're the victims, we find explanations outside ourselves.
    ANSWER: T   TYPE: T   COG: R
15. *Empathy* is derived from two Greek words meaning "feeling with." *Sympathy* has Greek roots that mean "feeling inside."
    ANSWER: T   TYPE: T   COG: R
16. Empathy is the ability to recreate another person's perspective, to experience the world from her or his point of view.
    ANSWER: T   TYPE: T   COG: R
17. Self-serving bias is the term used by social scientists to label our tendency to judge ourselves in the most generous terms possible.
    ANSWER: T   TYPE: T   COG: R
18. There is a high correlation between perceived empathy and the level of intimacy in a relationship.
    ANSWER: T   TYPE: T   COG: R

19. When people are aware of both the positive and negative characteristics of another, they tend to be more influenced by the undesirable traits.

    ANSWER: T   TYPE: T   COG: R

20. Being open-minded is difficult because people confuse understanding another's position with accepting it.

    ANSWER: T   TYPE: T   COG: R

21. Perception checking is a tool to help us understand others accurately instead of assuming that our first interpretation is correct.

    ANSWER: T   TYPE: T   COG: R

22. Sex roles arise more from environmental influences than from physiological factors.

    ANSWER: T   TYPE: T   COG: C

23. Androgynous behaviors are solely the product of biological sexual differences.

    ANSWER: F   TYPE: T   COG: R

24. Empathy leads to increased self-esteem.

    ANSWER: T   TYPE: T   COG: R

25. Empathy can lead to greater tolerance and understanding.

    ANSWER: T   TYPE: T   COG: R

26. We cannot avoid making initial judgments, and we usually cling to these first impressions even if they are wrong.

    ANSWER: T   TYPE: T   COG: R

27. There is a lack of research to substantiate a link between empathy and ethics.

    ANSWER: F   TYPE: T   COG: C

28. Research shows us that it's hardest to empathize with people who are radically different from us.

    ANSWER: T   TYPE: T   COG: R

29. Interpretation plays a role in virtually every interpersonal act.

    ANSWER: T   TYPE: T   COG: R

30. Our emotional state has little relevance to how we view people and events.

    ANSWER: F   TYPE: T   COG: R

31. Problems arise with first impressions when the labels we attach are inaccurate and we tend to hang on to them.

    ANSWER: T   TYPE: T   COG: R

32. According to the textbook, imagination is a requirement for empathy.

    ANSWER: T   TYPE: T   COG: R

33. As a result of empathy, the gap between you and the other person is likely to grow.

    ANSWER: F   TYPE: T   COG: R

34. Each of us experiences the world in a unique way.

    ANSWER: T   TYPE: T   COG: R

35. Motives seldom influence how we perceive others.

    ANSWER: F   TYPE: T   COG: R

36. Your text recommends "decategorizing" as an antidote to stereotyping.

    ANSWER: T   TYPE: T   COG: R

37. Perceptual schema are tendencies to misinterpret data.

    ANSWER: F   TYPE: T   COG: R

38. When a relationship is happy it is less likely that your partner will have a negative interpretation of your behavior.

    ANSWER: T   TYPE: T   COG: R

39. Your mood can affect how you perceive an event.

    ANSWER: T   TYPE: T   COG: R

40. Climate has been shown to be a remarkably accurate predictor of communication behaviors.

    ANSWER: T   TYPE: T   COG: R

41. Emotional contagion is the ability to take on another's viewpoint.
        ANSWER: F   TYPE: T   COG: R
42. Empathy may have a biological basis.
        ANSWER: T   TYPE: T   COG: R
43. Empathy requires open-mindedness, imagination, and commitment.
        ANSWER: T   TYPE: T   COG: R
44. Gender is one of the most fundamental schema people use to organize their perceptions.
        ANSWER: T   TYPE: T   COG: R
45. When an instructor sees a group of students on the first day of class as motivated and interested in learning, (s)he is generalizing.
        ANSWER: T   TYPE: T   COG: A
46. Believing that all women are emotional or that all blondes are airheads is stereotyping.
        ANSWER: T   TYPE: T   COG: A
47. Research has shown that there is no correlation between the degree of empathy an individual exhibits and his/her tendency to commit violent crimes.
        ANSWER: F   TYPE: T   COG: R
48. Research cited in this text showed that perceptions of pictures were not significantly influenced by the mood of the perceivers.
        ANSWER: F   TYPE: T   COG: R
49. A study showed that males and females have similar interpretations for resistance messages sent by females.
        ANSWER: F   TYPE: T   COG: R

Multiple Choice

50. We attach meaning to our experiences using which of the following?
    a. physiology, culture, society
    b. selection, organization, interpretation and negotiation
    c. social roles, self-concept and perception
    d. empathy, sympathy and interpretation
    e. all of the above
        ANSWER: b   TYPE: M   COG: R
51. Which step of perception is based on the fact that we notice some messages and ignore others?
    a. selection
    b. organization
    c. interpretation
    d. negotiation
    e. none of the above
        ANSWER: a   TYPE: M   COG: R
52. We notice extremely short or tall people because of which factor of attention?
    a. motives
    b. change
    c. repetition
    d. organization
    e. intensity
        ANSWER: e   TYPE: M   COG: C

53. We notice a dripping faucet because of which factor of attention?
    a. motives
    b. contrast or change
    c. repetition
    d. intensity
    e. emotional state
        ANSWER: c   TYPE: M   COG: C
54. We take wonderful people for granted because of what factor of attention?
    a. motives
    b. contrast or change
    c. repetition
    d. intensity
    e. organization
        ANSWER: b   TYPE: M   COG: R
55. A hungry person sees restaurants everywhere because of which factor of attention?
    a. motives
    b. contrast or change
    c. repetition
    d. intensity
    e. organization
        ANSWER: a   TYPE: M   COG: R
56. Perceptual schema include which constructs?
    a. physical and role
    b. interaction
    c. psychological
    d. all of the above
    e. none of the above
        ANSWER: d   TYPE: M   COG: R
57. A form of organization used to identify causes and effects in interaction is called
    a. grammar
    b. syntax
    c. punctuation
    d. spelling
    e. capitalization
        ANSWER: c   TYPE: M   COG: R
58. Which step of perception is involved when you wonder if the person who smiles at you across the room is interested in romance or just being polite?
    a. selection
    b. organization
    c. interpretation
    d. negotiation
    e. none of the above
        ANSWER: c   TYPE: M   COG: A
59. Exaggerated beliefs associated with a categorizing system are known as
    a. empathy
    b. perspective taking
    c. stereotyping
    d. salience
    e. punctuation
        ANSWER: c   TYPE: M   COG: R

60. The process by which individuals influence each others perceptions through communication is known as _____.
    a. Selection
    b. Organization
    c. Interpretation
    d. Punctuation
    e. Negotiation
        ANSWER: e   TYPE: M   COG: R

61. Kim thinks her roommate Julie's constant cleaning is obsessive, and Julie thinks that Kim is a slob. Kim and Julie are experiencing a clash of _____.
    a. Role constructs
    b. Narratives
    c. Punctuation
    d. All of the above
    e. None of the above
        ANSWER: b   TYPE: M   COG: A

62. Cooper's research regarding male and female perceptions of *Thelma and Louise* reported all of the following *except*...
    a. male students saw the movie as a statement about sexism
    b. female students saw the movie as about women's marginalized status in society
    c. males saw the movie as an unfair exercise in male bashing
    d. both males and females perceive events and one another through the lenses of social roles and personal experiences
    e. the film's conclusion was perceived differently depending on the sex of the viewer.
        ANSWER: a   TYPE: M   COG: C

63. Which of the following sex types was *not* hypothesized by Sandra Bem?
    a. masculine
    b. male-female dichotomy
    c. feminine
    d. androgynous
    e. undifferentiated
        ANSWER: b   TYPE: M   COG: R

64. Which sex type is characterized by competitive interaction, seeing relationships as opportunities to win something?
    a. masculine
    b. male-female dichotomy
    c. feminine
    d. androgynous
    e. undifferentiated
        ANSWER: a   TYPE: M   COG: R

65. Which sex type differs little in perceptions of interpersonal relationships?
    a. masculine
    b. male-female dichotomy
    c. feminine
    d. androgynous
    e. undifferentiated
        ANSWER: d   TYPE: M   COG: C

66. Stanford psychologist Philip Zimbardo's experiment with young men, assigning some as prisoners and some as guards, was a dramatic example of the significance of which role in perception?
    a. sexual
    b. occupational
    c. mood
    d. self-concept
    e. cultural
        ANSWER: b   TYPE: M   COG: C

67. Tendencies that distort perceptions include
    a. being influenced by the obvious
    b. clinging to first impressions and assuming others are like us
    c. favoring negative impressions and blaming innocent victims
    d. being influenced by our expectations
    e. all of the above
        ANSWER: e   TYPE: M   COG: R

68. The value of empathy in communication for the target of empathy is
    a. increased self-esteem
    b. comfort
    c. increased trust
    d. all of the above
    e. none of the above
        ANSWER: d   TYPE: M   COG: R

69. The value of empathy in communication for the empathizer is
    a. comfort
    b. boosting your own knowledge and influence
    c. relational development and prediction
    d. all of the above
    e. b and c only
        ANSWER: e   TYPE: M   COG: R

70. The term social scientists use to describe the process of attaching meaning to behavior is
    a. selection
    b. attribution
    c. punctuation
    d. perception checking
    e. none of the above
        ANSWER: b   TYPE: M   COG: R

71. When we engage in self-serving bias,
    a. we tend to judge ourselves in the most generous terms possible
    b. we tend to blame others' problems on their personal qualities
    c. we find explanations outside ourselves when we have problems
    d. all of the above
    e. none of the above
        ANSWER: d   TYPE: M   COG: A

72. In Western cultures, such as the United States, silence is most often viewed as
    a. a sign of social grace
    b. an embarrassment
    c. an indication of communication competence
    d. a sign of physical strength
    e. all of the above
        ANSWER: b   TYPE: M   COG: R

73. If your application for a credit card is denied because of a credit report that contains only one derogatory comment along with much positive credit history, which mistake of perception is involved by the credit card company?
    a. influenced by the obvious
    b. cling to first impressions
    c. assume others are like us
    d. favor negative impressions
    e. blame innocent victims
        ANSWER: d   TYPE: M   COG: A
74. The country that is likely to have less talkative people is
    a. the United States
    b. Japan
    c. Mexico
    d. Germany
    e. Canada
        ANSWER: b   TYPE: M   COG: R
75. Which of the following does your text offer as an explanation as to why sex roles differ?
    a. Mothers are more stable communication models than are fathers.
    b. Early relationships for girls are less rewarding than are those for boys.
    c. Boys below the age of nine are encouraged to be more androgynous than are girls.
    d. Psychological differences are more important in the development of girls.
    e. None of the above is offered as an explanation.
        ANSWER: e   TYPE: M   COG: C
76. Which of the following is *not* a type of perceptual schema that allows us to organize the raw data we have selected?
    a. physical constructs
    b. role constructs
    c. interaction constructs
    d. psychological constructs
    e. selective constructs
        ANSWER: e   TYPE: M   COG: R
77. All of the following influence what we think of ourselves and others *except*
    a. self-concept
    b. socialization
    c. social norms
    d. mood
    e. none of the above
        ANSWER: c   TYPE: M   COG: R
78. The ability to understand others fully and to let them know it is
    a. perceptual organization
    b. selective perception
    c. empathy
    d. punctuation
    e. none of the above
        ANSWER: c   TYPE: M   COG: R
79. Influences on perception include
    a. physiological and psychological
    b. cultural and social
    c. selection and organization
    d. all of the above

e.   a and b only
        ANSWER: e   TYPE: M   COG: R

80. Maureen and Roland argue about where to spend the holidays. Roland argues because Maureen is unwilling to make concessions whereas Maureen argues because Roland isn't respecting Maureen's feelings. This is an example of
    a.   stereotyping
    b.   cognitive complexity
    c.   empathy
    d.   sympathy
    e.   punctuation
        ANSWER: e   TYPE: M   COG: A

81. When you explain to a friend why you think his or her parents acted in a certain way, you are engaging in
    a.   empathy
    b.   interpersonal communication
    c.   social cognition
    d.   social recognition
    e.   perception checking
        ANSWER: c   TYPE: M   COG: A

82. The term social scientists use to describe the power of a first impression to influence subsequent perceptions is
    a.   stereotyping
    b.   halo effect
    c.   empathizing
    d.   ambiguity reduction
    e.   attributions
        ANSWER: b   TYPE: M   COG: R

83. _____ narratives provide the best chance for smooth communication.
    a.   Organized
    b.   Psychological
    c.   Intense
    d.   Shared
    e.   Social
        ANSWER: d   TYPE: M   COG: C

84. When a person who is normally good-natured yells at us, we pay attention because of the quality of
    a.   salience
    b.   intensity
    c.   repetition
    d.   contrast
    e.   motives
        ANSWER: d   TYPE: M   COG: A

85. When you are thinking of buying a new car and suddenly become aware of all the car commercials, you are reacting to the attention quality of
    a.   salience
    b.   intensity
    c.   repetition
    d.   contrast
    e.   motives
        ANSWER: e   TYPE: M   COG: A

86. Which of the following is *not* one of the constructs of perceptual schema?
   a. physical
   b. mental
   c. role
   d. interaction
   e. psychological
      ANSWER: c   TYPE: M   COG: R

87. Schemata are useful in what two ways?
   a. as reality and fantasy
   b. as empathy and sympathy
   c. to unite and separate
   d. to classify and predict
   e. to unite and diversify
      ANSWER: d   TYPE: M   COG: R

88. Rather than focus on who started a conflict, it might be more productive to ask,
   a. what can we do to make things better?
   b. who is most at fault?
   c. whose perceptions are most accurate?
   d. all of the above
   e. a and c only
      ANSWER: a   TYPE: M   COG: R

89. The Walter Lippman quote, "For the most part we do not see first and then define; we define first and then see," means
   a. blind people have difficulty with definitions
   b. normally, we see something, then make sense out of it
   c. our mental processes affect our senses
   d. the phases of perception can occur in differing sequences
   e. c and d
      ANSWER: e   TYPE: M   COG: C

90. Scientists developed _____ to describe how a person's position in a society shapes his or her view of society and of specific individuals.
   a. Social theory
   b. Interaction theory
   c. Standpoint theory
   d. Social role theory
   e. Self concept theory
      ANSWER: c   TYPE: M   COG: R

91. If after several months you begin to lose patience from empathetically listening to a friend's constant family problems, you may be experiencing _____.
   a. Compassion fatigue
   b. Empathetic termination
   c. Sympathetic termination
   d. Reflection fatigue
   e. Perception fatigue
      ANSWER: a   TYPE: M   COG: A

92. Treating people as individuals instead of assuming they possess the same characteristics as every other member of the group to which you assign them is called
    a. Punctuating
    b. Decategorizing
    c. Empathizing
    d. Sympathizing
    e. Stereotyping
        ANSWER: b   TYPE: M   COG: C

93. Empathy consists of
    a. perspective taking
    b. emotional contagion
    c. concern
    d. a, b, and c
    e. a and c only
        ANSWER: d   TYPE: M   COG: R

94. Which of the following is not a factor that affects how we interpret other people's behavior?
    a. Assumptions about human behavior
    b. Degree of involvement
    c. Knowledge of others
    d. Past experience
    e. Intelligence
        ANSWER: e   TYPE: M   COG: R

95. Jake is embarrassed to find that the "Dumb Blond" jokes he told in class was offensive to several of his classmates. John made the common perception mistake of
    a. Being influenced by the obvious.
    b. Clinging to first impressions.
    c. Assuming others are like us
    d. Incorporating the halo effect
    e. None of the above
        ANSWER: c   TYPE: M   COG: A

96. Which component is missing from the following perception checking statement?
    "When you hung up on me I got mad. What were you feeling?"
    a. A request for clarification for how to interpret the behavior?
    b. An empathizing statement.
    c. Providing two possible interpretations of the behavior.
    d. Emotional contagion.
    e. No components are missing
        ANSWER: c   TYPE: M   COG: A

97. "Being open-minded" means
    a. finding something to love in everyone
    b. being able to agree with most people
    c. being easily persuaded
    d. being able to set aside your beliefs and consider those of someone else
    e. having no set opinions
        ANSWER: d   TYPE: M   COG: R

98. Immediately disliking a blind date after hearing negative evaluations about him from others is an example of how perception is
    a. Influenced by the obvious
    b. Influenced by our expectations.
    c. Influenced by negative impressions.
    d. Influenced by self-serving bias.
    e. None of the above
        ANSWER: b   TYPE: M   COG: A
99. Empathy requires
    a. open-mindedness
    b. imagination
    c. commitment
    d. all of the above
    e. a and c only
        ANSWER: d   TYPE: M   COG: R

Essay

100. Provide an example for your own experience of how each of the following factors affects perception and, hence, your interpersonal communication:
    a. psychological sex types
    b. occupational roles
    c. cultural differences
    d. physiological factors
        ANSWER: TYPE: E   COG: A

101. Briefly explain the concept of selective perception and give one example of it in action.
        ANSWER: TYPE: E   COG: A

102. Select and explain two constructs you would use to classify the students in this class. How would your relationship to them be affected differently by the two constructs?
        ANSWER: TYPE: E   COG: C

103. The text divides the act of perception into a three-part process. Name each of these parts, then, using an event from your own experience, describe how each part functions.
        ANSWER: TYPE: E   COG: A

104. What skills and attitudes does an empathic person possess? Use examples to distinguish and empathic person from a nonempathic person.
        ANSWER: TYPE: E   COG: A

105. Here is a situation: Your best friend has just arrived to pick you up for a movie date. For the fifth time in a row, he is more than fifteen minutes late. Write a perception checking statement that you might use in this situation. Indicate the parts of the statement.
        ANSWER: TYPE: E   COG: A

106. There are several factors that cause us to interpret a person's behavior in one way or another. Identify three of these factors and explain how they affect interpretation.
        ANSWER: TYPE: E   COG: R

107. How we select, organize, and interpret data about others is influenced by a variety of factors. Explain how your perceptual judgments are affected by physiology, culture, social, and psychological factors.
        ANSWER: TYPE: E   COG: A

Matching

108. Match the interpretation of a rock on the left with the person most likely to hold it on the right.

     _____ 1. What a unique mineral content!
     _____ 2. Looks like the area this came from could contain gold
     _____ 3. This would really hurt if I hit someone with it
     _____ 4. Someone could fall on this and get hurt

    a. Person feeling physically threatened
    b. Store owner
    c. Investor
    d. Geologist
        ANSWER: d, c, a, b   TYPE: K   COG: C

CHAPTER FOUR: LANGUAGE

True/False

1. The "study of symbols" would be an accurate description for the "study of language."
        ANSWER: T   TYPE: T   COG: C
2. Words are arbitrary symbols that have no meaning in themselves.
        ANSWER: T   TYPE: T   COG: R
3. An important task facing communicators is to establish a common understanding of the words they use to exchange messages.
        ANSWER: T   TYPE: T   COG: C
4. Because of the static, unchanging nature of our grammar, we often regard people and things as never changing.
        ANSWER: T   TYPE: T   COG: R
5. English defines many nonsexual concepts as male.
        ANSWER: T   TYPE: T   COG: R
6. To the extent that our language is both sexist and racist, our view of the world is affected.
        ANSWER: T   TYPE: T   COG: C
7. English syntactic rules require every word to contain at least one vowel.
        ANSWER: T   TYPE: T   COG: R
8. Syntax deals with structure; semantics govern meaning.
        ANSWER: T   TYPE: T   COG: R
9. As a group, women are likely to use conversation to enhance relationships, whereas men are likely to use conversation to exchange information or accomplish a task.
        ANSWER: T   TYPE: T   COG: C
10. Coordinated management of meaning (CMM) theory describes some types of pragmatic rules that operate in everyday conversation.
        ANSWER: T   TYPE: T   COG: R
11. Ogden and Richards' "triangle of meaning" shows a direct relationship between a word and the thing or idea it represents.
        ANSWER: F   TYPE: T   COG: R
12. A common theme in all-male talk is a feeling of empathy and understanding; the most common theme in all-girl talk is appreciation of the practical value of conversation.
        ANSWER: F   TYPE: T   COG: C

13. An important task facing communicators is to establish a common understanding of the words they use to exchange messages.
    ANSWER: T   TYPE: T   COG: R
14. Research indicates that names shape the way others think of us, the way we view ourselves, and the way we act.
    ANSWER: T   TYPE: T   COG: R
15. The preconceptions we hold about people because of their names have little influence on our behavior toward them.
    ANSWER: F   TYPE: T   COG: C
16. The labels we choose for ourselves and encourage others to use say a great deal about who we think we are and how we want others to view us.
    ANSWER: T   TYPE: T   COG: C
17. Research shows that linguistic differences are often more a function of sex roles than of the speaker's biological sex.
    ANSWER: T   TYPE: T   COG: C
18. In the study of communication, the terms "sex type" and "gender" are interchangeable.
    ANSWER: F   TYPE: T   COG: R
19. Stafford and Kline found that women's married name choices are associated with perceptions of loss of personal self.
    ANSWER: F   TYPE: T   COG: R
20. The Dr. Fox hypothesis suggests that credibility is more a function of style than of ideas expressed.
    ANSWER: T   TYPE: T   COG: R
21. Communication researchers call the process of adapting one's speech style to match that of others with whom the communicator wants to identify as "divergence."
    ANSWER: F   TYPE: T   COG: C
22. Powerful speech is most likely to get desired results regardless of the country in which it is used.
    ANSWER: F   TYPE: T   COG: C
23. The use of "powerful" or "powerless" language affects how competent speakers are judged.
    ANSWER: T   TYPE: T   COG: R
24. On the average, men and women discuss about the same range of topics.
    ANSWER: F   TYPE: T   COG: C
25. Language can shape the way we perceive and understand the world.
    ANSWER: T   TYPE: T   COG: C
26. Competent communicators understand that ambiguity and vagueness can sometimes serve useful purposes.
    ANSWER: T   TYPE: T   COG: R
27. Behavioral descriptions are less specific than abstract ones.
    ANSWER: F   TYPE: T   COG: R
28. Recent studies show that there is no significant difference in the self-esteem or relationship power balance between marriages in which women kept their own names and marriages in which women assumed the names of their husbands.
    ANSWER: T   TYPE: T   COG: C
29. CMM (Coordinated Management of Meaning) theory describes pragmatic rules operating in everyday conversations.
    ANSWER: T   TYPE: T   COG: R
30. Ogden and Richard's "triangle of meaning" shows that there is a direct relationship between a word and the thing or idea it claims to represent.
    ANSWER: F   TYPE: T   COG: R
31. The language we use describes our perceptions but does not affect our perceptions.
    ANSWER: F   TYPE: T   COG: C

32. Research suggests that common names are generally viewed as being more active, stronger, and better than unusual ones.
    ANSWER: T   TYPE: T   COG: R
33. Like equivocation, high-level abstractions also can help communicators find face-saving ways to avoid confrontations and embarrassment by being deliberately unclear.
    ANSWER: T   TYPE: T   COG: R
34. The negative effect of unusual names seems to be more damaging to men than to women.
    ANSWER: T   TYPE: T   COG: R
35. Low-level abstractions can increase the chances of a serious misunderstanding.
    ANSWER: F   TYPE: T   COG: R
36. Research suggests that a mixture of powerful and polite speech is usually more effective than powerful-only or polite-only styles.
    ANSWER: T   TYPE: T   COG: C
37. The goal of language is always to be perfectly clear to another person.
    ANSWER: F   TYPE: T   COG: C
38. Language that is open to several interpretations should not be used by a competent communicator.
    ANSWER: F   TYPE: T   COG: C
39. High-level abstractions can help communicators avoid confrontations and embarrassment.
    ANSWER: T   TYPE: T   COG: R
40. "I" language reflects the speaker's willingness to take responsibility for her or his beliefs and feelings.
    ANSWER: T   TYPE: T   COG: R
41. Research suggests that "I" language in large doses can sound egotistical.
    ANSWER: T   TYPE: T   COG: C
42. Research shows that I/we combinations are strongly endorsed by college students, particularly for confrontations in romantic relationships.
    ANSWER: T   TYPE: T   COG: C
43. "The climate in Portland is better than in Seattle" is an example of a factual statement.
    ANSWER: F   TYPE: T   COG: A
44. Studies suggest that men ask more questions in mixed-sex conversations than do women.
    ANSWER: F   TYPE: T   COG: C
45. In a survey about conversational frequency, nearly 50 percent of the women said they called friends at least once a week just to talk, whereas less than half as many men did so.
    ANSWER: T   TYPE: T   COG: R
46. In same-sex conversations, men use more questions and personal pronouns; women use more directives and interruptions.
    ANSWER: F   TYPE: T   COG: R
47. Research suggests that both men and women are equally likely to discuss personal appearance, sex, and dating in same-sex conversations.
    ANSWER: T   TYPE: T   COG: R
48. In mixed-sex dyads, men tend to talk longer than women.
    ANSWER: T   TYPE: T   COG: C
49. Gender research indicates that there is no significant difference between male and female speech in areas such as the use of profanity, qualifiers, and vocal fluency.
    ANSWER: T   TYPE: T   COG: R
50. Differences between the way men and women speak are determined by a wide variety of factors that may have little or nothing to do with biological sex.
    ANSWER: T   TYPE: T   COG: C

Multiple Choice

51. The features that characterize all languages are
    a. symbolic
    b. rule-governed
    c. subjective
    d. all of the above
    e. a and b only
    ANSWER: d   TYPE: M   COG: R

52. The notion that words are arbitrary and have no meaning in themselves refers to which characteristic of language?
    a. symbolic
    b. rule-governed
    c. meanings in words, not people
    d. equivocal
    e. static
    ANSWER: a   TYPE: M   COG: R

53. Rules that tell us what uses and interpretations of a message are appropriate in a given context are:
    a. phonological rules
    b. syntactic rules
    c. pragmatic rules
    d. equivocal rules
    e. none of the above
    ANSWER: c   TYPE: M   COG: R

54. The fact that the words "whiskey makes you sick when you're well." when arranged differently, "Whiskey, when you're sick, makes you well." Create a totally different meaning is related to which rule of language?
    a. pragmatic
    b. syntactic
    c. phonological
    d. semantic
    e. none of the above
    ANSWER: b   TYPE: M   COG: R

55. Brandon's stomach begins to churn when his boss pokes his head in his office and says "I want to see you." because of which language rule?
    a. pragmatic
    b. syntactic
    c. phonological
    d. semantic
    e. none of the above
    ANSWER: c   TYPE: M   COG: A

56. The fact that "love" means many things, ranging from "eros" (romantic love) to agape (selfless love) suggests which quality of troublesome language?
    a. equivocal
    b. static
    c. inferential
    d. emotive
    e. relative
    ANSWER: a   TYPE: M   COG: A

57. Alfred Korzybski suggested the linguistic device of "dating" to cope with which form of troublesome language?

      a.   ambiguous
      b.   static
      c.   inferential
      d.   emotive
      e.   relative

      ANSWER: b   TYPE: M   COG: A

58. Terms like "angry" or "exciting" that announce the speaker's attitude point to which quality of troublesome language?

      a.   equivocal
      b.   static
      c.   inferential
      d.   emotive
      e.   relative

      ANSWER: d   TYPE: M   COG: A

59. When Sarah, a newspaper editor, opened her e-mail up she found a message typed in capital letters filled with curse words, criticizing her view of a local issue and insulting her personally. This is an example of computerized

      a.   emotion
      b.   flaming
      c.   equivocation
      d.   abstraction
      e.   none of the above

      ANSWER: c   TYPE: M   COG: A

60. Problems that arise when we speak too generally are solved by

      a.   avoiding static evaluation
      b.   distinguishing facts from inferences
      c.   making behavioral descriptions
      d.   using euphemisms sparingly
      e.   using emotive words with caution

      ANSWER: c   TYPE: M   COG: C

61. Overly abstract language causes which of the following problems?

      a.   stereotyping
      b.   confuses others
      c.   appreciation can suffer
      d.   leaves you unclear about your own thoughts
      e.   all of the above

      ANSWER: e   TYPE: M   COG: C

62. Language shapes our impression of

      a.   credibility
      b.   status
      c.   power
      d.   racism and sexism
      e.   all of the above

      ANSWER: e   TYPE: M   COG: R

63. The Dr. Fox hypothesis is an example of language shaping our impression of
    a.   credibility
    b.   status
    c.   power
    d.   racism
    e.   sexism
    ANSWER: a   TYPE: M   COG: R

64. Professor Henry Higgins' transformation of Eliza Doolittle in *My Fair Lady* is an example of language shaping our impression of
    a.   credibility
    b.   status
    c.   power
    d.   racism
    e.   sexism
    ANSWER: b   TYPE: M   COG: A

65. Which of the following is the *least* likely to influence use of language?
    a.   gender
    b.   occupation
    c.   sexual orientation
    d.   orientation toward problem solving
    e.   All are equally likely to influence language
    ANSWER: a   TYPE: M   COG: C

66. Research on naming reveals that
    a.   common names are viewed as being less strong and active than unusual names
    b.   hypothetical people with common names were given higher grades than those with uncommon names
    c.   unusual names tend to be more damaging to women than to men
    d.   a and b
    e.   all of the above
    ANSWER: b   TYPE: M   COG: R

67. Statements that have the effect of canceling the thought that precedes it are
    a.   questions
    b.   but statements
    c.   if statements
    d.   you statements
    e.   we statements
    ANSWER: b   TYPE: M   COG: R

68. Language can express an unwillingness to take responsibility through the use of
    a.   if
    b.   you
    c.   we
    d.   but
    e.   all of the above
    ANSWER: e   TYPE: M   COG: R

69. The statement, "Claudia is a beautiful person," is an example of which troublesome characteristic of language?
    a.   the Dr. Fox hypothesis
    b.   how language shapes our reality
    c.   semantic bypassing
    d.   static evaluation

e. none of the above

ANSWER: d   TYPE: M   COG: A

70. If we fail to recognize that words are only generalized symbols, we are in danger of making which of the following invalid assumptions?
   a. words have only one commonly accepted definition
   b. words are what they symbolize
   c. people and things do not change
   d. words have specific referents
   e. all of the above apply

ANSWER: e   TYPE: M   COG: C

71. Euphemisms are
   a. pleasant words substituted for blunt ones
   b. terms such as freedom, truth, and democracy
   c. words that appear to describe but actually announce a speaker's attitude
   d. words that gain their meaning by making comparisons
   e. not defined by any of the above

ANSWER: a   TYPE: M   COG: R

72. Which of the following statements is the lowest-level abstraction of the word "considerate"
   a. she helps me around the house
   b. she calls me on Fridays before she goes shopping to see if I need anything
   c. she thinks of others
   d. she always follows the rules of politeness
   e. she follows the Golden Rule

ANSWER: b   TYPE: M   COG: A

73. The statement, "Americans are materialistic," is an example of which problem caused by overly abstract language?
   a. a euphemistic statement
   b. syntactic confusion
   c. the Sapir-Whorf hypothesis
   d. stereotyping
   e. none of the above

ANSWER: d   TYPE: M   COG: A

74. Teaching kids to "go potty" instead of "urinating in the toilet bowl" is an example of:
   a. ambiguous language
   b. euphemism
   c. emotive language
   d. static evaluation
   e. relative language

ANSWER: b   TYPE: M   COG: A

75. Being surprised at paying $20 a plate at your friend's suggested "inexpensive" restaurant reflects which type of language?
   a. ambiguous language
   b. euphemism
   c. emotive language
   d. static evaluation
   e. relative language

ANSWER: e   TYPE: M   COG: A

76. The statement, "For me, a good dinner is fresh seafood, white wine, and French pastry," is an example of
    a.   emotive language
    b.   behavioral description
    c.   intentional orientations
    d.   semantic ambiguity
    e.   a euphemistic statement
    ANSWER: b   TYPE: M   COG: A

77. Language usage that has a high frequency of terms implying superior male traits and inferior female traits or a high frequency of terms of superior female traits and inferior male traits is known as
    a.   metacommunication
    b.   androgynous language
    c.   paralanguage
    d.   sexist language
    e.   none of the above
    ANSWER: d   TYPE: M   COG: R

78. The implication of the statement, "Sign language is symbolic, not literal," is:
    a.   that there are many different sign languages because there are many possible symbols for each concept
    b.   that there is only one correct sign language because the signs are universally recognized
    c.   the connection between a concept and its visual representation is obvious and direct
    d.   experts should work more to unify the major sign languages
    e.   sign language is more impersonal than verbal language
    ANSWER: a   TYPE: M   COG: C

79. The rules which tell us what interpretation of a message is appropriate in a given context are
    a.   syntactic
    b.   semantic
    c.   pragmatic
    d.   all of the above
    e.   a and b
    ANSWER: c   TYPE: M   COG: R

80. Ambiguous language refers to the fact words have
    a.   unique sounds
    b.   unique spellings
    c.   one commonly accepted definition
    d.   more than one commonly accepted definition
    e.   different levels of abstraction
    ANSWER: d   TYPE: M   COG: R

81. In the statement, "Mekelle is a good student," the word that is troublesome due to static evaluation is
    a.   Mekelle
    b.   is
    c.   a
    d.   good
    e.   student
    ANSWER: b   TYPE: M   COG: A

82. Arguments often result when we label our inferences as:
    a.   facts
    b.   inferences
    c.   ambiguous language
    d.   personal
    e.   descriptive
         ANSWER: a   TYPE: M   COG: R
83. Saying "You look nice" instead of "That color of dress looks good on you" is an example of
    a.   a euphemism
    b.   abstracting
    c.   emotive language
    d.   a behavioral description
    e.   a hedge
         ANSWER: b   TYPE: M   COG: A
84. Which statement does not contain powerless language?
    a.   I really hope you can understand
    b.   This assignment is not too difficult
    c.   Call me later, won't you?
    d.   This may not be fair, but I don't like Charlyce
    e.   Let's meet for lunch tomorrow
         ANSWER: e   TYPE: M   COG: A
85. Research findings suggest that characteristically feminine speech is a function of:
    a.   female preferences
    b.   euphemisms
    c.   women's historically less powerful positions
    d.   gender
    e.   none of the above
         ANSWER: c   TYPE: M   COG: R

Essay

86. Climb down the "abstraction ladder" by suggesting three successively more concrete meanings for the following words: independent, selfish
         ANSWER: TYPE: E   COG: A
87. Identify the language problem(s) illustrated in the following statement: "Camille is insensitive." Rewrite it to be less troublesome, adding any necessary information.
         ANSWER: TYPE: E   COG: A
88. The statement, "Raj, you're doing a great job," is an abstract description of an appreciative message. Rewrite the sentence to make it a behavioral description as discussed in the text. Suggest one reason why using the behavioral description (or a combination of both) is preferable to using just the abstract description.
         ANSWER: TYPE: E   COG: A
89. Discuss two ways of eliminating sexist language.
         ANSWER: TYPE: E   COG: C
90. Emotive language seems to describe something but really describes the speaker's attitude toward it. The following is a statement of a personality trait: "My child is high-spirited." Give two versions to show how the trait can be viewed wither favorably or unfavorably, according to the label people give it.
         ANSWER: TYPE: E   COG: A

91. Words that use "man" generically to refer to humanity at large or to occupations are sexist/problematic because they imply that humanity is composed only of men or that certain occupational roles are only filled by men. Replace the following words with language that includes both sexes:

Congressman   Mankind   Manpower   Policeman   "Men Working"   Chairman
　　　ANSWER:　　　TYPE: E　　　COG: A

92. Rewrite the following statements so that the speaker takes responsibility for the feelings expressed:
    a. "It's really annoying to have to wait for people."
    b. "You never know what's going to happen with Marlon."
    c. "We really should get going."
    d. "Are you doing anything later?"
　　　ANSWER:　　　TYPE: E　　　COG: A

93. Explain and give an example of the disruptive language concept "Fact-opinion confusion."
　　　ANSWER:　　　TYPE: E　　　COG: A

94. Using the word "but" in a statement has the effect of canceling everything that came before it. Rewrite the following two statements so that they more clearly express the speaker's thoughts and feelings:
    a. "I really enjoy the time we spend together, but I think we should see other people more"
    b. "You're a good worker, but your habitual lateness makes it hard for your co-workers to do their jobs."
　　　ANSWER:　　　TYPE: E　　　COG: A

95. Explain, using the Coordinated Management of Meaning hierarchy, how the question, "How are you?" could have very different meanings.
　　　ANSWER:　　　TYPE: E　　　COG: A

96. Your close friend has a habit of interrupting you whenever you try to share a personal story. Offer an example of how you might describe this problem to your friend, using "I," "You," and "We" language as recommended in the text.
　　　ANSWER:　　　TYPE: E　　　COG: A

97. Distinguish between phonological, syntactic, semantic, and pragmatic rules. Provide an example of each.
　　　ANSWER:　　　TYPE: E　　　COG: A

98. Explain the relationship between language use and gender roles.
　　　ANSWER:　　　TYPE: E　　　COG: A

Matching

99. Label the following as facts (F) or inferences (I).

　　　_____ Bernie's face is turning red.
　　　_____ Shameeka's happy she won the prize.
　　　_____ You're ten minutes late.
　　　_____ You didn't call me last night.
　　　_____ You only like me because I'm a football star
　　　ANSWER: F, I, F, F, I   TYPE: K　　　COG: C

100. Identify the levels of the Coordinated Management of Meaning hierarchy, with 6 representing the highest (broad) level and 1 representing the lowest (basic) level.

     _____ Relational Contract
     _____ Content
     _____ Speech Act
     _____ Cultural Archetype
     _____ Episode
     _____ Life Script
     ANSWER: 4,1,2,6,3,5 TYPE: K   COG: R

CHAPTER FIVE: NONVERBAL COMMUNICATION

True/False

1. Nonverbal communication is best defined as "messages expressed by nonlinguistic means."
    ANSWER: T   TYPE: T   COG: R
2. In real life, spontaneous nonverbal expressions are frequently unclear and difficult to interpret.
    ANSWER: T   TYPE: T   COG: C
3. What we say often conveys more meaning than what we do.
    ANSWER: F   TYPE: T   COG: C
4. Most nonverbal messages are carefully chosen and consciously sent.
    ANSWER: F   TYPE: T   COG: C
5. Nonverbal messages arrive in a sequential manner.
    ANSWER: F   TYPE: T   COG: C
6. 6.   Emblems are usually delivered intentionally.
    ANSWER: T   TYPE: T   COG: R
7. In one study, less than a quarter of experimental subjects who had been instructed to show increased or decreased liking of a partner could describe the nonverbal behaviors they used.
    ANSWER: T   TYPE: T   COG: R
8. Researchers have found that people who hear content-free speech can consistently recognize the emotion being expressed, as well as identify its strength.
    ANSWER: T   TYPE: T   COG: C
9. All behavior has communicative value.
    ANSWER: T   TYPE: T   COG: R
10. Gesturing has little bearing on persuasiveness.
    ANSWER: F   TYPE: T   COG: C
11. Persuasiveness increases when one person mirror's another's movements.
    ANSWER: T   TYPE: T   COG: R
12. Although early studies seemed to indicate that touch was important for infant survival, more recent research shows that touch may overstimulate infants and be detrimental.
    ANSWER: F   TYPE: T   COG: C
13. It is possible to understand the attitudes or feelings of others, even if you aren't able to understand the subject of their communication.
    ANSWER: T   TYPE: T   COG: C
14. Social scientists use the term "paralanguage" to describe nonverbal vocal messages.
    ANSWER: T   TYPE: T   COG: R
15. In the United States, the amount of touching usually decreases with age.
    ANSWER: T   TYPE: T   COG: R

16. Listeners pay more attention to the content of words than to paralanguage when asked to determine a speaker's attitudes.

      ANSWER: F   TYPE: T   COG: R

17. Cognitively complex people are better at decoding nonverbal behavior than are those who are less cognitively complex.

      ANSWER: T   TYPE: T   COG: C

18. Sarcasm is one instance in which we use both emphasis and tone of voice to change a statement's meaning to the opposite.

      ANSWER: T   TYPE: T   COG: C

19. Research shows that people who probe deceptive communicators with questions are better at detecting lies than those who don't probe.

      ANSWER: F   TYPE: T   COG: R

20. Research suggests that observers of a conversation recognize deceit better than the communicators who are involved in the conversation.

      ANSWER: T   TYPE: T   COG: R

21. Intimate partners aren't very good at recognizing one another's lies.

      ANSWER: T   TYPE: T   COG: C

22. Dress has no nearing on how likely we are to obey or follow the suggestions of others.

      ANSWER: F   TYPE: T   COG: C

23. Clothing-based assumptions aren't always accurate.

      ANSWER: T   TYPE: T   COG: C

24. Proxemics is the term social scientists use to describe the study of how people communicate through bodily movements.

      ANSWER: F   TYPE: T   COG: R

25. Research shows that we tend to comply with requests when they are delivered at a rate that is not similar to our own speaking rate.

      ANSWER: F   TYPE: T   COG: R

26. The way housing projects are designed controls to a great extent the contact neighbors have with each other.

      ANSWER: T   TYPE: T   COG: A

27. Watching how people use an already existing environment can be a way of telling what kind of relationship they want.

      ANSWER: T   TYPE: T   COG: C

28. While it's possible to avoid verbal communication, it's impossible to stop sending nonverbal messages.

      ANSWER: T   TYPE: T   COG: R

29. Most nonverbal communication expresses feelings; most verbal communication expresses thoughts.

      ANSWER: T   TYPE: T   COG: R

30. If a person's verbal and nonverbal messages are contradictory, the verbal aspect is most likely to be believed.

      ANSWER: F   TYPE: T   COG: R

31. Nonverbal behavior may both repeat and substitute for verbal communication.

      ANSWER: T   TYPE: T   COG: R

32. Appropriate touch increases liking and boosts compliance.

      ANSWER: T   TYPE: T   COG: C

33. People who use fewer gestures are viewed as less enthusiastic, considerate, and likeable in the United States.

      ANSWER: T   TYPE: T   COG: R

34. *Paralanguage* is a scientific term given to speech that includes slang peculiar to a specific group.

      ANSWER: F   TYPE: T   COG: R

35. Territory and personal space are used interchangeably to describe the invisible bubble that serves as an extension of our physical being.

ANSWER: F   TYPE: T   COG: R

36. Proxemics is the study of how people use the space around them.

ANSWER: T   TYPE: T   COG: R

37. Emblems are culturally understood substitutes for verbal expressions.

ANSWER: T   TYPE: T   COG: R

38. The higher a person's intellectual skills, the more likely it is that sarcasm will be understood.

ANSWER: T   TYPE: T   COG: C

39. To be labeled *nonverbal communication,* a gesture must be intentional.

ANSWER: F   TYPE: T   COG: R

40. As we get to know more about people and like them, we start to regard them as better looking.

ANSWER: T   TYPE: T   COG: C

41. Chronemics is the study of how people use color.

ANSWER: F   TYPE: T   COG: R

Multiple Choice

42. All of the following are characteristics of nonverbal communication *except*
    a. all behavior has communicative value
    b. nonverbal communication is primarily relational
    c. nonverbal communication is ambiguous
    d. nonverbal communication is specific
    e. all of the above are characteristics of nonverbal communication

ANSWER: d   TYPE: M   COG: R

43. Which of the following functions illustrate how verbal and nonverbal communication are interconnected?
    a. nonverbal behavior repeats verbal messages
    b. nonverbal messages can substitute for verbal messages
    c. nonverbal messages can complement and accent verbal statements
    d. nonverbal behaviors can control verbal interaction by regulating it.
    e. all of the above

ANSWER: e   TYPE: M   COG: C

44. The fact that it is impossible to think about and control all nonverbal behavior suggests which characteristic of nonverbal communication?
    a. multiple channels
    b. continuous
    c. unconscious
    d. ambiguous
    e. nonverbal impact

ANSWER: c   TYPE: M   COG: R

45. The fact that most nonverbal cues are vague implies which characteristic of nonverbal communication?
    a. multiple channels
    b. continuous
    c. ambiguous
    d. unconscious
    e. nonverbal impact

ANSWER: c   TYPE: M   COG: R

46. When compared to truth-tellers, deceivers typically
    a. make more speech errors
    b. blink their eyes more often
    c. shift their posture
    d. fidget with their hands
    e. all of the above
        ANSWER: e   TYPE: M   COG: R
47. Emblems satisfy which function of nonverbal communication?
    a. repeating
    b. substituting
    c. complementing and accenting
    d. regulating and contradicting
    e. all of the above
        ANSWER: b   TYPE: M   COG: R
48. Turn-taking signals fall under which function of nonverbal communication?
    a. repeating
    b. substituting
    c. complementing and accenting
    d. regulating and contradicting
    e. all of the above
        ANSWER: d   TYPE: M   COG: R
49. Which of the following are nonverbal signals that indicate a speaker has finished talking and is ready to yield to a listener?
    a. lack of change in vocal intonation
    b. a drawl on the first syllable
    c. a drop in vocal pitch or loudness
    d. all of the above
    e. a and b only
        ANSWER: c   TYPE: M   COG: C
50. Which type of nonverbal communication is considered the most noticeable?
    a. face
    b. posture and gesture
    c. touch
    d. voice
    e. proxemics and territoriality
        ANSWER: a   TYPE: M   COG: R
51. Research shows that when teachers reduce the spatial distance between themselves and their students
    a. the students are less likely to follow the teacher's instructions
    b. the students are less likely to be satisfied with the class
    c. the students are less likely to be satisfied with the teacher
    d. all of the above
    e. none of the above
        ANSWER: e   TYPE: M   COG: R
52. People who gesture appropriately often create impressions of being more
    a. formal
    b. warm and agreeable
    c. analytic
    d. distant
    e. logical
        ANSWER: b   TYPE: M   COG: C

53. Research by Berger and diBattista showed that when communicators gave directions that weren't followed, in their second attempt the would
    a. change their wording
    b. talk faster
    c. talk louder
    d. use more gestures
    e. talk softer
        ANSWER: c   TYPE: M   COG: R
54. When Chandra is finished speaking, she lowers her pitch and nods toward Barret to show that it is now his turn to speak. Chandra is using nonverbal cues for the function of
    a. regulating
    b. substituting
    c. repeating
    d. emphasizing
    e. contradicting
        ANSWER: a   TYPE: M   COG: A
55. While he plays with his fingers and fidgets in his chair, Travis tells the interviewers that he is not nervous. Travis is using nonverbal cues for the function of
    a. regulating
    b. substituting
    c. repeating
    d. emphasizing
    e. contradicting
        ANSWER: e   TYPE: M   COG: A
56. The ability to consider more than one possible interpretation for nonverbal behavior is a characteristic of
    a. cognitive complexity
    b. ambiguity
    c. paralanguage
    d. proxemics
    e. kinesics
        ANSWER: a   TYPE: M   COG: R
57. The voice communicates through
    a. tone and pitch
    b. speed and volume
    c. pauses and disfluencies
    d. all of the above
    e. a and b only
        ANSWER: d   TYPE: M   COG: R
58. Edward T. Hall considers intimate distances to be
    a. 0 to 18 inches
    b. 18 inches to 4 feet
    c. 4 feet to 12 feet
    d. 12 feet to 25 feet
    e. 25 feet and beyond
        ANSWER: a   TYPE: M   COG: R

59. At which distance can you keep someone "at arm's length?"
    a. intimate
    b. personal
    c. social
    d. public
    e. none of the above
                    ANSWER: b   TYPE: M   COG: C
60. Edward T. Hall considers social distance to be
    a. 0 to 18 inches
    b. 18 inches to 4 feet
    c. 4 feet to 12 feet
    d. 12 feet to 25 feet
    e. 25 feet and beyond
                    ANSWER: c   TYPE: M   COG: R
61. Which is *not* barrier behavior?
    a. touch
    b. sneeze
    c. cough
    d. scratch
    e. backing away
                    ANSWER: a   TYPE: M   COG: R
62. Women who are perceived as more attractive
    a. have more dates
    b. receive higher grades
    c. persuade males easier
    d. receive lighter court sentences
    e. all of the above
                    ANSWER: e   TYPE: M   COG: R
63. Which messages are *not* conveyed by clothing?
    a. economic and educational levels
    b. analytical and logical
    c. trustworthiness and moral character
    d. sophistication and social position
    e. level of success
                    ANSWER: b   TYPE: M   COG: R
64. The effect of an attractive room on the people working in it is an example of which type of nonverbal communication?
    a. environment
    b. territoriality
    c. proxemics
    d. touch
    e. paralanguage
                    ANSWER: a   TYPE: M   COG: R
65. When studying the relationship between clothing and self worth, researchers found :
    a. The relationship between clothes and self worth was greater for men than women.
    b. No correlation between clothes and self worth for either men and women.
    c. An equally positive correlation between clothes and self worth for both sexes.
    d. The relationship between clothes and self worth was greater for women than men.
    e. A and B
                    ANSWER: a   TYPE: M   COG: C

66. Culturally understood substitutes for verbal expressions are known as
    a. emblems
    b. illustrators
    c. regulators
    d. paralinguistic cues
    e. none of the above
        ANSWER: a   TYPE: M   COG: R
67. Behaviors that complement or reinforce a verbal statement are known as
    a. emblems
    b. illustrators
    c. regulators
    d. paralinguistic cues
    e. none of the above
        ANSWER: b   TYPE: M   COG: R
68. Which distance is being used when a child sits on your lap?
    a. intimate
    b. personal
    c. social
    d. public
    e. territorial
        ANSWER: a   TYPE: M   COG: A
69. Which distance is typically used when a teacher lectures in front of a large lecture class?
    a. intimate
    b. personal
    c. social
    d. public
    e. territorial
        ANSWER: d   TYPE: M   COG: A
70. At what distance a re a couple of friends likely to stand when in public?
    a. intimate
    b. personal
    c. social
    d. public
    e. territorial
        ANSWER: b   TYPE: M   COG: A
71. John thinks Sue is beautiful after getting to know her even though he wasn't initially attracted to her. This is an example of how _____ theory works.
    a. Attraction and Interaction
    b. Interaction Appearance
    c. Interaction Overtime
    d. Interaction Affection
    e. Interaction Development
        ANSWER: b   TYPE: M   COG: A
72. The term "proxemics" refers to the study of the effects of
    a. the social relationship between two or more individuals
    b. the spatial relationship between two or more individuals
    c. the spatial relationship between people and objects
    d. the spatial relationship between one object and another
    e. none of the above
        ANSWER: b   TYPE: M   COG: R

73. Which distance is being used when an employer talks with an employee as they are seated across from each other at an office desk?
    a. intimate
    b. personal
    c. social
    d. public
    e. territorial
        ANSWER: c   TYPE: M   COG: A

74. Which kind of distance is used most often in business situations?
    a. intimate
    b. personal
    c. social
    d. public
    e. none of the above
        ANSWER: c   TYPE: M   COG: C

75. Nonverbal messages are best at communicating
    a. thoughts
    b. ideas
    c. feelings
    d. concepts
    e. negative emotions
        ANSWER: c   TYPE: M   COG: R

76. Nonverbal messages are
    a. sequential
    b. multichannel
    c. simultaneous
    d. all of the above
    e. b and c only
        ANSWER: e   TYPE: M   COG: R

77. Morton & Trehub's study on children's interpretation of mixed messages concluded:
    a. Children rely on nonverbal cues more than words for understanding.
    b. Children rely on words more than nonverbal cues for understanding.
    c. Children became confused when words and nonverbal cues contradicted each other.
    d. Children were more accurate than adults at interpreting mixed messages.
    e. None of the above
        ANSWER: b   TYPE: M   COG: C

78. Speakers regulate conversation and indicate they are finished talking by
    a. looking at the conversational partner
    b. glancing at the listener and then looking away
    c. blinking at the listener and then looking away
    d. looking at the listener when talking, then looking down when at the end of a message
    e. an increase in volume
        ANSWER: a   TYPE: M   COG: C

79. Which type of problem can arise regarding territory?
    a. Territorial contamination
    b. Territorial Invasion
    c. Territorial violation
    d. Both b and c
    e. A, B and C
        ANSWER: e   TYPE: M   COG: C

80. When asked if she's angry, LeAnne responds by slamming her hand on the table and loudly saying, "NO, I'M NOT MAD." LeAnne's nonverbal behavior is _____ her verbal words.
    a. Regulating
    b. Accenting
    c. Repeating
    d. Complementing
    e. Contradicting
        ANSWER: e   TYPE: M   COG: A
81. When detecting deception, women are
    a. more likely to probe messages of deceptive communicators
    b. more accurate at detecting lying
    c. more accurate at determining underlying truth
    d. all of the above
    e. b and c only
        ANSWER: e   TYPE: M   COG: R
82. When Russ gives Joel "the finger," he is using a nonverbal cue known as a(n)
    a. illustrator
    b. adaptor
    c. emblem
    d. manipulator
    e. none of the above
        ANSWER: c   TYPE: M   COG: A
83. When researching the nonverbal behavior of liars, the Mayo Clinic discovered that:
    a. There is no physical difference between liars and truth-tellers nonverbal behaviors
    b. The pupils of liar's eyes become more constricted than truth-tellers.
    c. The pupils of liar's eyes are more dilated than truth-tellers.
    d. The temperature of liar's skin is the same as truth-tellers.
    e. The temperature of liar's skin around the eyes was higher than truth-tellers.
        ANSWER: e   TYPE: M   COG: C
84. Which of the following is *not* included in the term *kinesics*?
    a. paralanguage
    b. body movement
    c. posture
    d. gesture
    e. physical orientation to others
        ANSWER: a   TYPE: M   COG: R
85. Some social scientists claim that _____ were the first form of human communication.
    a. gestures
    b. paralinguistics
    c. manipulators
    d. regulators
    e. proxemics
        ANSWER: a   TYPE: M   COG: R
86. Which of the following is not a social function of nonverbal communication?
    a. It defines the type of relationship we want with others
    b. It conveys emotions we may be unwilling or unable to express
    c. It involves identity management
    d. All of the above
    e. Both b & c
        ANSWER: d   TYPE: M   COG: C

87. Which of the following conclusions can be reached from the study showing those touched lightly on the arm were 70 percent more likely to sign a petition?
    a. touching someone lightly is more persuasive than a heavier touch
    b. touching someone on the arm is the most persuasive location for compliance
    c. touch increases compliance
    d. touch increases understanding
    e. if you touch someone, she or he will do what you want.
    ANSWER: c   TYPE: M   COG: C

88. Realizing that students are bored in class by noticing their slumped postures and vacant facial expressions is an example of how:
    a. Proximity impacts mood
    b. Nonverbal behavior involves identity management
    c. Nonverbal messages repeat verbal messages.
    d. All nonverbal behavior communicates messages.
    e. Nonverbal behavior lacks ambiguity.
    ANSWER: d   TYPE: M   COG: A

89. Paralanguage includes the vocal qualities of
    a. rate and pitch
    b. disfluencies and pauses
    c. tone and volume
    d. all of the above
    e. a and c only
    ANSWER: d   TYPE: M   COG: R

90. The conclusion that can be drawn from the study of comfortable conversation distance, which found that happily married couples stood 11.4 inches apart and unhappy ones 14.8 inches apart, is
    a. personal space bubbles vary in size according to the person we're with
    b. unhappy couples don't like to be touched
    c. happy couples prefer to be able to see details of the partner
    d. happiness makes people less aware of the distance between them
    e. all of the above
    ANSWER: a   TYPE: M   COG: C

Essay

91. Assume you are at a restaurant with a friend. He or she flirts with the server. Write a one-sentence statement you could use to check out your interpretation of this nonverbal communication. Assume you will say the sentence to your friend.
    ANSWER: TYPE: E   COG: A

92. Discuss the implications of the fact that children born deaf and blind display a broad range of expressions: smiles, laughter, and tears.
    ANSWER: TYPE: E   COG: C

93. Discuss how nonverbal communication is influenced by culture. Provide an example of how understanding can be impacted as a result of cultures having different nonverbal behaviors.
    ANSWER: TYPE: E   COG: C

94. Certain gestures have been shown to increase persuasiveness. List three of them and explain why you feel each would have that effect. Think of and explain a situation in which there would be an exception to one of them. When would the use of that gesture not increase effectiveness?
    ANSWER: TYPE: E   COG: C

95. Give an example of a type of touch typical of the following types of relationships:
      functional/professional
      social/polite
      friendship
      love
      sexual arousal
      ANSWER: TYPE: E   COG: A

96. Anthropologist Edward T. hall defined four distances we use in our everyday lives. Name and briefly describe each of the four distances. Provide an example of the kind of communication that goes on at each range.
      ANSWER: TYPE: E   COG: A

97. For each of the settings below, describe how the environment is likely to be designed to suit the needs of the person who manages it.
      a.   a fast-food restaurant
      b.   airport waiting areas
      c.   a professor's office
      d.   a gambling casino
      e.   a movie theater
      ANSWER: TYPE: E   COG: A

98. Describe the technological advances that must take place in order for the Internet (and similar technology) to become a more useful tool for communicating relational messages.
      ANSWER: TYPE: E   COG: A

99. Explain and provide an example for three of the five functions that nonverbal communication can serve.
      ANSWER: TYPE: E   COG: C

100. Which specific nonverbal behaviors suggest a communicator is attempting an act of deception?
      ANSWER: TYPE: E   COG: A

Matching

101. Some countries or regions are characterized by high levels of touching, others by lower levels. Indicate which in the list below (E) encourage touching or (D) discourage it.

      _____ Canada
      _____ Latin America
      _____ Northern Europe
      _____ Southern Europe
      _____ United States

      ANSWER: D,E,D,E,D   TYPE: K   COG: C

CHAPTER SIX: LISTENING

True/False

1. Of the four types of communication activities, we spend more time listening than on reading, writing, and speaking combined.
      ANSWER: T   TYPE: T   COG: R

2. Hearing is the process that gives meaning, whereas listening is a physiological process.
      ANSWER: F   TYPE: T   COG: R

3. Research indicates that executives spend approximately 60 percent of their communication time listening.

      ANSWER: T   TYPE: T   COG: C

4. True listening involves much more than the passive act of hearing.

      ANSWER: T   TYPE: T   COG: R

5. Despite the frequency with which we use listening, listening skills tend to be recognized as of little importance by business leaders.

      ANSWER: F   TYPE: T   COG: C

6. In committed relationships, listening to personal information in everyday conversation is considered an important ingredient of satisfaction.

      ANSWER: T   TYPE: T   COG: C

7. Listening is a communication skill that can be developed and improved through instruction and training.

      ANSWER: T   TYPE: T   COG: R

8. Effective listening builds better relationships.

      ANSWER: T   TYPE: T   COG: C

9. "Failing to take the other's perspective when listening" is one of the most frequent marital communication problems.

      ANSWER: T   TYPE: T   COG: R

10. Listening is the process wherein sound waves strike the eardrum and cause vibrations that are ·transmitted to the brain.

      ANSWER: F   TYPE: T   COG: R

11. Listening is a natural activity that people do without conscious effort.

      ANSWER: F   TYPE: T   COG: R

12. Because every person interprets data uniquely, we have to accept the fact that we can never completely understand another person.

      ANSWER: T   TYPE: T   COG: R

13. Research indicates that the average person spends much more time speaking than listening in a normal day.

      ANSWER: F   TYPE: T   COG: R

14. The ability to make sense of messages is closely related to the listener's intelligence.

      ANSWER: T   TYPE: T   COG: R

15. Personality traits of listeners do not affect their ability to understand messages.

      ANSWER: F   TYPE: T   COG: R

16. While most people recall very few details of their conversations, they do retain an overall impression about the speaker, especially in important relationships.

      ANSWER: T   TYPE: T   COG: C

17. The process of listening involves hearing, attending, understanding, remembering, and responding.

      ANSWER: T   TYPE: T   COG: R

18. Evaluative responses have the best chance of being received when the person with the problem hasn't requested an evaluation.

      ANSWER: F   TYPE: T   COG: C

19. A major difference between effective and ineffective listening is the kind of feedback offered.

      ANSWER: T   TYPE: T   COG: R

20. At the same time that we receive messages, we also send them.

      ANSWER: T   TYPE: T   COG: C

21. The ability to repeat a statement you just heard doesn't guarantee that you understood it.

      ANSWER: T   TYPE: T   COG: R

22. There are times when the best response is no response.

      ANSWER: T   TYPE: T   COG: R

23. While passive listening gives speakers a chance to be heard, it doesn't guarantee that they will be understood.

        ANSWER: T   TYPE: T   COG: R

24. Clark and Delia found that college students prefer that their friends be silent listeners or ask noncommittal questions rather than asking probing questions about troubling situations.

        ANSWER: T   TYPE: T   COG: R

25. Sincere questions are attempts to send a message rather than receive one.

        ANSWER: F   TYPE: T   COG: R

26. The meaning and intent of any statement is shaped by its context.

        ANSWER: T   TYPE: T   COG: R

27. The best way to improve your listening skills is to concentrate more intensively on your surroundings.

        ANSWER: F   TYPE: T   COG: C

28. Questioning is an example of a listening response from the "more reflective/less evaluative" end of the listening response continuum.

        ANSWER: T   TYPE: T   COG: R

29. Hasting's research tells us that the best way to support parents who have had a child die is to encourage them to move on in life.

        ANSWER: F   TYPE: T   COG: C

30. Listening is less automatic than hearing.

        ANSWER: T   TYPE: T   COG: R

31. Most communicators accurately evaluate their ability to listen and understand others.

        ANSWER: F   TYPE: T   COG: C

32. Paraphrasing is feedback that restates, in your own words, the message you thought the speaker sent.

        ANSWER: T   TYPE: T   COG: R

33. Sympathizing is a response style listeners use when they want to show that they identify with a speaker.

        ANSWER: F   TYPE: T   COG: R

34. Counterfeit questions aren't always bad; they sometimes can be used as face-saving devices.

        ANSWER: T   TYPE: T   COG: R

35. Physiological factors do not contribute to listening since listening is a psychological process.

        ANSWER: F   TYPE: T   COG: C

36. Empathizing requires both understanding of and agreement with another person's message.

        ANSWER: F   TYPE: T   COG: C

37. When paraphrasing, it is important to use the speaker's exact words.

        ANSWER: F   TYPE: T   COG: R

38. People who are seeking an empathic listener usually also want advice.

        ANSWER: F   TYPE: T   COG: C

39. Women are more prone than men to give supportive responses when presented with another person's problem.

        ANSWER: T   TYPE: T   COG: A

40. In analyzing a situation, the listener offers an interpretation of a speaker's message.

        ANSWER: T   TYPE: T   COG: R

41. Research on listening reveals that people only remember about half of what they hear immediately after hearing it.

        ANSWER: T   TYPE: T   COG: C

42. Communicators should use the one or two response styles at which they are the most skilled.

        ANSWER: F   TYPE: T   COG: R

43. Another name for pseudolistening could be counterfeit communication.

        ANSWER: T   TYPE: T   COG: R

44. When approached with another's problem, the most common reaction is advising.
        ANSWER: T   TYPE: T   COG: R
45. Advice isn't always helpful.
        ANSWER: T   TYPE: T   COG: R

Multiple Choice

46. Recall is related to which component of hearing?
    a. hearing
    b. attending
    c. understanding
    d. remembering
    e. all of the above
    ANSWER: d   TYPE: M   COG: R

47. The ability to recall is a function of
    a. the number of times information is repeated
    b. how much information there is
    c. whether the information may be "rehearsed"
    d. all of the above
    e. a and b only
    ANSWER: d   TYPE: M   COG: R

48. Reasons for improving listening skills include:
    a. to understand and retain information
    b. to build and maintain relationships
    c. to help others
    d. to evaluate messages
    e. all of the above
    ANSWER: e   TYPE: M   COG: R

49. Postman and Weingartner's concept of "crap detecting" is an example of which reason for listening?
    a. to understand and retain information
    b. to build and maintain relationships
    c. to help others
    d. to evaluate messages
    e. all of the above
    ANSWER: d   TYPE: M   COG: R

50. Silent listening is the best response to use when
    a. You aren't sure if the other person wants to discuss an unpleasant situation.
    b. You don't want to encourage a speaker to keep talking.
    c. You are open to the speaker's ideas and interjecting isn't appropriate.
    d. You want the speaker to talk through their own solution to a problem
    e. All of the above.
    ANSWER: e   TYPE: M   COG: C

51. Barriers to listening include
    a. information overload
    b. rapid thought and noise
    c. other-affirmation
    d. all of the above
    e. a and b only
    ANSWER: e   TYPE: M   COG: R

52. Which of the following is not a contributing factor for understanding messages?
    a. Knowledge about the source of the message.
    b. The listener's mental abilities.
    c. The context of the message.
    d. The volume of the message.
    e. Both a and b
    ANSWER: d   TYPE: M   COG: R

53. The fact that we spend five or more hours a day listening contributes to
    a. hearing problems
    b. information overload
    c. personal concerns
    d. rapid thought
    e. noise
    ANSWER: b   TYPE: M   COG: R

54. Distractions presented by our physical and mental worlds contribute to
    a. hearing problems
    b. noise
    c. personal concerns
    d. rapid thought
    e. information overload
    ANSWER: b   TYPE: M   COG: R

55. After hearing about the car accident that Dan was in, Jenny responded with "What did you do then?." This type of questioning response is used to:
    a. Clarify meanings
    b. Learn about others' thoughts, feelings and wants
    c. Encourage elaboration.
    d. Encourage discovery
    e. Gather more fact and details.
    ANSWER: e   TYPE: M   COG: A

56. When asking children leading vs. free-recall questions after viewing a video of a theft, Bjorklund and his colleagues found that:
    a. Children had less accurate recall when asked leading questions.
    b. Children had less accurate recall when asked free-recall questions.
    c. Children had more accurate recall when asked statement types of questions.
    d. Children had more accurate recall when asked assumptive questions.
    e. None of the above.
    ANSWER: a   TYPE: M   COG: C

57. Fatigue or other forms of discomfort can be which barrier to listening?
    a. hearing problems
    b. information overload
    c. personal concerns
    d. rapid thought
    e. noise
    ANSWER: e   TYPE: M   COG: R

58. Susan's professors think she is always listening to their lectures because of her eye contact, nods, and note-taking. In reality, Susan is using the class time to catch up on her personal diary. Susan is guilty of
    a. pseudolistening
    b. filling in the gaps
    c. insulated listening
    d. defensive listening
    e. none of the above
    ANSWER: a   TYPE: M   COG: A

59. Barry is more concerned about how much and how long he can talk, rater than listening to others. Barry is guilty of
    a. pseudolistening
    b. insensitive listening
    c. stage hogging
    d. ambushing
    e. selective listening
    ANSWER: c   TYPE: M   COG: A

60. At least four of his friends have told Spencer that his girlfriend is dating others, but Spencer never seems to hear what they are saying. Spencer is probably a(n)
    a. pseudolistener
    b. insulated listener
    c. stage hogger
    d. defensive listener
    e. ambusher
    ANSWER: b   TYPE: M   COG: A

61. Which of the following is an example of a question that carries a hidden agenda:
    a. "Are you busy Sunday evening?"
    b. "You called her back already?"
    c. "Why don't you ever listen?"
    d. "Do you think my new haircut is nice?"
    e. "Are you going to let him get away with that?"
    ANSWER: a   TYPE: M   COG: A

62. It's hard to talk to Edie because she always seems to take things the wrong way and to try to support herself and her side of the story. Edie is a(n)
    a. pseudolistener
    b. insulated listener
    c. stage hogger
    d. defensive listener
    e. ambusher
    ANSWER: d   TYPE: M   COG: A

63. It's hard to talk to Kit because she never really seems to listen; she is just waiting for you to make a mistake and then she pounces. Kit is a(n)
    a. pseudolistener
    b. insulated listener
    c. stage hogger
    d. defensive listener
    e. ambusher
    ANSWER: e   TYPE: M   COG: A

64. Restating in your own words what you thought a speaker has told you is known as
     a. emphatic communication
     b. paraphrasing
     c. pseudolistening
     d. stage hogging
     e. empathizing
     ANSWER: b   TYPE: M   COG: R

65. In comparing listening, speaking, reading, and writing, which of the following is true?
     a. listening is most used but taught least
     b. speaking is used most but taught least
     c. reading is used most and taught most
     d. writing is used most and taught most
     e. reading is taught most and used least
     ANSWER: a   TYPE: M   COG: R

66. The listening response that involves staying attentive while being nonverbally responsive is known as
     a. silent listening
     b. questioning
     c. paraphrasing
     d. interjecting
     e. advising
     ANSWER: a   TYPE: M   COG: R

67. Which response style is associated with the "less reflective/more evaluative" end of the listening response continuum?
     a. questioning
     b. empathizing
     c. paraphrasing
     d. analyzing
     e. none of the above
     ANSWER: d   TYPE: M   COG: R

68. Reflecting a speaker's thoughts, feelings, and wants is associated with which type of listening response?
     a. paraphrasing
     b. analyzing
     c. advising
     d. evaluating
     ANSWER: a   TYPE: M   COG: R

69. Which of the following is *not* a misconception about listening?
     a. listening is a skill that can be taught
     b. listening and hearing are the same thing
     c. listening is easy
     d. all listeners receive the same message
     e. none of the above is applicable
     ANSWER: a   TYPE: M   COG: R

70. Which of the following was *not* used in the text as an example of counterfeit listening?
     a. "Are you finally off the phone?"
     b. "Are you busy Friday night?"
     c. "Honey, do you think I'm overweight?"
     d. "Why aren't you listening to me?"
     e. "You said we were going too fast. Could you be more specific?"
     ANSWER: e   TYPE: M   COG: R

71. Paraphrasing means
    a. using gestures, nods, and facial expressions to respond to the speaker
    b. restating, in your own words, the message you think the speaker just sent
    c. repeated use of questions
    d. mentally questioning the speaker's intentions and arguments
    e. all of the above
    ANSWER: b   TYPE: M   COG: R

72. All of the following represent the "more reflective/less evaluative" end of the listening continuum
    except
    a. questioning
    b. paraphrasing
    c. empathizing
    d. supporting
    ANSWER: d   TYPE: M   COG: R

73. Which of the following is *not* one of the five components of listening mentioned in your text?
    a. hearing
    b. attending
    c. understanding
    d. advising
    e. responding
    ANSWER: d   TYPE: M   COG: R

74. Hearing is physiological; attending is
    a. sociological
    b. psychological
    c. entropological
    d. physical
    e. biological
    ANSWER: b   TYPE: M   COG: R

75. When listeners attempt to show solidarity with the people to whom they are listening, they are using
    which listening response style?
    a. silent listening
    b. paraphrasing
    c. supporting
    d. analyzing
    e. evaluating
    ANSWER: c   TYPE: M   COG: R

76. The residual message is the
    a. most important component
    b. least important component
    c. message "lost" through lack of recall
    d. part of the message we remember
    e. connections listeners make with their own culture
    ANSWER: d   TYPE: M   COG: R

77. A listening model that includes responding is a _____ model.
    a. transactional
    b. transmission
    c. residual
    d. proactive
    e. nonverbal
    ANSWER: a   TYPE: M   COG: R

78. Which of the following is the most accurate example of an empathizing response?
   a. "Don't worry about it."
   b. "Hey, it's only a game."
   c. "You'll feel better tomorrow."
   d. All of the above
   e. None of the above
   ANSWER: e   TYPE: M   COG: R

79. Which of the following is *not* a "less reflective/more evaluative" listening response?
   a. supporting
   b. questioning
   c. analyzing
   d. advising
   e. evaluating
   ANSWER: b   TYPE: M   COG: R

80. Which statement about the conversation below is accurate?
   Speaker: Trent is such a jerk; he always takes me for granted.
   Listener: You're disgusted with the way Trent has been treating you.
   a. the listener used pseudolistening
   b. the listener gave a poor paraphrase because it doesn't use the speaker's words
   c. the listener should have used a question before trying to paraphrase
   d. the listener used a paraphrase to try and understand the speaker's message
   e. both a and b are accurate
   ANSWER: d   TYPE: M   COG: A

81. The difference between an empathizing response and a supporting response is
   a. a supporting response is less effective
   b. an empathizing response is less effective
   c. an empathizing response is more evaluative and directive
   d. a supporting response is more evaluative and directive
   ANSWER: d   TYPE: M   COG: C

82. Which is *not* an example of a counterfeit question?
   a. questions that make statements
   b. questions that carry hidden agendas
   c. questions based on unchecked assumptions
   d. questions that gather more facts and details
   ANSWER: d   TYPE: M   COG: R

83. When offering a supporting response it is important to
   a. use touch as well as verbal support
   b. be sure your support is sincere
   c. be sure the speaker can accept your support
   d. all of the above
   e. b and c only
   ANSWER: e   TYPE: M   COG: R

84. When offering an analyzing response it is important to
   a. use tentative phrasing
   b. be reasonably sure you are correct
   c. be sure the other person will be receptive
   d. be sure your motive for offering an analysis is truly to help
   e. a, b, and c
   ANSWER: e   TYPE: M   COG: R

85. Which of the following is an analyzing response phrased in a tentative way?
   a. I think your teacher doesn't understand you
   b. Perhaps your teacher wants you to work harder
   c. You need to talk to the teacher
   d. Most teachers are like that
   e. What did your teacher say?
      ANSWER: b   TYPE: M   COG: A

86. When offering advice it is important to be sure
   a. the advice is correct
   b. the speaker is ready to accept it
   c. the speaker won't blame you if it doesn't work
   d. all of the above
   e. a and b only
      ANSWER: d   TYPE: M   COG: R

87. When offering a judging response it is important
   a. that you have experienced the same problem
   b. that the speaker has requested the evaluation
   c. that the judgment is constructive
   d. all of the above
   e. b and c only
      ANSWER: e   TYPE: M   COG: R

Essay

88. Discuss the following quotation in terms of what you know about listening: "If you think communication is all talk, you haven't been listening." Ashleigh Brilliant
      ANSWER: TYPE: E   COG: C

89. Give examples of three counterfeit questions, explain what makes them counterfeit rather than sincere, and then offer sincere alternatives for each.
      ANSWER: TYPE: E   COG: A

90. The text states that there are several styles of listening that people typically use when trying to help someone deal with a problem. Discuss the following four helping strategies in terms of their potential disadvantages: advising, analyzing, evaluating, and supporting.
      ANSWER: TYPE: E   COG: C

91. Imagine that you are explaining the listening unit of this course to friends or family. They want to know why it's important to be a good listener and why (since they all hear) it is possible they're not good listeners.
      ANSWER: TYPE: E   COG: C

92. Tori and Lamar are discussing where they will go to eat dinner. Lamar has an opinion, but is concealing it behind counterfeit questions. Offer two types of counterfeit questions Lamar might ask, with examples of each.
      ANSWER: TYPE: E   COG: A

93. Your text gives several reasons why paraphrasing assists listening. Cite three of these reasons, briefly explaining each.
      ANSWER: TYPE: E   COG: R

94. Your friend has just told you about a death in her/his family. Offer two responses that would fall into categories of non-empathizing identified in the text. Explain what makes them non-empathic, then offer and explain two empathizing alternatives.
      ANSWER: TYPE: E   COG: A

95. You and your partner are having a discussion about your relationship. Your partner says the following to you: "I don't like the way things are going between us. You don't treat me like you used to and you embarrassed me in front of my friends last night. It seems to me like I care about you a lot more than you care about me." Explain in detail why the following responses would *not* be examples of active listening.
   a. "You're upset because you're tired. Why don't we talk about this tomorrow when I know we'll both feel a lot better?"
   b. "Don't worry. What happened last night won't happen again."
   c. "Hey, you're not the only one unhappy about this relationship."
           ANSWER: TYPE: E   COG: A
96. Respond to each of the following statements with a more reflective/less evaluative listening response.
   a. "You just never stop to think of me…it's just work, work, work, as if that's all there is to life."
   b. "Frankly, I'm leaving because I'm looking for a job where my talents will be recognized and my contributions valued."
   c. "I don't know how you expect me to believe you care when you leave me waiting here for three hours."
   d. "I'm such a jerk! If I hadn't opened my big mouth, Bob and Barb would be together right now!"
           ANSWER: TYPE: E   COG: A
97. Give five different types of responses to your friend who says to you: "That professor wants me to think of him as God or something. He thinks nobody could possibly know anything prior to entering his classroom." Choose from the following: advising, analyzing, supporting, empathizing, questioning, and evaluating. Be sure to identify the style that each example illustrates.
           ANSWER: TYPE: E   COG: A
98. Explain the habits of people who listen ineffectively.
           ANSWER: TYPE: E   COG: A
99. Explain two advantages and two disadvantages of evaluating as a listening style.
           ANSWER: TYPE: E   COG: A
100. Explain the essential differences between "more reflective/less evaluative" listening responses and "less reflective/more evaluative" listening responses. In your answer, give two examples from each end of the listening continuum.
           ANSWER: TYPE: E   COG: A

CHAPTER SEVEN: EMOTIONS

True/False

1. Daniel Goleman's concept of "emotional intelligence" refers to the ability to understand and manage one's own emotions and to be sensitive to others' feelings.
           ANSWER: T   TYPE: T   COG: R
2. The most basic emotional expressions are universal.
           ANSWER: T   TYPE: T   COG: C
3. Not all physical changes that accompany emotions are universal.
           ANSWER: T   TYPE: T   COG: C
4. There is no apparent difference between the way that men and women experience and express their emotions.
           ANSWER: F   TYPE: T   COG: R

5. People from warmer climates tend to be more emotionally expressive than those in colder climates.
   ANSWER: T   TYPE: T   COG: C
6. 6.   Facial expressions indicating fear, sadness, happiness, and pain appear to be universally understood from one culture to another.
   ANSWER: T   TYPE: T   COG: R
7. Plutchik's "emotion wheel" suggests that many feelings need to be described using a single term.
   ANSWER: F   TYPE: T   COG: R
8. Failure to express emotions plays a part in physical as well as mental health.
   ANSWER: T   TYPE: T   COG: A
9. Individuals who label themselves as "shy" tend to exhibit distinctly different behavioral patterns than those who label themselves as "not shy."
   ANSWER: F   TYPE: T   COG: R
10. Pretending to be angry can actually make us become angry.
    ANSWER: T   TYPE: T   COG: R
11. Our interpretation of any event is a more important determinant of feelings than is the even itself.
    ANSWER: T   TYPE: T   COG: R
12. As a group, women are more likely than men to use emotions to clarify their feelings in e-mail than are men.
    ANSWER: T   TYPE: T   COG: R
13. Women are consistently better than men at detecting nonverbal emotional cues.
    ANSWER: T   TYPE: T   COG: R
14. Because we talk ourselves into debilitative feelings, it is possible to talk ourselves out of feeling bad.
    ANSWER: T   TYPE: T   COG: C
15. Both men and women express anger equally but men are less bashful about revealing their strengths and positive emotions.
    ANSWER: T   TYPE: T   COG: C
16. The ability to express emotions verbally is of minor importance to effective communication.
    ANSWER: F   TYPE: T   COG: R
17. There are some situations in which you may (correctly) choose never to express your feelings.
    ANSWER: T   TYPE: T   COG: R
18. Many people think they're clearly expressing their feelings when in fact their statements are emotionally counterfeit.
    ANSWER: T   TYPE: T   COG: C
19. Most people find it easier to express negative emotions than positive ones.
    ANSWER: F   TYPE: T   COG: R
20. The comment "I feel as if you're trying to hurt me" is a clear statement of the speaker's feelings.
    ANSWER: F   TYPE: T   COG: A
21. Beyond physiological benefits, a primary advantage of expressing emotions effectively is the chance of improving relationships.
    ANSWER: T   TYPE: T   COG: R
22. Intimacy is a desirable goal for every relationship.
    ANSWER: F   TYPE: T   COG: R
23. Close relationships require a constant exchange of emotions.
    ANSWER: T   TYPE: T   COG: C
24. Skillful expression of emotions increases the quality of problem solving.
    ANSWER: T   TYPE: T   COG: R
25. Facilitative emotions hinder or prevent effective communication.
    ANSWER: F   TYPE: T   COG: R
26. Strong emotions sharpen your thinking ability.
    ANSWER: F   TYPE: T   COG: C

27. Recent research by Bushman suggests that people who act out angry feelings actually feel worse than those who experience anger without lashing out.
ANSWER: T   TYPE: T   COG: R

28. One of the important guidelines for expressing emotions is the ability to recognize the difference between feeling and acting.
ANSWER: T   TYPE: T   COG: R

29. Facilitative emotions hinder or prevent effective performance.
ANSWER: F   TYPE: T   COG: R

30. The difference between facilitative and debilitative emotions often isn't one of quality so much as degree.
ANSWER: T   TYPE: T   COG: R

31. Robert Plutchik developed the "emotion wheel" to illustrate the relationships between the eight primary emotions and the many combinations of mixed emotions.
ANSWER: T   TYPE: T   COG: R

32. It is best to express our emotions spontaneously and completely in all circumstances.
ANSWER: F   TYPE: T   COG: C

33. Being rushed, tired, or disturbed by some other matters are not adequate reasons for postponing the sharing of a feeling.
ANSWER: F   TYPE: T   COG: C

34. Catastrophic thinking often takes the form of rumination.
ANSWER: T   TYPE: T   COG: C

35. Failure to express emotions plays a part in physical as well as mental health.
ANSWER: T   TYPE: T   COG: R

36. First order emotions are triggered by "emotional scripts" we have learned as part of our socialization.
ANSWER: F   TYPE: T   COG: R

37. Competent communicators should be able to handle any situation with complete confidence and skill.
ANSWER: F   TYPE: T   COG: R

Multiple Choice

38. Components in our emotions include
    a. physiological changes
    b. nonverbal manifestations
    c. cognitive interpretations
    d. a and b
    e. a and b and c
    ANSWER: e   TYPE: M   COG: R

39. An increased heartbeat, a rise in blood pressure, and an increase in adrenaline secretions are all part of which emotional component?
    a. physiological changes
    b. nonverbal manifestations
    c. cognitive interpretations
    d. verbal expressions
    e. all of the above
    ANSWER: a   TYPE: M   COG: C

40. Rebecca tearfully apologizes to her history professor for showing up 30 minutes late to class. Rebecca is experiencing a(n)
    a. First order emotion
    b. Second order emotion
    c. Fallacy of causation
    d. Emotional contagion
    e. Fallacy of should
        ANSWER: b   TYPE: M   COG: A

41. First order emotions are triggered by
    a. Primary feelings
    b. Secondary feelings
    c. Social knowledge of what's right and wrong
    d. Environmental stimuli
    e. None of the above.
        ANSWER: d   TYPE: M   COG: R

42. Facial expression, body positioning, and distance are all indicative of which emotional component?
    a. physiological changes
    b. nonverbal manifestations
    c. cognitive interpretations
    d. verbal expressions
    e. all of the above
        ANSWER: b   TYPE: M   COG: R

43. _____ is the best predictor of the ability to detect and interpret emotional expression.
    a. Biological sex
    b. Cultural similarity
    c. Willingness to self-disclose
    d. Academic background
    e. Non-verbal communication
        ANSWER: a   TYPE: M   COG: C

44. People fail to express the full range of their feelings because of
    a. society and models
    b. social and sexual roles
    c. inability to recognize and feel emotions
    d. fear of self-disclosure
    e. all of the above
        ANSWER: e   TYPE: M   COG: R

45. Benefits that can follow from sharing feelings appropriately are
    a. physical health
    b. increased intimacy
    c. conflict resolution
    d. lower cholesterol
    e. all of the above
        ANSWER: e   TYPE: M   COG: R

46. Debilitative feelings are caused by fallacies of
    a. perfection, repeating, and shoulds
    b. overgeneralization and causation
    c. helplessness and catastrophic expectation
    d. all of the above
    e. b and c only
        ANSWER: d   TYPE: M   COG: R

47. It's been a year since Mark and Tracy broke up. Mark is still depressed and gets irate if anyone even mentions Tracy's name. Mark is experiencing:
    a. First order emotions
    b. Self talk
    c. Facilitative emotions
    d. Debilitative emotions
    e. None of the above
        ANSWER: d   TYPE: M   COG: A

48. Using situational clues to label symptoms is characteristic of which emotional component?
    a. physiological changes
    b. nonverbal manifestations
    c. cognitive interpretations
    d. verbal expressions
    e. all of the above
        ANSWER: c   TYPE: M   COG: R

49. The little voices in your head that talk to you constantly is called:
    a. Self-talk
    b. Cognitive performance
    c. Cognitive talk
    d. Irrational thinking
    e. Debilitative thinking
        ANSWER: a   TYPE: M   COG: R

50. Recognizing your _____ is an important step in minimizing debilitative emotions.
    a. Personality style
    b. Feelings
    c. Self-concept
    d. Activating events
    e. None of the above
        ANSWER: d   TYPE: M   COG: R

51. Feeling apologetic when you are not at fault is a symptom of which fallacy?
    a. approval
    b. causation
    c. shoulds
    d. helplessness
    e. catastrophic expectations
        ANSWER: c   TYPE: M   COG: C

52. If people insist that the world can operate just as they want it to, they have fallen into which fallacy?
    a. approval
    b. causation
    c. shoulds
    d. helplessness
    e. catastrophic expectations
        ANSWER: c   TYPE: M   COG: R

53. Being lost in the dark in a sudden blackout is an example of
    a. Social convention affecting emotions
    b. Defensive retaliation
    c. First order emotion
    d. Second order emotion
    e. Fallacy of should
        ANSWER: c   TYPE: M   COG: A

54. Sharon tells Mary everything about her sexual past. However, Mary doesn't reciprocate since she's afraid that Sharon might use the information against her some day. Mary is demonstrating one of the reasons people
    a. See social roles differently
    b. Cognitively process emotions differently
    c. Fear self disclosure
    d. Experience debilitative emotions
    e. Experience the fallacy of helplessness.
         ANSWER: c   TYPE: M   COG: A

55. Charles Darwin's observation that humans and certain other creatures behave in similar ways when enraged contributes to our understanding of which emotional component?
    a. physiological changes
    b. nonverbal manifestations
    c. cognitive interpretations
    d. verbal expressions
    e. all of the above
         ANSWER: b   TYPE: M   COG: C

56. Science has established a clear relationship between _____ and the way people experience and communicate emotions.
    a. Academic background
    b. Personality
    c. Social Status
    d. Biological Sex
    e. Intelligence
         ANSWER: b   TYPE: M   COG: C

57. Instead of saying "You are so boring," it is better to say _____ when your friend talks about shopping again.
    a. "I think you are boring"
    b. "I'm a little bored"
    c. "I am bored with you"
    d. You are boring when you talk about shopping"
    e. "I get bored when you talk about shopping"
         ANSWER: e   TYPE: M   COG: A

58. Being obsessed with "shoulds" can
    a. cause unnecessary expectations
    b. keep you from changing unsatisfying conditions
    c. build a more positive climate with others
    d. all of the above
    e. a and b only
         ANSWER: e   TYPE: M   COG: R

59. "I don't have a thing to wear!" is a statement of which fallacy?
    a. causation
    b. overgeneralization
    c. shoulds
    d. helplessness
    e. catastrophic expectations
         ANSWER: b   TYPE: M   COG: A

60. If you feel you should do nothing that can hurt others because it would make them feel a particular way, you have fallen into which fallacy?
    a. causation
    b. overgeneralization
    c. shoulds
    d. helplessness
    e. catastrophic expectation
         ANSWER: a   TYPE: M   COG: A
61. If people see themselves perpetually as victims, they have fallen into which fallacy?
    a. causation
    b. overgeneralization
    c. shoulds
    d. helplessness
    e. catastrophic expectations
         ANSWER: d   TYPE: M   COG: A
62. Guidelines on expressing your feelings include all of the following *except*
    a. recognize your feelings
    b. always express your feelings spontaneously
    c. accept responsibility for your feelings
    d. choose the best place and time for expressing feelings
    e. speak unambiguously
         ANSWER: b   TYPE: M   COG: R
63. Monitoring self-talk is a way to
    a. recognize your feelings
    b. share multiple emotions
    c. accept responsibility for your feelings
    d. choose the best time and place for expressing your feelings
    e. speak unambiguously
         ANSWER: a   TYPE: M   COG: R
64. The recognition that others don't cause your feelings helps you
    a. recognize your feelings
    b. share multiple emotions
    c. accept responsibility for your feelings
    d. choose the best time and place for expressing your feelings
    e. speak unambiguously
         ANSWER: c   TYPE: M   COG: R
65. Members of collectivist cultures are more likely to
    a. discourage expression of negative emotions
    b. feel comfortable revealing their feelings
    c. speak openly abut problems
    d. share personal ideas and feelings
    e. b and c and d
         ANSWER: a   TYPE: M   COG: R
66. Which of the following is the most genuine expression of emotions?
    a. "It's inconvenient to be kept waiting."
    b. "We really need to get going."
    c. "I'm worried about my brother."
    d. "I feel like we've been seeing too much of each other."
    e. "I didn't get to study last night."
         ANSWER: c   TYPE: M   COG: A

67. Storming out of your bedroom to yell at your loud roommates at 3:00am is a violation of which guideline to expressing feelings appropriately?
    a. Recognize the difference between feeling and acting.
    b. Choose the best time and place to express feelings.
    c. Share multiple feelings
    d. Recognize your feelings
    e. None of the above
        ANSWER: b   TYPE: M   COG: A
68. One result of a life spent avoiding the expression of emotion may be
    a. a debilitating fear of self-disclosure
    b. the limiting of behavior to stereotyped roles
    c. the inability to recognize and act on one's emotions
    d. failure to acknowledge strong feelings
    e. all of the above
        ANSWER: e   TYPE: M   COG: A
69. Which of the following is a benefit of sharing feelings?
    a. an increase in the quality of problem solving
    b. a decrease in other-directedness
    c. an increase in static evaluations
    d. a need for deciding when to self-disclose
    e. none of the above ·
        ANSWER: a   TYPE: M   COG: R
70. Debilitative emotions can be distinguished from facilitative emotions by their
    a. low intensity and brief duration
    b. low intensity and extended duration
    c. high intensity and extended duration
    d. high intensity and brief duration
    e. variable intensity and duration
        ANSWER: c   TYPE: M   COG: R
71. A cognitive model of emotions includes
    a. event, intention, action
    b. activating event, thought, consequences
    c. thought, rationalization, consequences
    d. intention, interpretation, action
    e. intensity, interpretation, duration
        ANSWER: b   TYPE: M   COG: R
72. All of the following guidelines for expressing emotions are provided in the textbook *except*
    a. recognize your feelings
    b. choose the best language
    c. share multiple feelings
    d. accept responsibility for your feelings
    e. express your feelings ambiguously
        ANSWER: e   TYPE: M   COG: R
73. The first step in Ellis's approach to cutting down on irrational thinking is to
    a. think about stopping negative self-talk
    b. express any emotion any time it is felt
    c. learn to distinguish what is from what should be
    d. monitor your emotional reactions
    e. sacrifice personal principles to the relationship
        ANSWER: d   TYPE: M   COG: C

74. Acknowledging attraction to certain men or women, even though you might not choose to act on these feelings, is an example of how to
    a. distinguish feeling from acting
    b. share multiple emotions
    c. accept responsibility for your feelings
    d. choose the best time and pace for expressing feelings
    e. speak unambiguously
        ANSWER: a   TYPE: M   COG: A

75. According to Ellis's theory, the experience of fright, joy, or anger comes primarily from
    a. the symptoms experienced
    b. the cause of the emotion
    c. the label we give these experiences
    d. the situation
    e. attribution theory
        ANSWER: c   TYPE: M   COG: C

76. Ellis's theory is most directly linked to which fallacy?
    a. perfection
    b. overgeneralization
    c. approval
    d. causation
    e. "shoulds"
        ANSWER: d   TYPE: M   COG: C

77. "It's no big deal" is a response that
    a. is cognitively complex
    b. is rational rather than emotional
    c. denies the listener the right to interpret the speaker's feelings
    d. is face-saving
    e. reflects debilitative feelings
        ANSWER: c   TYPE: M   COG: A

78. Crying can be helpful because it
    a. encourages sympathy from others
    b. makes you appear weaker than you are
    c. washes debris from the eyes
    d. rids the body of chemicals caused by stress
    e. prevents mental illness
        ANSWER: d   TYPE: M   COG: C

79. The fallacy of overgeneralization:
    a. confuses "is" with "might"
    b. results from trying to obtain everyone's approval
    c. bases a belief on a limited amount of evidence
    d. exaggerates shortcomings
    e. c and d
        ANSWER: e   TYPE: M   COG: R

80. "If I take chemistry, I'll probably get an 'F'." This statement is an example of the fallacy of
    a. overgeneralization
    b. perfection
    c. causation
    d. shoulds
    e. catastrophic expectations
        ANSWER: e   TYPE: M   COG: A

81. The difference between the stimulus-response model and the cognitive model of emotional response is
    a. the thought or belief component
    b. the nature of the activating event
    c. the intensity of the reaction
    d. the nature of the consequence
    e. the environment in which the event occurs
         ANSWER: a   TYPE: M   COG: C

82. George has refused to continue to teach Interpersonal Communication because he sometimes has conflicts in his own relationships. George may be a victim of the fallacy of
    a. overgeneralization
    b. perfection
    c. causation
    d. shoulds
    e. catastrophic expectations
         ANSWER: b   TYPE: M   COG: A

Essay

83. What is the difference between perfection and competence? What are the implications for communication?
         ANSWER: TYPE: E   COG: C

84. The text states that "the fallacy of perfection" is an irrational belief that leads people to think they must perform perfectly in any situation or they are failures. Using your own experience, describe two debilitative emotions that can result from subscribing to this belief.
         ANSWER: TYPE: E   COG: A

85. Explain what is meant by the following statement: "Anger suppressed can literally 'eat away at our guts.'"
         ANSWER: TYPE: E   COG: A

86. Imagine you are a student in a class for which participating in discussions is a central requirement for a good grade. You are a relatively outgoing person but you have always had a hard time speaking up in class to offer your comments, opinions, criticisms, and so on. In fact, you almost never do so, not even when you are completely familiar with the material. Using Ellis's model, identify 1] the activating event and the 2] emotional reaction. Then offer three examples of the negative self-talk that represents the irrational belief this student is probably operating on, and finally, dispute those irrational beliefs with three coping statements.
         ANSWER: TYPE: E   COG: A

87. Briefly describe and provide an example of each of the four components of emotion.
         ANSWER: TYPE: E   COG: R

88. Briefly explain the influence of sex and culture on emotional expressiveness and sensitivity.
         ANSWER: TYPE: E   COG: C

89. Discuss two personal examples of facilitative and debilitative emotions.
         ANSWER: TYPE: E   COG: A

CHAPTER EIGHT: DYNAMICS OF INTERPERSONAL RELATIONSHIPS

True/False

1. According to Charles Berger, even ritualistic exchanges between customers and servers at a fast-food restaurant count as "personal" relationships.
   ANSWER: F   TYPE: T   COG: R

2. Your text suggests that a relationship is less a *thing* than a *process*.
   ANSWER: T   TYPE: T   COG: R

3. While e-mail may be helpful in sending information, its use seldom leads to any kind of sustained interpersonal relationship.
   ANSWER: F   TYPE: T   COG: C

4. A recent study has shown that the most universally preferred approach in initiating a romantic relationship is the use of a cute or flippant remark.
   ANSWER: F   TYPE: T   COG: C

5. Individuals in a couple relationship usually agree upon the specific events that caused turning points in their relationship.
   ANSWER: F   TYPE: T   COG: R

6. Research by Virginia Richmond asserts that satisfied couples talk more to one another than do less satisfied ones.
   ANSWER: T   TYPE: T   COG: C

7. The relational dimension of messages makes statements about how the parties feel toward one another.
   ANSWER: T   TYPE: T   COG: R

8. Metacommunication is communication about communication.
   ANSWER: T   TYPE: T   COG: R

9. Average-looking people with pleasing personalities are likely to be judged as attractive.
   ANSWER: T   TYPE: T   COG: C

10. Generally, the similarity between husbands and wives is significantly less than the amount the partners assume to exist.
    ANSWER: T   TYPE: T   COG: C

11. Appearance is especially important in the early stages of a relationship.
    ANSWER: T   TYPE: T   COG: R

12. We don't appreciate other people if their liking is insincere or doesn't fit our own self-concept.
    ANSWER: T   TYPE: T   COG: R

13. Exchange theory suggests we seek out people who can give us rewards that are greater than the costs we encounter in dealing with them.
    ANSWER: T   TYPE: T   COG: R

14. The best way to gain the liking of others is to be good at what you do and to deny your mistakes.
    ANSWER: F   TYPE: T   COG: C

15. Self-disclosure is a good measure of the depth of a relationship.
    ANSWER: T   TYPE: T   COG: R

16. The keys to satisfying self-disclosure are reciprocity and timing.
    ANSWER: T   TYPE: T   COG: C

17. Relationships, once invented and defined, cannot be reinvented and redefined.
    ANSWER: F   TYPE: T   COG: R

18. Ironically, people with high self-esteem tend to seek out relationships with people who treat them poorly.
    ANSWER: F   TYPE: T   COG: R

19. For adults, similarity is more important to relational happiness than even communication ability.
ANSWER: T   TYPE: T   COG: C
20. In terminating the least intimate relationships, one partner simply withdraws; in terminating the most intimate relationships, the initiator typically expresses grief.
ANSWER: T   TYPE: T   COG: R
21. Differences strengthen a relationship when they are complementary.
ANSWER: T   TYPE: T   COG: R
22. When partners are radically different, the dissimilar qualities that at first appear intriguing later become cause for relational breakups.
ANSWER: T   TYPE: T   COG: C
23. Exchange theory suggests that we often seek out people who can give us rewards that are greater than or equal to the costs we encounter in dealing with them.
ANSWER: T   TYPE: T   COG: R
24. Aronson's research suggests that competent people who blunder are rated as less attractive than competent people who don't blunder.
ANSWER: F   TYPE: T   COG: C
25. The relational stages described by Mark Knapp are most appropriate for describing professional rather than personal relationships.
ANSWER: F   TYPE: T   COG: R
26. Telling others important information about yourself can help build liking.
ANSWER: T   TYPE: T   COG: R
27. According to Knapp's theory, small talk is a meaningless pastime engaged in at initial stages of relationships.
ANSWER: F   TYPE: T   COG: R
28. Social scientists agree that relationships generally develop and dissolve in phases.
ANSWER: T   TYPE: T   COG: R
29. Relationships that are particularly strong usually have a high degree of understanding and empathy, but many satisfactory relationships operate quite well without a high degree of these traits.
ANSWER: T   TYPE: T   COG: R
30. The study of dialectical tensions emphasizes the ongoing maintenance of a relationship, rather than how a relationship develops in stages.
ANSWER: T   TYPE: T   COG: R
31. Dialectical tensions are conflicts that occur when two opposing or incompatible forces exist simultaneously.
ANSWER: T   TYPE: T   COG: R
32. Dialectical tensions are confined to external conflicts in which the desires of two relational partners clash with one another.
ANSWER: F   TYPE: T   COG: R
33. The dialectical tensions of stability and change involve our conflicting desires for connection and independence.
ANSWER: F   TYPE: T   COG: R
34. When we are unsure how to react to an unexpected response from an intimate friend, we are being affected by the predictability-novelty dialectic.
ANSWER: T   TYPE: T   COG: A
35. Deciding how to openly respond to a touchy question is related to the expression-privacy dialectic.
ANSWER: T   TYPE: T   COG: A
36. Vagueness and humor are techniques that might be used to disqualify apparent dialectical tensions in a relationship.
ANSWER: T   TYPE: T   COG: R

37. By age one, most infants understand that they can influence the actions of others through their behavior.

        ANSWER: T   TYPE: T   COG: R

38. Compliance-gaining strategies define negative tactics we use to coerce others to think or act in a desired way.

        ANSWER: F   TYPE: T   COG: R

39. The exchange and reciprocity approach can be either manipulative or supportive.

        ANSWER: T   TYPE: T   COG: C

40. The number and variety of compliance-gaining strategies decreases with age.

        ANSWER: F   TYPE: T   COG: R

41. Relational messages are usually expressed nonverbally.

        ANSWER: T   TYPE: T   COG: R

42. The influence of personal attractiveness begins early in life and continues well into middle age.

        ANSWER: T   TYPE: T   COG: C

43. Couples in successful marriages are similar enough to satisfy each other, but different enough to meet each other's needs.

        ANSWER: T   TYPE: T   COG: C

44. We like to be around talented people because we hope their abilities will rub off on us, but we are uncomfortable around people who are too competent.

        ANSWER: T   TYPE: T   COG: R

45. Proximity is the factor that maintains that we are likely to develop strong personal feelings or either like or dislike toward others whom we encounter frequently.

        ANSWER: T   TYPE: T   COG: R

Multiple Choice

46. According to Charles Berger, for a relationship to exist, the people involved must do all of the following *except*
    a.   be aware of each other
    b.   take each other into account
    c.   exercise some degree of influence with one another
    d.   have some agreement about social expectations
    e.   Berger recognizes all four of the above characteristics

        ANSWER: e   TYPE: M   COG: R

47. The similarity thesis is based upon which similarities between partners?
    a.   age and education
    b.   race and ethnic background
    c.   socioeconomic status
    d.   all of the above
    e.   a and b only

        ANSWER: d   TYPE: M   COG: R

48. Logical reasons for the similarity thesis include
    a.   social validation of ourselves
    b.   reduces uncertainty and anxiety
    c.   assume they like us, so we like them
    d.   all of the above
    e.   a and c only

        ANSWER: d   TYPE: M   COG: C

49. The old saying, "Opposites attract," suggests which reason for forming relationships?
    a.   appearance
    b.   similarity
    c.   complementarity
    d.   reciprocity
    e.   exchange
          ANSWER: c   TYPE: M   COG: C

50. The theory that explains relationship development using an economic model is
    a.   exchange
    b.   penetration
    c.   relational dialectic
    d.   all of the above
    e.   none of the above
          ANSWER: a   TYPE: M   COG: R

51. Which type of person was rated as the most attractive?
    a.   superior person who did not blunder
    b.   superior person who blundered
    c.   average person who blundered
    d.   average person who did not blunder
    e.   a and d only
          ANSWER: b   TYPE: M   COG: C

52. The fact that we are likely to choose a mate with whom we frequently cross paths often points to which reason for forming relationships?
    a.   appearance
    b.   similarity
    c.   complementarity
    d.   reciprocity
    e.   proximity
          ANSWER: e   TYPE: M   COG: C

53. Which stage of relational development is usually brief and follows conventional formulas?
    a.   initiating
    b.   experimenting
    c.   intensifying
    d.   integrating
    e.   bonding
          ANSWER: a   TYPE: M   COG: R

54. Which of the following are acceptable strategies for learning about others?
    a.   networking
    b.   offering
    c.   approaching
    d.   sustaining
    e.   all of the above
          ANSWER: e   TYPE: M   COG: R

55. Picking a seat in class near the person you'd like to get to know is an example of
    a.   networking
    b.   offering
    c.   approaching
    d.   sustaining
    e.   self-disclosing
          ANSWER: b   TYPE: M   COG: A

56. Jose is attracted to Phyllicia so he tries to discover as much as about her as he can from Phyllicia's friend Mel. Jerry is using a technique called
   a.   networking
   b.   offering
   c.   approaching
   d.   sustaining
   e.   all of the above
      ANSWER: a   TYPE: M   COG: A
57. Asking someone for the time is an example of
   a.   networking
   b.   offering
   c.   approaching
   d.   sustaining
   e.   all of the above
      ANSWER: c   TYPE: M   COG: A
58. Small talk is the hallmark of which stage of relationship development?
   a.   experimenting
   b.   intensifying
   c.   integrating
   d.   bonding
   e.   terminating
      ANSWER: a   TYPE: M   COG: R
59. When partners begin to refer to themselves as "we," they have moved into which relational stage?
   a.   initiating
   b.   experimenting
   c.   intensifying
   d.   integrating
   e.   bonding
      ANSWER: c   TYPE: M   COG: R
60. Business contracts or marriage licenses are found in which stage of relational development?
   a.   initiating
   b.   experimenting
   c.   intensifying
   d.   integrating
   e.   bonding
      ANSWER: e   TYPE: M   COG: C
61. Which of the following is not a factor to consider when choosing a compliance gaining strategy?
   a.   Level of intimacy
   b.   The level or reciprocity
   c.   Personal benefits to the persuader.
   d.   Resistance
   e.   Consequences of rejection.
      ANSWER: b   TYPE: M   COG: R
62. Working late at the office could be an example of which stage of relational development?
   a.   bonding
   b.   differentiating
   c.   circumscribing
   d.   stagnation
   e.   termination
      ANSWER: c   TYPE: M   COG: A

63. When your mother still calls you "my baby," even though you are in adult, she is *not* recognizing which principle about relationships?
    - a. they do change
    - b. they require attention
    - c. they meet expectations of participants
    - d. they can be improved
    - e. none of the above
    - ANSWER: a   TYPE: M   COG: A

64. Kahlil Gibran's statement, "Let there be spaces in your togetherness…The pillars of the temple stand apart, and the oak tree and the cypress grow not in each other's shadow," is indicative of which relational stage?
    - a. bonding
    - b. differentiating
    - c. circumscribing
    - d. stagnation
    - e. avoiding
    - ANSWER: b   TYPE: M   COG: A

65. We give up some characteristics of our old selves and become different people in which relational stage?
    - a. initiating
    - b. experimenting
    - c. intensifying
    - d. integrating
    - e. differentiating
    - ANSWER: d   TYPE: M   COG: R

66. Workers who have lost enthusiasm for the job reflect which relational stage?
    - a. bonding
    - b. differentiating
    - c. circumscribing
    - d. stagnation
    - e. avoiding
    - ANSWER: d   TYPE: M   COG: A

67. If Cal accuses Jaden of constantly interrupting him when they argue, Cal is engaging in
    - a. recalibration
    - b. reward and punishment
    - c. relational appeals
    - d. indirect appeals
    - e. metacommunication
    - ANSWER: e   TYPE: M   COG: A

68. "I've been sick lately and can't see you" is illustrative of which relational stage?
    - a. bonding
    - b. differentiating
    - c. circumscribing
    - d. stagnation
    - e. avoiding
    - ANSWER: e   TYPE: M   COG: A

69. The way a relationship ends depends on whether
    a.   the onset of problems is sudden or gradual
    b.   negotiations about disengagement are brief or lengthy
    c.   the outcome is termination or continuation in some other form
    d.   all of the above
    e.   a and c only
          ANSWER: d   TYPE: M   COG: R
70. "Movement is always to a new place." This means that
    a.   communication is irreversible
    b.   it is impossible to go back to the way a relationship was in the past
    c.   change is inherent
    d.   there is constant flux
    e.   all of the above are true
          ANSWER: e   TYPE: M   COG: C
71. Even after breaking up and getting back together again repeatedly, Susan and Jim are disappointed to discover they can't seem to recapture the exact excitement they felt when they first met. This example illustrates how
    a.   self-disclosure is necessary for relationships.
    b.   relationship are constantly changing
    c.   relational movement is always to a new place.
    d.   A and B
    e.   B and C
          ANSWER: e   TYPE: M   COG: A
72. Although she really loves Jon and enjoys being with him, Waynetta is beginning to feel trapped in her marriage to him. She is being pulled by the
    a.   altruistic-selfishness dialectic
    b.   integration-separation dialectic
    c.   stability-change dialectic
    d.   expression-privacy dialectic
    e.   similarity-complementarity dialectic
          ANSWER: b   TYPE: M   COG: A
73. Self-disclosure is most related to which dialectical tension?
    a.   altruistic-selfishness dialectic
    b.   integration-separation dialectic
    c.   stability-change dialectic
    d.   expression-privacy dialectic
    e.   similarity-complementarity dialectic
          ANSWER: d   TYPE: M   COG: C
74. At their marriage ceremony, Eva and Juan lit a candle to symbolize their unity. This ritual is related to the
    a.   altruistic-selfishness dialectic
    b.   integration-separation dialectic
    c.   stability-change dialectic
    d.   expression-privacy dialectic
    e.   similarity-complementarity dialectic
          ANSWER: b   TYPE: M   COG: A

75. "Quite frankly, this relationship is getting pretty boring. I always know exactly what Bev is going to do and say about everything." The boredom of this relationship is linked to the
    a. altruistic-selfishness dialectic
    b. integration-separation dialectic
    c. stability-change dialectic
    d. expression-privacy dialectic
    e. similarity-complementarity dialectic
    ANSWER: c   TYPE: M   COG: A

76. It is understood that every year Bob will plan a surprise evening for Cathy's birthday. Bob and Cathy are using the _____ strategy for managing the stability-change dialectic.
    a. recalibration
    b. integration
    c. segmentation
    d. alternation
    e. reaffirmation
    ANSWER: b   TYPE: M   COG: A

77. In order to manage dialectical tension in their marriage, Brianna and Enrique decide that they will dedicate certain times each week that they will spend together and other specific times to be on their own. They are using the strategy of
    a. selection
    b. cyclic alternation
    c. segmentation
    d. reframing
    e. moderation
    ANSWER: b   TYPE: M   COG: A

78. Cecelia enjoys romantic movies whereas Eddie prefers action films. They explain away their differences by saying that they both love movies. They are using the strategy of
    a. selection
    b. cyclic alternation
    c. segmentation
    d. re-framing
    e. moderation
    ANSWER: d   TYPE: M   COG: A

79. Gender research shows
    a. men want autonomy while women want connection
    b. men are more open while women are more closed
    c. men like stability while women prefer more novelty
    d. a and c
    e. all of the above
    ANSWER: a   TYPE: M   COG: R

80. Which label could be used to describe the communication when one partner in a relationship exclaims, "I can never discuss anything with you"?
    a. metacommunication
    b. responsiveness
    c. paralanguage
    d. other delegation
    e. none of the above
    ANSWER: a   TYPE: M   COG: A

81. Anna, who is counselor at a women's crisis center, says the reason she most often hears from battered wives for returning to their husbands is, "I don't have any other place to go." Which explanation of why people perform relationships best predicts this relationship?
   a. the similarity thesis that suggests we like people whom we perceive are like us
   b. the reciprocity thesis that suggests being liked by others is a strong source of attraction
   c. the competency thesis that suggests we are attracted to people we believe are competent
   d. exchange theory that suggests we form relationships through assessment of potential rewards and costs
   e. disclosure theory that suggests we are attracted to those who use disclosure appropriately
   ANSWER: d   TYPE: M   COG: A

82. Initiating relationships within on-line dating services has proven to be beneficial for people who are:
   a. competent
   b. shy
   c. extraverted
   d. close in proximity
   e. none of the above
   ANSWER: b   TYPE: M   COG: C

83. Which is not a strategy outlined by Hess for gaining distance from a relational partner?
   a. mentally dissociating
   b. showing antagonism
   c. name calling
   d. avoiding involvement
   e. expressing detachment
   ANSWER: c   TYPE: M   COG: R

84. The authors define an interpersonal relationship as an association in which the partners meet each other's social needs _____
   a. totally
   b. frequently
   c. to some degree
   d. that are relevant to the relationship
   e. that are specific to the relationship
   ANSWER: c   TYPE: M   COG: R

85. "I wish you wouldn't act like that. As your mother, it embarrasses me." This is an example of a(n)
   a. indirect appeal
   b. punishment
   c. exchange
   d. reward
   e. relational appeal
   ANSWER: e   TYPE: M   COG: A

86. When you send someone a birthday card because she or he sent you one, you are complying with the norm of
   a. equality
   b. reciprocity
   c. regularity
   d. collegiality
   e. familiarity
   ANSWER: b   TYPE: M   COG: A

87. Albert Camus said, "Charm is a way of getting the answer yes without asking a clear question." This quotation refers to
    a.   a balance of power
    b.   exchange and reciprocity
    c.   an indirect appeal
    d.   face maintenance
    e.   a relational appeal
    ANSWER: c   TYPE: M   COG: A

88. The fact that two people both like the same kind of books is most important during which relationship stage?
    a.   experimenting
    b.   integrating
    c.   bonding
    d.   circumscribing
    e.   terminating
    ANSWER: a   TYPE: M   COG: A

89. Although she has a boyfriend, Kim realizes she may be happier if she was single when she goes away to college. Kim is rating her relationship according to her
    a.   Reward level
    b.   Cost level of alternatives
    c.   Comparison level
    d.   Comparison level of alternatives
    e.   Social exchange level
    ANSWER: d   TYPE: M   COG: A

90. Distancing yourself from a friend because you notice they never reciprocate their thoughts and feelings like you do reflects a which of the reasons we choose relationships?
    a.   Competency
    b.   Proximity
    c.   Disclosure
    d.   Complementarity
    e.   Appearance
    ANSWER: c   TYPE: M   COG: C

91. Tactics we use to persuade others to act in a desired way are called _____ strategies.
    a.   social science
    b.   comprehension-checking
    c.   empathic
    d.   alienating
    e.   compliance-gaining
    ANSWER: e   TYPE: M   COG: R

92. In which type of compliance-gaining strategy are hints used most frequently?
    a.   direct requests
    b.   indirect appeals
    c.   exchange and reciprocity
    d.   reward and punishment
    e.   Relational appeal
    ANSWER: b   TYPE: M   COG: R

93. Behaving in a positive way, being open and assuring your partner that you're committed to the relationship are examples of _____
    a. Competency
    b. Small Talk
    c. Experimenting
    d. Initiating
    e. Relational Maintenance
    ANSWER: e   TYPE: M   COG: C
94. "Will you lend me your pen?" is an example of a(n)
    a. direct request
    b. indirect appeal
    c. reward
    d. act of face maintenance
    e. relational appeal
    ANSWER: a   TYPE: M   COG: A

Essay

95. List, describe, and give an example of three compliance-gaining strategies used to intensify dating relationships.
    ANSWER: TYPE: E   COG: A
96. Explain how exchange theory applies to relationships. Provide an example of how comparison level and comparison level of alternatives exists within a relationship.
    ANSWER: TYPE: E   COG: A
97. Identify the stage of a relationship in which you are currently involved using Knapp's model of stages. Briefly discuss how your communication pattern reflects the present relationship stage.
    ANSWER: TYPE: E   COG: A
98. Describe each of Knapp's five phases of coming together and five phases of coming apart. Illustrate them by tracing a real or imaginary relationship from initial formation to final dissolution, providing examples of communication at each phase.
    ANSWER: TYPE: E   COG: A
99. Identify a dialectical tension in one of your significant relationships. Describe the problem that this tension has created (or could create) in the relationship. Describe which strategy or strategies you have used (or could use) to manage this tension.
    ANSWER: TYPE: E   COG: A
100. Describe the ways content and relational messages are communicated in interpersonal relationships.
    ANSWER: TYPE: E   COG: R
101. Explain the reasons why people choose others as potential relational partners.
    ANSWER: TYPE: E   COG: C

CHAPTER NINE: INTIMACY AND DISTANCE IN RELATIONSHIPS

True/False

1. The content of self-disclosing communication is the other person.
    ANSWER: F   TYPE: T   COG: R
2. The percentage of messages that are self-disclosing is relatively high.
    ANSWER: F   TYPE: T   COG: R
3. The relative size of each area in our personal Johari Window stays the same throughout our lives.
    ANSWER: F   TYPE: T   COG: C

4. Most people's overall style of disclosure could be represented by a single Johari window.
      ANSWER: T   TYPE: T   COG: C
5. Some dyadic relationships may be impersonal and nonintimate.
      ANSWER: T   TYPE: T   COG: C
6. 6. Women are generally seen as being less disclosing than men.
      ANSWER: F   TYPE: T   COG: R
7. A well-documented conclusion from research is that one act of self-disclosure begets another—that self-disclosure is reciprocal.
      ANSWER: T   TYPE: T   COG: R
8. The four dimensions of intimacy are physical, intellectual, emotional disclosure, and shared activities.
      ANSWER: T   TYPE: T   COG: R
9. Lying may be so common because it provides an easy way to manage difficult situations.
      ANSWER: T   TYPE: T   COG: C
10. In general, men disclose more than women.
      ANSWER: F   TYPE: T   COG: R
11. Intimacy is the measure of relational satisfaction; we cannot have satisfying relationships that are not intimate.
      ANSWER: F   TYPE: T   COG: C
12. Sometimes we do not self-disclose because of fear of losing control.
      ANSWER: T   TYPE: T   COG: R
13. An obsession with intimacy can actually lead to less satisfying relationships.
      ANSWER: T   TYPE: T   COG: C
14. Even the strongest relationships need some distance.
      ANSWER: T   TYPE: T   COG: R
15. Parent-child relationships go through "Leave me alone" stages, while satisfied spouse-spouse relationships do not.
      ANSWER: F   TYPE: T   COG: C
16. One risk of self-disclosure is that it often leads to increased awareness and can expose a need to change, which might be painful.
      ANSWER: T   TYPE: T   COG: R
17. We like people with whom we reciprocally disclose, and we disclose with people whom we like.
      ANSWER: T   TYPE: T   COG: R
18. Female-female relationships generally contain more and deeper exchanges of information than any other type of relationship.
      ANSWER: T   TYPE: T   COG: C
19. Two of the most powerful factors influencing desired levels of intimacy are gender and culture.
      ANSWER: T   TYPE: T   COG: R
20. Research suggests that men tend to find and express relational intimacy through shared activities rather than through talking.
      ANSWER: T   TYPE: T   COG: C
21. Women, more than men, generally regard practical help as a measure of caring.
      ANSWER: F   TYPE: T   COG: C
22. Women tend to see sex as a means for expressing intimacy that has already developed; men tens to see it as a means for creating that intimacy.
      ANSWER: T   TYPE: T   COG: C
23. The notion of what is considered intimate is consistent across cultures.
      ANSWER: F   TYPE: T   COG: R
24. Because of the pervasiveness of nonverbal communication, we often self-disclose unintentionally.
      ANSWER: F   TYPE: T   COG: R

266

25. In terms of the Johari Window, the depth of a relationship is determined by the size of a person's "open" area.
    ANSWER: T   TYPE: T   COG: R
26. Asian and European cultures are quite similar in their approaches to showing emotions and expressing emotion in public.
    ANSWER: F   TYPE: T   COG: R
27. Because of its nature, self-disclosure is never self-serving.
    ANSWER: F   TYPE: T   COG: C
28. In research by Gudykunst, U.S. natives were found to be more disclosing than any culture studied.
    ANSWER: T   TYPE: T   COG: R
29. The benevolent lie is recognized as a popular and acceptable form of communication, and research indicates that most people tell them to save face and/or avoid conflict.
    ANSWER: T   TYPE: T   COG: R
30. While most people think of benevolent lies as benefiting the recipient, in reality, most communication behavior is to help the speaker achieve her or his goal.
    ANSWER: T   TYPE: T   COG: C
31. Both men and women prefer self-disclosure with members of the same sex.
    ANSWER: F   TYPE: T   COG: R
32. Self-disclosure can lead to a decrease in the satisfaction obtained from a relationship.
    ANSWER: T   TYPE: T   COG: C
33. We should be self-disclosing at all times, in all relationships.
    ANSWER: F   TYPE: T   COG: C
34. The relative size of each area of our Johari Windows changes according to our moods.
    ANSWER: F   TYPE: T   COG: C
35. The Japanese are generally high self-disclosers.
    ANSWER: F   TYPE: T   COG: R
36. The emotionally closer you are to someone, the stronger your expectation of honesty.
    ANSWER: T   TYPE: T   COG: C
37. Research shows that most conversations even among friends or intimate partners focus on mundane topics and impersonal information.
    ANSWER: T   TYPE: T   COG: R
38. Benevolent lies are defined as being non-malicious, or even helpful.
    ANSWER: T   TYPE: T   COG: R
39. If some self-disclosure is good, then more disclosure is better.
    ANSWER: F   TYPE: T   COG: C
40. Because females tend to exhibit more self-disclosing behavior, they tend to have more fulfilling close relationships than do males.
    ANSWER: F   TYPE: T   COG: C
41. Despite their superficiality, clichés serve several useful functions.
    ANSWER: T   TYPE: T   COG: R
42. Facts represent a deeper level of self-disclosure than opinions.
    ANSWER: F   TYPE: T   COG: R
43. Research on marital communication suggests that a moderate amount of openness produces better results than extreme disclosure or extreme withholding.
    ANSWER: T   TYPE: T   COG: C
44. A relationship can be defined as casual or intimate based upon its depth and breadth of disclosure.
    ANSWER: T   TYPE: T   COG: R
45. Successful liars, equivocators, and hinters can be said to possess a certain kind of communicative competence.
    ANSWER: T   TYPE: T   COG: R

Multiple Choice

46. The best chance for developing highly interpersonal relationships is found in a person who
    a. is neither receptive to feedback nor willing to self-disclose
    b. is open to feedback but does not voluntarily self-disclose
    c. discourages feedback but discloses freely
    d. is both open to others' ideas and willing to disclose information
    e. none of the above
        ANSWER: d   TYPE: M   COG: C

47. In a study of people dying in hospices or hospitals, 90 percent of the terminally ill people said this is what mattered most in their lives
    a. career success
    b. financial success
    c. personal achievement
    d. intimate relationships
    e. none of the above
        ANSWER: d   TYPE: M   COG: C

48. Which type of relationship is it impossible to be satisfied with unless there are at least moderate amounts of intimacy?
    a. co-workers
    b. friends
    c. neighbors
    d. family
    e. all of the above
        ANSWER: e   TYPE: M   COG: C

49. Being reserved, shortening interaction, and restricting topics are all ways of _____ in a relationship.
    a. maintaining intimacy
    b. maintaining reciprocity
    c. maintaining distance
    d. maintaining catharsis
    e. none of the above
        ANSWER: c   TYPE: M   COG: R

50. Brad does not answer a call identified by caller I.D. as his best friend Mark because he is not in the mood to talk to him. Brad is managing which dimension in their relationship?
    a. distance
    b. intimacy
    c. reciprocity
    d. self-disclosure
    e. none of the above
        ANSWER: a   TYPE: M   COG: A

51. Researchers Mark Morman and Kory Floyd (2002) note that in North America fathers are _____ with their sons than they were in previous generations.
    a. becoming more affectionate
    b. expressing the same amount of affection
    c. becoming more of a disciplinarian
    d. becoming less affectionate
    e. none of the above
        ANSWER: a   TYPE: M   COG: C

52. Which reason for self-disclosure is found in wanting "to get it off your chest?"
    a. catharsis
    b. self-clarification
    c. self-validation
    d. reciprocity
    e. impression formation
        ANSWER: a   TYPE: M   COG: R

53. Which reason for self-disclosure is frequently found in talking to bartenders or hairdressers?
    a. catharsis
    b. self-clarification
    c. self-validation
    d. reciprocity
    e. impression formation
        ANSWER: b   TYPE: M   COG: A

54. Which reason for self-disclosure is suggested by the parenthetical remark, "I think I did the right thing?"
    a. catharsis
    b. self-clarification
    c. self-validation
    d. reciprocity
    e. impression formation
        ANSWER: c   TYPE: M   COG: A

55. Which reason for self-disclosure is found in dating behavior, particularly on the first few dates?
    a. catharsis
    b. self-clarification
    c. self validation
    d. reciprocity
    e. impression formation
        ANSWER: e   TYPE: M   COG: C

56. Admitting to your spouse you had an affair because you feel guilty is an example of which reason for self-disclosure?
    a. catharsis
    b. self-clarification
    c. self-validation
    d. reciprocity
    e. social influence
        ANSWER: a   TYPE: M   COG: A

57. Eric discloses to his partner that he has just tested positive for AIDS. His reason for disclosing such information is most likely:
    a. impression formation
    b. reciprocity
    c. moral obligation
    d. self-validation
    e. none of the above
        ANSWER: c   TYPE: M   COG: A

58. Disclosing to your parents that you're expecting an "F" in math before the report card arrives is an example of which reason for self-disclosure?
    a. impression formation
    b. reciprocity
    c. moral obligation
    d. self-validation
    e. self-defense
        ANSWER: e   TYPE: M   COG: A
59. Not revealing something because you fear the other person will reveal the information to people you prefer not to know is an example of which risk of self-disclosure?
    a. decreased relational satisfaction
    b. loss of control
    c. hurt the other person
    d. rejection
    e. none of the above
        ANSWER: b   TYPE: M   COG: A
60. Which reason for self-disclosure is involved in wanting relationships to stay healthy and develop?
    a. reciprocity
    b. impression formation
    c. relationship maintenance and enhancement
    d. social control
    e. manipulation
        ANSWER: c   TYPE: M   COG: R
61. Telling the boss that another firm has made you an offer, in an effort to get a raise or promotion, reflects which reason for self-disclosure?
    a. reciprocity
    b. impression formation
    c. relationship maintenance enhancement
    d. social control
    e. catharsis
        ANSWER: d   TYPE: M   COG: A
62. The Social Penetration Model looks at self-disclosure in terms of
    a. breadth
    b. catharsis
    c. depth
    d. a & c only
    e. all of the above
        ANSWER: d   TYPE: M   COG: R
63. Whenever Steve and Amy get together, their conversations include a wide range of subjects from school to politics to their families. The Social Penetration Model would describe their interaction as having a lot of
    a. depth
    b. intellectual sharing
    c. breadth
    d. shared activities
    e. none of the above
        ANSWER: c   TYPE: M   COG: A

64. The Johari Window illustrates which of the following?
    a. building a relationship depends on the use of self-disclosure containing more information about another rather than the self
    b. building a relationship involves enlarging your blind and hidden areas while decreasing your free areas.
    c. building a relationship involves increasing complementary behaviors by helping the other person to decrease the number of hidden agendas as you decrease risk-taking.
    d. building a relationship involves enlarging your open areas while decreasing your blind and hidden areas
    e. None of the above illustrates it
        ANSWER: d   TYPE: M   COG: C

65. The key element characterizing intimacy in relationships is
    a. closeness
    b. honesty
    c. location
    d. independence
    e. romance
        ANSWER: a   TYPE: M   COG: R

66. Research by Rosenfeld and Kendrick indicates that the main reasons for self-disclosing to strangers are
    a. relationship maintenance and reciprocity
    b. catharsis and impression formation
    c. reciprocity and impression formation
    d. self-clarification and validation
    e. too risky to take the chance
        ANSWER: c   TYPE: M   COG: C

67. When communicating with a person who has very little open area in the Johari Window, the interpersonal communication can be best described as
    a. limited to certain topics
    b. highly emotional
    c. virtually impossible
    d. secretive
    e. risky
        ANSWER: c   TYPE: M   COG: C

68. One study has shown that the percentage of statements made that were totally honest was
    a. 10 percent
    b. 38 percent
    c. 52 percent
    d. 83 percent
    e. 94 percent
        ANSWER: b   TYPE: M   COG: R

69. "Saving face" of another person includes attempts to be
    a. kind
    b. tactful
    c. thoughtful
    d. protective
    e. all of the above
        ANSWER: e   TYPE: M   COG: C

70. Couples tend to _____ the amount of personal information their partners reveal
    a. underestimate
    b. overestimate
    c. be accurate about
    d. all of the above
    e. none of the above
        ANSWER: b   TYPE: M   COG: C
71. Which of the following is an equivocal response to the question, "How do you like my new hair-do?"
    a. "It looks great"
    b. " I don't like it"
    c. "I didn't even notice it"
    d. "Don King would be jealous"
    e. "It gives you a new look"
        ANSWER: e   TYPE: M   COG: A
72. The setting that tends to be especially risky for the revealing of personal thoughts and feelings is
    a. school
    b. bars
    c. family reunions
    d. parties
    e. the workplace
        ANSWER: e   TYPE: M   COG: C
73. In determining the appropriateness of self-disclosure, a person should consider all of the following guidelines, *except*
    a. is the other person going to self-disclose also?
    b. is the other person trustworthy?
    c. is the information helpful to the relationship?
    d. is there adequate time to develop and respond to the self-disclosure?
    e. None of the above is an exception
        ANSWER: e   TYPE: M   COG: R
74. To be considered self-disclosure, a communication act
    a. must contain personal information
    b. must be communicated verbally
    c. must have another person as a listener
    d. all of the above
    e. a and c only
        ANSWER: d   TYPE: M   COG: R
75. Self-disclosure is distinguished by which factor?
    a. honesty
    b. availability of information and context of sharing
    c. obliqueness
    d. all of the above
    e. a and b only
        ANSWER: e   TYPE: M   COG: R
76. Which part of the Johari Window represents information unrealized by both you and others?
    a. open
    b. blind
    c. hidden
    d. unknown
    e. none of the above
        ANSWER: d   TYPE: M   COG: R

77. Which part of the Johari Window represents information of which both you and the other person are aware?
    a. open
    b. blind
    c. hidden
    d. unknown
    e. none of the above
        ANSWER: a   TYPE: M   COG: R

78. Which part of the Johari Window represents information of which you are unaware but the other person knows?
    a. open
    b. blind
    c. hidden
    d. unknown
    e. none of the above
        ANSWER: b   TYPE: M   COG: R

79. Which part of the Johari Window represents information that you know but are unwilling to reveal to others?
    a. open
    b. blind
    c. hidden
    d. unknown
    e. none of the above
        ANSWER: c   TYPE: M   COG: R

80. Discovering that you have an unrecognized talent, strength, or weakness points to which part of the Johari Window?
    a. open
    b. blind
    c. hidden
    d. unknown
    e. none of the above
        ANSWER: d   TYPE: M   COG: A

81. A person who takes few risks and may appear aloof and uncommunicative is represented by which style of the Johari Window?
    a. neither receptive to feedback nor willing to self-disclose
    b. open to feedback but does not voluntarily self-disclose
    c. discourages feedback but discloses freely
    d. both open to others' ideas and willing to disclose information
    e. none of the above
        ANSWER: a   TYPE: M   COG: A

82. Which reason for self-disclosure is most likely to be involved when the target is a friend?
    a. moral obligation
    b. impression formation
    c. relationship maintenance and enhancement
    d. impression formation
    e. social influence
        ANSWER: c   TYPE: M   COG: C

83. Which of the following is a stage through which we repeatedly cycle, according to researcher Morris
    a. "Hold me tight"
    b. "Put me down"
    c. "Leave me alone"
    d. all of the above
    e. none of the above
        ANSWER: d   TYPE: M   COG: R

84. "The check is in the mail" is an example of which motivation for lying
    a. saving face
    b. avoiding tension or conflict
    c. guiding social interaction
    d. affecting interpersonal relationships
    e. achieving personal power
        ANSWER: a   TYPE: M   COG: A

85. "How nice to see you" (when it isn't) illustrates which motivation for lying?
    a. saving face
    b. avoiding tension or conflict
    c. guiding social interaction
    d. affecting interpersonal relationships
    e. achieving personal power
        ANSWER: c   TYPE: M   COG: A

86. "I gotta go…I have to study for a test tomorrow" (when you don't) is lying for which reason?
    a. saving face
    b. avoiding tension or conflict
    c. guiding social interaction
    d. affecting interpersonal relationships
    e. achieving personal power
        ANSWER: e   TYPE: M   COG: A

87. "No, I can't come…I'm booked up" (when you're not) is lying for which reason
    a. saving face
    b. avoiding tension or conflict
    c. guiding social interaction
    d. affecting interpersonal relationships
    e. achieving personal power
        ANSWER: e   TYPE: M   COG: A

88. The statement, "I am afraid to tell you who I am because if I tell you who I am, you may not like who I am, and that's all I have," best illustrates which risk of self-disclosure?
    a. rejection
    b. projection of a negative image
    c. decrease in satisfaction
    d. loss of control
    e. hurt the other person
        ANSWER: a   TYPE: M   COG: A

89. Which of the following is *not* a type of intimacy?
    a. physical
    b. financial
    c. emotional
    d. intellectual
    e. shared activities
        ANSWER: b   TYPE: M   COG: R

90. The positive relation between self-disclosure and marital satisfaction reflects which benefit of disclosure?
    a. better relationships
    b. mental health
    c. self-understanding
    d. all of the above
    e. none of the above
        ANSWER: a   TYPE: M   COG: C

91. When researchers conclude that there is a curvilinear relationship between liking and self-disclosure, they mean
    a. those who disclose too little or too much may both be disliked
    b. those who disclose too little are more likely to be disliked than those who disclose too much
    c. those who disclose too much are more likely to be disliked than those who disclose too little
    d. if some self-disclosure is good, more is better
    e. none of the above applies
        ANSWER: a   TYPE: M   COG: C

92. The dialectical tension that pulls against intimacy is the need for
    a. ambition
    b. satisfaction
    c. distance
    d. logic
    e. achievement
        ANSWER: c   TYPE: M   COG: R

93. The nature of a statement that comes from the setting points to which characteristic of self-disclosure?
    a. honesty
    b. availability of information
    c. context of sharing
    d. obliqueness
    e. none of the above
        ANSWER: c   TYPE: M   COG: R

94. Roxanne Parrott and her research associates investigated self disclosure in personal advertisements and reported which of the following?
    a. every ad contained information about appearance, background, and attitude/values
    b. many principles of face-to-face interpersonal communication also operate in the construction of personal ads
    c. most of what writers of personal ads revealed about themselves matched the qualities they were looking for in respondents
    d. all of the above
    e. none of the above
        ANSWER: d   TYPE: M   COG: R

Essay

95. The shape of the Johari Window is likely to change from relationship to relationship and from time to time within relationships. Pick a time in one of your relationships when one quadrant was predominant. Construct your Johari Window in that interaction and justify your selection by explaining your communication style in this interaction.
        ANSWER: TYPE: E   COG: A

96. The text provides several characteristics of and reasons why self-disclosure is an important part of the communication process. Select three that have been particularly relevant in your interpersonal relationships, and briefly describe them and their importance.
    ANSWER: TYPE: E   COG: A
97. The text suggests that there are several risks to people who self-disclose. Briefly discuss two that inhibited your own self-disclosure at one time or another, and discuss how legitimate they were.
    ANSWER: TYPE: E   COG: A
98. Effective interpersonal communication demands that those who would self-disclose carefully consider the act and its consequences before engaging in it. Below are cue words to the seven guidelines for self-disclosing presented in the text. Expand on each one and suggest possible consequences of not considering it prior to self-disclosing.
    a. Importance
    b. Risk appropriateness
    c. Relevancy
    d. Reciprocity
    e. Constructiveness
    f. Clarity
    ANSWER: TYPE: E   COG: C
99. Explain the Social Penetration Model
    ANSWER: TYPE: E   COG: R
100. Discuss the different ways to assess the ethics of hints, white lies, and equivocations. Provide examples.
    ANSWER: TYPE: E   COG: R

CHAPTER TEN: COMMUNICATION CLIMATES

True/False

1. The kinds of messages that affirm the value of others have been called confirming responses.
   ANSWER: T   TYPE: T   COG: R
2. According to studies, the most important single factor ensuring mental development and stability is confirmation.
   ANSWER: T   TYPE: T   COG: C
3. Communication climate refers to the social tone of a relationship.
   ANSWER: T   TYPE: T   COG: R
4. Research shows that while a positive communication climate makes a job more pleasant, it does not affect production or organizational commitment.
   ANSWER: F   TYPE: T   COG: C
5. It isn't *what* we communicate about that shapes a relational climate as much as *how* we speak and act toward one another.
   ANSWER: T   TYPE: T   COG: R
6. John Gottman's research found that complaining is usually a sign of a troubled relationship that is headed for divorce.
   ANSWER: F   TYPE: T   COG: C
7. A message that sounds disconfirming to one person can be a term of endearment to another person.
   ANSWER: T   TYPE: T   COG: C
8. Most researchers agree that it is psychologically healthier to have someone ignore us than to have them disagree with us.
   ANSWER: F   TYPE: T   COG: C

9. Communication researchers use the term "argumentativeness" to describe vicious and destructive interaction.

        ANSWER: F   TYPE: T   COG: R

10. Honest messages are confirming when they grow out of a sincere desire for the other person's welfare.

        ANSWER: T   TYPE: T   COG: R

11. Separate research by Clark, Veroff, and others have identified positive climate as the best predictor of marital satisfaction.

        ANSWER: T   TYPE: T   COG: R

12. It is possible to accept that principle upon which criticism is based and still continue to behave as you have been doing.

        ANSWER: T   TYPE: T   COG: C

13. Communication climate is determined by the degree to which people see themselves as valued.

        ANSWER: T   TYPE: T   COG: R

14. A disagreeing response may acknowledge the speaker's message but assert that it is incorrect.

        ANSWER: T   TYPE: T   COG: R

15. Communication spirals may be either positive or negative.

        ANSWER: T   TYPE: T   COG: R

16. When we don't look at our communication partner, we are denying recognition and are probably sending a negative, disconfirming message.

        ANSWER: T   TYPE: T   COG: C

17. Argumentativeness is defined as presenting and defending positions on issues while attacking positions taken by others.

        ANSWER: T   TYPE: T   COG: R

18. Defensiveness is the attempt to protect a presented image that we perceive is bring attacked.

        ANSWER: T   TYPE: T   COG: R

19. Because of the need to protect our self-esteem and maintain emotional stability, defensive behavior may be justified in some situations.

        ANSWER: T   TYPE: T   COG: C

20. Recognition, acknowledgement, and endorsement are three increasingly positive types of messages that have the best chance of being perceived as confirming.

        ANSWER: T   TYPE: T   COG: R

21. When satisfied couples complain, they usually offer complaints about behaviors rather than complaints about personal characteristics.

        ANSWER: T   TYPE: T   COG: C

22. Your text indicates that the most negative and destructive way to disagree with someone is by engaging in complaining.

        ANSWER: F   TYPE: T   COG: R

23. Using problem-orientation builds a negative communication climate.

        ANSWER: F   TYPE: T   COG: R

24. Paraphrasing is effective both in helping others handle their problems and as a way of responding to their criticisms of us.

        ANSWER: T   TYPE: T   COG: R

25. A communication climate begins to develop as soon as two people start to communicate.

        ANSWER: T   TYPE: T   COG: R

26. The strongest type of confirming message is acknowledgement.

        ANSWER: F   TYPE: T   COG: R

27. Your text suggests there are certain "foolproof" ways to create a positive communication climate, such as giving praise or offering help.

        ANSWER: F   TYPE: T   COG: R

28. The key for maintaining a positive climate while arguing is the way you present your ideas.
    ANSWER: T   TYPE: T   COG: R
29. Gibb regards neutrality as supportive because it involves being objective and rational.
    ANSWER: F   TYPE: T   COG: R
30. "Certainty" and "control" are both defensive components in Gibb's model.
    ANSWER: T   TYPE: T   COG: R
31. Supportive communication can be used for ulterior motives to restrict and control others.
    ANSWER: T   TYPE: T   COG: C
32. "We" language is usually associated with controlling communication.
    ANSWER: F   TYPE: T   COG: C
33. Gibb's notion of spontaneity means sharing whatever you're thinking as soon as it crosses your mind.
    ANSWER: F   TYPE: T   COG: R
34. Individualistic people are more likely to interpret others' messages as neutral or critical, while people with communal orientations are likely to interpret ambiguous messages as supportive.
    ANSWER: T   TYPE: T   COG: C
35. In order to give an endorsing response, it is necessary to agree with everything that the speaker is saying.
    ANSWER: F   TYPE: T   COG: R
36. It is easiest to identify disconfirming communication by observing responses to others' messages.
    ANSWER: T   TYPE: T   COG: R

Multiple Choice

37. Communication climates
    a.   are a function of the way people feel about one another
    b.   refer to the tone of a relationship
    c.   can change over time
    d.   all of the above
    e.   a and b only
    ANSWER: d   TYPE: M   COG: R
38. Saying hello, shaking hands, and making eye contact are examples of which level of confirming response?
    a.   recognition
    b.   acknowledgement
    c.   endorsement
    d.   all of the above
    e.   a and b only
    ANSWER: b   TYPE: M   COG: A
39. Foss & Griffen use the term _____ to describe a respectful approach that strives to understand others and invite them to see your point of view.
    a.   invitational rhetoric
    b.   neutrality
    c.   empathy
    d.   equality
    e.   spontaneity
    ANSWER: a   TYPE: M   COG: R

40. When an instructor listens carefully to your question in class, he or she is using which level of confirming message?
   a.   recognition
   b.   acknowledgement
   c.   endorsement
   d.   neutrality
   e.   all of the above
        ANSWER: b   TYPE: M   COG: A

41. All of the following are types of defense-arousing communication identified by Jack Gibb *except*
   a.   evaluation
   b.   control
   c.   strategy
   d.   neutrality
   e.   spontaneity
        ANSWER: e   TYPE: M   COG: R

42. Researchers who study argumentativeness
   a.   regard it as synonymous with aggressiveness
   b.   regard it as an attacking of issues, not an attacking of people
   c.   regard it as a negative trait
   d.   all of the above
   e.   none of the above
        ANSWER: b   TYPE: M   COG: R

43. The decision whether a message is perceived as confirming or disconfirming is:
   a.   all in the way a message is delivered
   b.   dependent on the context of a situation
   c.   not dependent on the receiver
   d.   in the eye of the beholder
   e.   none of the above
        ANSWER: d   TYPE: M   COG: C

44. All of the following are types of supportive communication identified by Jack Gibb *except*
   a.   description
   b.   problem orientation
   c.   empathy
   d.   certainty
   e.   equality
        ANSWER: d   TYPE: M   COG: R

45. If someone used on of Gibb's attacking behaviors on you, it is best to
   a.   use defensive strategy tactics
   b.   seek more information
   c.   use certainty tactics
   d.   respond with neutrality
   e.   evaluate the situation
        ANSWER: b   TYPE: M   COG: C

46. Research shows that aggressiveness is associated with
   a.   physical violence in marriages
   b.   juvenile delinquency
   c.   depression
   d.   all of the above
   e.   none of the above
        ANSWER: d   TYPE: M   COG: R

47. Acting as though you don't hear someone and not making any response is which type of disconfirming response?
    a.   impervious
    b.   ambiguous
    c.   tangential
    d.   impersonal
    e.   incongruous
         ANSWER: a   TYPE: M   COG: A

48. A monologue of intellectual, generalized statements is considered which type of disconfirming response
    a.   impervious
    b.   ambiguous
    c.   tangential
    d.   impersonal
    e.   incongruous
         ANSWER: d   TYPE: M   COG: A

49. The tendency to attack the self-concepts of other people in order to inflict psychological pain is referred to as
    a.   aggressiveness
    b.   assertiveness
    c.   argumentativeness
    d.   ambiguousness
    e.   acknowledgement
         ANSWER: a   TYPE: M   COG: R

50. Customer: "The amount of time I've been on hold is ridiculous. I'm going to cancel my service."
    Customer Service Representative: "It sounds like you're angry. Can you tell me about your problem?"
    The listener's response is an example of:
    a.   Paraphrasing the speaker's ideas.
    b.   Agreeing with the truth
    c.   Agreeing with the odds
    d.   Agreeing in Principle
    e.   None of the above
         ANSWER: a   TYPE: M   COG: A

51. Satisfied couples have a _____ ratio of positive to negative statements.
    a.   10:1
    b.   5:2
    c.   10:2
    d.   4:1
    e.   5:1
         ANSWER: e   TYPE: M   COG: R

52. Messages that communicate, "I know what's best for you, and if you do as I say, we'll get along" are associated with which Gibb component?
    a.   control
    b.   spontaneity
    c.   neutrality
    d.   strategy
    e.   problcm-orientation
         ANSWER: a   TYPE: M   COG: R

53. "You never take out the garbage unless I nag you" is an example of which type of disagreeing message?"
        a.   complaining
        b.   argumentativeness
        c.   aggressiveness
        d.   disconfirmation
        e.   irrelevant response
        ANSWER: a   TYPE: M   COG: A

54. Shawn: "Did you enjoy the movie?"
Katie: "Yeah, I loved it (rolling eyes)."
Katie's response is an example of
        a.   irrelevant response
        b.   tangential response
        c.   impersonal response
        d.   ambiguous response
        e.   incongruous response
        ANSWER: e   TYPE: M   COG: A

55. Generally, people respond with _____ when they are confronted with face threatening acts.
        a.   empathy
        b.   an impervious response
        c.   defensiveness
        d.   ambiguity
        e.   none of the above
        ANSWER: c   TYPE: M   COG: C

56. Counterfeit questions are associated with which Gibb component?
        a.   description
        b.   spontaneity
        c.   neutrality
        d.   strategy
        e.   problem-orientation
        ANSWER: d   TYPE: M   COG: R

57. "What do I do that's unfair?" is which way to seek additional information from your critics?
        a.   ask for specifics
        b.   guess about specifics
        c.   paraphrase the speaker's ideas
        d.   ask about the consequences of your behavior
        e.   ask what else is wrong
        ANSWER: a   TYPE: M   COG: A

58. Research suggests that men tend to be more defensive than women about messages regarding
        a.   their mental or physical errors
        b.   their weight
        c.   their clothes and hair
        d.   their personality
        e.   A and c
        ANSWER: a   TYPE: M   COG: C

59. Avoiding being too boring and predictable in a relationship is an example of which Gibb strategy for creating a positive climate?
   a.   Provisionalism
   b.   Evaluation
   c.   Strategy
   d.   Spontaneity
   e.   None of the above
       ANSWER: e   TYPE: M   COG: C

60. In order to create a confirming climate, a person needs to
   a.   agree with the other's position
   b.   acknowledge the other's position
   c.   praise the other's position
   d.   investigate the other's position
   e.   do none of the above
       ANSWER: b   TYPE: M   COG: R

61. Which of the following is *not* a level of confirming communication?
   a.   recognition
   b.   acknowledgement
   c.   compliment
   d.   endorsement
   e.   all four are levels
       ANSWER: c   TYPE: M   COG: R

62. Studies of married couples indicate that partners feel confirmed when their spouses communicate in
   a.   a direct way
   b.   an empathic way
   c.   a humorous way
   d.   all of the above
   e.   a and b
       ANSWER: e   TYPE: M   COG: R

63. Speaker: Lorinda makes me so mad when she's late.
    Listener: Lorinda? Yeah, but she's great. We went to a party together and had a fantastic time
    The listener's response is an example of
   a.   verbal aggression
   b.   a tangential response
   c.   an irrelevant response
   d.   an ambiguous response
   e.   an impersonal response
       ANSWER: b   TYPE: M   COG: A

64. Speaker: I'm really worried about trying to meet all of my obligations this semester. There's just SO much to do!
    Listener: Yeah, I guess we're all overwhelmed. I had to work every day last weekend.
    The listener's response is an example of
   a.   verbal aggression
   b.   a tangential response
   c.   am irrelevant response
   d.   an ambiguous response
   e.   an impersonal response
       ANSWER: e   TYPE: M   COG: A

65. Attacks against our presenting self are called
    a.   face-threatening acts
    b.   face-saving acts
    c.   defensive communication
    d.   offensive communication
    e.   focused communication
          ANSWER: a   TYPE: M   COG: R

Essay

66. Gerald Suttles claims, "Friendship is like a fishhook; the further it goes in, the harder it is to pull out." Think of an analogy you would use to explain friendship. Describe the analogy and how it helps explain the concept of a communication climate that fosters friendship.
    ANSWER: TYPE: E   COG: C

67. What are the implications of using the term "communication climate" (rather than communication situation, for instance)?
    ANSWER: TYPE: E   COG: C

68. Thoreau claims we should treat one another tenderly. How can your knowledge of communication climates help you to do this?
    ANSWER: TYPE: E   COG: C

69. Discuss, using concepts from the text, this quotation from Thomas Mann:
    "Speech is civilization itself. The word, even the most contradictory word, preserves contact; it is silence which isolates."
    ANSWER: TYPE: E   COG: C

70. An employee for whom you are responsible has a tendency to neglect assignments he is given at your weekly staff meetings. As a result, his projects often go uncompleted. Offer two comments about this problem that you could make during an annual review with this person; then explain how each comment reflects one of Gibb's supportive climate components.
    ANSWER: TYPE: E   COG: A

71. Despite your attempts to create a supportive climate in the preceding question, your employee gets defensive and starts criticizing you. Cite and give examples of two methods you could use to transform this negative climate into a positive one.
    ANSWER: TYPE: E   COG: A

72. Rewrite the following statements to decrease their defense-provoking potential by changing them from evaluations to descriptions.
    "You are so insensitive."
    "You're just not committed enough for a serious relationship."
    ANSWER: TYPE: E   COG: A

73. Respond to the following criticisms by drawing on two strategies from the "seeking more information" element and two strategies from the "agree with critic" element of the textbook's model for coping with criticism. Create the situational details from your own experience.
    "You're so callous in the way you deal with people."
    "You're so inflexible; it's impossible to discuss things with you."
    ANSWER: TYPE: E   COG: A

74. Briefly explain why it is important to be valued and confirmed.
    ANSWER: TYPE: E   COG: R

75. Provide three messages to correspond with each of the message types: confirming, disagreeing, and disconfirming.
    ANSWER: TYPE: E   COG: A

Matching

76. Match the terms in the left column with their category from the right column. (note: categories may be used more than once)

      _____ 1. recognition   a. confirming messages
      _____ 2. interrupting   b. disagreeing messages
      _____ 3. imperviousness   c. disconfirming messages
      _____ 4. endorsement
      _____ 5. argumentativeness
      _____ 6. aggressiveness
      _____ 7. acknowledgement

ANSWER: a, c, c, a, b, b, a TYPE: K   COG: R

77. Fill in the letters of the Gibb climate components that correlate most closely with the descriptions below. In each pairing, list the defensive component first and the supportive component second.
    a. Certainty
    b. Control
    c. Description
    d. Empathy
    e. Equality
    f. Evaluation
    g. Neutrality
    h. Problem-orientation
    i. Provisionalism
    j. Spontaneity
    k. Strategy
    l. Superiority

1. Counterfeit questions vs. genuine questions
    _____ vs. _____

2. Ideas evaluated on the basis of who contributed them vs. ideas evaluated on their own merit
    _____ vs. _____

3. Indifference vs. acceptance
    _____ vs. _____

4. "Must," "Always," "Can't" vs. "Might," "Perhaps," and "Maybe"
    _____ vs. _____

5. Being vague, brief, and abstract vs. being specific and concrete
    _____ vs. _____

6. Making decisions for others vs. making decisions with others.
    _____ vs. _____

ANSWER: 1. k,j; 2. l,e; 3. g,d; 4. a,i; 5. f,c; 6. b,h
TYPE: K   COG: A

78. Match the pronoun type from the left column with the associated Gibb component from the right column.

        _____ 1. "We" language   a. description
        _____ 2. "I " language   b. problem-orientation
        _____ 3. "You" language   c. evaluation
        ANSWER: b, a, c   TYPE: K   COG: R

CHAPTER ELEVEN: MANAGING CONFLICT

True/False

1. Although it is impossible to eliminate conflict, there are ways to manage it effectively.
     ANSWER: T   TYPE: T   COG: R

2. Research by Hocker and Wilmot asserts that all interpersonal conflicts share certain similarities regardless of the forms they may take.
     ANSWER: T   TYPE: T   COG: R

3. Reasonable people are usually able to see mutually satisfying answers to their problems.
     ANSWER: F   TYPE: T   COG: R

4. Conflict is an expressed struggle between at least two interdependent parties who perceive incompatible goals, scarce rewards, and interference from the other party in achieving their goals.
     ANSWER: T   TYPE: T   COG: A

5. People most likely to find themselves in a conflict are independent from each other.
     ANSWER: F   TYPE: T   COG: R

6. 6. Your text maintains that conflict is inevitable.
     ANSWER: T   TYPE: T   COG: R

7. Communication scholars usually describe beneficial conflicts as dysfunctional and harmful ones as functional.
     ANSWER: F   TYPE: T   COG: R

8. Most people view conflict as something to be avoided whenever possible.
     ANSWER: T   TYPE: T   COG: R

9. For functional problem-solving to occur it is wise to multi-task; that is, to work on multiple problems simultaneously.
     ANSWER: F   TYPE: T   COG: R

10. In sharing our needs with another person we should avoid the use of "I" language so as not to polarize the conflict.
     ANSWER: F   TYPE: T   COG: R

11. The inability or unwillingness to express thoughts or feelings in a conflict is called nonassertion.
     ANSWER: T   TYPE: T   COG: R

12. A student who dislikes a teacher but does not show it fits the textbook's definition of conflict.
     ANSWER: F   TYPE: T   COG: A

13. One advantage of indirect communication is that it can save face.
     ANSWER: T   TYPE: T   COG: R

14. Martin and his colleagues conducted research on verbal aggression among siblings and reported, "when verbal aggressiveness is present in a relationship there is less satisfaction and trust."
     ANSWER: T   TYPE: T   COG: R

15. Partners who use different but mutually reinforcing behaviors to manage their conflicts have a conflict style called *symmetrical.*
     ANSWER: F   TYPE: T   COG: R

16. Research by Cupach and Metts revealed that college students in romantic relationships who believed that conflicts are destructive were most likely to neglect or leave the relationship and less likely to seek a solution that couples who had less-negative attitudes.

ANSWER: T   TYPE: T   COG: R

17. Conflict rituals prevent successful conflict management.

ANSWER: F   TYPE: T   COG: R

18. Passive aggression occurs when a communicator expresses dissatisfaction in a disguised manner.

ANSWER: T   TYPE: T   COG: R

19. Avoidance is never an advisable conflict-resolution style.

ANSWER: F   TYPE: T   COG: R

20. A personal conflict style is similar to a personality trait in that it carries across most all situations.

ANSWER: F   TYPE: T   COG: R

21. Assertive individuals can respect and seek to satisfy their own needs and still respect and seek to satisfy the needs of others.

ANSWER: T   TYPE: T   COG: R

22. Research shows that unhappily married couples have conflicts but happily married couples do not.

ANSWER: F   TYPE: T   COG: R

23. Research suggests there is a significant connection between verbal aggression and physical aggression.

ANSWER: T   TYPE: T   COG: R

24. Research suggests that indirectness is effective for gaining compliance in intimate relationships, while directness works better in nonintimate relationships.

ANSWER: F   TYPE: T   COG: R

25. For men, friendship and aggression are mutually exclusive.

ANSWER: F   TYPE: T   COG: R

26. Women are more likely to use logical reasoning and bargaining than aggression in conflict.

ANSWER: T   TYPE: T   COG: R

27. Recent research shows that the differences in how men and women approach conflict are rather small and not at all representative of the stereotypical picture of the aggressive male and the passive female.

ANSWER: T   TYPE: T   COG: R

28. Compared to females, males use more competing behaviors with same-sex peers and more avoiding behaviors with opposite-sex peers.

ANSWER: T   TYPE: T   COG: R

29. Estimates are that the Japanese only have one lawyer for every 10,000 people, while in the United States there is one lawyer for every 50 people.

ANSWER: T   TYPE: T   COG: R

30. One Chinese proverb states, "The first person to raise his voice wins the argument."

ANSWER: F   TYPE: T   COG: R

31. Conflicts with a win-lose orientation are always destructive.

ANSWER: F   TYPE: T   COG: R

32. Assertive approaches to conflict are likely to seem rude to members of collectivist cultures.

ANSWER: T   TYPE: T   COG: R

33. High-context cultures place a premium on being direct during conflict.

ANSWER: F   TYPE: T   COG: R

34. Some cultures regard heated debates as a means of being sociable.

ANSWER: T   TYPE: T   COG: R

Multiple Choice

35. Partners in interpersonal relationships can use which of the following styles to manage their conflicts?
    a. complementary conflict style
    b. symmetrical conflict style
    c. parallel conflict style
    d. all of the above
    e. none of the above
       ANSWER: d   TYPE: M   COG: R

36. All of the following are elements of conflict *except*
    a. perceived incompatible goals
    b. perceived scarce rewards
    c. independence
    d. expressed struggle
    e. inevitability
       ANSWER: c   TYPE: M   COG: R

37. When children are involved in divorce, it intensifies which element Wilmot and Hocker's definition of conflict for the parents?
    a. expressed struggle
    b. perceived incompatible goals
    c. inevitability
    d. interdependence
    e. perceived scarce rewards
       ANSWER: d   TYPE: M   COG: R

38. Avoidance may be the best course
    a. if the risk of speaking up is too great
    b. if the issue is generally minor
    c. if the conflict occurs in an unimportant relationship
    d. all of the above
    e. none of the above
       ANSWER: d   TYPE: M   COG: R

39. Which of the following is (are) characteristics of dysfunctional conflict?
    a. biases are rampant
    b. participants see their actions as protective
    c. participants see the behavior of others as sneaky and distrustful
    d. all of the above
    e. a and c only
       ANSWER: d   TYPE: M   COG: R

40. Hinting to others instead of expressing ourselves outright is an example of
    a. nonassertion
    b. indirect communication
    c. passive aggression
    d. direct aggression
    e. assertion
       ANSWER: b   TYPE: M   COG: R

41. Character attacks are common to which style of handling conflict?
    a. nonassertion
    b. indirect aggression
    c. direct aggression
    d. assertion
    e. accommodation
        ANSWER: c   TYPE: M   COG: R
42. The style of handling conflict that maintains the self-respect of both parties is
    a. nonassertion
    b. indirect aggression
    c. direct aggression
    d. accommodation
    e. assertion
        ANSWER: b   TYPE: M   COG: R
43. If two co-workers are seeking promotion to the same job, they would likely fall into which methods of resolving disputes?
    a. win-lose
    b. lose-lose
    c. win-win
    d. avoidance
    e. accommodation
        ANSWER: a   TYPE: M   COG: R
44. Which kind of power can be used in win-lose problem solving?
    a. physical
    b. authority
    c. mental
    d. voting
    e. all of the above
        ANSWER: e   TYPE: M   COG: R
45. All of the following are components of Hocker and Wilmot's definition of conflict *except*
    a. perception of incompatible goals
    b. interdependence
    c. surplus rewards
    d. expressed struggle
    e. none of the above
        ANSWER: c   TYPE: M   COG: R
46. Which of the following is typical of boys (rather than girls) in conflict
    a. proposals beginning with the word "Let's"
    b. joint proposals
    c. assigning roles to others in pretend play
    d. giving reasons for suggestions
    e. none of the above
        ANSWER: c   TYPE: M   COG: R
47. Which of the following is a win-win strategy?
    a. avoid arguments that might lead to anger and hurt feelings
    b. know what you are willing to give up if the other person agrees to give up something
    c. determine what both parties need to get out of a negotiation
    d. vote and abide by majority decision
    e. none of the above is a win-win strategy
        ANSWER: c   TYPE: M   COG: R

48. Neither side is satisfied with the outcome in which method of problem-solving?
    a. win-lose
    b. lose-lose
    c. win-win
    d. avoidance
    e. accommodation
        ANSWER: b   TYPE: M   COG: R
49. The attitude of "we're all in this together" reflects the quality
    a. expressed struggle
    b. interdependence
    c. individuality
    d. caring
    e. nonassertion
        ANSWER: b   TYPE: M   COG: R
50. Unhappily married couples are more likely than happy couples to
    a. show concern for defending themselves
    b. use perception checking
    c. use evaluative language
    d. a and c
    e. all of the above
        ANSWER: d   TYPE: M   COG: R
51. Which of the following factors govern the selection and use of conflict style?
    a. the situation
    b. the other person
    c. your goals
    d. all of the above
    e. none of the above
        ANSWER: d   TYPE: M   COG: R
52. Accommodators deal with conflict by
    a. putting the other's needs ahead of their own
    b. putting their needs ahead of the other's
    c. ignoring the needs of others
    d. ignoring their own needs
    e. a and d
        ANSWER: a   TYPE: M   COG: R
53. Rolando and Laura had a fight last week about his working weekends. Today Laura is careful not to mention the coming weekend. She is using
    a. assertive behavior
    b. aggressive behavior
    c. accommodation
    d. avoidance
    e. a complementary conflict style
        ANSWER: d   TYPE: M   COG: A
54. Which of the following would be the most likely form of refusal in the Japanese culture?
    a. No
    b. No, not now
    c. I don't think so
    d. Maybe
    e. I will consider it and let you know
        ANSWER: e   TYPE: M   COG: A

55. Which of the following best reflect conclusions of a study of university students in Turkey regarding conflict-style preferences?
    a. friendship preferences revealed that aggression was the most preferred.
    b. friendship preferences revealed that aggression was the least preferred
    c. compromising was the most preferred
    d. compromising was the least preferred
    e. b and c
        ANSWER: e   TYPE: M   COG: A

56. "It seems like you don't want me to have a boyfriend and *that makes me feel like you want to keep me a little girl.*" In the above statement, the italicized portion is a(n)
    a. description of observable behavior
    b. interpretation of behavior
    c. feeling that arises from your interpretation
    d. consequence of the information shared
    e. intention statement
        ANSWER: c   TYPE: M   COG: A

57. Partners who use different but mutually reinforcing behaviors have a conflict style labeled
    a. complementary
    b. symmetrical
    c. parallel
    d. aggressive
    e. assertive
        ANSWER: a   TYPE: M   COG: R

58. When one partner says, "I want to talk about your treatment of me" and the other partner leaves, the conflict would be labeled
    a. pointless
    b. skewed
    c. symmetrical
    d. fight-flight
    e. flight-fight
        ANSWER: d   TYPE: M   COG: A

59. Research by Ann Ruvolo shows that women who avoid conflict feel _____ in their dating relationships than women who don't.
    a. less secure
    b. more secure
    c. no different
    d. more loved
    e. none of the above
        ANSWER: a   TYPE: M   COG: R

60. The type of couple most likely to communicate more positive and less negative information is
    a. separates
    b. independents
    c. traditionals
    d. a and c
    e. a and b
        ANSWER: c   TYPE: M   COG: R

61. Which of the following statements best summarizes the attitude expressed toward conflict by the text?
    a. conflict is natural and inevitable
    b. conflict can lead to stronger, healthier relationships
    c. negative attitudes about conflict are a result of socialization and lack of resolution skills
    d. conflict provides an outlet for feelings of frustration and aggression
    e. all of the above reflect the text's approach to conflict
        ANSWER: e   TYPE: M   COG: R

62. "I have tried everything in my power to make this relationship work, but it's impossible. It'll never work because you don't make any effort; you don't try at all." This statement is an example of which type of dysfunctional conflict?
    a. shortsightedness
    b. losing sight of the original issue
    c. unwillingness to cooperate
    d. polarization
    e. personalization
        ANSWER: d   TYPE: M   COG: A

63. Which of the following was *not* a finding in a study of college students on sex roles in handling conflict?
    a. men are better listeners
    b. women are more concerned with others' feelings
    c. mcn are more direct
    d. all of the above
    e. none of the above
        ANSWER: a   TYPE: M   COG: R

64. Which of the following choices has two components of an assertive message?
    a. accommodation and interpretation
    b. intention and consequence
    c. frustration and manipulation
    d. respect and avoidance
    e. none of the above
        ANSWER: b   TYPE: M   COG: R

65. The distinguishing characteristic in win-lose problem solving is
    a. power
    b. accommodation
    c. triumph
    d. compromise
    e. none of the above
        ANSWER: a   TYPE: M   COG: R

66. Whenever Bridget and Tony fight, Tony always brings up additional issues until the original issue gets lost. This is an example of
    a. escalation
    b. "kitchen sink fighting"
    c. integration
    d. foresight
    e. shortsightedness
        ANSWER: b   TYPE: M   COG: A

67. When Karen tries to talk about going visiting her family for the holidays, John changes the subject. This is an example of which individual conflict style?
    a. passive aggressive
    b. direct aggression
    c. drifting
    d. nonassertion
    e. none of the above
        ANSWER: d   TYPE: M   COG: A
68. Jack wants to limit their spending and Sandy wants to try a new restaurant. Which of the following would be an example of the indirect conflict style?
    a. "I think we should forget your stupid budget and go out to eat for once."
    b. "It's been so long since I've been in a restaurant I don't even think I'd know how to act."
    c. "That new restaurant looks good – I think you'd like their menu."
    d. "What would you like for dinner?"
    e. none of the above
        ANSWER: c   TYPE: M   COG: A
69. After much discussion, Chad finally agrees to go to the opera with his wife. As they are finding their seats he says, sarcastically, "Yeah, this is going to be a lot of fun." This is an example of which individual conflict style?
    a. avoidance
    b. assertion
    c. accommodation
    d. direct aggression
    e. passive aggression
        ANSWER: e   TYPE: M   COG: A
70. Paul and Stacy have a very volatile conflict style. They both are very forceful and inevitably end up hurling insults at each other until they both withdraw exhausted. This is an example of which conflict style?
    a. complementary
    b. parallel
    c. symmetrical
    d. assertive
    e. none of the above
        ANSWER: c   TYPE: M   COG: A
71. A pattern of managing disagreements that repeats itself over time is a(n):
    a. focusing
    b. confirmation
    c. foresight
    d. escalation
    e. relational conflict style
        ANSWER: e   TYPE: M   COG: R
72. Couples with a parallel conflict style
    a. use complementary styles
    b. use symmetrical styles
    c. shift back and forth between complementary and symmetrical
    d. always agree with each other
    e. none of the above
        ANSWER: c   TYPE: M   COG: R

73. Dave tells his girlfriend he wants to see a new action movie but goes along when she replies that she would rather see a romantic comedy. This is an example of:
    a. nonassertion
    b. passive aggression
    c. assertion
    d. direct aggression
    e. none of the above
         ANSWER: a   TYPE: M   COG: A

74. Which of the following is not a couple type identified by Mary and Fitzpatrick?
    a. separates
    b. intimates
    c. independents
    d. traditionals
    e. none of the above
         ANSWER: b   TYPE: M   COG: R

75. According to Mary Ann Fitzpatrick, during conflict separates tend to take which approach?
    a. nonintimate-nonaggressive
    b. intimate-aggressive
    c. intimate-nonaggressive
    d. nonintimate-aggressive
    e. none of the above
         ANSWER: a   TYPE: M   COG: C

76. A newly married husband and wife both want to spend Thanksgiving with their families. They decide to eat with her family at noon and his at 6:00. This is an example of:
    a. win-lose
    b. compromise
    c. lose-lose
    d. win-win
    e. none of the above
         ANSWER: d   TYPE: M   COG: A

77. Sherell and Monique have a disagreement about how to spend their end-of-the-year bonus. Sherell wants to go on a trip, and Monique wants to spend it on the house. Instead, they decide to buy a fishing boat. This is probably an example of
    a. avoidance
    b. compromise
    c. collaboration
    d. competing
    e. accommodating
         ANSWER: b   TYPE: M   COG: A

Essay

78. Suggest a possible mutually satisfying solution to the following conflicts:
    A teenager likes to wear make-up, and her parents don't want her to.
    A little boy likes to pop his gum, and the sound annoys his mother.
    A secretary likes to take her lunch hour from 11 to 12, but her boss finds this inconvenient.
    A man likes horror movies, and his wife likes comedies.
         ANSWER: TYPE: E   COG: A

79. What do you think Hugh Prather meant when he said, "Our marriage used to suffer from arguments that were too short?"

          ANSWER: TYPE: E   COG: C

80. Phrase the following request in a way that would not be offensive to a Japanese listener: "Lend me your textbook."

          ANSWER: TYPE: E   COG: A

81. Define a conflict ritual. Give an example of one and discuss what effect it might have on a conflict

          ANSWER: TYPE: E   COG: A

82. Define escalatory and de-escalatory spirals and explain how they relate to complementary and symmetrical styles.

          ANSWER: TYPE: E   COG: C

83. "Partners married 40 years or more report having fewer conflicts than earlier in their relationships, since many contested issues (such as children, in-laws, and money) are no longer present." Discuss this statement in relation to the common characteristics of the definition of conflict reviewed at the beginning of this chapter.

          ANSWER: TYPE: E   COG: C

84. Is a win-lose orientation always destructive? Explain your answer.

          ANSWER: TYPE: E   COG: C

85. Does compromising create win-win or lose-lose outcomes? Explain.

          ANSWER: TYPE: E   COG: C

86. Explain how the words we use to describe conflict can shape our perception of conflict.

          ANSWER: TYPE: E   COG: C

87. Explain three forms of the conflict style nonassertion.

          ANSWER: TYPE: E   COG: R

88. Explain the seven step approach to win-win problem solving

          ANSWER: TYPE: E   COG: R

89. Define the following characteristics of conflict and explain whether they are functional or dysfunctional.

    Polarization

    Confirmation

    Focusing

    Shortsightedness

          ANSWER: TYPE: E   COG: R

90. Explain how the Miss America Pageant could be viewed as a lose-lose, win-lose, or win-win conflict. Explain all three perspectives, then select one to defend.

          ANSWER: TYPE: E   COG: A

91. Explain the five elements of an assertive message.

          ANSWER: TYPE: E   COG: R

92. Each of the stages of the win-win problem-solving model requires the implementation of one or another of the repertoire of communication skills presented throughout the text. Below are seven steps. Identify at least one of the communication skills necessary to successfully negotiate each step.

    Step 1. Define your needs

    Step 2. Share your needs with the other person

    Step 3. Listen to the other person's needs

    Step 4. Generate possible solutions

    Step 5. Evaluate the possible solutions and choose the best one

    Step 6. Implement the best solution

    Step 7. Follow up on your solution

          ANSWER: TYPE: E   COG: C

93. The text suggests several reasons why people develop a view of conflict as unnatural and undesirable. Briefly describe three of these reasons to which you have subscribed.
    ANSWER: TYPE: E   COG: A

94. Dysfunctional conflict typically has three consequences. Name each, as labeled in the text, and, in one or two sentences, explain the "why" behind each.
    ANSWER: TYPE: E   COG: C

95. The fourth step of the seven-stage problem-solving model is labeled "Evaluate Possible Solutions." Identify the best strategy for doing this and outline the communication behaviors necessary for its success.
    ANSWER: TYPE: E   COG: C

96. The text discusses four styles of conflict behavior:
    a. nonassertion
    b. indirect aggression
    c. direct aggression
    d. assertion

    For each style, describe its basic characteristics; present at least one communication behavior for each style; and present an advantage and disadvantage of each.
    ANSWER: TYPE: E   COG: C

97. Identify the three possible positive outcomes of functional conflict.
    ANSWER: TYPE: E   COG: R

Matching

98. Match the phrase with the type of conflict style they typify

    _____ 1. I'm OK; you're not OK,   a. nonassertive
                 but I'll let you think you are   b. directly aggressive
    _____ 2. I'm OK; you're OK   c. passive aggressive
    _____ 3. I'm not OK; you're OK   d. indirect
    _____ 4. I'm OK; you're not OK   e. assertive
             ANSWER: c, e, a, b or d   TYPE: K   COG: R

99. Match the element of the assertive message with the message statements.

    _____ 1. It appears to me that you're jealous
    _____ 2. When you get angry because I go out with my friends…
    _____ 3. I need to talk about this
    _____ 4. I'm beginning to think this is a problem for our relationship
    _____ 5. Your reaction makes me wonder if you can trust me

    a. description of observable behavior
    b. interpretation of the behaviors
    c. feelings that arise from the interpretation
    d. consequences of the information shared
    e. intention statement
             ANSWER: b, a, e, d, c, TYPE: K   COG: A

100. Match the types of couples to the approach to conflict they most typically use.

```
_____ 1.  separates          a.  intimate-nonaggressive
_____ 2.  independents        b.  intimate-aggressive
_____ 3.  traditionals        c.  nonintimate-nonaggressive
```
ANSWER: c, b, a   TYPE: K   COG: R

101. Label the following as characteristic of functional (F) or dysfunctional (D) conflict resolution.

```
_____ 1.  Integration
_____ 2.  Isolation
_____ 3.  Coercion
_____ 4.  Cooperation
_____ 5.  Agreement
_____ 6.  De-escalation
_____ 7.  Drifting
_____ 8.  Focusing
_____ 9.  Polarization
_____ 10. Shortsightedness
_____ 11. Escalation
_____ 12. Foresight
```
ANSWER: 1-F, 2-D, 3-D, 4-F, 5-F, 6-F, 7-D, 8-F, 9-D, 10-D, 11-D, 12-F
                    TYPE: K   COG: R

CHAPTER TWELVE: CULTURE AND COMMUNICATION

True/False

1. Marshall McLuhan's "global village" metaphor suggests that the world's cultures are becoming increasingly disconnected and independent.
    ANSWER: F   TYPE: T   COG: R
2. In the first years of the new millennium, white females, minorities, and immigrants will constitute almost 85 percent of those entering the workforce.
    ANSWER: T   TYPE: T   COG: R
3. When people from different backgrounds interact, they face a set of challenges that are different from those that arise when members of the same culture try to interact.
    ANSWER: T   TYPE: T   COG: C
4. "Out-groups" are groups we perceive to be different from ourselves.
    ANSWER: T   TYPE: T   COG: R
5. In order to consider yourself part of a particular culture, you need only to share a number of characteristics with other members of the group.
    ANSWER: F   TYPE: T   COG: R
6. According to your text, intercultural communication occurs every time people from different cultures interact.
    ANSWER: F   TYPE: T   COG: R
7. High-context cultures rely more on nonverbal cues than do low-context cultures.
    ANSWER: T   TYPE: T   COG: R
8. Mainstream North American culture tends to be more low context than high context.
    ANSWER: T   TYPE: T   COG: R

9. There are many cases of interpersonal communication that are not influenced by intercultural considerations.

      ANSWER: T   TYPE: T   COG: C

10. Instead of classifying some exchanges as intercultural and some as free from cultural influences, it's more accurate to talk about degrees of cultural significance.

      ANSWER: T   TYPE: T   COG: R

11. Collective societies produce team players, whereas individualistic cultures are more likely to produce "superstars."

      ANSWER: T   TYPE: T   COG: C

12. Latin American and Asian cultures tend to be more collectivist than North American cultures.

      ANSWER: T   TYPE: T   COG: R

13. Leets's research on racist messages found that the kinds of messages that are most harmful are relatively the same from culture to culture.

      ANSWER: F   TYPE: T   COG: R

14. Autonomy, change, and initiative are associated with individualistic cultures.

      ANSWER: T   TYPE: T   COG: R

15. Compliance gaining strategies in collective cultures rely more on relational requests than in individualistic cultures, which are more likely to be more direct and straightforward.

      ANSWER: T   TYPE: T   COG: C

16. Individualistic cultures emphasize belonging to a few permanent in-groups, which have a strong influence over the person.

      ANSWER: F   TYPE: T   COG: R

17. Care for extended family before self is typical of collectivist cultures.

      ANSWER: T   TYPE: T   COG: R

18. "Power distance" describes the degree to which members of a society accept the unequal distribution of power among members.

      ANSWER: T   TYPE: T   COG: R

19. Cultures with high power difference believe in minimizing the difference between various social classes.

      ANSWER: F   TYPE: T   COG: R

20. Challenging authority is acceptable in cultures that endorse low power distance.

      ANSWER: T   TYPE: T   COG: R

21. China, Korea, and Japan exhibit a significantly lower degree of anxiety about speaking out in public than do members of individualistic cultures.

      ANSWER: F   TYPE: T   COG: R

22. Cultures with low power distance are not surprised or offended when children ask Why?"

      ANSWER: T   TYPE: T   COG: C

23. The desire to reduce uncertainty seems to be a trait shared by people around the world.

      ANSWER: T   TYPE: T   COG: R

.24. In countries that avoid uncertainty, deviant people and ideas are considered dangerous and intolerance is high.

      ANSWER: T   TYPE: T   COG: C

25. Nurturing societies emphasize cooperation and show little difference between the expected behaviors for men and for women.

      ANSWER: T   TYPE: T   COG: R

26. The impact of language on the self-concept is minimal.

      ANSWER: F   TYPE: T   COG: C

27. When offering identification information, one's personal name will be given before one's family name in every culture.

      ANSWER: F   TYPE: T   COG: C

28. According to research conducted on insult and aggression, Southern-raised participants are more likely to be upset and primed for aggression after the "hallway incident" than are Northern-raised participants.
    ANSWER: T   TYPE: T   COG: C
29. In the Chinese written language, the pronoun "I" looks very similar to the word for "good."
    ANSWER: F   TYPE: T   COG: R
30. Strong assertions and exaggerations that would sound ridiculous in English are a common feature of Arabic.
    ANSWER: T   TYPE: T   COG: C
31. Linguistic determinism asserts that culture is shaped and reflected by the language its members speak.
    ANSWER: T   TYPE: T   COG: R
32. Asian cultures tend to use more formality in their verbal communication styles than do North American cultures.
    ANSWER: T   TYPE: T   COG: C
33. Research suggests that bilingual speakers think differently when they change languages.
    ANSWER: T   TYPE: T   COG: C
34. Linguistic relativism is a more moderate version of the concept of linguistic determinism.
    ANSWER: T   TYPE: T   COG: R
35. Some languages contain words that have no English equivalents.
    ANSWER: T   TYPE: T   ·   COG: R
36. An example of a nonverbal cure that is universally understood is the "okay" sign made by joining the thumb and forefinger to form a circle.
    ANSWER: F   TYPE: T   COG: A
37. Edward Hall found that people in the Middle East stand much closer when conducting business than Americans do.
    ANSWER: T   TYPE: T   COG: R
38. People who use the term "African American" are more liberal than those who use the term "Black."
    ANSWER: T   TYPE: T   COG: R
39. Native Americans tend to value verbal and nonverbal animation while African Americans tend to value restraint.
    ANSWER: F   TYPE: T   COG: C
40. Members of a culture who use the culture's standard dialect when speaking are usually judged to be unintelligent and lacking in confidence.
    ANSWER: F   TYPE: T   COG: C
41. The way members of a culture are taught to think and reason shapes the way they interpret others' messages.
    ANSWER: T   TYPE: T   COG: R
42. Members of individualistic cultures tend to see the world in terms of dichotomies such as good-bad, right-wrong, and happy-sad.
    ANSWER: T   TYPE: T   COG: R
43. Tolerance for ambiguity is a characteristic of intercultural competence.
    ANSWER: T   TYPE: T   COG: R
44. Ethnocentrism is a characteristic of intercultural competence.
    ANSWER: F   TYPE: T   COG: C
45. Ethnocentrism is the attitude that one's culture is superior to others.
    ANSWER: T   TYPE: T   COG: R
46. The way members of a culture arc taught to think and reason has little to do with how messages are interpreted.
    ANSWER: F   TYPE: T   COG: C

47. Samovar and Porter suggest that attitude and motivation are more "culture general," while knowledge and skill are more "culture specific."

        ANSWER: T   TYPE: T   COG: R

48. When members of the same culture converse, their interaction management is usually unconscious and relatively smooth.

        ANSWER: T   TYPE: T   COG: R

Multiple Choice

49. Which factor(s) are leading us toward a "global village"
    a.   relatively cheap transportation
    b.   advances in communication technology
    c.   population and political pressures
    d.   all of the above
    e.   none of the above

        ANSWER: d   TYPE: M   COG: R

50. "The language, values, beliefs, traditions, and customs people share and learn." is known as
    a.   communication
    b.   culture
    c.   community
    d.   corporation
    e.   colonialism

        ANSWER: b   TYPE: M   COG: R

51. Teenagers may see the elderly as a(n):
    a.   co-culture
    b.   in-group
    c.   low context
    d.   out-group
    e.   none of the above

        ANSWER: d   TYPE: M   COG: A

52. The term Fred Casmir (1992) uses to refer to "a unique relationship shared by two or more people" when some degree of personal contact has been established is
    a.   achievement culture
    b.   third culture
    c.   nurturing culture
    d.   all of the above
    e.   none of the above

        ANSWER: b   TYPE: M   COG: R

53. Membership in a group that is part of an encompassing culture is known as a(n)
    a.   anti-culture
    b.   focus group
    c.   co-culture
    d.   inner group
    e.   none of the above

        ANSWER: c   TYPE: M   COG: R

54. In North American culture categories such as age, ethnicity, race, gender, sexual orientation, physical disabilities and religion are all considered
   a. anti-cultures
   b. focus groups
   c. co-cultures
   d. inner groups
   e. none of the above
       ANSWER: c   TYPE: M   COG: A

55. Rather than classifying some exchanges as intercultural and others as free from cultural influences, it's more accurate to talk about
   a. degrees of cultural significance
   b. high and low context
   c. power distance
   d. co-cultures
   e. none of the above
       ANSWER: a   TYPE: M   COG: C

56. Low-context cultures tend to value and emphasize
   a. straight talk and assertiveness
   b. face-saving and social harmony
   c. nonverbal cues
   d. all of the above
   e. none of the above
       ANSWER: a   TYPE: M   COG: R

57. High –context cultures tend to:
   a. value and emphasize subtle, often nonverbal cues to maintain social harmony
   b. value straight talk and assertiveness
   c. value verbal cues
   d. all of the above
   e. none of the above
       ANSWER: a   TYPE: M   COG: R

58. In which culture are people more likely to avoid saying "no?"
   a. United States
   b. Japanese
   c. Israel
   d. Canada
   e. None of the above
       ANSWER: b   TYPE: M   COG: A

59. When an Israeli views an Arab as being evasive while the Arab views the Israeli as overly blunt, they are encountering value differences primarily associated with
   a. high vs. low context
   b. individualism vs. collectivism
   c. power distance
   d. uncertainty avoidance
   e. achievement vs. nurturing
       ANSWER: a   TYPE: M   COG: A

60. Members of collective cultures
    a.   emphasize individual factors over their relationships with others
    b.   produce and reward team players rather than superstars
    c.   value honesty and directness
    d.   have little communication apprehension
    e.   all of the above
          ANSWER: b   TYPE: M   COG: R
61. When a North American answers the question "Who am I?" by citing individual factors, while an Asian person answers the same question by identifying groups in which she/he is a member, they are expressing value differences associated with
    a.   high vs. low context
    b.   individualism vs. collectivism
    c.   power distance
    d.   uncertainty avoidance
    e.   achievement vs. nurturing
          ANSWER: b   TYPE: M   COG: R
62. When Austrian students are praised for asking their teachers questions while Filipino students see questioning their teachers as inappropriate, they are exhibiting values associated with which concept?
    a.   high vs. low context
    b.   individualism vs. collectivism
    c.   power distance
    d.   uncertainty avoidance
    e.   achievement vs. nurturing
          ANSWER: c   TYPE: M   COG: A
63. The degree to which members of a culture feel threatened by ambiguous situations and try to stay away from them is known as
    a.   power distance
    b.   uncertainty avoidance
    c.   cultural perception
    d.   all of the above
    e.   none of the above
          ANSWER: b   TYPE: M   COG: R
64. The term that reflects the degree to which members of a culture feel threatened by ambiguous situations is
    a.   prejudice
    b.   individualism
    c.   power distance
    d.   uncertainty avoidance
    e.   ethnocentrism
          ANSWER: d   TYPE: M   COG: R
65. A "hard" culture is a culture that values
    a.   achievement
    b.   collectivism
    c.   low power distance
    d.   nurturing
    e.   high power distance
          ANSWER: a   TYPE: M   COG: R

66. When a German believes men should be "hard" and women should be "soft," while a Spaniard believes there is little difference between expected behaviors for men and women, they are experiencing value differences associated with
   a.   high vs. low context
   b.   individualism vs. collectivism
   c.   power distance
   d.   uncertainty avoidance
   e.   achievement vs. nurturing
   ANSWER: e   TYPE: M   COG: A

67. The Korean language has separate terms for older brother, oldest brother, younger sister, youngest sister, and so on. This is a reflection of:
   a.   cultural perspective
   b.   power distance
   c.   uncertainty avoidance
   d.   individualism vs. collectivism
   e.   none of the above
   ANSWER: b   TYPE: M   COG: C

68. Which of the following contrasting pairs is associated with features of verbal communication styles
   a.   directness/indirectness
   b.   elaborate/succinct
   c.   formal/informal
   d.   all of the above
   e.   none of the above
   ANSWER: d   TYPE: M   COG: R

69. The notion that the world view of a culture is shaped and reflected by the language its members speak is known as
   a.   prejudice
   b.   ethnocentrism
   c.   egocentrism
   d.   co-culture
   e.   linguistic determinism
   ANSWER: e   TYPE: M   COG: R

70. The fact that although Chinese speakers have five distinct words for what North Americans would simply call "shame," the North Americans are as capable as Chinese of experiencing distinct varieties of shame casts doubt on which extreme viewpoint?
   a.   prejudice
   b.   ethnocentrism
   c.   egocentrism
   d.   co-culture
   e.   linguistic determinism
   ANSWER: e   TYPE: M   COG: C

71. The Sapir-Whorf hypothesis is associated with
   a.   linguistic determinism
   b.   demographics
   c.   technology
   d.   in-groups
   e.   out-groups
   ANSWER: a   TYPE: M   COG: R

72. Cultural differences in decoding messages occur because of differences in
    a.   translation
    b.   attributional variations
    c.   patterns of thought
    d.   all of the above
    e.   none of the above
          ANSWER: d   TYPE: M   COG: R
73. Collectivist cultures, in comparison to individualist cultures, tend to
    a.   see the world in terms of either/or dichotomies
    b.   define themselves as part of a group
    c.   define themselves in terms of what they do
    d.   tolerate conflict easily
    e.   none of the above
          ANSWER: b   TYPE: M   COG: R
74. Most scholars believe intercultural competence requires
    a.   motivation and attitude
    b.   knowledge
    c.   skill
    d.   all of the above
    e.   none of the above
          ANSWER: d   TYPE: M   COG: R
75. Patiently dealing with the uncertainty that surrounds most intercultural encounters is a sign of
    a.   tolerance for ambiguity
    b.   intercultural competence
    c.   ethnocentrism
    d.   two of the above
    e.   all of the above
          ANSWER: d   TYPE: M   COG: R
76. Which of the following is *not* associated with intercultural competence?
    a.   tolerance for ambiguity
    b.   open-mindedness
    c.   interaction management
    d.   display of respect
    e.   stereotyping
          ANSWER: e   TYPE: M   COG: R
77. The ideas that al women are emotional and that all older people are out of touch with reality are examples of
    a.   patterns of thought
    b.   open-mindedness
    c.   stereotypes
    d.   power distance
    e.   none of the above
          ANSWER: c   TYPE: M   COG: A
78. Which of the following is associated with intercultural competence
    a.   interaction management
    b.   ethnocentrism
    c.   prejudice
    d.   intolerance for ambiguity
    e.   stereotyping
          ANSWER: a   TYPE: M   COG: R

79. Japanese insurance companies warn their policyholders who are visiting the United States to avoid their cultural tendency to say "excuse me" or "I'm sorry" if they are involved in a traffic accident because of cultural differences in
   a. translation
   b. attributional variations
   c. patterns of thought
   d. reflections of power distance
   e. none of the above
   ANSWER: a   TYPE: M   COG: A

Essay

80. Identify and explain three factors that are moving us toward McLuhan's notion of a "global village."
   ANSWER: TYPE: E   COG: R
81. Explain what is meant by culture being a matter of perception.
   ANSWER: TYPE: E   COG: C
82. Offer contrasting examples of two people from different cultures who are (a) engaging in intercultural communication and (b) not engaging in intercultural communication.
   ANSWER: TYPE: E   COG: A
83. Discuss, using examples, the relationship between ethnocentrism, prejudice, and stereotyping. In the process, define each term.
   ANSWER: TYPE: E   COG: C
84. Describe, using terms from the text, some difficulties that might occur in a business meeting with participants from the United States, Japan, and Saudi Arabia.
   ANSWER: TYPE: E   COG: A
85. Explain how Gudykunst & Kim's two-by-two matrix reflects the relationship between interpersonal communication and cultural significance.
   ANSWER: TYPE: E   COG: C
86. Explain the primary cultural influences that effect interpersonal communication. Include in your discussion the following:
   a. high versus low contexts
   b. individualism versus collectivism
   c. power distance
   d. uncertainty avoidance
   e. achievement versus nurturing
   ANSWER: TYPE: E   COG: A
87. Explain how a person's cultural tendency toward uncertainty avoidance could impact their tolerance for ambiguity.
   ANSWER: TYPE: E   COG: C
88. Identify three specific challenges faced by communicators when using different verbal and nonverbal communication systems.
   ANSWER: TYPE: E   COG: C
89. How might interpersonal conflict be viewed differently by high vs. low context cultures?
   ANSWER: TYPE: E   COG: A
90. Explain how the concepts "shyness" and "assertive" may be seen differently in individualistic cultures and collectivistic cultures.
   ANSWER: TYPE: E   COG: A
91. Explain why multinational companies need to consider fundamental difference in power distance when they set up shop in a new country.
   ANSWER: TYPE: E   COG: C

92. Explain how a country's need for uncertainty avoidance might affect innovation vs. imitation of products and ideas.
    ANSWER: TYPE: E   COG: C
93. What is the role of perception in intercultural communication?
    ANSWER: TYPE: E   COG: A
94. How does communication operate when members of different cultures interact?
    ANSWER: TYPE: E   COG: A
95. Explain how translation, attributional variations, and patterns of thought make the decoding messages especially difficult for communicators from different cultures.
    ANSWER: TYPE: E   COG: A
96. Compare and contrast ethnocentrism, prejudice, and stereotyping.
    ANSWER: TYPE: E   COG: A
97. Explain how the classroom atmosphere might be different given the following cultural influences:
    a. High vs. low context
    b. Power distance
    c. Individualism vs. collectivism
    ANSWER: TYPE: E   COG: C
98. Charles Berger identifies three specific strategies of increasing one's intercultural communication competence. Discuss the potential strengths and weaknesses of each in relation to the following cultural tendencies:
    a. High vs. low context
    b. High power distance
    c. Individualism vs. collectivism
    ANSWER: TYPE: E   COG: A
99. Your friend, Selwynn, is planning a trip to Germany. Selwynn has mastered textbook German but is concerned about intercultural communication competence. What *specific strategies* would you provide Selwynn to improve the three dimensions of intercultural communicative competence before the trip to Germany?
    ANSWER: TYPE: E   COG: A

Matching

100. Match the cultural values and norms with their definition.

_____ a. High vs. Low Context
_____ b. Individualism vs. Collectivism
_____ c. Power Distance
_____ d. Uncertainty Avoidance
_____ e. Achievement vs. Nurturing

1. The degree to which a culture views their primary responsibility as themselves or their group.
2. The degree to which societies place value on material success vs. support of relationships.
3. The degree to which people feel threatened by ambiguous situations.
4. The degree to which a culture values direct verbal communication or subtle, often nonverbal communication.
5. The degree to which members of a society accept an unequal distribution of power.
    ANSWER: a. 4; b. 1; c. 5; d. 3; e. 2
    TYPE: K   COG: R

CHAPTER THIRTEEN: COMMUNICATING WITH FAMILY AND AT WORK

True/False

1. A family is defined as "a system with two or more interdependent people who have a common past history, a present reality, and who expect to influence each other in the future.
   ANSWER: T   TYPE: T   COG: R

2. Of the three basic couple types outlined in your text, *Independent* couples have the highest marital satisfaction.
   ANSWER: F   TYPE: T   COG: C

3. Researcher Mary Ann Fitzpatrick asserts that *Independent* coupes do not avoid conflict.
   ANSWER: T   TYPE: T   COG: R

4. Sarah and Steve express their affection to each other frequently and report high levels of marital satisfaction. Steve and Sarah would be classified as a *Separate* couple type.
   ANSWER: F   TYPE: T   COG: A

5. Mixed couple types tend to have a moderately high marital satisfaction and moderately high expression of affection.
   ANSWER: T   TYPE: T   COG: C

6. Having a child has no influence on how couples communicate with each other, only on how they communicate with the new family member.
   ANSWER: F   TYPE: T   COG: C

7. Shared narratives help hold siblings together as well as clarify family events.
   ANSWER: T   TYPE: T   COG: R

8. Siblings' perceptions of family experiences are typically very similar when they grow up in the same household.
   ANSWER: F   TYPE: T   COG: C

9. In many families, parents have a tendency to have fewer expectations of intellectual achievements for their daughters than their sons.
   ANSWER: T   TYPE: T   COG: C

10. Sister relationships tend to be more competitive than brother relationships.
    ANSWER: F   TYPE: T   COG: R

11. Family members are interdependent. Each event is a reaction to the family's history, and each event shapes future interaction.
    ANSWER: T   TYPE: T   COG: R

12. Dave, an outgoing advertising executive, typically becomes very quiet when attending family reunions. This is indicative of the idea that a family is more than a sum of its parts.
    ANSWER: T   TYPE: T   COG: A

13. The nuclear family is the smallest family subsystem.
    ANSWER: F   TYPE: T   COG: R

14. Family systems are "closed" systems.
    ANSWER: F   TYPE: T   COG: R

15. According to Virginia Satir, four roles arise during family conflict: the blamer, the placater, the analyst and the distracter.
    ANSWER: F   TYPE: T   COG: R

16. Whenever there is an argument in his family, Chris is always quick to point a finger to the person he believes is responsible. He has taken on the role of *distracter.*
    ANSWER: F   TYPE: T   COG: A

17. The person in the conflict role of *computer* uses reasonableness and dispassion to defuse conflict.

    ANSWER: T   TYPE: T   COG: R

18. According to Satir, the person who placates during family conflict feels helpless and worthless without the other family member.

    ANSWER: T   TYPE: T   COG: C

19. Distracters use unrelated and pointless behaviors to mask their belief that nobody cares for them and there is no place for them in the family.

    ANSWER: T   TYPE: T   COG: R

20. According to Satir, the *blamer* acts cool and calm, but on the inside feels very vulnerable.

    ANSWER: F   TYPE: T   COG: R

21. Social Scientists refer to the family in which we grow up in as our *family of origin*.

    ANSWER: T   TYPE: T   COG: R

22. Adolescents in homes where there is wife abuse are particularly at risk of being physically abused themselves.

    ANSWER: T   TYPE: T   COG: C

23. People have a tendency to define family similarly across cultures.

    ANSWER: F   TYPE: T   COG: R

24. Families that interact freely, frequently, and spontaneously, without many limitations regarding topic or time spent interacting, are said to have a high conversation orientation.

    ANSWER: T   TYPE: T   COG: R

25. Conformity orientation refers to the degree to which family communication stresses uniformity of attitudes, values, and beliefs.

    ANSWER: T   TYPE: T   COG: R

26. Families low in both conversation orientation and conformity orientation are pluralistic.

    ANSWER: F   TYPE: T   COG: R

27. Stepchildren feel more satisfied with stepparents who can strike a balance between being authoritarian and permissive.

    ANSWER: T   TYPE: T   COG: C

28. Social scientists label families with too little cohesion as enmeshed.

    ANSWER: F   TYPE: T   COG: R

29. Families cope with dialectical tensions be creating boundaries – limits set on a family member's actions.

    ANSWER: T   TYPE: T   COG: R

30. Boundaries must always be openly negotiated if family members are going to accept them.

    ANSWER: F   TYPE: T   COG: C

31. Balanced and mid-range families generally function more adequately than extreme families.

    ANSWER: T   TYPE: T   COG: C

32. Gottman's studies show that satisfied couples consistently have a 5-1 ratio of positive to negative comments.

    ANSWER: T   TYPE: T   COG: R

33. Downward communication occurs when managers address messages to subordinates.

    ANSWER: F   TYPE: T   COG: R

34. Informal messages can supplement formal messages in a variety of ways.

    ANSWER: T   TYPE: T   COG: R

35. As long as team members have the ability to do their tasks skillfully, relational skills are not as important for a team to operate effectively.

    ANSWER: F   TYPE: T   COG: C

36. The following message illustrates an example of task coordination. "If you can get me the job tomorrow, I'll have it finished by Thursday."

    ANSWER: T   TYPE: T   COG: A

37. "They say the deadline is Friday, but first thing Monday morning is O.K." is an example of informal communication that confirms a formal message.

          ANSWER: F   TYPE: T   COG: A

38. The reinforcement stage occurs when members accept a team's decision.

          ANSWER: F   TYPE: T   COG: R

39. During upward communication, negative information can get distorted and put in a positive light.

          ANSWER: T   TYPE: T   COG: C

40. Informal relationships are often more efficient and accurate than formal networks in the workplace.

          ANSWER: T   TYPE: T   COG: C

41. Virtual teams refer to team membership that transcends the boundaries of location and time.

          ANSWER: T   TYPE: T   COG: R

42. Electronically mediated relationships are becoming less common in the work setting as we learn how important face to face communication is to relationships.

          ANSWER: F   TYPE: T   COG: C

43. Formal communication refers to rules that govern how language should be used in the workplace.

          ANSWER: F   TYPE: T   COG: R

44. Although everyone has unique communication styles, most groups go through a predictable set of stages when they work together.

          ANSWER: T   TYPE: T   COG: C

45. Working groups and entire organizations have their own unique cultures.

          ANSWER: T   TYPE: T   COG: C

46. Emotional support and tolerance for new ideas are dimensions or organizational culture.

          ANSWER: F   TYPE: T   COG: R

47. The reinforcement stage in-group decision-making is when members attempt to persuade other team members to agree with their ideas.

          ANSWER: F   TYPE: T   COG: R

48. Only a designated leader has the ability to influence the effectiveness of a group.

          ANSWER: F   TYPE: T   COG: C

49. It is usually a good idea to clarify an interviewer's goals before the interview actually takes place.

          ANSWER: T   TYPE: T   COG: C

50. Group decision-making occurs in a linear rather than a circular process.

          ANSWER: F   TYPE: T   COG: C

51. Referent power refers to the authority that leaders have to recommend individuals for promotion.

          ANSWER: F   TYPE: T   COG: C

52. It is an outdated idea to think that first impressions can make or break an interview.

          ANSWER: F   TYPE: T   COG: R

53. It is better to under dress for an interview rather than risk being seen as too formal for an organization's culture.

          ANSWER: F   TYPE: T   COG: R

54. During an employment interview, it is customary for the interviewer to talk the majority of the time.

          ANSWER: F   TYPE: T   COG: C

55. According to the survey in your text, employers identified communication as the most important skill a job candidate could possess.

          ANSWER: T   TYPE: T   COG: R

56. A common source of conflict in many families is actually related to how to handle conflicts.

          ANSWER: T   TYPE: T   COG: R

Multiple Choice

57. Which couple type strives to maintain stability by upholding a conventional belief system that values traditional sex roles, interdependence, and conflict avoidance?
    a. traditional couples
    b. independent couples
    c. separate couples
    d. mixed couples
    e. enmeshed couples
    ANSWER: a   TYPE: M   COG: R

58. Which couple type avoids adhering to traditional sex roles and maintains their psychological distance?
    a. traditional couples
    b. independent couples
    c. separate couples
    d. mixed couples
    e. enmeshed couples
    ANSWER: b   TYPE: M   COG: R

59. Which couple type places a higher value on their individual freedom than their relationship?
    a. traditional couples
    b. independent couples
    c. separate couples
    d. mixed couples
    e. enmeshed couples
    ANSWER: c   TYPE: M   COG: R

60. Which of the following roles is usually not present in sibling relationships?
    a. playmate
    b. confidant
    c. role model
    d. adversary
    e. all of these roles are present in sibling relationships.
    ANSWER: e   TYPE: M   COG: C

61. Which of the following is not a characteristic of how families are like systems?
    a. Family members are interdependent
    b. A family is more than the sum of its parts
    c. Families have systems within the larger system
    d. Family systems are affected by their environment
    e. All of the above are characteristics
    ANSWER: e   TYPE: M   COG: R

62. During family conflict, the role of the distracter is to
    a. judge others and hold them responsible for anything that goes wrong
    b. agree with whatever the other person says
    c. stay cool and calm while using reason to defuse the conflict
    d. say something irrelevant so the threat will be forgotten
    e. none of the above
    ANSWER: d   TYPE: M   COG: R

63. During family conflict, the role of the computer is to
    a. judge others and hold them responsible for anything that goes wrong
    b. agree with whatever the other person says
    c. stay cool and calm while using reason to defuse the conflict
    d. say something irrelevant so the threat will be forgotten
    e. none of the above
       ANSWER: c   TYPE: M   COG: R

64. Whenever Stacey gets into an argument with her sister, she is always the first to back down because she doesn't want to make her sister angry. Stacey is playing the conflict role of
    a. blamer
    b. placater
    c. computer
    d. distracter
    e. laissez-faire
       ANSWER: b   TYPE: M   COG: A

65. Which of the following is not a family conflict role outlined by Virginia Satir in your text?
    a. blamer
    b. placater
    c. computer
    d. distracter
    e. laissez-faire
       ANSWER: e   TYPE: M   COG: R

66. Making comments such as "You never do anything right. What is the matter with you?" is indicative of which family conflict role?
    a. blamer
    b. placater
    c. computer
    d. distracter
    e. laissez-faire
       ANSWER: a   TYPE: M   COG: A

67. The degree to which families favor an open climate of discussion of a wide array of topics is termed
    a. conversation conformity
    b. conversation orientation
    c. communication orientation
    d. communication conformity
    e. none of the above
       ANSWER: b   TYPE: M   COG: R

68. The degree to which family communication stresses uniformity of attitudes, values, and beliefs is termed
    a. conversation conformity
    b. conversation orientation
    c. communication orientation
    d. communication conformity
    e. none of the above
       ANSWER: a   TYPE: M   COG: R

69. Families high in both conversation orientation and conformity are
    a. consensual
    b. pluralistic
    c. protective
    d. laissez-faire
    e. none of the above
       ANSWER: a   TYPE: M   COG: R
70. Families high on conversation orientation and low in conformity orientation are:
    a. consensual
    b. pluralistic
    c. protective
    d. laissez-faire
    e. none of the above
       ANSWER: b   TYPE: M   COG: R
71. Families low in conversation orientation and high in conformity orientation are:
    a. consensual
    b. pluralistic
    c. protective
    d. laissez-faire
    e. none of the above
       ANSWER: c   TYPE: M   COG: R
72. Families low in both conversation orientation and conformity orientation are:
    a. consensual
    b. pluralistic
    c. protective
    d. laissez-faire
    e. none of the above
       ANSWER: d   TYPE: M   COG: R
73. Which of the following is outlined in your text as guidelines for effective communication in families?
    a. strive for closeness while respecting boundaries
    b. strive for a moderate level of adaptability
    c. encourage confirming messages
    d. deal constructively with family conflict
    e. All of the above are outlined
       ANSWER: e   TYPE: M   COG: C
74. A family rule prohibiting entering a bedroom without knocking first is an example of a
    a. conformity
    b. pluralism
    c. boundary
    d. laissez-faire
    e. none of the above
       ANSWER: c   TYPE: M   COG: A
75. Families cope with dialectical tensions be creating
    a. boundaries
    b. chaotic rules
    c. family of Origin
    d. laissez-faire rules
    e. none of the above
       ANSWER: a   TYPE: M   COG: C

76. When adaptability is too high, the result may be what the Circumplex Model labels a(n)
    a. disengaged family
    b. rigid family
    c. enmeshed family
    d. chaotic family
    e. none of the above
       ANSWER: c   TYPE: M   COG: R

77. Gottman's studies show that satisfied couples have the following ratio of positive-to-negative communication:
    a. 1-1
    b. 1-2
    c. 1-5
    d. 1-10
    e. none of the above
       ANSWER: b   TYPE: M   COG: R

78. Many family conflicts center of which of the following issues?
    a. power struggles
    b. differences in intimacy needs
    c. interaction difficulties
    d. A & B
    e. all of the above
       ANSWER: e   TYPE: M   COG: R

79. Which of the following is identified as a relational role that every group needs at some time to operate efficiently?
    a. relieving tension
    b. giving praise
    c. encouraging participation
    d. both a and b
    e. all of the above are roles
       ANSWER: e   TYPE: M   COG: C

80. Once a group has worked through a period of conflict, it typically enters a(n) _____ stage where members accept a team's decision.
    a. reinforcement
    b. emergence
    c. conflict
    d. orientation
    e. remediation
       ANSWER: b   TYPE: M   COG: R

81. Even though they live and work across the country from each other, Katrina and Dan are writing a new training manual together. This is an example of how _____ teams operate.
    a. virtual
    b. isolated
    c. horizontal
    d. reinforcement
    e. none of the above
       ANSWER: a   TYPE: M   COG: R

82. Communication that occurs between people who don't have direct supervisor-subordinate relationships is called
    a. lateral communication
    b. peer communication
    c. horizontal communication
    d. informal communication
    e. none of the above
    ANSWER: c   TYPE: M   COG: R

83. Downward communication messages can include
    a. job instructions
    b. job rationale
    c. Feedback
    d. manager announcements to subordinates
    e. all of the above
    ANSWER: e   TYPE: M   COG: R

84. Because Susan is the only one in the office that knows the new inventory software program, she possesses_____ power.
    a. reward
    b. coercive
    c. referent
    d. expert
    e. technical
    ANSWER: d   TYPE: M   COG: A

85. It is usually a good idea to bring which materials to a job interview:
    a. letters of recommendation
    b. copies of past work
    c. extra copies of your resume
    d. performance reviews
    e. all of the above
    ANSWER: e   TYPE: M   COG: R

86. Research shows that many interviewers form their opinions about candidates within the first _____ minutes of conversation.
    a. 10
    b. 4
    c. 2
    d. 15
    e. 5
    ANSWER: b   TYPE: M   COG: R

87. One of the qualities that distinguishes winning teams is a(n) _____ climate in which team members trust each other.
    a. collaborative
    b. virtual
    c. emergence
    d. disconfirming
    e. formal
    ANSWER: a   TYPE: M   COG: C

88. Jennifer provides weekly reports to her supervisor on her team's sales numbers. This is an example of
    a. downward communication
    b. horizontal communication
    c. informal communication
    d. upward communication
    e. confirming communication
    ANSWER: d   TYPE: M   COG: A

89. John refuses to stay late and help Janice finish the print layout since he is angry that Janice didn't invite him to a department lunch. John is using _____ power.
    a. coercive
    b. retaliation
    c. negotiation
    d. punishment and reward
    e. none of the above
    ANSWER: a   TYPE: M   COG: A

90. Interviews are different from everyday communication because of their
    a. structure
    b. tone
    c. control
    d. both a & b
    e. both a & c
    ANSWER: e   TYPE: M   COG: R

91. Rebecca and Linda are managers for the same company, but work in different departments. While talking at a friend's birthday party, Rebecca tells Linda that her team will be rolling out a new product line. This is an example of how _____ communication occurs within an organization.
    a. virtual
    b. downward
    c. informal
    d. cohesive
    e. systematic
    ANSWER: c   TYPE: M   COG: A

Essay

92. Explain the basic differences between Mary Ann Fitzpatrick's three couple types (traditional, independent, and separate).
    ANSWER: TYPE: E   COG: R

93. Your text outlines seven influence patters that develop with the birth of a couple's first child. List and give an example of three of them.
    ANSWER: TYPE: E   COG: C

94. Discuss the idea that families are "systems."
    ANSWER: TYPE: E   COG: C

95. Discuss the idea that a family is "more than the sum of its parts."
    ANSWER: TYPE: E   COG: C

96. List and explain the differences between Virginia Satir's four family conflict roles.
    ANSWER: TYPE: E   COG: R

97. Discuss how "family narratives" can affect family communication.
    ANSWER: TYPE: E   COG: A

98. What role do *boundaries* play in family interaction?
          ANSWER: TYPE: E   COG: R

99. Explain the differences between upward, downward and horizontal communication.
          ANSWER: TYPE: E   COG: R

100. Discuss, using examples, the various stages that groups go through when they work together.
          ANSWER: TYPE: E   COG: R

101. Describe, using terms from the chapter, the various types of power and influence that individual members can have within organizational groups.
          ANSWER: TYPE: E   COG: C

102. Your friend just told you she has her first job interview next week and would like some advice from you. What guidelines and strategies would you provide regarding preparation before, during and after the interview?
          ANSWER: TYPE: E   COG: A

103. Briefly explain how informal messages can confirm or contradict formal messages within organizations. Provide an example of each type of statement.
          ANSWER: TYPE: E   COG: C

104. Outline two of the four general principles of conflict management discussed in your text.
          ANSWER: TYPE: E   COG: R

PART VI STUDY GUIDES

CHAPTER ONE: INTERPERSONAL PROCESS STUDY GUIDE

Communication Meets Four Needs

What are the four needs?

How does each of them affect our communication?

The Communication Process

How have communication models changed over time?

Define: encoding, decoding and feedback

What are the four insights from the Communication Model?

Define: communicator, environment, three types of noise, and channel

Communication Principles

Name and define three communication principles

Communication Misperceptions

Name and define four communication misperceptions.

When is Communication Interpersonal?

Define: Quantitative Definition

Define: Qualitative Definition

Define: Impersonal communication

Interpersonal vs. Impersonal

Identify and define the features that distinguish qualitative interpersonal communications from less personal exchanges.

Personal and Impersonal Communication

What is the balance?

Interpersonal Communication and Technology

What are the pros and cons of Computer-Mediated Communication (CMC)?

Communication Competence

What are the two dimensions of communication competence?

What are three characteristics of communication competence?

Define: The seven common denominators that characterize effective communication in most contexts.

CHAPTER TWO: COMMUNICATION AND THE SELF STUDY GUIDE

Communication and the Self-Concept

Define: Self-Concept

Define: Self-Esteem

How the Self Concept Develops

Define: The two theories that describe how self-concept develops.

How do <u>significant others</u> and <u>reference groups</u> fit into and function in these two theories?

Characteristics of the Self-Concept

Describe the three characteristics of the self-concept.

List the reasons why some people have a self-concept that is unrealistically favorable or unfavorable.

Self-fulfilling Prophecy

Define: The two types of self-fulfilling prophecy.

What does an observer have to do to create a self-fulfilling prophecy for the target person?

Describe the influence of self-fulfilling prophecy.

Changing Your Self-Concept

List the four ways to help change your self-concept.

Presenting the Self

Define: identity management

Define: perceived self

Define: presenting self

Define: face and facework

Identity Management

Identify the four characteristics of identity management.

Discuss why we manage impressions.

Identify the way we manage impressions in two communication channels.

Discuss the ethics of impression management.

CHAPTER THREE: PERCEIVING OTHERS STUDY GUIDE

The perception process has four steps

What are the four steps?

What are the factors that help us select messages?

Name the four types of perceptual schema?

Define: stereotyping and punctuation.

What are the factors used to interpret behavior?

Define: narratives

Influences on perception

Define: The four influences

Define: The six physiological influences.

Define: The two psychological influences.

Give two examples of cultural differences and their influence.

Define: The three social influences.

Common tendencies in perception

Define: six common tendencies.

More accurate perceptions of others

What are the two tools to use?

Write out the three steps of a perception check.

Create two examples of a perception check.

Why and when would we use a perception check?

Define: empathy.

List the three payoffs for the recipient of empathy.

Name the skills and attitudes that are needed to develop stronger empathy?

Define: compassion fatigue.

CHAPTER FOUR: THE NATURE OF LANGUAGE STUDY GUIDE

The Nature of Language

What is meant by the statement "language is symbolic?"

Language is Rule-Governed

What are the 4 types of rules?

Define: Coordinated Management of Meaning (CMM) Theory

What is meant by the statement "language is subjective?"

Define: triangle of meaning

Define: computerized flaming

The Impact of Language

How do names shape the way others think of us, the way we view ourselves, and the way we act?

How does the Fox Hypothesis illustrate the use of credibility and status in language?

Define: convergence, divergence

Define: power - powerless speech mannerisms

How does racism and sexism affect perception?

Uses (And Abuses) of Language

Define each of the following terms:

    ambiguous language

    abstractions (abstraction ladder)

    euphemisms

    relative language

    static evaluation

    "it" statements

    "I" language

    "but" statements

"I," "you, " and" we" language

Explain each of the following types of disruptive language:

fact-opinion confusion

fact-inference confusion

emotive language

Male and Female Language Use

Explain the similarities and differences between the following factors of female and male language use:

content

reasons for communicating

conversational style

nonsex variables

CHAPTER FIVE: NONVERBAL COMMUNICATION STUDY GUIDE

What is the Definition of Nonverbal Communication?

Characteristics of Nonverbal Communication

Why do we believe that "all behavior has communicative value?"

Why do we believe that "nonverbal communication is primarily relational?"

Define: the three social functions of nonverbal communication.

Explain how "nonverbal communication is ambiguous."

Explain how nonverbal communication is influenced by culture.

Functions of Nonverbal Communication

Define the following terms.

repeating

substituting

complementing and accenting

emblems

illustrators

regulating

contradicting

deceiving

Types of Nonverbal Communication

Define and explain how the following terms and concepts affect human communication.

face and eyes

body movement

kinesics

manipulators

gestures

touch

voice

paralanguage

disfluencies

proxemics and territoriality

personal space – What are the four distances we use in our every day lives?

territory – What problems can arise?

time

chronemics

physical attractiveness

interaction appearance theory

clothing

environment

CHAPTER SIX: LISTENING STUDY GUIDE

The Importance of Listening

How much time do we spend communicating, how much is spent listening?

What are the four reasons for listening?

The Challenge of Listening

Explain the difference between listening and hearing.

Define: The 5 listening barriers.

Define: The seven poor listening habits.

Components of Listening

Define: The five components of listening

Types of Listening Responses

Define: silent listening

Define: questioning

What are the five reasons to ask sincere questions?

Define: counterfeit questions

What are the five types of counterfeit questions?

Paraphrasing

Define: paraphrasing

What are the three types of paraphrasing statements?

Explain the two levels at which you can paraphrase messages

Empathizing

Define: empathizing.

Identify four non-empathizing behaviors.

Supporting

List the types of support.

What are the circumstances under which supporting is helpful?

Analyzing

Discuss the two problems with analyzing.

What are the guidelines to follow for helpful analysis?

Advising

Define: advising

Identify the four conditions for offering advice.

Evaluating

Define: evaluating

List the two conditions for acceptance.

Which Style to Use?

What responses should you begin with?

What are the three factors to consider in choosing the best style?

CHAPTER SEVEN: EMOTIONS STUDY GUIDE

What are Emotions?

Define: the four components of emotion

Types of Emotions

Define: three ways of looking at emotions.

Influences on Emotional Expression

Explain how each of the following influence emotional expression:

personality

culture

biological sex and gender

social conventions

social rules

fear of self-disclosure

emotional contagion

Guidelines for Expressing Emotions

Identify and explain the following six suggestions given to help you decide when and how to express your emotions.

Recognize your feelings

Choose the best language

Share multiple feelings

Recognize the difference between feeling and acting

Accept responsibility for your feelings

Choose the best time and place to express your feelings

Managing Difficult Emotions

Define: facilitative and debilitative Emotions

Thoughts cause feelings: Define the rational-emotional approach

Irrational Thinking and Debilitative Emotions: define the following terms:

The fallacy of perfection

The fallacy of approval

The fallacy of should

The fallacy of overgeneralization

The fallacy of causation

The fallacy of helplessness

The fallacy of catastrophic expectations

Minimizing Debilitative Emotions

Explain the four steps to practice cutting down on the self-defeating thinking that leads to debilitative emotions.

CHAPTER EIGHT: DYNAMICS OF INTERPERSONAL RELATIONSHIPS
STUDY GUIDE

Why We Form Relationships

Define each of the seven reasons why we form relationships.

Identify the three parts of "similarity."

Define: exchange theory.

Communication and Relational Dynamics

Developmental Model of Relational Development

Define the ten steps of Knapp's model

Draw a diagram of the ten steps illustrating their relationships.

Dialectical Perspectives on Relational Development

Define: the internal and external dialectical tensions.

What are the eight strategies for managing the dialectics?

Characteristics of Relational Development

What are the two characteristics that are true of every interpersonal relationship?

Communicating About Relationships

Define: content and relational messages

How do we express relational messages?

Compliance Gaining Strategies

Define and be prepared to explain the following terms:

direct requests

indirect appeals

reciprocity

reward and punishment

face maintenance

relational appeals

Which Strategies to Choose

Identify the repertoire of strategies identified in the text.

What are the three principles that can help choose an approach for gaining compliance?

CHAPTER NINE: INTIMACY AND DISTANCE IN RELATIONSHIPS
STUDY GUIDE

Intimacy and Distance: Striking a Balance

Dimensions of Intimacy

Define the four qualities of intimacy.

Dimensions of Distance

What are the six common avoidance tactics?

The Dialectics of Intimacy and Distance

How much intimacy is the right amount? Be prepared to explain.

Influences on Intimacy and Distance

Male and Female Intimacy Styles

What are the two ways that men and women create intimacy?

How do you think these differences would affect men and women's perception of intimacy?

Culture

How are the United States' cultural views on intimacy changing?

Cultural influences on intimacy: Prepare examples of cultural differences.

Self-Disclosure in Relationships

Define: self-disclosure

What are the four factors that distinguish self-disclosure from other types of communication?

Degrees of Self-Disclosure

What are the two dimensions of the social penetration model?

What are the factors that make the disclosure in some messages deeper than others?

How much disclosure is good?

A Model of Self-Disclosure

Define and explain the elements of the Johari Window.

Define: the four Johari styles of disclosure

Risks and Benefits of Self-Disclosure

Define: the nine benefits of self-disclosure

Define: the seven risks of self-disclosure

Alternatives to Self-Disclosure

Lies

Define: lying

Define: benevolent lies

List and explain the five major reasons for lying.

What are the effects of lies?

Define: equivocation

Define: hinting

The Ethics of Evasion: What should be considered?

Guidelines for Self-Disclosure

What are the seven guidelines for self-disclosure?

CHAPTER TEN: COMMUNICATION CLIMATE STUDY GUIDE

How Communication Climates Develop

Define: communication climate

Define: confirming messages and disconfirming messages.

Identify and explain the three confirming messages.

Define and explain the three disagreeing messages

Define and explain the seven disconfirming messages.

Define defensiveness. Explain "face-threatening acts."

What are climate patterns? Explain the concept of the "spiral."

Creating Positive Climates

Be prepared to explain Gibb's categorization of supportive and defensive behavior.

Define and develop examples for the following terms:

evaluation vs. description

control vs. problem orientation

strategy vs. spontaneity

neutrality vs. empathy

superiority vs. equality

certainty vs. provisionalism

Transforming Negative Climates

What is the rationale behind seeking more information as a response to a critical attack?

What are the six ways in which a person may seek more information from a critic? Explain.

What is the rationale behind realizing that there are several different types of agreement?

Explain the four ways that a person may agree with the critic.

CHAPTER ELEVEN: MANAGING CONFLICT STUDY GUIDE

What Is Conflict?

Define: Conflict

Define: The five parts of the definition.

Functional and Dysfunctional Conflict Styles

Define: the eight symptoms that distinguish functional from dysfunctional conflicts.

What are the two consequences of dysfunctional conflicts?

What are the positive outcomes of functional conflicts?

Individual Conflict Styles

Define: the five styles of conflict behavior.

List the five elements of assertion.

What are the three factors that govern the conflict style to use?

Conflict in Relational Systems

Define: the three styles that can be used to manage relationships

Define: intimate and aggressive styles

Define: "conflict rituals."

Variables in Conflict Styles

Define: the two variables that affect the way people manage conflict

Be prepared to explain the variables.

Methods of Conflict Resolution

Define: the four approaches to resolving conflicts

Explain the seven-step approach to a "Win – Win" solution.

CHAPTER TWELVE: CULTURE AND COMMUNICATION STUDY GUIDE

Why Study Intercultural Communication?

List and explain the four reasons.

Fundamental Concepts

Define: culture

Define: in-groups

Define: out-groups

Intercultural Communication

Define: intercultural communication

Define: co-culture

Interpersonal and Intercultural Communication

Define: "degrees" of cultural significance?

Cultural Norms and Values

Define and provide an example for each of the following terms:

high vs. low context

individualism vs. collectivism

power distance

uncertainty avoidance

achievement vs. nurturing

Codes and Culture

Define and provide an example for each of the following terms:

Language and Identity

Directness vs. Indirectness

Elaborate vs. Succinct

Formality vs. Informality

Linguistic Determinism

Sapir-Whorf Hypothesis

Linguistic Relativism

Nonverbal Codes

Decoding Messages: Translation

Attributional Variations

Patterns of Thought

Intercultural Communication Competence

Define each of the following terms:

tolerance for ambiguity

ethnocentrism

prejudice

stereotyping

passive observation

active strategies

self-disclosure

CHAPTER THIRTEEN: COMMUNICATING WITH FAMILY AND AT WORK STUDY GUIDE

Communication in Families

Define: family

Types of Family Communication

Spouses/Partners

Define: the three couple types

Parent-Child

Explain the effect on dyads

Siblings

Define: shared narratives

How can sibling experiences differ?

Elements of Family Communication

Define: the five characteristics of family systems

Define: the four roles family members can play in conflict situations

Define: family narratives

Define: family of origin

Communication Rules

Define: conversation orientation

Define: conformity orientation

Explain the four types of families that result

Effective Communication in Families

Define: boundaries, enmeshed, disengaged, chaotic, rigid,

Explain the importance of confirming messages

List the repeating issues of family conflict

List and explain the four general principles of family conflict

Communicating in Organizations

Formal and Informal Relationships

Define: the three types of formal communication

How does informal communication supplement formal communication?

Face-to-Face and Mediated Relationships

Define: Virtual teams

Relationships in Work Groups
Define: the six groups roles?

Define: the four stages of group work communication

What dimensions of communication exist in the culture of working groups?

Define: designated leader

What are the four types of power in groups?

Interviewing

What are the four qualities that distinguish interviews from other types of communication?

What are the responsibilities of the interviewer and interviewee before, during, and after they meet?